With Ballot
and Bayonet

With Ballot and Bayonet

THE POLITICAL SOCIALIZATION OF
AMERICAN CIVIL WAR SOLDIERS

Joseph Allan Frank

The University of Georgia Press
Athens & London

© 1998 by the University of Georgia Press
Athens, Georgia 30602
All rights reserved
Designed by Walton Harris
Set in 11/14 Bulmer by G & S Typesetters, Inc.
Printed and bound by Braun-Brumfield, Inc.

The paper in this book meets the guidelines for
permanence and durability of the
Committee on Production Guidelines for Book Longevity
of the Council on Library Resources.

Printed in the United States of America

02 01 00 99 98   C   5 4 3 2 1

Library of Congress Cataloging in Publication Data

Frank, Joseph Allan.
    With ballot and bayonet : the political socialization of American Civil War
soldiers / Joseph Allan Frank.
        p.   cm.
    Includes bibliographical references and index.
    ISBN 0-8203-1975-9 (alk. paper)
    1. United States.   Army—History—Civil War, 1861–1865.   2. Political
socialization—United States—History—19th century.   3. Soldiers—United
States—Attitudes—History—19th century.   4. Motivation (Psychology)—
United States—History—19th century.   I. Title.
E491.F83   1998
973.7′41′0922—dc21   97-52644

British Library Cataloging in Publication Data available

Contents

Preface

With Ballot and Bayonet: The Political Socialization of American Civil War Soldiers seeks to identify the defining attribute that kept the people's armies, composed largely of volunteers to enlist and fight, in the nation's most bloody conflict. Most of the men who constituted this highly motivated core of the armies had volunteered during the first year of the conflict and remained true to their obligations despite the high desertion rates among others, such as bounty men, substitutes, and conscripts. (However, the letters and diaries of later enlistees seldom acknowledged that the men were bounty men, substitutes, or conscripts.)

Even after three years of slaughter, instead of walking away from the horrors with all honors due a veteran, many put their lives on the line yet again by re-enlisting for the duration of the conflict. Offers of furloughs and promises of service with comrades in veteran volunteer regiments were hardly sufficient incentives for taking such a momentous decision. What motivated the men and characterized the battalions that fought from the Mississippi Valley to the Atlantic? This book contends that politics was the defining feature of the people's armies of the North and South: politics steeled mens' souls and shaped their armies. American political tradition of local recruitment and distrust of standing armies, along with more prosaic necessities like patronage, was the mold in which the citizens' armies were cast. In addition, political convictions served an important role in motivating the men and gauging the loyalty of the officers. Furthermore, political considerations affected the way the armies fought by promoting the use of irregular troops and by selecting politically symbolic objectives whose capture would undermine enemy civilian morale. Finally, politics was a decisive factor affecting relations between the home front and the men in the ranks: troops demanded that the home front suppress dissidents who undermined the parent society's resolve and jeopardized its support for the army.

While most soldiers' letters typically were not reflective and were usually brief anecdotal descriptions of life in camp and on the march interspersed with personal matters, this study relies on the letters and diaries of 1,013 soldiers who reflected on broader political questions and the military issues of the war for the obvious reason that this correspondence was the most interesting. Furthermore, though their degree of interest and resoluteness varied, these soldiers were the politically informed elements among the troops. Their steadfastness had an additional anchor to hold them to the cause. Not all were volunteers: many may have joined to gain a bounty or avoid the draft. Besides the usual motivations such as personal gain, fear of punishment for desertion, unit loyalty, small group bonds, and a personal sense of duty, some of the men were additionally animated by political convictions. This reinforced their resolve and was one more animus strengthening their commitment to see the thing through as the war dragged on into its third year. By 1863, volunteering was down, bounties were rising to overcome resistance, and many feared death in battle more than the provost marshal. Unit loyalty was wearing thin when some regiments were consolidated with other worn battalions. Loyalty to campmates also withered as more and more comrades died or did not reenlist. While glory and adventure were long gone, political and strategic issues became more pressing as the war took new twists and turns. However, no claim is made that those who discussed political issues typified all soldiers. After all, most of them did not write anything, and the majority of those who did write letters or diaries did not keep them, or their correspondence was lost over the decades. Nor, as mentioned above, were most of these soldiers interested in politics. But this study focuses only on politically motivated citizen-soldiers whose political ideas reinforced their determination to fight for the cause. Ranking them according to three indicators of political awareness, political acuity, scope of interest, and sense of political effectiveness, this study examines their comments on the political features of the citizen armies of the American Civil War.

A final point to be made about the soldiers' letters and diaries is that in a few cases quoted letters and diaries were edited with spelling or punctuation changes to make them more readable. Many soldiers had highly idiosyncratic spelling, little if any punctuation, and unusual syntax and phrasing that sometimes made the letters and diaries difficult to decipher. Such changes were made only to clarify the meaning of the soldier's comments.

To provide new insights, this study uses social science categories for identifying politically aware soldiers and then defining and classifying the levels of political socialization to provide new insights. (Since this book was written, James M. McPherson has published an insightful work, *For Cause and Comrades*, that I was unable to use.) This research also contests American historiographical exceptionalism by examining the American Civil War armies in world historical context and comparing these armies with other politically motivated armies of citizen-soldiers—the French Revolutionary armies and the Cromwellian army in the English Civil War. Finally, the research tries to verify its findings with statistical tests of probability of error and strength of association between factors. However, statistical checks are relegated to the endnotes to avoid encumbering the flow of the argument.

The author wishes to express his appreciation to the Canadian Social Sciences and Humanities Research Council for its generous funding for travel to more than twenty archival holdings in fifteen states. I especially thank my wife, Brigitte, for her help in collecting the material, for reading the manuscript, and generally for her encouragement and interest. The author also wishes to express his gratitude to Dr. Richard Sommers at the U.S. Army Military History Institute for his help and advice. The Institute was rich in its collection, and Dr. Sommers expertly guided the researcher. In addition, the author would like to express particular appreciation to Cheryl Schnirring, curator at the Illinois State Historical Library; Wayne C. Moore and Ann Alley, archivists, Tennessee State Library and Archives; Gary Arnold, archivist, Ohio Historical Society; Dr. Wilbur E. Meneray, assistant university librarian for special collections, and Leon Cahill Miller, manuscripts librarian, at the Howard-Tilton Memorial Library, Tulane University; Randy Roberts, manuscripts curator, and his assistants, Cindy Stewart and Diane Ayotte, at the Western Historical Manuscript Collection, Columbia, Missouri; Richard Shrader, reference archivist, and John White, assistant reference archivist, Southern Historical Collection, University of North Carolina; Bill Erwin, senior reference librarian, and Janie Morris, reference and processing archivist, Special Collections Library, Duke University; and finally, James Holmberg, curator, and James Trace Kirkwood, manuscript assistant, the Filson Club, Louisville, Kentucky.

*With Ballot
and Bayonet*

1 The Sword of the Republic

THE CHARACTERISTICS OF PEOPLE'S ARMIES

With Ballot and Bayonet is about why men fought in the Civil War, but, more importantly, it seeks to find out why they chose to persevere after years of inconclusive conflict even though its horrors now had become familiar to them. This book seeks to explore the ideas and values that inspired the men and provided the fortitude to endure and to identify the key motivator that induced soldiers to reenlist even though their time in the ranks had expired and they could have returned home with all honors. The key to answering these questions is to be found in the nature of the army in which the men served and the mix of motivators that provided the chief source of morale. The armies in America's Civil War were essentially composed of volunteer citizen-soldiers. These short-service troops responded to a national political crisis and were motivated by the issues associated with the confrontation.

Every major revolutionary rupture in eighteenth- and nineteenth-century history had a mass people's army as its agent. These mass military organizations were the first instruments for mobilizing the citizenry behind a common cause. Only later in the nineteenth century did mass political parties parallel the national mobilization begun by people's armies. Until the 1840s in the United States and the 1870s in France and England, political parties were elite clubs rather than large popular organizations. Until political parties came into their own right, the people's army of short-service troops was the sole means to mobilize the populace. For this reason, the chief revolutionary instrument in the eighteenth and nineteenth centuries was people's armies rather than political parties. The revolutionary impulse that mass mobilizations unleashed was the reason for the important political role played by people's armies in the American Civil War.

Union outfits including the 20th Massachusetts and the 109th Illinois were composed of many Democrats and were derisively called Copperhead regiments. Their men denounced emancipation policy and called for war only to reestablish the Union. Other units had large Republican contingents that drafted resolutions supporting emancipation and radical policies. The Confederate army also had units from conquered border states whose more radical soldiers called for invasion of the North to reclaim their homes. Other soldiers from the South advocated a purely defensive war and a compromise peace. Politics thus played an important role in motivating Union and Confederate troops, more so than in other types of armies. Armies differ and so does the mix of motivators that vitalizes their morale. The volunteer people's armies of the American Civil War required a nucleus of highly politically aware soldiers to keep up morale and define the issues that were at stake in the struggle. With a high level of political consciousness, these soldiers generated zeal among the other volunteers and encouraged them to continue in times of defeat. Later they set an example when they voluntarily reenlisted to fight on until the issue was conclusively decided.

The political issues that motivated many Civil War soldiers did not play as significant a role in the conscript armies of the two world wars in which draftees tended to be motivated by inchoate patriotic feelings and a crude sense of grievance against the enemy. A third type of army is the professional armies of long-service troops that fought Europe's colonial wars and dynastic conflicts and that today are the instrument of the developed countries of the world. These armies fight whenever and wherever the state needs them. Their area of operations ranges the world from Somalia to Bosnia or to the Persian Gulf. They are composed of professionals motivated by professional pride and unit loyalty. The regulars who staff these armies have little time to acquaint themselves with the complex issues behind the conflicts as they move from one hot spot to another. Their main loyalty is to their comrades, to their unit, and to their own military world and only secondarily is it underpinned by an undefined sense of patriotism.

The focus of this book is the people's armies of the American Civil War. Such mass forces of citizen-soldiers gained supremacy on battlefields from the late eighteenth to the mid-twentieth centuries. Political motives were central to these new armies. Many soldiers were engaged by the issues leading to the war, such as the right to secede from the Union, the question of slavery, the arming of black soldiers, and the attitude toward the occupied areas in the South. During the last phase of the war, occupation policy also segued into debates about how the occupied South should be treated by the conquering army and how it should be "reconstructed" after the war had ended.

Political considerations became defining organizational features of the new people's armies. Such concerns often prevailed over purely military needs in organizing and mobilizing the armies. Rather than use the regular army as the cadre for a uniform federally recruited force, the new army was locally recruited to provide state leaders with patronage plums and to build on local militia traditions. Political issues like slavery and secession induced many citizens to enlist in the republic's armies. Loyalty to the cause was a key factor in vetting officers for their political reliability. The rank and file often questioned their officers' devotion to the administration's policies on slavery and on the conduct of the war and reported those suspect of disloyalty to the authorities. The political dimension also emerged in the tensions between the army and its parent society over war aims and the community's support of the political and military leadership. Finally, politics affected the way a people's army fought. Political objectives often were more important than purely military ones. Capturing a politically symbolic place like Richmond, the Confederate capital, or Charleston, where the war began, could affect enemy morale and was often as important as gaining a purely military objective. Warring on the civilian population would undermine the enemy society's support for the political leaders and the army as much as defeating the enemy's army. The impact of the political dimension on a people's army was a direct measure of the level of citizen-soldiers' political sophistication, which raises the problem of gauging soldiers' political competence. The problem of measuring soldiers' political awareness will be addressed in chapter 2.

The peoples' armies of the nineteenth and twentieth centuries gained preeminence on European battlefields in the wake of the French Revolution. This upheaval inaugurated a modern age, an era of unrestricted wars fought by armies of citizen-soldiers. This new type of recruit trooped to the colors as an agent of powerful ideas such as democracy, liberty, and national independence. Armies became democratized. They were recruited from all classes. Their officers now included men who had risen through the ranks. The aristocracy's domination of the officer corps ended with the French Revolution. Democratization of the officer corps was more hesitant in the South's Civil War armies because of the enduring influence of the landed gentry and especially the first families of Virginia who saw themselves as *primi inter pares* among the ruling elites of the South. The Virginian ruling groups believed that the Old Dominion's gentry should dominate the civilian and military administration of the Confederacy. General Robert E. Lee and George Wythe Randolph, secretary of war in 1862, exemplified this ruling class, inordinately drawn from among the landed gentry or aristocracy. They justified their claim to primacy by invoking the historical role Virginians had played in founding the republic. Armed with this historical status, they were able to impose their values and lifestyle on other Confederates who came to work in the capital in Richmond. The landed gentry remained a cohesive influential elite tied throughout the war by kinship, success in public life, and shared military service preceding the struggle. They continued to define themselves as country squires by maintaining rural residences while spending their professional lives in the cities. Aspiring Southern officers from less estimable backgrounds tried to emulate the gentry's romantic, chivalrous style.[1] No such defining class model stood out in the North's army to shape the officer corps coming up from the ranks.

Many of the new officers were civilians who served only during the national emergency and intended to return to their civilian pursuits after the war. They did not share the aristocracy's idea that military service was a lifelong vocation. Though an army is by its very nature a hierarchical institution, the people's armies of the American Civil War did not set boundaries between the officers and the rank and file as inflexibly as did the professional armies of Europe, best epitomized by the British regular forces at the turn of the nineteenth century, in which the officer corps came overwhelmingly from the aristocracy and officers never gave orders directly to the men but had their commands transmitted by the noncommissioned officers.[2] These citizen-soldiers acquired a dual role during the revolution and the democratization of politics that followed it. Citizens gained a role in deciding their country's future. They had a civilian role as voters and direct participants in the political process, and they took on new military obligations associated with citizenship as defenders of their newfound liberties against foreign and domestic threats.[3] Service in the armed forces was the military equivalent of citizens' political participation. The army was the embodiment and spearhead of the democratic idea. The army was organized democratically with an officer corps and the rank and file drawn from all strata of the parent society, thus representing it.

Though there were regular units such as the Confederate Battalion at Shiloh, marine units, and "regulars" in the Union's III Corps, these troops nevertheless were citizen-soldiers. They were short-service troops who had volunteered or were conscripted for federal organizations rather than state outfits under national control. Though such units were organized directly by the national authorities and discipline was more stern, their recruits were often inducted locally just like state militia. E. R. Kellogg, for example, initially joined the 24th Ohio Volunteers but resigned during the West Virginia campaign complaining that the regiment was run by "tired politician soldiers and military cabals." He joined the U.S. Infantry's 1st Battalion of the 16th Regiment, which was organizing in Columbus, Ohio. He rose to the rank of lance sergeant in Company B. He thought a federally organized Ohio outfit would do more fighting and less politicking. He got his wish at Shiloh a short time later.[4] These units were composed of a new type of soldier who not only fought to protect his own country and its government but also was the agent of the democratic idea in the rest of Europe still benighted by aristocratic rule. Republican and Napoleonic France forged armies of soldier-citizens that spread the democratic idea and defeated the monarchs' professional armies. They also compelled the monarchs to copy the

French model. American political and military tradition paralleled the French idea of a revolutionary people's army during the American War of Independence and the Civil War. In some ways America's forces came closer to the ideal than the French armies. In France mixed brigades of "white" formerly royal battalions of regulars joined with a "blue" battalion of revolutionary volunteers in demi-brigades.[5] In the American Civil War, however, the armies' units were composed entirely of citizen-soldiers.

The people's armies that fought in Europe and America were products of their age. It was an age of mass participation in electoral politics. The industrial revolution also mobilized the population into the factory system, imposing collective discipline and mechanical skills on the workforce. The industrializing democracies also relied on mass participation to man their large armies. Democracy and industrialization correlated with the rise of people's armies. Without democracy and mass production it would have been impossible to organize and arm such enormous armies.[6] Industrialization made possible large-scale production of standardized cheap weaponry that society used to equip the entire male citizenry during a general mobilization.

Nineteenth-century people's armies relied on several manpower systems to fill the ranks. They used a cadre/conscript system, a militia system, or a combination of both to fill the ranks of the new armies.[7] In the American Civil War, both sides initially relied on a poorly organized militia system. At the outbreak of the war, militia organizations in the North and the South were a patchwork of units whose quality ranged from fair to miserable.[8] Yet the United States and the Confederacy had little choice, since the existing militia framework was more extensive than the minuscule organizational capacity of the standing army at the outbreak of the war. Moreover, the situation in 1861 required a rapid mobilization to prevent the border states from seceding, and the militia was all that was available.[9] At the Civil War's outbreak, the sixteen thousand–man regular army was scattered along the frontier. The federal army also had many officers of southern origin whose political reliability was uncertain. Yet another reason for relying on the militia system instead of using the regular army as a framework for the mobilization was that the militia system was a truer reflection of the country's political culture. Though the American militia system originated with the English Muster Law of 1572, the Americans integrated the militia system into the political framework after the country gained independence.[10] The American political culture valued decentralization and mistrusted strong central government and its corollary, a large standing army of professional soldiers whose ethos was alien to the democratic ideals of the republic. By contrast, Americans came to believe that a territorially recruited militia system would regionalize autonomy. It would integrate society and its army, assuring that the army and society would share the same values. The militia would also engage in the life of the community as participant in its political process and in the defense of its ideals. Americans' distrust of a strong central government and its standing army gained credence during the War of Independence, and these ideas governed the military structure that prevailed at the outbreak of the Civil War.

The state militia organizations were essential to the war effort, though their record appears more favorable in the North than in the South, where it seems it was more difficult to coordinate state and national efforts and tensions between state and national authorities occurred.[11] Nevertheless, the militia system was an essential part of the military organization of the North and the South. It provided manpower, training, organized equipment, and leadership to federalized volunteer units. State militia forces were required to meet on a monthly or weekly basis for training and also were required to participate in encampments for intensive training. They provided an important reserve for the North's federal forces. At the close of hostilities, there were about one million militia drawn into federal service. The militia organizations also provided units of nonfederalized state troops who were mobilized in emergencies, such as during Morgan's raid and the Gettysburg campaign. The militia also undertook garrison duty under federal authority outside their states, guarded prison camps at home, and provided an internal security force against threatened uprisings or subversion. The minuteman thus remained a defining characteristic of the armies fielded in the Civil War. Rhode Island, Massachusetts, Kansas, and Missouri even imposed active militia service on their entire male population not inducted into federal military service.

This phenomenon distinguished the American forces from those in Europe. Besides the armies raised during the *levée en masse* during the French Revolution, most European armies continued to rely on professional long-service troops and did not reach down as deeply and extensively into their manpower pools. Thus, the militia system was the source of many of the American federalized forces and also provided approximately two hundred thousand state forces by the end of the war. Finally, Northern state militia forces were not only an important source of volunteers, but they also provided conscripts for federal service because state militiamen were not exempt from the federal draft at the time it was instituted.[12]

Later, however, the American system moved closer to the French model, which gave a more important role to the national government. Like the French during the latter stages of their revolution, Americans increasingly resorted to conscription and to bounties to fill the ranks. The *levée en masse* that brought so many to the colors in America in 1861 and France in 1793 could no longer fill the manpower needs in the final years of the Civil War. By then, the national bureaucracy had become more efficient. It became more proficient in using coercion and in using taxes to provide monetary inducement to fill the ranks. The citizens' sense of duty to volunteer was the backbone of the American manpower system, but it had to be supplemented with financial inducements in the form of bounties for enlisting or by resorting to enforced conscription.[13] The French exemplified the trend away from volunteer service and toward reliance on conscription. Ultimately, they expanded their brigades from a dual structure to a tripartite structure by adding a battalion of conscripts to serve alongside the battalion of regulars and the battalion of volunteers.[14] The American system relied on conscripts as well, but never in the same measure. Political tradition in the United States may have been more adverse to obligatory military service than in France, where peasants already had been mustered into service under the *ancien régime.* Probably, however, American people's armies remained essentially volunteer forces because neither the Confederacy nor the Union ever created a national bureaucracy that equaled the effectiveness of France's public administration under the republic and the empire. Consequently, neither the Confederacy nor the federal government implemented conscription very efficiently. Only 5 to 7 percent of the Union army's combat effectives were conscripts.[15] Many men avoided enlistment by paying commutation fees. Others bought substitutes through a network of brokers, while still others dodged the draft or deserted.[16]

The draft drew less than .25 percent of the North's total population into the army because there were so many ways to avoid conscription. Failing the physical examination was of course one way; another was to pay a substitute or pay a commutation fee of three hundred dollars, a sum that most individuals were capable of assembling. Thus, the draft was not a direct stimulus to volunteering though it did have an indirect effect by engendering a bidding war to summon recruits to fill town quotas.[17] Communities competed for recruits by raising additional local bounties. These sums exceeded an average workingman's annual wage. A man of modest means could not overlook the financial considerations before volunteering. He knew that a soldier's wages were not keeping up with inflation, and there were no government agencies like those that arose during World War II to implement price controls or an allotment system to protect a soldier's family from hardship. The bounty was an important and honorable way for the volunteer to see to his family and at the same time carry out his patriotic duty. Most bounty men were neither bounty jumpers nor profiteers: they were men seeing to their families before embarking for the front. They may have welcomed the draft as a way to increase the money available for their families when they decided to enlist.[18] The only bounty men who may have been less reliable usually did not enlist as substitutes in their own towns. If they jumped their bounties, there was less chance that their fellow townsmen would find out about it after they returned. Locally drafted levies were considered more reliable than bounty men because they enlisted from their own towns and were exposed to neighbors' and kinsmen's pressure to behave honorably and not desert.[19]

For these reasons, the backbone of the Civil War armies remained the volunteer citizen-soldier, which had significant implications for organizing and motivating the army. The decentralized political framework of the country meant that the army would be recruited and organized at the state and local levels under the direction of governors and county political leaders. The volunteer nature of the armies also signified that getting people to join and keeping up morale in the ranks would require greater reliance on political motivators rather than coercing conscripts into line. Politically sophisticated soldiers would be more responsive to the country's call. Politically aware citizen-soldiers would be more sensitive to the issues in the conflict and would be convinced that they had a stake in the outcome. They would be more motivated to join up and stay the course until the issues were resolved. They would volunteer to fight. The citizen-soldier volunteer did not need to be conscripted or bought off with bounties.

The citizen-soldier ideal originated long before the French Revolution. It existed as far back as Athens and Rome. Niccolo Machiavelli's *Discourses on the First Ten Books of Titus Livius* revived the ideal in the sixteenth century in his work glorifying the idea of the Roman republic and its citizen-soldiers.[20] In the eighteenth century, the ideal received a romantic and revolutionary patina in painter Louis David's *Oath of the Horatii* and in the political theory of Jean-Jacques Rousseau's *On the Origin of Inequality*.[21] For revolutionaries like David and Rousseau, the ideas of democracy and military service conjoined with republican tradition. According to the new principles, the government, like its army, had to mirror its population. The volunteer system never became a perfect reflection of its parent society, however. The poor were not fully represented because they were less likely to volunteer. They had to stay home to support families.[22] The lower class was also underrepresented because immigrants enlisted at lower rates than did native-born Americans.[23]

The minuteman ideal made military service an honorable endeavor. Contrary to the eighteenth century's image of a military in which professional soldiers were foreign to civil society and only came in contact with civilians during boisterous bouts of whoring, drinking, and general mayhem, democratic society held up the soldier-citizen as the epitome of republican virtue.[24] For example, Maine denied the right to vote in the field to its enlistees in the regular army but accorded that right to its volunteer militia.[25]

During the American Civil War and the French Revolution, national crises unleashed waves of patriotic fervor and stimulated a general mobilization of volunteer militia. The power of shared political beliefs in motivating politically

Centrality of politics in the mobilization of people's armies. The Billy Wilson Zouaves rallying to the colors at Tammany Hall, New York, April 24, 1861. Louis Shepard Moat, ed., *Frank Leslie's Illustrated Famous Leaders and Battle Scenes of the Civil War* (New York: Mrs. Frank Leslie, 1896), 80.

engaged militiamen could hardly be underestimated. Despite the disorder and turmoil that tore the sections asunder in America and ripped the classes apart in France, the two countries' citizenry clambered over the debris of their shattered societies to join the colors and set things right. Their fighting faith was essential to their fighting prowess. Neither superiority in weapons nor bigger battalions guarantees that an army will fight if the soldiers are not motivated. History confirms the importance of political motivators in mass armies. The effectiveness of the German army in the last stages of World War II underscores the importance of a minority of politically motivated soldiers' high commitment to fighting on to the bitter end.[26] And political motivation among elements in the South's and the North's armies in times of adversity in turn steeled the souls of the rest of the troops.

Politics was thus central to a people's army, which was the armed manifestation of a political idea. Politically motivated Civil War soldiers, for example, voiced an interest in every dimension of the conflict. The most evident form of political comment was their expressions of deep patriotic attachment to their homeland and its political institutions. But beside these rather inchoate feelings, there were more specific comments from the politically sophisticated soldiers. They discussed the overall strategic situation and the implications of events in far-off theaters of war for the general progress of the war effort. They evaluated—and often denounced—the military leadership's conduct of the war. They often raised questions about the country's manpower policy, demanding that the nation mobilize every segment of society to share in the burden of the struggle. They sought to demonstrate to their satisfaction that this was indeed a just war and warranted committing their lives and fortunes to it. They discussed the impact of national and local elections on the country's war effort. They supported and condemned candidates according to their impact on the national war effort. The men debated the purpose of the war. Was it, for example, a revolutionary struggle to destroy slavery in the South, or was it a conservative, limited war to reestablish the Union? War aims also were the focus of discussions among the South's soldiers, when in 1864 and 1865 the men questioned the ultimate purpose of the war. Was it being fought to defend the South's "peculiar institution" or was the war being fought for a progressive ideal—for the new country's independence? Yankees and Rebels wondered about the purposes of the conquest of the South. Would it be a purely military affair, or would the North use the army as a revolutionary instrument to "reconstruct" southern society? The question also arose in the Southern ranks when the troops debated the idea of freeing slaves to serve in the Confederate forces to fill manpower shortages.

The citizen-soldiers also discussed political issues abroad, wondering whether France or Britain would intervene. They questioned the loyalty of people back home and wondered about the resolve and political and economic conditions in the enemy's society. The troops on both sides also evaluated the terms and the chances of success of peace feelers during the long conflict. These are some of the topics that the politically motivated volunteer citizen-soldiers raised in their letters and diaries. The soldiers had to sort out these political issues to clarify their own reasons for fighting and to assess the chances of their side's success and, above all, to motivate them to continue to fight.

In this study, I define *politics* in its broadest sense. *Politics* encompasses all areas of human life where the state organizes society to pursue a collective endeavor, be it by war or by peaceful means.[27] By definition, politics is the determining context of war.[28] War is an instrument of policy for achieving national independence, democracy, or any other great purpose to which the people may set themselves. Serving as a German auxiliary in Napoleon's Grand Army invading Russia, Karl von Clausewitz was among the first to examine the new types of military forces unleashed in the French Revolution. His study was based on personal experience. In the Napoleonic Wars, he saw people's armies of hundreds of thousands of soldiers hurled against each other in Napoleon's army. Entire nations had taken up arms in the name of millennial ideas that inspired their soldiers. A country's survival in these nation-to-nation and peoples-against-peoples conflicts depended largely on the political motivation of its citizen-soldiers. Where it faltered, so did the national will, and with it the chances of surviving the struggle.

Politics was thus central to the new people's army in five ways: (1) in its recruitment and organization, (2) in the combat motivation of its soldier-citizens, (3) in assuring the political reliability of officers and rank and file, (4) in the need to secure the political solidarity of the home front, and (5) in formulating strategies and tactics that were suited to the new armies.

First, politics affected recruitment and organization of the Civil War's armies. Recruits enlisted because they believed that the cause was worthwhile, many voicing a strong attachment to the government and its policies. Any who were held to be politically unreliable, who did not seem to demonstrate appropriate zeal for the cause, were challenged by the rest of the rank and file. The soldiers were also voters, and they would not countenance half-hearted military or political leadership. They not only demanded and obtained the right to participate in elections for the civilian leadership, but they also voted in their militia units to select company-grade officers. As late as 1864, veterans were demanding that they retain the right to elect their officers in return for reenlisting.[29] A Republican operative in Elkhart County, Indiana, rejoiced that 90 percent of those answering the latest draft call were Republicans, but it would "slaughter" the party at the polls if the men could not vote in the field.[30] Local political leaders supervised the decentralized recruitment system and used it for political patronage, offering militia commands to political allies. Governors jealously held on to their right to hand out colonelcies. Local leaders also saw militia appointments as a source of local influence. During the race to fill the ranks, local leaders poached on each other's pools of young men to fill their quotas and increase the number of units from their area and thus the number of posts they could offer to friends and political supporters. Leaders undermined their competitors' credibility by spreading rumors questioning the political reliability of leaders in other towns.[31] It is not surprising, then, that the war nourished the political patronage system and that it endured throughout the ordeal. Thus, an important reason for the persistence of political patronage was that creating new regiments instead of providing replacements for existing ones increased the number of patronage plums for state political leaders.[32] Even in 1863, Tennessee Unionist Andrew Johnson, keeping his political influence unhindered by military considerations, obtained exclusion from review board examination for all Tennessee officers seeking to command U.S. Colored Troops. The Lincoln administration had accorded Johnson full control of patronage for all Union Tennessee units to secure his pro-Union base in Tennessee.[33]

Besides motivating men to enlist, politics also induced the soldiers of the

American Civil War to fight. Personal and social values have always played a key role in motivating recruits in mass armies.[34] In the twentieth century, Nazi ideology contributed significantly to the effectiveness of the German army in World War II, underscoring the importance of shared political values about the nature of their society and its polity in inspiring soldiers.[35] Donald Lang has classified society's values, those that are also internalized by the most politically motivated troops during a war, into four categories: (1) those that are based on personal beliefs, such as duty, patriotism, or—in the Civil War—abhorrence of slavery; (2) those values that are logically founded, such as the conviction among soldiers in the Union army that even if they personally abhorred conferring political and personal equality on the ex-slaves, slaves had to be freed to undermine the South; (3) those that are shared by the community concerning war aims, and finally, (4) those hedonistic interests associated with material gains such as promotion, pay, and bounties for enlisting.[36]

During the American Civil War, the first three of Lang's value categories— personal beliefs, logically based principles, and consensus-based values of the community—played a significant role in motivating the more politically aware volunteers. James H. Meteer, campaigning in Georgia in 1864, exemplified the idealism of the average citizen-soldier. He cursed slavery as the source of every villainy in the inventory of evil. Meteer's war experience sharpened his political acuity by bringing into focus the profound moral issues that were at stake in the conflict. When he had to hand over a runaway slave to an owner, he was subject to the slaveowner's lamentations about the condition of a recaptured slave. The slaveowner whined that he had paid $300 to buy a full-grown man who now had been returned in an emaciated state weighing only sixty pounds and worth very little. Apparently, the slaveholder expected the army not only to serve as slave catcher but also to care and feed his property to maintain its value.[37] The war brought men into direct contact with the moral questions that gave rise to the conflict. For the first time, the soldiers confronted this issue in all its reality. Heretofore, it had been an abstract question that they had only read about in the newspaper or discussed with friends. The experience in their campaigns sharpened the men's awareness of the issues and increased their political perceptiveness. As a case in point, capture during the battle of Gettysburg occasioned arguments between Union prisoners and their Confederate captors over the issues of the war.[38] In another instance, Private Edgar Walters of the 150th Pennsylvania Volunteer Infantry remembered marching into Muttontown on the Mason-Dixon line between Maryland and Pennsylvania and being greeted by a banner supporting the McClellan-Pendleton ticket. The marching columns quickly made their opposition known to the inhabitants of the Democratic stronghold when they unleashed three hardy cheers for the American flag and the Lincoln-Johnson ticket.[39]

Yet another political dimension of people's armies is vetting candidates for commissions for their political reliability. When the fortunes of war turned against the people's army, cleavages quickly began to appear in the ranks. In France, there were desertions and rumors of treason in the officer corps. Paris rushed political commissioners to stamp out antigovernment intrigue. The civilian authorities also sought to eliminate all professional military symbols and institutions that stood between the soldier and civil society. The French authorities discouraged unit flags and other military insignia that fostered esprit de corps and separateness from society. The political leadership feared that the army might grow distant from society. In the Union army, there also were rumors of Bonapartist tendencies, but they never went beyond talk. The Union also had its *comités de salut public* in the Union Leagues and in the Joint Committee on the Conduct of the War. There were also political differences between professional officers and militia officers and militiamen. As a rule, regular army officers are inclined to have a conservative outlook, while short-service troops frequently adopt a democratic and progressive political attitude. The differences between regular officers and their men arise over war aims and strategy. Both the French revolutionary army and American Civil War armies were plagued with tensions between the volunteers and regular officers over political and military issues. They were made severe, for instance, when the officers were almost all Democrats but the rank and file were Republicans. Muttering, arguments, and open animosity between rank and file and officers could poison camp life.[40] Political discord so strained relations between soldiers and officers that the civil authorities had to take measures to oust suspect officers.[41] Political issues divided the officers too. When rumors circulated that some divisional commanders of the Army of Tennessee had challenged the high command by calling a meeting to draft a petition advocating emancipation for slaves who enlisted in the Confederate service, President Jefferson Davis sided with Major General Braxton Bragg and Brigadier General William H. T. Walker in squelching the idea.[42] Political differences among officers also arose in the North's armies. The rank and file and the people back home suspected some officers of being cool to Lincoln's Emancipation Proclamation. They informed on the officers, filling state adjutants general files with political denunciations.[43]

Politics also plays a role in the relations of a people's army with the home front. Ideally, a people's army reflects the society whose interests it serves.[44] Generally, the Confederate and Union armies came close to achieving this ideal.[45] The morale of a people's army relies to a large extent on its ties to its parent community. Contrary to a professional army, which is more self-sufficient and is able to generate its own morale by emphasizing unit pride and the military ethos, a people's army depends to a great degree on the home front for its sense of purpose. The military is the armed will of its society, an instrument that has been forged to attain certain objectives. If the parent society breaks solidarity with its army and renounces the cause that the army bleeds for, there are immediate repercussions on morale. The bonds between army and society separate, and the army becomes alienated from civil society. Ultimately this rupture may give rise to Bonapartist muttering among the officers against the constitutional civilian political authorities and Spartacist complaints among the men, accusing the government and the officer corps of serving the interests of a ruling oligarchy at the expense of the people.[46] During the American Civil War, when some home folk questioned war aims, the men felt betrayed and demanded that civilian authorities take stern measures against recalcitrant elements in imposing home-front solidarity.

Finally, politics affects the fighting style of a people's army. The magnitude of the forces that are mobilized in a people's war also expand the violence. When an entire people takes up arms, its armies not only fight each other but also wage war against the opposing population. It gradually becomes apparent to both sides that such a large enemy army cannot be destroyed in battle as long as it can obtain moral and material sustenance from its parent society. The army must wage war against civilians to reduce society's ability to make war. Grand strategy and even battle tactics are politically driven. Strategists seek out politically significant objectives that will undermine the enemy's economic capabilities and the enemy society's will to fight. Strategy is often directed at political objectives because patriotism at home among the enemy is a source of morale. The destruction or capture of major symbolic objectives like an enemy's great cities will undermine the opposing people's will to fight. Commanders resort to blockade, pillage, destruction of transportation facilities, and any other means to bring a society to its knees. Strategists also seek out certain politico-military objectives to sustain their side's morale and strengthen the war party in a coming election. Success in the field feeds the will to fight at home, which loops back to encourage the army. And as the war progresses, a circular relationship gradually emerges between the army and the society. Initially, the people's army is a reflection of its parent society, but society is later molded by its army to reflect the army's aims.

Contrary to long-service troops in professional armies, the American Civil War armies never totally transformed their citizens into soldiers. The close ties between the men and their communities prevented the total absorption of the citizen-soldiers into the military culture. Regimentation thus never totally transformed the new recruits. The men remained civilians and shared many of the political interests of their fellow citizens at home. The home front had an important role in mobilizing and in motivating the army. The voluntary militia organizations reflected the political values of the American polity with their emphasis on local initiative and community pride dovetailing with national patriotism. The communal character of the militia companies and regiments reflected the entire country's traditions. Though Civil War militia outfits were military organizations, they continued to have civilian purposes as well. Soldiers formed literary and political societies, created religious associations, set up libraries, held prayer meetings, and tried to arrange mutual aid, mirroring fraternal organizations back home. These civilian attitudes were reinforced by ties to their communities through letters as well as through newspapers mailed to soldiers that discussed problems at home but also national political issues. Political exchanges in letters between friends and relatives and the men at the front, along with exchanges in letters to the editor and visits by relatives and friends to the camps, sharpened the political awareness of troops.[47] Lizzie Little wrote to her future husband, George Smith Avery, a sergeant and later a captain in an Illinois outfit, arguing that the war was not only a war for the Union, as her husband believed, but it was also a crusade against slavery. When George tired of war and complained that it was losing its attraction, Lizzie steeled his resolve, reminding him why he had enlisted: "I knew you could not wait and see your rights defended by others without lending a helping hand." In a subsequent letter she called on him to show revolutionary zeal, declaring: "I would rather have you marching to the music of freedom than living a life of ease & luxury. I do not believe God gave us souls to be 'aproned waiters' . . . and pampering our baser natures. We should have higher aims & what can be nobler than purchasing Freedom."[48] Few went as far as Louicy Ann May Eberhart, who followed her husband, Uriah, chaplain of the 20th Iowa, to the front to become a missionary teacher for freedmen.[49]

These strong ties gave the community considerable influence over its soldiers. Newspapers reported successes. Personal failures, such as desertion, or group failures, when the unit did not perform well in battle, also appeared in the local press. The men knew they brought shame and disappointment to family and friends back home. Disgrace at the front would also jeopardize the men's chances for setting up a postwar business or career. Reid Mitchell also points out that home-front pressure encouraged the men to reenlist, fearing the community's opprobrium if they returned before the war was over.[50]

The very intensity of the ties between the soldiers and their communities also caused tensions when soldiers came to believe that the people back home were not bearing their share of the burden. Soldiers railed against the stay-at-homes and profiteers. They lamented the community's lack of attention when friends and family did not write or did not show interest in the situation of the men.[51] Yet the tensions also served to intensify the communications between the home front and the army. The recriminations from the front and the responses from home sharpened the issues on both sides and increased the political awareness of the army and the community.

However, as the war went on, the army began to have an impact on its parent society. The war made heavy demands on society, requiring a high degree of social discipline on the home front to assure efficient mobilization of society's resources. War collectivizes a polity and a society. Community values, such as unity and discipline, gained ascendence over individualism. The political system became more efficient as it became centralized as its bureaucracy grew. All great revolutionary and civil wars strengthened the national government and created a more efficient bureaucracy, according to Theda Skocpol's study of the French, Russian, and Chinese Revolutions.[52] This process also occurred during the American Civil War. Additionally, people's wars affect policy by polarizing society between conservatives and radicals. To assure a conclusive victory, the army demands revolutionary war aims that would restructure the enemy society. Radical war aims could only be implemented after a total victory. They required a prostrate enemy to restructure the defeated society to prevent the same social and economic forces from ever again challenging the victor. Such views were probably not typical of all soldiers. Yet those who voiced an interest in these questions constituted an important minority. They had an influential role in motivating fellow soldiers and in holding the army to its purpose. They were able to perceive a collective mission in the struggle and articulate it to comrades at the front and to people back home.

One way of assessing the impact of the American Civil War on the soldiers' political awareness is to read through soldiers' letters and diaries looking for political content. I defined political content in the broadest sense, including comments on the conduct of the war, the military leadership, as well as the political leaders and policies. An argument may be made that the correspondence that has survived came from the most articulate soldiers and officers. I did not find this to be the case in examining more than two thousand soldiers' letters and diaries in three studies. Many were banal and full of clichés and hence were probably typical. It is true, however, that the letters and diaries that survived in print were those of the most articulate soldiers, but the vast majority of the collections used in this study came from unpublished collections, and they are more representative of the rank-and-file soldiers and officers. I gave more attention to soldiers' comments in the last two and a half years of the struggle in order to appraise the war's impact on their political awareness. More than three-fourths

(76 percent) of the correspondence in this study's 1,013 soldiers' letters and diaries was written after 1863. There is of course the caveat that only those who could read or write could be included in this study. Nonetheless, given the population's 85 percent literacy rate in 1860, the sample is representative of politically articulate soldiers.[53] Sixty percent of the material came from Union soldiers and 40 percent from Confederates. The sample's ratio of infantry to other arms of service also was approximately representative, with 82 percent of the soldiers serving in infantry units and the rest assigned to the artillery, cavalry, or special duties. The letters and diaries, however, overrepresent officers, who constituted 37 percent of the total. Many officers had been enlisted men at the outset of the war, however, and gained their commissions during the later years of the conflict. Nor were they necessarily better educated than the rank and file: they came from the same small communities. In such homogeneous localities, rank was not always clearly distinguishable. Officer straps were not always an accurate proxy for social class or for political articulateness. I began with the assumption that officers and enlisted men shared the same image of their role as citizen-soldiers because the vast majority of the troops were militiamen. Consequently, they reflected a similar level of political awareness. This assumption will be probed in chapter 2.

In this chapter I have defined the topic by arguing the centrality of politics as the principal trait of the people's armies that fought in the American Civil War. *With Ballot and Bayonet* also contends that politics influenced the organization of the army by relying on mass mobilization through conscription and volunteering through the country's militia system. The militia system's decentralized organization dovetailed with local politicians' interest in patronage and in the population's preference for enlisting through local associations. In the following chapter, I will discuss how politics pervaded other aspects of the army besides its organization. I will explore how politics played a pivotal role in recruiting the armies' politically motivated and resolute soldiers.

2 *"Les armées délibérantes"*

THE POLITICAL AWARENESS OF CITIZEN-SOLDIERS

The American Civil War's citizen-soldier believed he was a cut above bounty men, conscripts, and regulars. He was a "volunteer," a symbol of civic duty and patriotic virtue. He was superior to other types of soldiers. He offered his life out of a sense of republican duty rather than for personal gain or out of fear of the provost guard. He scorned the conscripts he saw herded under guard on the wharfs of New York. He distrusted men who enlisted for money, who only served to gain promotion, pay, or privilege, and who shirked their duty at every opportunity; such soldiers only saw war as a means for gaining personal ends. Bounty men and conscripts were fair-weather patriots who avoided their duty or deserted when the march music stopped and their blood money ran out; they were not in for the long haul. Bounty men's and conscripts' perspective was strictly personal interest; their outlook came down to a parochial assessment of their own risks and benefits. Bounty men were opportunists seeking their own ends and never thinking of the higher collective aims at stake in the war. As for professional soldiers, they also fought for self-interest: war was a career opportunity in which the death of a superior meant a promotion to higher rank or a more comfortable posting.[1] (However, it should be noted that volunteer officers often had political ambitions and were jockeying with fellow officers for promotion and favorable comment in the press back home. Nevertheless, the level of political altruism among the volunteers, especially at the outset of the war, was inspiring when compared to the cynical late twentieth century.)

James Horrocks, a Civil War soldier, epitomized the apolitical mercenary abhorred by idealistic volunteers. Master James was the son of well-to-do English parents. He had left a young lady pregnant back home and fled to the New World in 1863. There he joined the 5th New Jersey Battery. To avoid any dangerous or arduous duty, he finagled a promotion to a comfortable position as quartermaster sergeant in charge of the baggage train, well away from danger, deeming it the *"smart thing"* to do.[2] John Vestal Hadley, an Indiana infantry officer, condemned men like Horrocks who gained such special privileges. He centered his disdain on officers who solicited special space allotments in the baggage train while caring not at all about their men's comfort.[3] The idea of a patriotic volunteer expecting personal privileges or seeking private gain was equally repugnant to Henry W. Gay of the 15th Maine. Gay rejected the idea of using subterfuge to obtain personal advantage through military service. Gay wrote to his father: "Never have I seen the time that I would give one cent to get out of it only to get in again to make more money [by accepting a bounty]."[4]

In this chapter I will examine the values and beliefs of volunteers like Gay and Hadley and see how they learned these principles through their community and family life. I also will design some indicators for assessing their level of political awareness to find out how highly politically motivated the soldiers were and how important their numbers were among the troops.

The principles that buttressed their political outlook and their ideas of patriotic obligation is the logical starting point. Honor and character were central to the citizen volunteer persona. Such soldiers were far more reliable than professionals in defending the country's cause. Reaching back to republican traditions dating to antiquity, the American Civil War volunteers believed that the most reliable soldiers were citizens, and they shared Polybius's and other Greeks' distrust of mercenaries.[5] American civic culture echoed Plato's disdain for professional soldiers, whom Plato deemed insolent, brutish, and a threat to civil society.[6] Early American leaders also echoed British historian Edward Gibbon's views on the unreliability of professional soldiers and mercenaries. Gibbon associated the Roman empire's decline with its increasing reliance on mercenaries. Such troops were rootless. They were men without honor or morality. Their values were those of a nomadic multitude, blindly attaching themselves to whatever leader held sway in camp or whatever ad hoc aims emerged in the field. By contrast, the civilian volunteer's ethos was rooted in the moral values of his community. His principles were firmly held because they had been instilled in him from childhood. His credo was duty and honor. He enlisted in a political cause that he and his fellow citizens had shared in defining and to which he pledged his life.[7]

For the volunteer, military obligation was enmeshed in an idea of citizenship stemming from ancient Greece and Rome. In antiquity, military service was a component of citizenship. The Greeks and Romans assumed that only a citizen who was qualified to vote should bear arms because citizens had a political stake in the polity. They were more patriotically motivated than the rest of the populace. Citizens alone had a vested interest in defending the system of laws because they had a share in enacting them.[8] The ideal citizen-soldier emulated the Roman Cincinnatus, who dropped his plow and took up his sword when the republic was in danger.[9] American Civil War volunteers shared this image of the citizen soldier. Robert Franklin Bunting, chaplain in the 8th Texas Cavalry, evoked the classical conception of the soldier: the "Greeks have taught us on the plains of M[a]rathon and by the rocks of Salamis, that the numbers of the tyrant will not avail against freemen [who] fight for their altars and hearthstones."[10]

Like the French revolutionary army and Cromwell's New Model Army, the volunteer forces of the American Civil War were the military instruments of the people. But they were also, as the French revolutionaries described them, "armées délibérantes."[11] Their camps often resounded with the American equivalent of the Roundheads' Putney debates as the men pondered the purposes of the war, voted resolutions putting forward their views, and demanded a say in the selection of their leaders. When they were prisoners of war and unable to participate in the election process, the men in the ranks held mock elections to reaffirm their citizenship. John W. Northrop described such an election in Andersonville. The Yankee prisoners produced two sacks of beans. There was a white bag for McClellan ballots and a black bag for Lincoln votes. The two bags were hung up: "The men . . . marched in by squads of thousands. . . . The Democracy leaders (Irish police) were loud in their cry for 'Mac', the Rebels looking on with envious interest. Then whole hundreds went in for 'Abe' . . . but when a party seperated & stopped at the white bean bag shouting 'Mac! Mac!' They [the Confederate guards] clapped their hands & gave a shrill rebel yell. . . . About 1,800 votes were cast, Lincoln receiving about two & half to McClellan one."[12]

The Civil War soldier was a more reflective soldier, meshing ideas and action for gaining universal political ends for which he enlisted to fight. In this fight for the "New Jerusalem," he held that the reaffirmation of freedom and the progress of republican America served as a beacon for the rest of the world. If the United States failed to preserve the republic, the lamp of liberty would disappear as a beacon for the rest of the world benighted in tyranny.[13] The citizen-soldier needed a special kind of courage, the courage of the virtuous free citizen serving the republic and aware of the issues at stake in the struggle. The army could not rely on his blind obedience as with professional soldiers. Bravery was defined differently in the citizen army. The ancient Greeks contended that an army of citizen-soldiers fought best when its members understood the strategic and tactical situation and when they could gauge the risks for themselves.[14] A people's army was an army of politically informed citizens who fought best when they understood the big picture and when they knew what was at stake in the conflict. Hiram Howe, serving with the 10th Missouri (U.S.), had a diary that not only recorded his thoughts but, more significantly, also included an assortment of information that a citizen-soldier would need to be politically competent to understand the war's issues. It held the tax revenue records of his county. It listed his elected leaders. It included a reference directory of the principal governments around the world, classifying them as absolutist, federal, hereditary, and republican or constitutional monarchies. And it contained a rousing patriotic poem about marching off to slay treason's hosts.[15] Such information helped Howe, the citizen volunteer, to make informed judgments about where his duty lay. His courage involved a reasoned calculation that the cause merited the risk; his response was grounded in his character and in the education with which his family and community had endowed him.[16] The polity defined and nurtured his bravery. Thus, courage was not merely the personal form of behavior that Gerald F. Linderman so eloquently describes in *Embattled Courage*. It was more than an individual show of fearlessness under fire, an exhibition of gallantry, coolness, or daring.[17] Courage was also a politically defined idea. It was a purposeful political act, used to attain transcendental ends like saving freedom and republican government in the world. It was inspired, defined, nurtured, and demanded of virtuous citizens by the democratic polity. Knowing how to die was a sign that the citizen-soldier embodied the grace of republican virtue.

Patriotic courage was reasoned bravery. It was collectively defined valor, not the rash impulse of primitive warriors. Demosthenes' perorations to his fellow Athenians exemplified the idea of the citizen's patriotic obligation when he enjoined his fellow Athenians to take arms for the city's glory. Only their collective commitment could defend the city from foreign foes.[18] Yet patriotic exhortation was not enough. Though idealism played a role in encouraging enlistments, defeat and the dreary hardship of camp life steadily eroded popular enthusiasm. Machiavelli was among the first to apprise political leaders of the brittleness of popular morale. He advised a prince that with their immense size, people's armies could quickly overwhelm the opponent in a short war. If, however, the campaign failed, morale became fragile. So Machiavelli warned the ruler that a country could not sustain the soldiers' will to fight in times of adversity without grounding military obligation on a more sound ideological footing.[19]

Republican doctrine predicated success in war on the state's ability to convince its citizenry to die well,[20] to give their lives for a meaningful transcendental purpose in a publicly endorsed cause. The polity and its leaders had to establish a convincing reason for their people to be willing to give their lives for the state. Dying well had to become part of the civic culture. The citizen had to go to battle bearing an image—no matter how naive—of the proper way to die as a soldier of the republic. It was a patriotic ritual. Thomas W. Hardin, 37th Georgia, believed he knew how to die well. He explained to his wife, Kate, that it was important for the volunteer to make all preparations for an honorable death on the battlefield. Hardin believed principled behavior was the defining quality of the virtuous citizen and soldier. Hardin gave up his life at Pine Mountain, Georgia.[21] Like the Roman Horatius, Colonel William Orme of the 94th Illinois also used a classical republican metaphor for picturing "the Glory of a manly Death" in the name of a great cause.[22]

Both Earl J. Hess and Reid Mitchell point out that Americans North and South shared a common republican ideology. They were all capitalists believing firmly in the benefits of private property; they shared a belief in self-government, individualism, political equality, and democracy. Both sides drew on the shared traditions of the Revolutionary War in defining their cause.[23] Both drew on their respective citizens' sense of patriotic duty. Both the Confederacy and the Union used three principles for binding their citizen-soldiers to the cause. First, the leaders argued that the soldier was constitutionally obligated to defend the polity. The soldier affirmed this obligation by an oath of loyalty and by his signature on his enlistment papers. Second, the polity based military obligation on the idea that the state was advancing universal goals such as national sovereignty, liberty, and constitutional legality to which its citizen-soldiers subscribed. Shortly before his death, Captain Thomas Stuart Garnett of the 48th Virginia defined the cause and his expectations of his children. He commanded his wife to raise their children "preferring Constitutional liberty and independence gained though it be by much suffering to inglorious peace under the vile Yankee." And should he fall and should the cause fail, Garnett entreated his wife and their children never to "sink so low in this contest as to rebuke their ancestors for 3 generations . . . by taking up the craven song of union."[24] A third measure that the community used to bind the soldier to the cause was to instill the idea that love of community outweighed personal interest.[25] As Captain George S. Avery, 3d Missouri Cavalry (U.S.), told Lizzie Little, his future wife: "our Country has the first right [on me] & I am ready to say that Lizzie has [only] the next."[26] Lieutenant Colonel Harvey Graham, 22d Iowa, also put country before personal considerations. To Graham, the republic's survival outweighed all other considerations. Echoing the ancient Greek idea voiced by Plato, Graham believed that his welfare and that of his family was embedded in the survival of the republic. Without its benevolent institutions, not only would his family and his business wither but so would the possibility of leading a principled and civilized life.[27]

Western political thought since Plato's *Republic* had argued that individual development could only be nurtured in a harmonious and just political community. Later French revolutionary idealists like Jean-Jacques Rousseau provided a philosophical justification for a citizen's military obligation. Rousseau argued that there was a concordance between self-interest and public interest. Like the Greeks, Rousseau contended that the state had a transcendental value in itself.

It was more than a contractual arrangement between citizens to best attain mutual personal interests: the democratic state was also the source of civilized existence and had a transcendental purpose extending beyond any single individual's pursuit of happiness. Without the state, social life was not possible. Returning to Plato's ideas, the French revolutionaries argued that man was a political animal who could not reach his potential outside democratic society.[28] Citizenship meant a higher level of existence without which a man could never realize his full potential. Defending the polity was essential to civilized life. Breaking the social contract by shirking military obligation or by deserting was the highest of crimes, a crime against the progress of civilization; it was a crime few Civil War volunteers countenanced.[29] Witnessing the execution of deserters at Pine Bluff, Arkansas, Texas Captain Elijah P. Petty thought they got their "just doom" for betraying the cause.[30] John H. Burrill, a member of a New Hampshire regiment, believed that deserters did not merit even a trial and should be shot out of hand.[31]

Not every polity could demand such sacrifices, but republican government was democratic and could legitimately impose what the French called the *impôt du sang*. Contrary to a monarchy, a democracy benefited the whole population. Its wars became, ipso facto, people's wars. The community's interests and those of the individual were synonymous.[32]

Republican tradition further maintained that military service itself served as a school for citizenship. War increased the citizen-soldier's political awareness and buttressed his patriotic convictions. Rousseau argued that military service sharpened the patriotic zeal of freemen and that it cultivated their taste for liberty.[33] The republic formulated an ideal image of the citizen-soldier that originated in the War of Independence, a tradition that continued to prevail during the Civil War. As Mitchell has shown, the Civil War volunteer emulated the Revolutionary War's minuteman ideal. He remained a citizen who did not put aside his civilian identity and his moral and political principles when he enlisted.[34] Echoing Benjamin Franklin's maxims to guide the virtuous republican citizen, Illinois Sergeant Benjamin Hieronymous carried a list of the principles drawn from civilian life that were to help him pattern himself on the ideal citizen-soldier: "Never lose time, Never err the least in Truth, Never say an ill thing of a person, Never be irritable or unkind to any-one, Never indulge in luxuries that are unnecessary, [and] Do all things with consideration."[35]

The American Civil War occurred in the middle of great political changes sweeping both Western Europe and America. The monarch's subject became a citizen, a voter, a participant in civil affairs. As the citizen peopled the political arena and as the political elites solicited his vote, he also began to man the armies of Europe and America as a new type of soldier—the citizen-soldier.

Parallels between the people's armies of the American Civil War appeared with other people's armies such as the French revolutionary army and Lord Kitchener's citizen army at the Somme. Like the people's armies of the American Civil War, the French and British citizen-soldiers were inspired by patriotic ideas associated with their citizen duty. The soldiers of the French Revolution and the Somme had a morality grounded in a set of firmly held values that included patriotism, honor, probity, constancy, sobriety, morality, and self discipline.[36]

American Civil War soldiers' correspondence proclaimed the ideas that were embodied in the idea of a citizen-soldier's patriotic duty: "My whole Soul is wrapt up in this our Country's caus[e]."[37] Patriotic duty was instilled at home and was based on each citizen's personal moral code. After reminding his sons that he had been among the volunteers, Alabama infantryman Thomas S. Taylor recorded his code of conduct for his sons to remember: "Try to live at all times with a conscience void of offence toward God or your fellow man. . . . Be useful to your fellow man. . . . Be useful to Society to the world & to yourselves."[38] It all came down to a sense of personal responsibility, of duty to one's family, home, and country. Ephraim S. Holloway affirmed his sense of citizen responsibility to his wife, declaring: "I feel that it is the duty of every man whose circumstances are such that he can leave home to go forth with a strong arm to crush out this rebellion."[39] Repeating the idea that duty was central to correct behavior and that a good soldier never avoided an unpleasant duty, Samuel Augustus Wildman's father admonished his son for trying to sabotage his work as army clerk so that he could get into the line and join in the fighting. Though his father understood Samuel's zeal, the father warned his son to do his duty wherever he was assigned and not risk censure, for he must emerge from the army with an unblemished record and character.[40]

A citizen's duty was not easy. It required character, personal discipline, and the ability to ward off the temptations of soft living. Jesse B. Connelly admonished himself in his diary when he found himself lounging in bed late. He warned himself that this was a "dangerous habit."[41] And if personal awareness did not show the path of citizen virtue, God would guide the citizen along the straight and narrow course to integrity and steadfastness. An Illinois man, Henry Clinton Forbes, affirmed that when an honorable citizen-soldier did his duty from authentic motive, he was in service to God and under God's guidance.[42] Thus, a reliable citizen-soldier was a morally true soldier who believed in God and followed his commandments.

Benjamin F. Ashenfelter lamented from the banks of the Rappahannock with the 201st Pennsylvania Volunteers that church attendance was declining by 1863.

Desertions were up, but Ashenfelter had no pity for those who were shot for failing to do their patriotic duty. The stern moral code of the citizen-soldier must prevail.[43] When John W. Baldwin's wife wrote that she feared that the years of war were corroding the virtue of the citizens who had "gone a soldiering," Baldwin assured her that he had not changed, that his behavior in camp was no different than at home, and that he comported himself the same way as a soldier or citizen—as a good Christian! He promised her that he never behaved in a manner unbecoming a Christian and a gentlemen: the men in his command could attest to it. He assured her he had never set up a "partnership" with anyone but her. Obviously, he could have made more money by staying home, but he went to war not for profit but for love of country. He remained loyal to his principles. War had not undermined his civilian values.[44]

But most of the men stood the test. Most were not sunshine patriots. In Chattanooga, though besieged, an Ohio regiment passed the requirements of patriotic duty when over three-fourths of its men reenlisted; Sergeant Nathaniel Parmeter declared with pride that with an army of such men, the cause could not be lost.[45] Across the lines at Chattanooga, George Phifer Erwin was utterly fed up with the war, but he too demonstrated the same fortitude. He felt it his patriotic obligation to stand to his duty until the demonic enemy was driven from the land.[46] As the war entered 1864, its bloodiest year, Dewitt Clinton Loudon reaffirmed his patriotic duty: "I am thankful that I had the moral courage to stand by my convictions without counting the cost & so preserved my self respect & the approval of my own conscience."[47]

This new type of soldier could not be motivated only by coercion and material reward, as had been the case with peasant conscripts and regular troops. The people had to be politically socialized to assimilate the patriotic values embodied in the ideal soldier-citizen and to voluntarily acknowledge the legitimacy of democracy's claim on a citizen's life. Coercion was pointless in the face of death at the front. Courage was a societal motivator. Military obligation had to be embedded in the government's legitimacy and the justice of its cause. The population tacitly acknowledged its government's legitimacy by obeying its laws and upholding its ideals. Social expectations weighed heavily on citizens of military age, but there were other sources of military obedience. Self-esteem and personal character, along with devotion to comrades and unit pride, also played a role in forging the soldier's steadfastness. These inducements came into play at different moments in a soldier's military experience. Social expectations and the ideal-soldier model initially were the key factors motivating citizens to enlist.[48] The citizen-soldier in the American Civil War had internalized civic values in the common school, in the church, by reading newspapers, and by participating in elections. One father named his child Liberty Independence; the son bore the name proudly on the muster roll of the 26th Alabama Infantry at Shiloh.

Psychologists Theodor Adorno, Hans J. Eysenck, and Rupert T. Wilkinson, who examined the psychological sources of political behavior and democratic versus authoritarian attitudes, argue that these political beliefs and civic behavior are associated with child-rearing practices and that these customs differ from culture to culture and from era to era.[49] Family life, the church, and the school were the principal agents in the early political socialization of the soldier-citizen, which began in childhood.

As Jean H. Baker has pointed out, although public schools tried to avoid partisan content in the curriculum, they nevertheless had an important role in inculcating civic virtues among their pupils. The country's Founding Fathers believed that a public-school system had to be created to inculcate republican values among the youth or the great democratic experiment would fail. Only a school program could obviate the risks of haphazard socialization by the family or in the church. Professional and patriotic training went hand in hand in the school system. There were many media, but such education mostly came from lessons on the country's political institutions and the Constitution along with American history to idealize the great leaders and the country's enterprise in building the republic. The school material had underlying themes imparting virtues such as obedience, self-control, social order, loyalty, and personal responsibility. Students also were given individual responsibilities in the school. They were awarded honorific appointments as monitors and early on learned the significance of winning office and gaining the admiration of their peers. Extracurricular activities also socialized students into the political process through literary societies, debating clubs, and mock elections.[50]

Families, however, were the chief source of political socialization and partisan training. Political leaders like John Quincy Adams encouraged parents to teach their children the principles of American republicanism and the ideas embodied in the Constitution. The importance of inculcating civic virtues at home gave the mother a particularly important role. Books and periodicals like *Parenting Magazine* on raising children encouraged mothers to foster rectitude and public spirit in their young and counseled mothers that a republic could not survive without a solid family structure to groom its children to become good citizens. While the mother was the chief definer of civic principles, the father became the source of the children's partisan attachments. The community engendered the earliest and deepest partisan attachments. Pella, Iowa, for example, with its Dutch immigrant population and Dutch-style homes, supported Democrats election after election with percentages ranging from 72 to 82 percent. Because there were fewer sources of entertainment in small communities, the youth soon joined their fathers in supporting candidates, developing partisan loyalties, and absorbing the prevailing partisan ties in their towns.[51]

The 1840s, however, were a period of turmoil over child-rearing practices. Two schools of thought collided. The traditional school, represented by the writings of Joseph Hale, advocated a stern approach to child rearing. This Calvinist-inspired doctrine assumed that God had already branded children with the mark of Cain, so they needed stern discipline to restrain their passions and keep them on the straight and narrow moral road. Coercion and control were central to this school of child rearing. Nevertheless, this doctrine was rapidly losing ground to a new naturalist school that reflected the ideas in Rousseau's *Emile*. Horace Mann, the Massachusetts educator, was this philosophy's principal exponent in America. Mann, a naturalist like Rousseau, argued that child rearing should rely less on coercion and more on instilling proper behavior by showing affection and by setting an example instead of using the strap. The naturalists assumed that children were endowed with innate goodness. The parent had only to encourage good behavior by example and allow these positive traits to come out spontaneously. There was no need to formally inculcate them.[52]

Naturalist ideas were beginning to appear in popular child-rearing manuals. Lydia Maria Child's *The Mother's Book*, first published in 1831, admonished mothers for giving rules instead of inspiring sentiments. Good education should not use guilt, fear, or pain as pedagogical vehicles. Instead, it should rely on love and affection. Education by example was far more effective than direct rules and prohibitions. Also, education had to consider each child's individual personality and take into consideration individual character differences. It was better to avoid rigidly imposing uniform rules, and if punishment had to be inflicted, it always should be carried out as temperately as possible. It is difficult to say how much headway these ideas were making in the rural communities of the West, but judging by the success Mann's ideas were having in Massachusetts and by Child's book sales, these new theories were certainly gaining dominance in the northeastern part of the country.[53]

These new child rearing ideas dovetailed with the belief that virtuous republican behavior was supposed to be self-generated. A virtuous soldier was guided by his own reasoned obedience.[54] The citizen-soldier would stay the course not because of externally imposed discipline but in great measure because he believed he was doing the right thing. This inner-generated sense of civic duty motivated the men to volunteer and even reenlist after their initial terms of service had expired. They believed they knew their duty, and they did not need their superiors to define it for them.

Religion also played a role in socializing the citizen-soldier. Some families prayed together and took turns reading Bible passages. They inculcated a moral code in the children, at the same time teaching them reading skills.[55] Soldiers maintained this custom in the field. For example, John Joyes Jr., a Confederate in Byrnes's Battery who was captured during Morgan's ill-fated raid into Ohio, sustained his morale by reading a chapter of the Bible each day.[56] Civic values were propounded from the pulpit and were explained in Sunday school. There were more than thirty thousand Sunday school libraries disseminating uplifting reading material to the country's youth at the outbreak of the war.[57] Church activity itself, more than the contents of religious teaching per se, politicized the citizenry. It was another form of community participation and socialization.

Common schools also were increasing literacy at a rapid pace. Illiteracy ranged from a low of 2.58 percent in Maine to a high of 25.78 percent in Delaware. High literacy rates made it far easier to train a people's army of raw recruits. Both officers and men were literate enough to read military manuals and so were able to improve their skills on their own.[58] Schools, however, did more than teach reading skills. They fostered civic virtues, assuming that an ignorant citizenry could never sustain a republic. The foundation of republican government was universal education, which inculcated moral and civic principles in its future citizens.[59] Only such an educated class could avert anarchy and live in harmony. The most important republican virtue was self-control in society. A self-controlled citizenry was essential for self-government to work. Civic virtue would prevent democracy from dissolving into chaotic selfish interests. Horace Mann advised teachers to encourage good behavior in their pupils by showing that disciplined, right-minded action is essential to the functioning of republican polity. Laws were the manifestation of a moral social order.[60] In his 1848 report, Mann advised: "Nothing would be easier to follow in the train of so many writers to demonstrate by logic, by history, and by the nature of the case, that a republican form of government, without intelligence in the people, must be, on a vast scale, what a mad-house, without superintendent or keepers, would be, on a small one;—the despotism of a few succeeded by universal anarchy."[61]

Schoolbooks went beyond defining character attributes. They also bore ideological content.[62] Hess reminds us that Civil War–era textbooks were filled with ideological lessons emphasizing devotion to the common good. Children also were exposed to a burgeoning popular culture that provided inexpensive dime novels, many of which told of the heroic deeds of their forefathers during the Revolutionary War, providing a conclusive definition of patriotic devotion.[63] The most popular common school text was the *McGuffey Reader*. It first appeared in 1836 and by the beginning of the next century 122 million copies had been printed.[64] Initially, it was a response to the inroads that Mann's and Child's permissive ideas were making in the more progressive northeastern school systems. Mann's and Child's teachings were collateral to the rise of Jacksonian democracy.[65] The spread of progressive naturalism in the schools, however, halted in the backward regions of the country. *McGuffey Readers* held sway in the rural areas. Its teaching doctrine was less permissive. To retain its foothold in the conservative southern market, the readers were ambivalent on slavery while broaching progressive naturalist ideas alongside an emphasis on discipline.[66] Ambiguity permitted soldiers on both sides of the Mason-Dixon line to find ideas that corresponded to their own regional peculiarities.

Besides ambivalence on the slavery issue, the civic principles inculcated by schools in the North were generally similar to those in the South. Thus, the two sections did not have noticeably different civic canons taught in their respective public schools. However, there were deeper social cleavages between classes in the South, because the wealthy spent disproportionately more on educating their offspring, tending to sequester their children away from the common folk by enrolling them in private academies, where spending per pupil was more than ten times as high as in the common schools.[67] This separation of rich and the rest in parallel school systems likely fostered elitist attitudes among the southern planter-class youths. Class differences were probably less sharply drawn in the North. Nevertheless, common soldiers—North and South—shared essentially the same civic values. Even if the politically aware Southern recruit's grammatical style and spelling skills left much to be desired, he was just as aware of his political beliefs and just as intent on voicing his opinions.

After the young man left Sunday school and the classroom, he continued to come in contact with political principles through membership in a militia company. These military organizations had undergone a renewal of interest in the 1850s.[68] Patriotism mixed with martial posturing and good fellowship at the local tavern enlivened the weekend for young men in many a dreary rural hamlet.

A youth's political socialization did not rely entirely on the structured formalized process of a militia organization. Young men could absorb political culture by reading about national heroes and visiting their shrines. By the 1840s the United States had gained enough historical maturity to begin formulating its own patriotic mythology. Monuments were being erected on Bunker Hill, and the U.S. Capitol building was in progress, along with other sanctified places that could serve as the object of patriotic pilgrimages.[69] Patriotic festivals commemorating historical events such as Washington's birthday and Independence Day were being celebrated across the country.

The average young man of the 1840s and 1850s did not have to go far afield to absorb political values. Political parties were beginning to reach out to the electorate as property barriers were falling and the franchise expanded to most white adult males. At the same time, political campaigns were becoming increasingly partisan. Every village witnessed a traveling political road show in which stump speakers outdid each other with patriotic oratory while they jousted in political debate.[70] While community life in European villages centered on religious occasions, American community life revolved around honoring historic, patriotic occasions and election rallies. Much of the political entertainment was in the local broadside newspaper; even the remotest township had its newspaper if it were linked to the world by telegraph. John Blair of the 80th Tennessee Infantry exemplified the rise in newspaper readership. His diary entries reflected his eager perusal of the local paper for war news: "no knews of a warlike character," and later "no war knews."[71] Soldiers had a great deal of time on their hands between campaigns. Camp life occasioned political discussions fed by fresh information from the newspapers. News vendors hawked the large city dailies in the camps. These publications reached the front in one to four days, and they cost about five cents. Where there were illiterates in camp, the company or mess often appointed a reader to give the news to illiterate comrades. The U.S. Christian Commission also provided field libraries that were transported to the front in wooden boxes that opened into three-sided bookcases. The chaplain or surgeon distributed them. Some units even operated portable presses for printing administration forms for the military bureaucracy but also for publishing camp newspapers.[72] The local newspaper was not only a significant source of political issues but more importantly, a significant vehicle for political participation.[73] Before the war, many young men already took part in political life by contributing copy to newspapers. At the outset of the war there were more than three thousand newspapers in circulation and more than two hundred periodicals.[74] During the war, soldiers continued reporting on events as stringers for their local newspapers. Sometimes they earned a modest fee for the service. The *Chicago Tribune* paid William H. Bradbury of the 129th Illinois five dollars per letter. The young reporter was eager to get the money, but he realized that he risked reprisals from his commander. Officers disapproved of their men communicating with the press.[75]

Small isolated communities exercised an important role in framing the political outlook of America's soldiers in the nineteenth century. Ethnically and culturally homogeneous, the social space of these communities was very narrowly defined. Every aspect of a youth's life was subject to his fellow townspeople's scrutiny. Conformity was the norm. Any serious breech of social norms meant humiliation, ostracism, and expulsion. Community pressure imposed standards of patriotic behavior and therefore pushed youth to enlist. The community had a large repertoire of ways to impose expectations on its young men. For example, neighbors sent recalcitrant youth women's undergarments, signifying a lack of manliness, and made disparaging comments on the street.

The press unleashed a flood of patriotic rhetoric, exhorting the community's young men to answer their country's call and castigating those who failed to show requisite alacrity in joining up. The *South Western Baptist* in Tuskegee, Alabama, chided those who had not enlisted: "Why do you stay at home while others are in the field? Are they not as good as you? . . . Examine yourselves and see if selfishness or cowardice or some unworthy motive is not at the bottom of all your excuses. If you have any mettle in you let it be seen now. The time has come and you know it. . . . Would you let women and children hoot you into the army?"[76] In February 1862 a woman wrote to the *Memphis Daily Appeal* demanding to know what was holding the men of Memphis back. Memphis was about to be taken by the Yankees and the youth of the city were walking about as if nothing had happened. She goaded them, asking: "Are you really willing . . . to be slapped in the face, snubbed, pricked with bayonets . . . and insulted by every epithet that a gloating jubilant Yankee can manufacture?"[77] Another Southern Valkyrie told the *Memphis Daily Appeal* that excuses like staying home to protect the women would not wash. The mothers, sisters, and sweethearts could see through such cowardly excuses. The young men of the city should shed pusillanimous subterfuges and do their duty. The best way to protect their womenfolk was to shoulder muskets and go to the front.[78] Henry Morton Stanley, later a famed explorer, was a resident of Arkansas and was caught by his townswomen's bellicosity. When the local female fire-eaters found his patriotism wanting, they sent him a parcel with women's underclothes so that he could dress appropriately as a fainthearted stay-at-home. Stanley got the message and hurriedly enlisted in the 6th Arkansas in time to get shot at and captured at Shiloh.[79]

The community continued to keep a watchful eye on its men to see that they did their duty after they left for the front. When they failed to fulfill their responsibility as citizen-soldiers, they sullied their regiment's honor and that of the community they represented. Fellow soldiers reported on comrades who failed to measure up to the standards expected of citizen-soldiers. Second Lieutenant William Vaught of the 5th Company of Louisiana's Washington Artillery sent his mother a list of the men who had "skipped away" during their first engagement at Shiloh. On the other side, a soldier of Company A, 14th Illinois, who fought in the same battle recorded the names of the twenty-two men in the company who had failed to behave in a "manner worthy of a son of Illinois."[80] The men's letters reflected their community's power over them. For example, William Goodrich James, Battery C, 1st Wisconsin Heavy Artillery, assured his father in a letter from Chattanooga: "I have not been in the guard house and I have more respect for my folks than to make a fool of myself."[81]

The soldier was a product of his community and felt obliged to conduct himself so that he would maintain its respect and support. The community had defined his obligations and had instilled his initial political awareness. Once he took the field, the issues arising from the war widened the scope of a soldier's political outlook and sharpened his understanding of politics. And later, once the first flush of campaigning was over and both sides realized that it would be a long and costly struggle, the rank and file began to devote more thought to the conduct of the war and to defining the war aims. The ensuing debate was more intense in the Union army, because by 1863 the North had to address more issues than the South did. Northern soldiers not only had to consider what was the best way to win the war, but they also had the further burden of defining the kind of peace that they wanted to impose on the South. With the Emancipation Proclamation in January 1863, the war was no longer a conservative struggle to reunite the country and reimpose old institutions. It had become a revolutionary conflict to change the South's class relations by destroying the wealth and power of its ruling landed oligarchy and confiscating its slaves. After the ruling class was overthrown, the army installed pro-Union regimes in the occupied states. These measures generated new issues such as arming the slaves, setting peace terms, keeping the home front behind the war, and suppressing dissent in the ranks. In addressing these complex issues, the Northern soldiers broadened their political outlook, and they became more politically sophisticated. Conversely, fewer dilemmas confronted the Confederates. They saw no alternative to fighting to defend their homes. Choices seemed simpler for them, and they faced fewer issues that would have expanded their political awareness. For this reason, they were slightly less politically sophisticated.

This study defines political awareness in its broadest sense. The idea includes all areas of human life in the state, including war, so it is more encompassing than definitions that restrict politics to government affairs.[82] Politics is "the womb in which war is developed."[83] War is simply another dimension of politics. The scope of the soldiers' outlook includes their views about elections and their judgments about political leaders, but it also includes their appraisals of military leadership and the strategic situation. And a soldier's ideas did not have to be ideologically sophisticated to be contained in the collection of letters and diaries. Few soldiers had an ideologically sophisticated worldview, one that had a precise and coherent belief structure and an articulate system of convictions that fit all the soldier's opinions together logically.[84] Most soldiers' and officers' outlooks were imprecise and inchoate, and they often included mutually contradictory ideas. For example, combatants believed in liberty and justice for all and wanted the war brought to a close expeditiously. Many also thought this aim could best be achieved by arming blacks. At the same time, however, they opposed political equality with the freedmen. Such contradictory views are not surprising. An ideology is a particularly sophisticated belief system that systematically lays out its assumptions and explains how they relate to each other.[85] Though the distinction between ideologies and near ideologies is ultimately arbitrary, as a rule, ideologies are usually articulated by intellectuals. Such belief systems are coherent and reduce contradictions. Few enlisted men or even field-grade officers were sophisticated enough to resolve such contradictions.

Several elements shaped the soldiers' worldview, including the political situation at home, the war effort, war aims, and peace terms. Politically aware soldiers also held opinions about their political and military leadership's capabilities. Furthermore, soldiers wanted to know how the big picture was unfolding. Politically aware soldiers also had considerable interest in manpower policy, bounties, and the draft. They commented on enemy military capabilities and speculated about the deployment of the armies. Concerns about the duration of the war and the chances of survival also appeared in their letters and diaries. Gaining insight on these various issues had practical implications for the soldiers; it helped them assess risks and gauge their chances of surviving the war.

I have used three measures of political awareness in assessing letters and diaries for this study: first, the precision or acuity appearing in the soldiers' political and military outlook; second, the breadth of the men's interest in the world around them; and third, the degree to which the men expressed a sense of political effectiveness.

Political acuity, the first measure of the soldiers' awareness, provided two levels of military and political sophistication. At the lowest level were soldiers who only mentioned inchoate patriotic symbols like the Union, the Constitution, and freedom. Such soldiers were politically aware but inarticulate; they did not provide a reasoned explanation for their statements. Their comments were usually straightforward descriptions or unreflective opinions. This low level of political sophistication also included soldiers who expressed a narrow interest in the war. They were only concerned with what directly affected them. With little interest in broader issues, they focused only on conditions along their immediate front. They were not inclined to take a broader view of the war. For example, one soldier noted that Vicksburg had fallen, but he did not comment on the strategic implications of its capture. The soldier seemed unaware that it meant opening the Mississippi or cutting the Confederacy in two. Other soldiers cursed Grant but never expressed any reasons for making the judgment. Finally, this lowest level of political sophistication included soldiers who gave uninformed opinions about the political conduct of the war. For example, one unsophisticated combatant made no effort to explain why the Copperheads were dangerous and how their activities affected the war effort.

Politically aware soldiers, on the other hand, not only made judgments about

"Les armées délibérantes." *Frank Leslie's Illustrated Newspaper,* October 22, 1864. Soldiers gather to read political handbills during the 1864 presidential election.

political or military issues but went beyond these assessments to give a coherent and reasoned explanation for their views. These more sophisticated soldiers tried to understand how issues, leaders, and events were related and how they affected the progress of the war. They tried to comprehend the consequences and the causes of military policies and events. For example, more politically sophisticated soldiers not only voiced opinions about emancipation but also tried to assess its impact on Southern morale and manpower supply. A politically sophisticated soldier was a reflective observer of events.[86]

Having described the outlook of the politically motivated soldiers, how can we define political awareness and then establish indicators for measuring its components—political acuity, scope of interests, and sense of political effectiveness? Then I will estimate how many of the troops were politically motivated and what percentage of this group were the most highly politically motivated.

More than a third (34.5 percent) of the soldiers exhibited a higher level of political sophistication in their correspondence. There was little difference between Confederates and Unionists: Northerners were only slightly more articulate than the Southerners (36 percent to 32 percent), though the conclusions are tentative.[87] Nonetheless, these figures call into question the presumption that the South's inferior school system had made Confederate soldiers less politically articulate. The similar level of political articulateness among Southern soldiers suggests that they had other means for sharpening their political awareness, such as conversations with friends and family, attending political gatherings, or listening to speeches. Second, the figures challenge the idea that there was an atrophied party system in the South after the collapse of the Whig Party.[88] In fact, political tensions intensified in both sections. In the North the Democratic and Republican Parties continued to function. In the case of the Democrats, deep splits emerged between war and peace factions. Opposition to Lincoln's administration coalesced around the latter group. The South had no two-party system to speak of, and there was no national organization around which the opposition could cohere. Dissidence took the form of scattered regional groups using a wide repertoire of collective action that ranged from contesting state and local elections to organizing seditious associations, for example, William Holden's bid as a peace candidate in North Carolina's gubernatorial race. By contrast, with a national party system more or less intact in the North, opponents could operate nationally and mobilize behind national parties and support like the McClellan-Pendleton Democratic ticket.

New England was reputed to be the most progressive region in the country. It had the best schools and the most influential abolitionists. New Englanders, it could be assumed, would be more politically articulate than soldiers from other regions. Yet when troops from Maine, Massachusetts, Rhode Island, Vermont, and New Hampshire were compared with those from Ohio, Indiana, Illinois, and Iowa, the midwesterners scored higher than the Yankees. Thirty-six percent of the midwesterners were politically sophisticated, compared to 30 percent of the New Englanders,[89] possibly because dissenter movements were more vocal in the midwestern states than in New England. For example, Copperhead leader Clement Laird Vallandigham was known throughout the Midwest. The peace Democrats had paralyzed the legislatures in Indiana and Illinois. These events elicited more interest among the Midwestern volunteers, who vociferously condemned the peace movement.

Upper-class soldiers (those who had university degrees or who came from important wealthy families) tended, not surprisingly, to show a higher level of political sophistication. Fifty-six percent of the 112 soldiers from such families displayed acute political perception and made reflective comments.[90] Since it was often impossible to determine a soldier's social background, like James M. McPherson I have been obliged to use rank as a proxy for class, with the evident caveat that by the middle of the war many men of modest background had been promoted from the ranks to company-grade commissions.[91] Again not surprisingly, the results indicated that officers were proportionately more articulate than the rank and file: officers were nearly twice as likely to be politically articulate as the enlisted men, 45.7 percent to 28 percent.[92] This was lower than the score registered in the cross-tabulation, which included both upper-class soldiers and officers, suggesting that class was a more important determinant than rank in deciding an individual's political sophistication (56 percent by class and 45.7 percent by rank). The lower percentage for officers as opposed to upper-class soldiers may be attributed to the increasing number of officers who came from modest backgrounds and who rose from the ranks in the second half of the war.

A second indicator of soldiers' political awareness was the breadth of political interest shown in letters and diaries. I assessed the number of different types of topics in the correspondence. Since people may have a large range of opinions, most which may only be understood superficially, breadth was not always a very accurate measure of political competence. Generally, however, a large range of topics suggests a higher level of political sophistication, especially if a soldier also scored well on the first indicator, related to his political acuity. The soldier's range of interests was divided into two categories: a soldier with a narrow range of interests limited his preoccupations to only one or two types of topics, whereas soldiers with a broad range of interests commented on three or more types. Ultimately, however, an organized political outlook requires an ideology. The greater the amount and range of information, the more the need for a coherent worldview to systemize the soldier's opinions and information. Moreover, an ideology makes retention easier.[93]

The range of topics in the soldiers' correspondence and diaries included several issues: the military situation on other fronts, an assessment of the high command's conduct of the war, demands for more energetic measures, the justice of the cause, state and local political issues, the quality of political leadership, national election issues and the soldier vote, emancipation, disloyalty at home and in the army, foreign affairs, conditions in the enemy camp, the chances that recent peace feelers might succeed, Lincoln's assassination, the implications of defeat, inchoate patriotic symbols, and the state of morale at home.

Only 28.6 percent of all soldiers had a broad political outlook, 28.5 percent of Southerners and 28.7 percent of Northern troops.[94] Conversely, there was a larger difference between the New Englanders, only 19 percent of whom displayed a broad range of interests, and the Midwesterners (almost 27 percent) than between Confederates and Unionists.[95] Here again, the stronger dissenter movements in the Midwest probably intensified political interest in that region. There was virtually no difference between officer (51 percent) and rank and file (49 percent) breadth of interest.[96] Promotions from the ranks reduced differences between enlisted men and officers. Such continuity is important for a people's army, because a common outlook between the men and their officers prevents the rise of Bonapartist tendencies in the officer corps or Spartacism among the rank and file. There was, however, a larger difference in breadth of interest between the upper-class volunteers (54.5 percent of whom had a wide range of interests) and the rest of the soldiers (45.5 percent).[97]

A soldier's sense of political effectiveness is also an indicator of his level of political awareness. Soldiers who were politically passive did not feel that they could affect the outcome of the situation. However, politically passive soldiers were not mute, and the tenor of their views had a different tone. Their correspondence evoked themes of powerlessness, victimization, and inability to change things. They saw themselves as pawns on the military chessboard. Despite some knowledge about what was going on and some interest in the big picture, they did not believe they could make a difference. They took less interest in the causes and consequences of important events. They only sought to survive the ordeal. These soldiers believed they were only cannon fodder. Zeal was pointless; they were prisoners of great forces, they were victims of the war. Such soldiers spoke as observers rather than as agents of history.[98] They did not take political initiatives or formulate resolutions condemning Copperheads; they obediently signed whatever resolutions the officers put before them.[99]

As citizen-soldiers, however, most Civil War volunteers were by definition motivated by the belief that they were agents of history who were defending noble principles. They generally fit into the second category of political effectiveness: They were active participants in the political process. Among Northern states, Indiana, Illinois, and Ohio had the most active soldiers based on enlistment rates.[100] High enlistment rates coincided with high electoral turnouts in these three states, where voter participation ranged from 85 to 90 percent in presidential elections.[101] The mid-nineteenth-century American political culture was highly participatory. Citizens exhibited a high level of confidence in their civic competence and political effectiveness. Alexis de Tocqueville observed the American propensity to organize social groups through church, clubs, schools, local frontier governments, and militia companies.[102] The Civil War soldiers personified this national characteristic. The soldiers' letters frequently expressed pride in being volunteers and in doing their patriotic duty. They scorned those who stayed behind and passively stood by. Humphrey Hughes Hood, a surgeon with the 117th Illinois, voiced his belief that he was an important and effective agent of history who was saving the republic and advancing democracy and individual liberty in the world. He saw every victory as a personal accomplishment and every war aim as a personal obligation. Hood also took time to draft resolutions supporting the Republican governor of Illinois, Richard Yates, against the peace Democrats.[103]

The vast majority of the soldiers in both armies believed that they were playing a significant role in a historic struggle, though the sense of political effectiveness was 9 percent higher among Northerners than it was among South-erners.[104] This slight disparity may be partly attributed to religious differences between the two sections. Southerners exhibited more religiosity. As things got worse at the front, it fostered otherworldliness among Confederates. Pietism rose in parallel with frequent defeats after 1863, which in turn fostered political passivity in the Confederate army. Sergeant Major Philip H. Powers, 1st Virginia Regiment of the Head Quarters Cavalry Corps, expressed his pietism when he wrote from northern Virginia in early 1864: "Each day teaches me the leson more impressively that all our help must come from God"—not from bigger bat-talions.[105] Private Constantine Hege, Company H, 48th North Carolina Infan-try, also reflected this inclination among Southerners when he put himself in God's hands. As Lee fell back after Gettysburg, Hege wrote to his parents that he had lost faith in his leaders and saw little chance of victory. Only fatalistic duty kept him in his place: "I am sometimes almost out of courage and sometimes almost tempted to desert, but then I think of that wont do. then I think of the providence of God.... I hope this war may soon close and pray that the almighty may preserve my and your lives."[106] Though Northern troops also expressed re-ligious themes, pietism and fatalistic devotion to duty did not appear as fre-quently among them as it did among Southerners.[107]

At the outbreak of a war, the banner is unfurled, and all reason is in the trum-pet. At the beginning of the Civil War, however, few had very clear ideas about political issues. Each side marshaled its forces in the name of idealistic patriotic rhetoric. The Unionists went to war for the Constitution and Union, while the South fought to repel the northern invader. As the war went into its second year, however, more specific issues emerged. Questions arose over the quality of the military and political leadership, over the best strategy for winning the war, over how to get support at home and thwart the rising tide of dissent. Defining war aims became a burning issue in the North. These questions stimulated discus-sions in the ranks and raised many soldiers' political consciousness. A compari-son of 241 soldiers' letters and diaries written during the first year of the war with those of 772 soldiers serving between 1863 and 1865 showed that the percentage of soldiers who had a high level of political acuity almost doubled from 21.6 per-cent to 38.6 percent.[108]

The war experience also broadened the volunteers' political awareness. The number of soldiers whose political outlook became more comprehensive nearly tripled from 12.9 percent in 1861–63 to 33.5 percent by the second half of the war.[109] Yet the war simultaneously reduced other soldiers' sense of empower-ment. These soldiers who came to believe they were only cogs in the war ma-chine increased fivefold from only 2.5 percent during the initial patriotic excite-ment to 11 percent as the war reached its midpoint.[110]

What portion of all the soldiers were politically aware? My previous studies of soldiers at Shiloh and of Wisconsin troops found that 23 percent of Shiloh's combatants and 33 percent of the Wisconsin men were politically motivated. If this ratio is representative of the army at large, we can then extrapolate that the 1,013 politically aware soldiers in this current study also comprise between 23 and 33 percent of all soldiers.

After assessing the soldiers' political acuity, breadth of interest, and sense of political effectiveness, how many of them scored highly on all three measures of political awareness? Nineteen percent of soldiers (197 of 1,013) simultaneously exhibited a high level of political acuity and a broad scope of interests and a sense of personal empowerment. This 197-soldier highly articulate subgroup represented perhaps 5 to 6 percent of all soldiers.[111] Although this group may seem small, its members defined the political ideas for the rest of the soldiers. The subgroup contained the true believers, the nucleus that sustained army morale and explained events to others. They read and interpreted the news for their illiterate comrades. They led discussions around the campfire. They were the political backbone of a people's army.

In summary, people's armies like those that fought the Civil War relied heavily on political motivation to rally their soldiers to the colors. These highly politically motivated soldiers were the backbone of the army. About 25 percent of the soldiers were interested in politics, and their political awareness came from child-rearing practices, schooling, public festivals, and local political life. Soldiers' political awareness can be assessed through political acuity, scope of interest, and sense of political effectiveness. Among the 1,013 politically aware soldiers who were gauged according to these three indicators of political sophistication, approximately 15 percent registered a high level of awareness for all three. These were the true believers, the most articulate and most important in motivating their fellow citizen-soldiers. Chapters 3 and 4 will survey the topics that constituted the politically aware soldiers' outlook.

3 The Strategic Picture

SOLDIERS' VIEWS ON GENERALS AND THEIR
CONDUCT OF THE WAR

The overall military situation was the most frequent topic in the politically motivated soldiers' correspondence during the Civil War. The subject appeared in over a third of the letters and diaries examined. L. F. Davis, a Confederate based at Fort Pillow near Memphis, sensed the strategic wind shifting in spring 1862: "The times look squally. . . . If the Yanks whips us at Corinth we are gone up for they will have all the advantage of us."[1] Davis appeared to realize that the loss of Corinth would disrupt the railroad network into western Tennessee, cut off Memphis, and threaten his own position at Fort Pillow. Politically aware soldiers like Davis followed the progress of their campaigns as well as movements on other fronts. Scanning the strategic situation from the Mississippi to the Atlantic, Ordnance Sergeant James Albright, 12th Virginia Battery, recorded in his diary in June 1864 that "the news from the West is very cheering—Forrest has given the enemy a severe flogging. Hampton has, also, whipped them in the Valley. [And] Grant is thought to be coming over to see us [south of the James]."[2] The men badgered the people back home to send newspapers so that they could keep abreast of the "big picture."[3] The men realized that the general military situation had an impact on many political issues, such as the public attitude toward the government, the chance that their localities might be invaded, and the chance for the opposition party to gain in the next election. The "big picture" was thus closely tied to the political situation.

Confederate citizen-soldiers were significantly more interested in the big picture (43 percent) than were their Union foes (31.8 percent).[4] The Confederates were more immediately affected by the strategic situation: their homes lay in the path of invading Northern forces. In addition, political issues were less complex for the Southerners. For the Confederates, who were defending their homes, the central focus of the war remained above all a military one. Conversely, the Northern troops' concerns were more varied and complex. As the attackers, they were not merely fighting for survival. General strategy had to be calibrated with important political questions, such as the type of war aims to pursue. If the war aims were to be revolutionary and radical enough to destroy the slavery-based social system in the South, then the war had to be an unrelenting assault on all fronts and against all elements of the enemy society. If the war had only limited political and strategic aims, it could be fought with surgical strokes against key strategic military objectives. For this reason, the overall military situation had important political implications.

Among the strategic concerns that appeared in the correspondence of Southern and Northern troops were the deployment and capabilities of the opposing side. Junius Newport Bragg of the 33d Arkansas carefully measured each side's advantages in the light of the Confederacy's twin defeats at Gettysburg and Vicksburg. He wondered if the Confederacy could still reverse the situation. Bragg believed that even though the North had the advantage in numbers and materiel, the South retained strategic superiority. It could use its inner lines of communication to improve its leverage against the larger federal forces by concentrating its troops against weak points of the Union deployment.[5]

Looking across the 31st Iowa's trenches toward the enemy at Vicksburg, Private Joseph Kohout, a Czech, summed up the Confederate situation: "The Rebels got 2 Generals [against them] and the best one . . . is General Starvation."[6] As the 1864 campaign season opened, Captain Elias Davis, Company B, 8th Alabama Regiment, also took measure of the enemy and its leadership, writing home: "If Gen'l Grant's *pole* is long enough to knock down the persimon [Richmond] that McClenan's Popes' Burnsides' Hookers' and Meades' were not long enough to reach the [tree] we will admit that Genl Grant wags the longest *pole* in America."[7] Others took their analysis of the military situation much further. They contemplated the political repercussions associated with victories and defeats. Reading the federal press, Bragg thought that the North was having manpower problems because of low morale and heavy losses, which would have explained why the Union abandoned Tennessee Governor Andrew Johnson's plan to liberate East Tennessee.[8] A year earlier, Captain Henry Clinton Forbes, Company B, 7th Illinois Cavalry, weighed the effects of the strategic reverses on the political situation in the North. Things were bleak after the Union defeats before Vicksburg and Fredericksburg in late 1862. Forbes feared that because of these events the Copperheads would be able to take over the Democratic Party. "I am afraid that the democrats are going to betray us," he warned his sister.[9] This same belief kept Confederate hopes alive until summer 1864. Captain William Biggs, Company A, 17th North Carolina Troops, who was fighting in the trenches at Petersburg, thought General Jubal Early's campaign up the Shenandoah Valley might "turn the tables" on General Ulysses S. Grant and strengthen Democratic election prospects. He hoped Early's move would force

Grant to weaken his grip on Petersburg in order to relieve pressure on Washington.[10] Confederates like Biggs had a fairly good idea of the electoral ramifications arising from the situation on the battlefield in summer 1864. Commanding a Texas Battery in Georgia, Major James Postell Douglas thought General Robert E. Lee's stubborn defense of Richmond and General Joseph E. Johnston's stand before Atlanta would divide moderate and radical Republicans and occasion Abraham Lincoln's defeat.[11]

Instead, the South's military situation began to deteriorate even further in fall 1864, so Edwin W. Bearse, Company E, 40th Massachusetts Volunteer Infantry, thought that the tightening Union grip on Petersburg and Atlanta would assure a Republican victory at the polls. Bearse also realized that hunger was Lincoln's ally, noting that each decline in the Rebels' caloric intake improved Lincoln's chances of winning the election and gaining his war aims.[12] Humphrey Hughes Hood, surgeon, 3d U.S. Colored Troops, shared the rising optimism over the favorable nexus between the political and military situations. "The capture of Mobile, Petersburg or Charleston, would send McClellan stock down fifty percent below its present rate. While the defeat of Lee and the capture of Richmond would drive it quite out of the market. . . . Sherman's victories in Georgia have depressed it terribly and now it remains for Grant to annihilate it."[13] Confederate Commissary Major John A. Hooper of Walthall's Brigade was equally aware of the South's declining fortunes. He could only hope that the South could hang on a little longer and that some military success would strengthen the peace movements in the North: "If we can hold our ground until after the election, I am of the opinion it will result in an out and out Peaceman, or the splitting up of the remaining United States, either of which will be of incalculable value to us."[14]

Yet despite their political savvy, hope and desperation often colored the accuracy of the men's perception of the big picture. The Confederates looked beyond the lines for relief in illusions about political divisions in the North leading to an early peace. In 1863 Martin Malone Gash, 65th North Carolina Troops, vainly believed that General Sterling Price was on his way to Richmond to act as mediator for the northwestern states. Gash harbored the forlorn hope that the states of the old Northwest would secede from the Union after the defeats in late 1862.[15] Some Confederates grabbed at other straws. Robert Patrick of the 4th Louisiana thought Northern politics was less important than the attitude of foreign powers. Ultimately, Patrick desperately believed the issue would be decided by French intervention.[16]

Along with observing the demoralizing effect of political dissident movements in the enemy camp and the enemy's ability to conduct the war, soldiers also assessed the competence of new commanders and weighed their effect on the course of the war. Lieutenant Benjamin J. Ashenfelter of the 35th Pennsylvania took stock of the latest round of appointments in the Army of the Potomac: "[Now] the Removal of [General Ambrose E. Burnside]. In My Opinion Old Joe Hooker is the best of the two. But Both he & Burnsides is not worth One McClellan." [17] Besides exhibiting a broader military perspective that extended to tactical and strategic levels, politically aware soldiers also were more inclined to criticize the high command. In so doing, they were extending the conventions of their civilian political life to the military arena. A democracy gave its citizen-soldiers the right to share in selecting political leaders, and the men assumed that the same right extended to judging their commanders' military abilities.

Interest in the competence of the high command was just as intense as interest in the overall strategic picture. The men were keenly aware of the political fallout from a failed command, the implications of such bungling for the course of the war, and their repercussions for the survival of the republic. Approximately one-third (31 percent) of the troops made judgments about the quality of their military leaders, and even more (36 percent) commented on the military situation. A total of 318 soldiers and officers discussed the quality of the military leadership. Surprisingly, 58.4 percent of their comments were favorable. Neither army was especially dissatisfied with its commanders. Nevertheless, the Southern troops felt somewhat more favorably toward their high command, 62 percent to 58 percent. When Confederate soldiers from the western theater (Texas, Missouri, Tennessee, Arkansas, Alabama, Mississippi, Kentucky, and Louisiana) were compared with Rebel troops in the eastern theater (Georgia, Florida, North and South Carolina, and Virginia), many of whom were fighting under Lee, not surprisingly the eastern Confederates were more confident in the high command than the western troops, 69.1 percent to 55.7 percent. [18]

The difference between western troops and eastern troops in the Union army was more surprising. Contrary to expectations, the easterners (men from Pennsylvania, Vermont, New Hampshire, Maine, Connecticut, New Jersey, and New York) had more favorable opinions of their commanders than their western counterparts (soldiers from Iowa, Illinois, Indiana, Kansas, Missouri, Ohio, and Wisconsin). Almost two-thirds (65.1 percent) of the easterners voiced support for their military leaders, compared to only 50.1 percent of the western troops. [19] The eastern Unionists' high level of support for their generals is surprising yet comprehensible. After July 1863, the Army of the Potomac never again was defeated. Despite heavy losses under Grant, there was a feeling of inexorable progress against Lee. As early as spring 1863, when Joseph E. Hooker commanded the army, the men appreciated Hooker's efforts to improve their lot. Many also

Soldiers regularly wrote home recording their views of the progress of the war, their opinions on political issues, and their assessment of political and military leaders. Here soldiers of the 41st Massachusetts Regiment with Banks's expedition write home from the hurricane deck of the transport *North Star* upon their arrival at Ship Island in the Gulf of Mexico. Louis Shepard Moat, ed., *Frank Leslie's Illustrated Famous Leaders and Battle Scenes of the Civil War* (New York: Mrs. Frank Leslie, 1896), 330.

admired Hooker's aggressive tactics as a divisional commander during the Seven Days' battles and later as a corps commander at Antietam. Conversely, the western troops were not all fighting under rising stars like Grant and William Tecumseh Sherman, and these two generals were not always successful. Grant's and Sherman's relations with the press often were rocky, and the soldiers read the papers. The Army of the Tennessee had also had some near disasters in 1862, including those at Shiloh and the failed attack at Vicksburg. Furthermore, many western commanders received little or no favorable coverage in the press because their theaters of operations were remote. And among other leaders, General William Starke Rosecrans was associated with near defeat at Stone's River, the debacle at Chickamauga, and the humiliating siege at Chattanooga, while General Nathaniel Prentiss Banks was pilloried for the disastrous Red River operation.

The men's assessment of the high command ranged from opinions about the entire command system to judgments about specific commanders. Soldiers were often cognizant of the political favoritism that led to one general's appointment over another. The men complained that patronage prevailed over competence in choosing commanders.[20] Others believed that petty jealousies among generals jeopardized strategic coordination. The soldiers criticized generals for not supporting each other's movements or accused them of sacrificing their men to further their ambitions.[21] Still others suspected that many generals were corrupt and used their positions for private gain. George H. Fifer, a lieutenant in the 33d Illinois Infantry serving in Arkansas, recounted how his brigade spent most of its time seizing cotton to sell in the North. The proceeds, Fifer believed, went into the pockets of the colonel and the high command. "I tell you there is just as much corruption in this war, as there was in our government, that is among the leading officers." He had come to conclude that the South was right when it condemned Northerners for only caring about money. He chastized his colonel and other officers who appropriated cotton to ship north and used "boats and other public property, and hazard the lives of soldiers for their private benefit."[22]

The commanding general's persona was deemed an important indicator of his capabilities. It was the one observable measure available to every soldier who had the chance to scrutinize a leader. Certain traits inspired confidence. Virginia gunner James E. Albright was impressed by Lee's appearance. He looked like a "noble plain old man." Albright was reassured by such a man and was ready to leave his fate in Lee's hands, believing that he could rely on this wise father figure.[23] Henry Livermore Abbott of Massachusetts was comforted by the paternal persona that General George Gordon Meade projected. He looked like a "good sort of a family doctor" thought Livermore, as he watched Meade in action at Gettysburg.[24] Colonel James W. Ames of the 11th U.S. Infantry was more specific when he described Meade's appearance and was ready to forgive Meade his Pennsylvania antecedents. Ames scorned the Pennsylvania militia as mere "cattle" but portrayed Meade as "a little slim man, with spectacles and ornithological style of face and carriage, he rides with his head way forward . . . he looks as if about to grumble or scold constantly,—but then he fights, and sees a long way thro his specs."[25]

The commander's moral character also came in for comment, another way of taking the measure of a leader. Letters often resembled report cards, giving detailed inventories of commanders' strengths and weaknesses. General William Franklin was intelligent; Hooker was a "plucky Yankee" but "inordinately vain" and entirely "unscrupulous." German Republicans would fight better under true believers like John C. Frémont or Franz Sigel.[26] Every imaginable trait and general's action came under the citizen-soldier's scrutiny. General George B. McClellan was too cautious, General Henry Wager Halleck and Lincoln were "caterpillars on the Commonwealth."[27] General John H. Morgan was "brave, generous . . . & daring."[28] General Fitz-John Porter had let petty jealousy and personal pique deter him from aiding General John Pope's army at Second Manassas and had caused the needless death of many men.[29]

The petty political intrigues in the high command raised disgust among the field-grade and company-grade officers. They had few illusions about some of the men who held their lives and that of the republic in their hands. Amongst the most damning descriptions of the high command came from George M. Barnard Jr., a young Massachusetts officer with access to the highest levels of command in the Army of the Potomac. Barnard recounted the talk at a generals' dinner: "Hooker was present and got tight and amused the crowd by running down Sumner, Heintzleman & Keyes." Well in his cups, Hooker lacerated his commanders as fools whose only merit was to have survived their more competent fellow officers. He then turned on those present, declaring that if his subordinates had "the same spirit that my old brigade had at the beginning of the war, why G——damn it we would go clear to New Orleans." Barnard compared Hooker unfavorably with McClellan, concluding that Hooker was a "pretty low fellow" whose lack of dignity bordered on the vulgar. Yet Barnard regretfully decided that a drunken Hooker was more competent on the battlefield than a sober Burnside.[30]

In contrast to Hooker, Grant left a good impression because he looked intrepid but avoided the bluster and posturing of some of his predecessors. Grant matched the ideal of the unpretentious democratic-republican soldier. He got the job done without seeking self-aggrandizement or political privilege. He conducted the war in a businesslike manner; he seemed cool, competent, and methodical in carrying out his intentions. He "plans as father does by the results of his game of chess," 17th Connecticut surgeon Robert Hubbard noted perceptively.[31]

Unfettered by censorship, the men in the ranks could usually express their views unhindered. Citizen-soldiers who were risking their lives to save the country believed that they had every right to make uncompromising judgments about leaders who put personal interest ahead of the cause. The soldiers judged their commanders' military ability as well as character. Brought up with the belief that moral rectitude went hand in hand with citizens' capabilities, soldiers condemned officers who did not measure up to the image of the selfless republican leader. Such opportunists sullied the righteous cause for which their men were laboring; their actions corroded the great political ideals of the struggle. Joseph Kohout of Iowa thought General Alvin Peterson Hovey was a reprehensible profiteer who "traded niggers for cotton."[32]

Last and most important, as politically aware citizen-soldiers, the men had the right and capability to rate their commanders' accomplishments in the field. With the press reaching the camps in a day or two, the men could rely not only on their own personal ground-level views of the actions of their leaders, but also on reports confirming their assessments of the military leadership. This was the first war fought by a literate citizenry, a rank and file that had access to inexpensive large-circulation dailies for evaluating its leaders. Newspaper stories also offered a broader view of the situation in which generals were operating. In addition, there was the virulent criticism generated by a defeat, and the soldiers' views were sharpened by the press reports in the existing partisan environment. McClellan scored poorly, for example, with the rank and file speaking disparagingly of "Little Bonaparte's" "masterly retreats."[33] Burnside got hooted during a futile "mud march" in January 1863: "Put him out, put him out," rang the refrain from his mud-covered columns as the general and his entourage slid past them.[34]

The rank and file also condemned Hooker for dividing his forces at Chancellorsville. They believed he had underestimated the force facing General John Sedgwick's corps at Salem Church. Finally, some troops of the Army of the Potomac thought that Hooker had retired prematurely during the second day's fighting at Chancellorsville.[35] Private William Hamilton, 2d Pennsylvania Reserve, summed up views about Hooker: "'Fighting Joe' is completely in the dark" about Lee's army.[36]

Meade got good reports for defeating what many Union troops thought was a larger army at Gettysburg, but others chastised him for letting Lee escape.[37] Rosecrans got mixed reviews: some stoutly defended him despite his repulse at Chickamauga. John W. Baldwin, a lieutenant in Company C, 74th Ohio Infantry, believed that the press was too harsh in condemning Rosecrans. Baldwin credited the general with great skill in evicting the Confederates from Chattanooga. His only fault, Baldwin argued, was to have outrun his supply line.[38] Others thought Rosecrans had an undeserved good reputation. Emerson Opdycke would have removed the general after Murfreesboro, which would have obviated Rosecrans's next disaster at Chickamauga, where Opdycke judged that the general had allowed gaps to form in his lines. He had not personally inspected his lines and had failed to verify their strength and the location of his units. Finally, Opdycke believed that Rosecrans had panicked and lost heart. He had scurried off to safety in Chattanooga, abandoning his army though two-thirds of its effectives remained intact and on the field. He withdrew although his commanders pleaded with him to continue the fight.[39]

Grant had his share of detractors, too. Even men from his own state gave him mixed reviews. While some, like James F. Drish, a colonel with the 122d Illinois, thought Grant was the "biggest *Bull* in the Ring," soldiers from the Democratic stronghold of Little Egypt near the confluence of the Ohio and the Mississippi distrusted Grant. Southern Illinois soldiers of the mutinous 109th Illinois Regiment accused Grant of botching the Yazoo expedition to get at Vicksburg from the rear. One of the unit's soldiers sent an indictment to the hometown

Jonesboro Gazette: "The idea of forcing an expedition over five hundred miles through the crookedest water course known to man; filled with sunken trees and so narrow that the boats could not pass without knocking their chimneys and cabins off against the trees off shore and with a certainty that their passage would be disputed at every suitable point, is about on par with other brilliant plans and expeditions which have rendered this war on the part of the North a stupendous farce."[40] When Grant moved to the eastern theater, many veteran officers of the Army of the Potomac remained unconvinced. They judged his conduct of the May–June 1864 campaign "useless slaughter." George M. Barnard Jr. thought Grant would never measure up to McClellan. If Congress had given as much support to McClellan as it was providing Grant, McClellan would have been victorious, too.[41]

Sherman was better liked than Grant because he seldom threw his troops into futile frontal assaults against improved or entrenched positions after the debacle at Kennesaw Mountain. Sherman relied on maneuver, and the men appreciated it. Sergeant Daniel Bishard of the 8th Iowa Cavalry found that even the Confederates shared his admiration for "Uncle Billy." Bishard described an encounter with a Confederate across a no-man's-land before Atlanta: "A Rebel hollered and asked what General Commandes you. when I replied Sherman is our Co-mander. Well Said the Rebb He is auer Comander too. I Said I guess Not. Yess He is[,] Said the Rebb[,] for When He telles us to git out of a place We ar Suer to Do it."[42] James A. Connolly, a major with the 122d Illinois, rated Sherman equal to Napoleon.[43] Many citizen-soldiers strongly supported Sherman's hard-war policy during his march through Georgia. Humphrey Hughes Hood defended Sherman against Democratic newspaper accusations that he was waging a war of unparalleled cruelty. Hood repeated Sherman's view that it was hypocritical to claim to fight a war without cruelty. Hood stated: "I grow desperately in love with any man whom the rascally Copperheads vituperate."[44]

One of Sherman's adversaries, however, was nearly universally disliked by his own troops. General Braxton Bragg was a "bird of evil omen."[45] Larry J. Daniel cites a few examples of soldiers who had some good things to say about their commander's military capacity, but earlier he quotes just as many who denounced the general.[46] The materials examined in this study, however, overwhelmingly support the latter attitude. Not one of the soldiers who wrote these documents was favorable to Bragg, which is hardly surprising given Bragg's persona and failed campaigns. Some of the men may have thought him a good general, but even they would hardly have held any affection for him. He treated the men brutally, and he was heartily despised in return. The men even cheered when it was rumored that his wife died.[47] Nor was there any confidence in his conduct of the war. Bragg's men castigated him for letting himself be maneuvered out of Tennessee.[48] They "cursed" him for not following up his victory at Chickamauga and quickly seizing Chattanooga while he had the chance.[49] Bragg nevertheless had a few defenders. Captain Joseph Branch O'Bryan, commanding Company B of the 1st Tennessee, came to Bragg's defense, arguing that his fellow generals had sabotaged his plans.[50] But most of the troops shared a young Kentucky surgeon's view. The physician, Lunsford Pitt Yandell Jr., who was serving with the 4th Tennessee, concluded after Chickamauga that "it would be a godsend for the country" if Bragg were removed.[51]

In contrast to Bragg, Confederate General Joseph E. Johnston was much loved. Like Sherman, Johnston valued the citizen-soldier's blood. He would not squander it in battle. Even after Johnston had been driven back to Atlanta, O'Bryan wrote: "The army has still the most unbounded confidence in General J[ohnston]. . . . We are satisfied that Gen Johnston will not fight under disadvantage. His men are too precious to usefully sacrifice. Whenever he says fight all will be satisfied that the proper time has arrived & will go at it with all their might."[52] Nevertheless, others began to question Johnston's ceaseless retrograde movements. Georgia Private John A. Johnson continued to support Johnston, but "Gen. J's continual falling back is not pleasant or encouraging and I am like the patient that is having a limb amputated. [He] may have great confidence in the surgeon before and after the operation is performed but can not help mistrusting and inwardly censuring while it is being done."[53]

Though the repulse at Gettysburg may not have been a disaster of the same magnitude as the capitulation of Vicksburg, as Gary W. Gallagher has cogently argued,[54] the heavy losses and Lee's failure to dislodge the Union army after a string of victories since Fredericksburg nonetheless raised concerns in the ranks. There was much talk in the South about gallant charges and shrill applause for the heroic but ineffective charges that bordered on tactical posturing. For example, Confederates tried to persuade themselves that the North's army had not dared take the fight to the men in gray but instead had remained on the defensive throughout the fight; further, Southerners found solace in the claim that the federals had benefited from strong defensive positions.[55] But no amount of protestation could sublimate the hard facts: Lee had not carried his putative objective; after all was said and done, he had to withdraw and leave the battlefield to the enemy, and he was in charge when the army bore the heavy costs seen everywhere on the battlefield and in the wagons of wounded rumbling south. After Gettysburg, even the marble hero's reputation began to crack and chip. Though Lieutenant James E. Green, 53d North Carolina Troops, thought the army unbeaten at Gettysburg, he believed that Lee had sacrificed too many men in the battle. "I think he had better let it a loan or not a fought them right where we did," Green concluded.[56] Major Franklin Gaillard of the

2d South Carolina Regiment concurred. He thought the attack on the third day was "injudicious" and regretfully concluded: "the greatest misfortune is that it destroyed the unbounded confidence reposed in Gen. Lee. Before, the army believed he could not err. They now see that he can." [57]

Politically articulate Northern soldiers believed in the need for unrestricted violence for revolutionary purposes. They wanted to sweep aside the old social structure of the South and build anew on the wreckage. They wanted to break the grip of the slaveowning oligarchy. Campaigning in Alabama with the 7th Illinois Cavalry, Henry Clinton Forbes summed up the idea when he wrote: "There is no permanent peace except in the *absolute banishment* of the principle slave holders from the soil of our common country. Expel the leaven from the measure of meal and *there* the fermentation will cease." [58] By contrast, Southern soldiers were fighting a defensive war, a war to maintain the conservative status quo. They were not endeavoring to conquer the North and impose their social system beyond the Mason-Dixon line. Their aims were not revolutionary. Therefore, 25 percent fewer Confederate soldiers advocated harsh war than their Northern counterparts. [59]

Rebel and Yankee envisioned the war as a test of wills between two peoples. The side that could sustain the most punishment would emerge victorious. A Bay Stater, Corporal Samuel Storrow of the 44th Regiment, wrote that ultimately it came down to which side had the will to outlast its opponent. [60] To break the enemy's will, invading forces not only had to wreck the opposing army but also had to punish the enemy citizenry so severely that their morale would be forever broken and they would never again challenge the Union. When Lee carried out his second invasion of the North, this time the Southern soldiers did not refuse to cross the Potomac. In 1862 they had claimed that they had only enlisted in a defensive war. By 1863, many now relished invading the North and ravaging Pennsylvania. They saw the second invasion of the North as retribution, a reprisal for the destruction wrought by Northern generals like David Hunter in the Shenandoah Valley. It was also a strategic decision aimed at undermining the Northern people's morale. [61] On the other side, Charles Jackson Paine, 30th Massachusetts, supported the idea of waging a war against Southern civilians. The only way to quell the rebellion was to make war on every man, woman, and child in the South, to carry the fighting from the battlefield to every hearth in the enemy's country, to scourge all generations and genders. Only then could victory be achieved. [62]

Fighting the war *à outrance* would require complete unity at home, because a total war demanded mobilizing more resources than a limited war. The whole country shared in the endeavor. In a limited war, however, some could stand aside and profit from others' efforts. In a people's war, everyone had to share the burden. Everyone was mobilized. Only by forging unity of action between army and society could the nation prevail. The soldiers denounced malingerers and angrily demanded that society get behind the war effort. Private Wilbur Fisk, serving with the 2d Vermont Infantry, complained to his local newspaper: "The poorest soldier can't help seeing [t]hat if the North would only rise now like a lion conscious of his strength, we might smash the Confederacy all to atoms and in a short time. But instead of that the North hangs back." [63] One way to purge society of skulkers was to enroll them in the army. Total war mobilized and disciplined society. It steeled it for the long and arduous struggle to batter the enemy into submission. Merciless destruction would leave the South's collective memory scarred forever by the defeat. The lesson would be remembered for generations to come. [64] When General Banks appeared to be pursuing a conciliatory occupation policy by allowing Louisiana planters to grow sugar for the North, a member of his command complained that neither southerners' property nor their lives should stand in the way of military operations. None and nothing should be spared. Homes should be burned; cotton and sugar should be seized, as Banks had done; the planter class should be destroyed because only such cruel methods would put an end to the rebellion. [65] And when Sherman signed an appeasing armistice with Johnston at the end of the war, there was more grumbling. The men believed that Sherman was contravening the government's all-out war policy. [66] This course had been proclaimed the previous year at the Baltimore convention and in the Republican Congressional Committee during the election. [67] Politically motivated Northern soldiers demanded adherence to radical policies. They demanded complete destruction of the South's slaveholding aristocracy before reconstructing democracy in the South.

Besides assessing the military leadership and forming distinct views on the conduct of the war, politically aware citizen-soldiers also wanted their compatriots to join the colors to sustain the military effort. As the 57th North Carolina emerged from the maelstrom of Chancellorsville and was girding itself for even more losses as the campaign season began, a private from Company D wrote with bitter humor: "If the war continues much longer there wont be men enough to suply the young widdows when the war ends as they will beat the young girl all hollow. . . . There will be a powerful push to get husbands before long and the girls will take anything which hops." [68] The people's armies of the Civil War were far larger than the European professional armies of the eighteenth century. The war of attrition occasioned severe manpower shortages in the American Civil War. The size and strategic unwieldiness of such large armies of amateur soldiers transformed battles into bloody brawls, and it raised some concerns among volunteers: should the government impose conscription, and should the government enroll former slaves?

Troops on both sides of the Mason-Dixon line overwhelmingly advocated that the draft be rigorously implemented, with 89 percent of Unionists and 82 percent of Confederates supporting conscription.[69] They vociferously demanded that there be no exception from obligatory military service. Universal conscription was the only effective way to bring to bear the overwhelming force needed to vanquish the enemy.[70] But by fall 1864, Private Andrew R. Linscott, Company K, 39th Massachusetts Volunteers, concluded that all who would come forward voluntarily already had done so. The hundred-day men were useless, costing the government more than they were worth. The draft was the only remaining source of replacements to fill the gaps in the ranks. Linscott's support for Lincoln and the radical war aims proclaimed at the Chicago convention was conditional on a tough draft policy. Without it, Linscott believed, the North could not achieve its ambitious objectives.[71] Otherwise, the North would have to accede to a Copperhead-inspired armistice and a negotiated peace. Company D of the 34th Ohio Volunteer Infantry also drafted resolutions supporting a sweeping conscription policy.[72] Moreover, the men believed that the burden must be equally shared. They scorned able-bodied men who stayed behind and profited from war-induced prosperity. Soldiers insisted on an accounting. They demanded to know who was shirking. "The Conscription bill suits me exactly," wrote John H. Stibbs from Benton Barracks, near St. Louis: "I want to see some of your Morgan County traitors toe the mark now."[73] Captain Tilmon D. Kyger, Company C, 73d Illinois Infantry, believed that the stay-at-homes should be at the front, where they would learn to cringe and cower soon enough. Kyger also desperately hoped that these shirkers would not find substitutes. The men in the line looked forward to giving Copperheads an appropriate welcome.[74] Benjamin F. Ashenfelter took perverse pleasure in receiving the list of inductees from home. He delighted in the thought of getting the chance to drill them himself.[75]

The conscription system was not efficient.[76] Neither the North nor the South could muster enough draftees. The armies remained mainly volunteer forces. The men who had freely joined in the first year and a half of the war remained the backbone of the army. In the Northwest, Indiana and Wisconsin were the only states that had to resort to conscription to fill their quotas. And even when they did, many fish slipped through the net. One-third of Wisconsin's draftees did not even report to the induction centers.[77] Another third of those eligible for the draft were excluded because of health and other reasons.[78] Some men evaded the draft, while still others deserted. Those with bounties often escaped to enlist again. According to James M. McPherson, only 7 percent of all draftees ever saw active service.[79] Allan Nevins found fewer than 170,000 draftees who went into the Union army in 1863–64.[80] The military authorities claimed that the draft took as many men to enforce it as it provided for service.[81]

The men in the ranks supported the draft but questioned its implementation. The bounty system was unjust because it brought in unreliable replacements. The wealthy could buy substitutes through brokers or could pay exemptions; only the poor were certain to be conscripted.[82] Conscripts reacted with scorn and sullen anger to this arrangement. Volunteers resented substitutes, who received large sums while the volunteers were subsisting on eleven dollars a month. Inflation was skyrocketing along with the price of substitutes. The market went from fifteen hundred dollars to ten thousand dollars in the Confederacy.[83] In the North, the market also rose. Communities had to bid against each other to lure bounty men to fill their quotas and avoid conscripting their residents. Westerners were jealous of eastern substitutes and bounty men from large wealthy cities who received bounties twice as large as their western comrades. The men in the ranks grew angry. They drafted petitions denouncing inequalities.[84] Poorer communities could not afford the large bounties to fill their quotas. They had to conscript more of their inhabitants. Furthermore, neighboring towns drained poor communities' manpower pools with high bounties forcing them to draft a larger percentage of those who remained.[85]

Meanwhile, recalcitrant conscripts and substitutes resorted to desperate measures to avoid the trenches. When Henry C. Metzger boarded a transport to rejoin Company G of the 184th Pennsylvania Volunteer Infantry, he embarked with a contingent of bounty jumpers and recaptured deserters who tried to blow up the ship.[86] At the front, three hundred men of the 37th Massachusetts fled "with the greatest enthusiasm" during an engagement at Pegram's Farm. Commanders had to put draftees and substitutes in "enclosed works" at night so that they could not sneak off to surrender to the Confederates: rumors circulated among these unwilling soldiers that Lee was granting safe passage to Europe to any who would desert.[87] The bounty men and conscripts were uncontrollable. Near Decherd, Tennessee, Company A, 5th Connecticut, composed of a large number of conscripts, stole wine from a hospital train and got as drunk "as any N.Y. rioters." When officers tried to quell the revelry, the troops drew their weapons and fired on their fellow soldiers. The miscreants were too numerous to be punished and too unreliable for service at the front. They finally were detached for duty in the rear. This type of soldier was as dangerous as the enemy.[88] New Hampshire's John H. Burrill wondered how the republic could fight a war with the "outscourings" of society.[89]

Speaking for many soldiers, William Pedrick of Company K, 115th New York, called for an end to bounties and the use of substitutes because the system discriminated against the poor.[90] Besides, the idea of paying men to fight for their country was demeaning and unrepublican.[91] "Money is the last thing a man should enlist for," wrote Voleny G. Barbour, a divisional provost guard in the

Union XIIth Corps.[92] It was shameful to see men follow the substitute market waiting for a profitable moment to offer their services.[93] The Confederacy exempted whites from the draft if they had more than twenty slaves, which caused resentment among the poor classes. The smaller Confederate states, with a pioneer tradition and small holdings, harbored the most widespread opposition to the planter-class law. Discontent was especially strong in Arkansas. A political agent reported to Governor Harris Flanagin that the draft law was a "festering sore of discontent. No wonder," he wrote, "the people use every equivocation possible to evade the law. . . . As it is, the cry of poor men being obliged to fight for the rich may be heard on all sides."[94] The volunteers demanded that all exemptions be abolished, that the draft be rigorously enforced, and that all substitute laws be eliminated.[95]

Another aspect of manpower policy that attracted the attention of politically motivated soldiers was arming blacks.[96] More than 70 percent of my sample of Union soldiers supported arming the black population.[97] Captain Isaac Plumb, a gold pen salesman from Hamilton, New York, serving with the 61st New York Infantry, was impatient with Congress for its slow progress toward arming blacks.[98] Union men demanded that all possible measures be used—including emancipation and arming of blacks—to suppress the rebellion.[99] Captain John Lynch, serving with the 6th Illinois Cavalry near La Grange, Tennessee, contended that the government should use "every means that it can to protect the lives of its white citizens and the Government will be weakened less by the loss of three Negroes than it would be the loss of one white Man."[100] Arming the blacks also had partisan political advantages. It was an issue that Republicans could use against the Democrats. Democrats opposed conscription, but that position left blacks as the only remaining untapped manpower pool. By acquiescing in arming the blacks, Democrats were put in an embarrassing position. When they reduced the pressure to conscript whites by arming and emancipating blacks, they moved closer to radical abolitionist policy, alienating their own constituency. Republicans relished the Democrats' discomfiture.[101]

The idea of arming the blacks also arose in the Confederate camps. Some Southerners recognized their dilemma. Would they free the slaves, fight alongside them, and thus acknowledge their equality as fellow soldiers? If the military duties of citizenship were extended to Negroes, would their political rights follow close behind? Would black political empowerment also ensue? Would such measures run counter to the initial war aims of the South? Captain Felix Pierre Poché, serving with General Jean-Jacques Mouton's Louisiana command, summed the Confederacy's dilemma in 1865: "I adhere to slavery as we had it; but I hold still more to a separation from the vile Yankee and independence for our young nation and to achieve that independence I would sacrifice all, excluding honor, consequently I would make it at the cost of abolishing slavery. So I think is the spirit of our people. Her motto is 'Independence at any price even to the abolition of Slavery.'"[102] Samuel F. Richards, a Union soldier with the 16th Connecticut, saw supreme irony in calling on the Confederacy's slave population to come to the aid of its oppressors. As early as summer 1863, a prescient rumor circulated in the Union camps that Jefferson Davis would call up five hundred thousand blacks and give them freedom and fifty acres in exchange for serving the Confederacy. Richards derisively expressed Union troops' reaction: "I do think the Southerners better shift places [and] let the niggers be the masters and they be the slaves for a while. . . . Three fourths of the whites at the south do not know as much as the niggers anyway."[103]

Ideas clashed in both armies about the fighting prowess of the black troops. Many thought blacks were unfit for combat.[104] Lieutenant Caleb Hadley Beale, a Bay Stater with the 107th New York Infantry, wrote that blacks could never become soldiers, even if "you white-wash um."[105] Private Alonzo G. Rich, another soldier from Massachusetts, thought the black troops had failed dismally to exploit the breach at the Crater battle and had thus proved their military inferiority.[106] Humphrey Hughes Hood deemed blacks slightly better than Irish laborers.[107]

Other Union citizen-soldiers came to accept blacks as fellow combatants. Byron M. McClain of the 2d Iowa thought that the black troops he saw around Memphis looked well-drilled and showed pride in their uniform, but he found they were careless with their firearms, shooting more of their fellow soldiers than the enemy.[108] Issashar Davis, 39th Iowa, nonetheless thought the blacks had proved that they were as good as white soldiers.[109] Corporal Samuel Storrow of the 44th Massachusetts served alongside black troops on the North Carolina coast. He observed that many of those who had previously opposed emancipation were now serving alongside blacks. Storrow believed that the blacks would fight tenaciously to hold the Union foothold along the North Carolina coast, knowing that if they were overrun the Southern troops would grant no quarter.[110]

Confederate assessments of black fighting prowess varied. Chaplain Robert S. Webb, who served with the 44th North Carolina at Petersburg, was impressed by black troops' aggressiveness in imposing their dominance over no-man's-land. They constantly tried to provoke their former masters into firefights: the "negroes sometimes jump out [of the trenches] and dance and hollow our men, call them rebels, saying they are free as we are."[111] Other Confederates thought that a position opposite black-held trenches was safer because those skirmishers were less aggressive.[112]

Politically motivated soldiers were able to form a comprehensive appraisal of the military situation because they could see how interrelated things were and how such connections determined the outcome of the war. These soldiers reflected on the overall disposition of the armies as they tried to make sense out of maneuvers on various fronts. They took interest in the order of battle of the opposing side. They weighed the chances of success in their area while speculating as to how the war was proceeding on other fronts. And they registered the effect of victories and defeats on army morale, realizing how important it was in strengthening or undermining the fighting ability of their fellow citizen-soldiers. Because politically aware men were more reflective, they also tried to measure their leaders' ability to handle forces effectively. They gauged their officers against the strategic tasks that lay before them. The citizen-soldiers' standards were not limited to the purely military considerations. The professional competence of the commander was important, but for the politicized soldier the officer was not only a military technician pursing military objectives: he was also the instrument and emissary of a fighting concept, the idea of armed justice. He was an agent of the republic in all its righteous majesty. As such, he had to comport himself accordingly. He had to show bravery, commanding bearing, and dignity. His persona had to be worthy of the nobility of the cause. Politicized soldiers called on their commanders to conduct a hard war against civilians if that was necessary to bring victory in so virtuous a cause. The citizen-soldiers supported blockades that starved the citizenry; they were not repelled when they saw their artillery shell homes in Atlanta or Petersburg; they foraged vigorously to supply themselves at the expense of enemy civilians. Finally, they believed that they could only bring victory if the entire society stood behind them by sending all available men to join the army. In the North and among some in the South, this included the black population as well. War on this scale required total mobilization. The military outlook of these soldiers thus combined the balance of power on the battlefield, the effectiveness of the leaders' conduct of the war, and the mobilization of the entire society's human and material resources. As losses mounted, manning the army became tied to broader policy issues extending beyond the effectiveness of the military effort. Soldiers raised broader questions about the justice of the cause. They sought to clarify the principles that were at stake in the war and to define the policies most appropriate for these tenets.

4 Fighting for the Right

PATRIOTISM, PRINCIPLES, AND POLICIES

Neither pay nor privilege were enough for men to risk life and limb. Money was everywhere to be made in the expanding wartime economy, and many people remained behind to reap the benefits of the new wealth. Adventure, the sight of new places, and camaraderie were not sufficient motivators to induce men to spend years living in discomfort, monotony, and danger. For excitement and bonding, young men could head west, and many did. None of these traditional incentives could justify the devotion and steadfastness of the soldiers of the people's armies in the American Civil War. Camaraderie, pay, and adventure were more important in the old professional armies than in the new people's armies in the era of democracy and mass ideologies. Career soldiers rely more on organizational and material incentives, while people's armies depend more on political motivation: political principles, policies, and patriotic symbols. While ideals such as patriotism had some role in inspiring the British regulars during their colonial campaigns and coercion was used to assure discipline in the American Civil War armies, certain types of motivators play a particularly important role in a people's army.

At the most rudimentary level, inchoate patriotic symbols initially attracted volunteers to the colors. These political metaphors included an assortment of vague ideas and objects such as Union, flag, and constitution. Even later in the war, these symbols remained the political lingua franca of the less politically knowledgeable rank and file. Patriotic symbols were assimilated by reading newspapers, attending school, visiting patriotic historical monuments, participating in festivals such as Fourth of July ceremonies, and joining in militia activities as a weekend soldier.[1] John W. Green was a Kentuckian who enlisted in the Confederate cause during the last desperate days of the Confederacy. He typified the average soldier, declaring that *"duty* to *God* & our Country" were the reasons he was in the fight.[2]

Ambiguous ideas like love of country, the "glorious republic," its flag, its cause, its leaders, and even the advance of humanity reverberated in the men's correspondence.[3] David Logan Houser in the 14th Iowa Infantry reflected this ardent idealistic but intuitive patriotism when he explained to his girlfriend, Malvina, what was at stake for a patriotic citizen-soldier: "What would riches be worth without a Country? What value has land when national integrity and Liberty are lost?" He concluded by assuring her that he loved her but confessed he loved the flag even more. Green believed the national ensign embodied the ideal most noble, the idea of "free government." It transcended personal love, because without free government none could reach "the completest development of each part & each individual."[4]

Idealistic patriotism remained a strong influence throughout the war. Two-thirds of the soldiers believed that important principles and ideals were at stake in the conflict, an attitude that persisted even during the last years of the war.[5] A comparison of the level of patriotic feeling in the Union and Confederate armies suggests that the Confederates were less idealistic than Union soldiers. Disenchantment was emerging among the many rebels, who were almost twice as likely (48 percent to 26 percent) to believe that the war was being fought only in the interest of a privileged minority.[6] This Confederate disillusionment may partly be due to defeats in the last two years of the war. Inequalities inherent in Southern society, such as sharp class differences, also generated cynics among the troops. The war accentuated these cleavages. Many Southern soldiers became increasingly aware that the planter class defined the civic culture. The centrality of the planter class made the small independent farmer, who manned the South's armies, politically marginal. Thus, the small farmer did not identify as closely with the government and was more likely to become demoralized and disillusioned. He was inclined to feel victimized by the Confederacy's policies. The Confederates were politically mature enough to perceive that some were sacrificing more than others, and many able-bodied men were remaining at home to take advantage of opportunities arising from the war. This growing disillusionment was particularly injurious to morale in a people's army.

Politically informed Southerners and Northerners alike understood the issues and forces that had brought on the war. These soldiers became disenchanted with the cause and came to regard the war as a tragic conflict provoked and sustained by two fanatical minorities: proslavery aristocratic hotheads in the South and fire-breathing abolitionists in the North. Trying to survive in Andersonville prison, John W. Northrop of Company F, 103d Ohio Volunteer Infantry, whiled away his time reading *Paradise Lost* and reflecting on the causes of the war that got him into his present predicament. He believed that a clique of conservative Southerners dragged the country into a "hoe-cake secession." In

Northrop's view, the Southern conservatives assumed they could use the fire-eaters to frighten the Unionists and bargain a better deal for themselves after the 1860 election. At the same time, the North's conservatives mistakenly believed they could negotiate a compromise with the secessionists, leaving the radicals in the North and the South isolated and excluded from power. But Northrop saw that conservatives on both sides of the Mason-Dixon line underestimated the volatility of the situation, and they lost control of events. They underestimated the Southern fire-eaters' ability to use abolition as a red herring to stir up secessionist sentiment.[7]

Such ideas about the cause of the war suggested a conservative outlook. This worldview drew on the Burkean idea that a happy polity is anchored to a centrist pole, which is rooted in the country's historical traditions and in its patterns of social intercourse. Violent upheavals like wars and revolutions tear apart the skein that holds together the country's political culture. War thus destroys more than it achieves. Furthermore, such upheavals ultimately lead to a return to political community's traditional moorings. The circularity of the revolutionary process is a tragedy as brother kills brother; war wrecks civilization and provides nothing better to replace it with. By some vague homeostatic process, society ultimately returns to its original values.

Soldiers with a conservative political outlook tended to see themselves as actors participating in this tragedy, a debacle that would only lead to the destruction of what had been good in the prewar society. They sought to obviate this disaster by proposing to negotiate a return to the status quo ante bellum, thereby protecting the country's precious traditions. During the Atlanta campaign, Robert W. Henry of the 26th Iowa lamented the horror and futility of an all-out war. It was a Manichean war where one side monopolized the right while the enemy embodied the wrong. He argued that the issues leading to the war could have been resolved through existing institutions: "Glorious war . . . if its so good and just why have Courts, why have law! The theory and practice is alike through domestic and national affairs, if a nation's differences can be settled justly, but by 'steel' then my wronging neighbor will find his deserts as equally just in the cold steel of the army."[8]

Some Unionist Democrats like Voleny G. Barbour shared Northrop's view that the Republicans had hijacked the war to instigate a servile rebellion. Republicans had transformed the war from the original conservative aim of restoring the Union to the revolutionary purpose of abolishing slavery.[9]

Others among the rank and file did not resort to complex analyses of the political maneuvering that preceded the conflict. They were less concerned with who caused it than with who benefited from it. Some Union soldiers opposed emancipation using Locofocoist arguments. Like their New York namesakes, who blamed the rich (bankers) for the panic of 1837, these men believed that the wealthy classes were directing the war to their own selfish ends. A soldier in the 13th Wisconsin Infantry wrote: "This is not a war to restore the country to its former condition, but it has degenerated into a war to make money for fat contractors and contractors' cousins."[10] Though many Southerners initially believed the war was part of the historical struggle to save republican government from the urban avaricious individualism of the North, this view began to fade in the latter stages of the war. Confederate soldiers started to complain about profiteering and privileges for the well-to-do while ordinary people were shouldering most of the burden. Marcus Hefner, a farmer fighting with the 57th North Carolina Troops and living off starvation rations, saw the struggle as a war that profitted the rich but that was fought by the poor.[11] Southerners who blamed the rich for the war fought only to protect their homes from invasion. Men like Confederate gunner Macon Bonner saw the issue as a defensive struggle.[12] Some deserted; others changed sides and joined the Union army. They came to believe that this war was not being fought in their interest. A former Confederate who had joined the U.S. 1st Mississippi Mounted Rifles summed up his reasons for deserting to fight against the South: "I got tired of fighting for a lot of old Rich Planters here in the South where I was fighting to save their Negroes and Property and them remaining at home living all the luxuries of life."[13]

Opposing the conservative outlook, with its metaphor of national tragedy and betrayal, idealistic radicals envisaged the conflict in an entirely different light. It was a millennial struggle to further democracy. America was the agent leading the effort on behalf of humankind. If it faltered, the beacon would be extinguished, and the nation would have failed to consummate the role that God had confided to the new republic when he launched its vocation during the revolution four score years earlier. Thwarting God's will were the Southern slavers, the devil's agents, obstructing progress toward the democratic ideal. Expressing this millennial creed, Union soldiers sang songs celebrating the "Year of Jubilo" and proclaiming their fighting faith: for example, the "Battle Hymn of the Republic" proclaimed that "as Christ had died to make men holy, let us die to make them free." Union soldiers perceived themselves as custodians of the nation's salvation, while the Southern leadership believed they were also fighting to redeem a pristine ideal of the original republican ideal that had become perverted during recent decades. For the North, however, the war was an apocalyptic event, a struggle over an issue of biblical scale. In the mind of many Union troops, armed with a faith nourished by republican evangelism and fighting to save the Union and spread the gospel of republicanism in the South, emancipation played only a supporting role beside the higher ideal of saving the Union.

The emerging American nationalism that advanced this ideal fused three components: a political one based on parliamentary democracy and majority rule, an economic one founded on acquisitive entrepreneurial capitalism, and a civic one founded on the central role of the citizen-soldier.[14] This worldview assumed that history was following a linear tangent, not the conservatives' circular vision. This Hegelian outlook conceived of the war as part of a struggle toward a higher level of human development. The soldiers believed themselves agents battering down yet another obstacle to human progress. Like his Confederate counterpart, the Union soldier was also an actor on history's stage. But the plot was not a tragedy; instead, he played the hero in a melodrama where good opposed evil, and he was the principal hero and the rebel regime was the arch villain. John N. Strayer of the Army of the Potomac expressed this view when he declared that he was fighting against oppression and for the survival of the Union. He was struggling to save American democracy, which was an advance over the tyrannies and monarchies of the Old World. It was a revolutionary conflict to speed human progress toward democracy, liberty, and good government. Strayer and his comrades were in a messianic struggle to save the American republic, which was the highest level of political development yet reached in human history.[15] Victory would assure the "lasting good of humanity."[16] Ohio surgeon William H. Philips of the 118th Regiment was among the most articulate protagonists of this idealistic and revolutionary worldview. He saw slavery as the chief impediment to the progress of democracy. Southern society had to be completely reconstructed. A new middle class of literate yeomen farmers would be encouraged to replace the old planter aristocracy.[17]

The radicals in the ranks resembled the moral citizen-soldier of Maximilien Robespierre's *république de la vertu*. The war was a historic struggle of good against evil, of progress over reaction, of freedom over tyranny. It was waged by citizens who knew their duty and would not shirk it or give countenance to any who did not share their zeal. The wicked would receive their just retribution in a war without mercy; those who refused their duty would pay. Even if men expressed revulsion when they saw deserters executed, few doubted the propriety of shooting deserters by the score. The war was a crusade that required absolute devotion to its high aims. It generated a moral catharsis and inspired a rebirth of patriotism and the idea of civic duty.[18]

Idealistic citizen-soldiers challenged arguments that the war was merely another human disaster caused by unrestrained ambitions among certain groups who were using the conflict to further their interests. Before embarking on a war, citizen-soldiers had to answer three questions for themselves about the morality of the conflict: Was the cause justified? Was the war waged by a legitimate government? And was the war conducted appropriately by using force proportionate to the level of resistance? Politically motivated soldiers on both sides responded positively.

Southerners believed they were victims of the North's determination to interfere in their institutions. By refusing to let the South go in peace and by trying to hold onto military installations on Southern territory, the North had provoked the war. Moreover, the North was an alien society, composed of "descendants of witch burners," wrote a soldier in the 18th Louisiana.[19] Thus, the South had to choose between liberty and subjugation.[20]

Union troops also believed that they were fighting a justifiable war. They were defending democracy against a section of the country whose civic culture was alien to the North's democratic principles. The Southern slavocracy would not acknowledge majority rule. It had refused to acknowledge the results of the 1860 democratic election of Abraham Lincoln. Furthermore, the South was undermining democracy by endeavoring to extend slavery into the territories. "We have nursed the scorpion for years and it is about to sting us," declared William Foster, serving with the 126th Ohio Volunteer Infantry.[21] In addition to securing democracy at home, the North was protecting democracy's progress in the world by defending democracy from European monarchism's stalking horse in North America—Southern slavocracy. Orderly Sergeant John Wesley Marshall of the 97th Ohio Volunteers warned that Southern slavery was a threat to all men's freedom and democracy: "None others are safe. . . . Nothing but monarchy, & that nearly absolute, promised [the slaveholders] security against the mudsills, as they termed the working masses. . . . Their theory that slavery is the normal condition of mankind, that capital should in all cases own labor really makes no distinction between the white & black laborer. The argument which would enslave a negro would enslave a white man."[22]

The soldiers on both sides also justified the war by affirming the legitimacy of their governments. For the North, the American republic was the bright hope of oppressed people, a beacon of freedom in the world.[23] Its constitution had proven durable over several generations. This sacred document embodied the national identity and defined its legitimacy. Defending the Union meant more than maintaining the country's territorial integrity. It was an idealistic crusade to prove the viability of republican democracy in the world.[24] The legitimacy of the republic's struggle was founded on "the decisions of an untrammeled people at the ballot box," wrote Levi A. Ross while campaigning with the 86th Illinois.[25]

Southern troops justified their struggle by invoking conservative ideas. They summoned up Whig constitutional procedures. They claimed protective rights for the elite minority against the onslaught of a volatile majority. They maintained that the South was the font of tradition and wisdom. "The Confederacy was the Roman part of the old Government. She gave its statesmen and heroes [George Washington, Thomas Jefferson, and John C. Calhoun], who made the old flag respected all over the world," contended 8th Texas Cavalry Chaplain Robert Franklin Bunting.[26] Like England in Europe, the South was a bastion against mudsill rule.

If the Southern cause was just and if its government was legitimate, it had every right to use whatever means it could muster to save itself. This justified an all-out war that employed irregular forces like those used ninety years earlier against the British. Total war was commensurate with the importance of the cause. Northern soldiers, for their part, justified waging an implacable war for great ideals as well. All means were justifiable when great principles were at stake. The war quickly became a no-holds-barred struggle between peoples as well as their armies.

Having concluded that the cause was just, that their government was a legitimate expression of the popular will, and that they were right in using all force needed to crush an immoral enemy, the citizen-soldiers of the North and the South at first flocked to the colors. Later, however, after the first flush of idealism passed, each side sought new aims to warrant the rising costs of the conflict. The war grafted new goals on those that initially had been advanced by the political leaders. Northern war aims were increasingly revolutionary and maximalist. The war was fought for a zero-sum outcome that could only be achieved by bludgeoning the enemy into submission. All capacity for organized resistance had to be destroyed to open the way for imposing the victor's maximalist war aims. Defining the issues of the war in terms of moral absolutes increased the ferocity of the struggle. No compromise could corrupt the integrity of the principles at stake. Millenialist moralism brooked no concessions or compromise. Corporal Samuel Storrow of the 44th Massachusetts Infantry in New Bern, North Carolina, expressed the soldier's moral absolutism: no compromise was possible with a felon who was bent on taking something precious. Either he had to yield his ill-gotten gain or the victims had to cede their property. It was not negotiable.[27]

The fundamental divide in the North was an ideological question about the purpose of the war. Was it a war to reestablish the status quo ante bellum, the Union as it was? Or was it a war for the Union as it ought to be? Conservatives and most moderate Republicans and Democrats took the former view, while radicals advocated the latter belief.[28] The Civil War opened a deep ideological fissure in the American body politic dating back to the revolution.[29] The conflict raised again the question of the nature of the revolution and the government it had created. Was the American republic a conservative nation established as a reaffirmation of existing rights that had been transgressed by the mother country, or was it a revolutionary advance in democracy, a political experiment, an entirely new form of government?

The cleavage between revolution and conservatism influenced party politics during the Civil War. By 1862 the Republicans were divided into three factions: conservatives, who hoped for the eventual collapse of slavery or the return of blacks to Africa; the moderates, including Lincoln, who opposed slavery but feared a white backlash if the slaves were freed; and abolitionists like Wendell Phillips, who called for seizing and freeing the slaves.[30] The abolitionists represented the revolutionary tradition of American politics, and they justified their revolutionary convictions on the irreconcilability of bondage and liberty.[31]

The size and scope of the war worked in favor of the radicals. The war had not only to defend freedom but also to extend it to the benighted black population.[32] The hard-war policy aimed to destroy the South's ability to sustain its army bolstered the radical demand that slaves be seized and used against the Confederacy. Furthermore, revolutionary Republicans believed that freeing the South's blacks would also free the small, oppressed farmers from the tyranny of the ruling slaveowners. A reconstructed South would be founded on a newly empowered class, yeoman farmers whose love of liberty was certified by Jeffersonian traditions. But its power could only be implanted on a cleared field where the weeds of slavocracy had been ripped out, according to radical senators like Charles Sumner. Otherwise republicanism could not take root.[33]

The moderate *New York Times* began to cover abolitionist meetings in 1862.[34] Abolitionists also began to notice that it was easier to find publishers for their tracts.[35] Both phenomena were signs that the political leadership and the people were shifting toward radical war aims. It also was becoming increasingly clear that the slavery issue could no longer be isolated from the broader question of national survival. The source and power of the rebellion was its access to cheap slave labor. Consequently, the war had to be redirected against the source of the South's strength.[36] Support began to grow for Frederick Douglass's contention that slavery supported the South's war effort and that only by knocking that support from under the slavocracy could the war be won. But military necessity was a more palatable argument to Democrats and moderate Republicans. Racist and constitutional arguments could be overcome if abolition became a strategic essential. Advocates of abolition insisted that emancipation would undermine or deprive the South of half its labor force.[37] Soldiers saw slaves run away and realized that slavery was crumbling and bringing about the South's internal destruction.[38] This assessment was confirmed by the army's experience. As the Northern armies pierced deeper into the South and contrabands sought their refuge, the military used black labor and saw how useful the ex-slaves could be for the war effort. Their plight also elicited sympathy among many Union troops.[39]

In summer 1862, even conservative Republicans like Senator John Sherman were coming around to this view. Conservative newspapers like the *Boston Advertiser* also acknowledged it. Abolition soon gained ground in Congress. Members from New England and from the Upper Midwest, where Free-Soilers and abolitionists were the strongest, were particularly effective. This situation served as a backdrop to the Emancipation Proclamation.[40] Meanwhile, Democrats despaired as their pro-peace newspapers were closed, their children were abused in school, and some of their members were arrested and denied the protection of habeas corpus. Their presidential candidate, George B. McClellan, refused to subscribe to the party's peace plank. Support for a negotiated peace was evaporating. The conservative peace wing of the party was appeased with the empty gesture of selecting George Pendleton as McClellan's running mate.[41]

Despite the lack of military progress and the costly losses in summer 1864, and notwithstanding murmurs in Republican ranks that it would be a disastrous mistake to reject a Southern peace overture accepting the Union but rejecting abolition, the government reaffirmed abolition as a war aim on July 9, 1864.[42] And after his reelection, Lincoln pressed for adoption of the Thirteenth Amendment.[43] The revolutionary wing of the party had triumphed.

The politically motivated soldiers in people's armies fight all-out wars because they need moralist and maximalist war aims to generate popular support and justify the enormous human costs of total war. When citizen-soldiers fight, the public expects the war's high moral aims to be commensurate with its huge costs. The cause must be comprehensive and idealistic. Arcane legalism or prosaic interests were the stuff of dynastic wars fought for incremental ends. Such limited wars lent themselves to a negotiated compromise. At first, Lincoln and many Democrats hoped to wage this kind of conservative war.[44] But the Civil War was being fought with people's armies motivated by idealism. The people would not tolerate incremental results through a negotiated compromise. They demanded new aims that measured up to the costs and scope of the endeavor. Specifically, this meant complete independence for the South to put an end to the Northern majority despotism. In the North, it meant punishing a criminal part of the population that had embarked on treason to maintain an immoral institution—slavery. There could be no middle course possible. The positions were diametrically opposed. Neither army would have accepted limited war aims by 1863. Iowa Sergeant Eugene Marshall summed up this view: "I can see no way of retreat from the proposition that the faith of the nation is pledged to the negroes of the seceded states, and that no peace can be made that does not recognize their freedom in all these states. Consequently I can see no way of settling the policy of peace."[45]

After the massive engagements of summer 1862 and the tremendous losses that they engendered, the war was no longer subservient to policy. Now policy became entirely subservient to war, and the driving force of the war was the people's army. Whatever the political leaders may have intended, whatever their domestic priorities, by late 1862 the parameters of their policies were set by their armies and by the dynamic of the conflict. Once the people had been mobilized, the politicians no longer could control strategy or unilaterally define the objectives of the war. Unlike a dynastic conflict between two eighteenth-century rulers fighting with small armies of professionals, this was a people's war with a people's army goals defined by the citizen-soldiers who bore its cost, not by the ruling elites. The people now bore the cause and defined the issues and the nature of the war. The Union citizen-soldiers demanded that the 1864 election campaign in the North be fought on radical principles, and any Democrats or Republicans who could not subscribe to the Union ticket's principles were traitors. Moderates like Thurlow Weed, who had been chairman of the New York Republican Party in 1860, understood the turn of events in the 1864 election campaign. He resigned.[46] The South did not hold any presidential elections during the war. Nevertheless, the war also forced it to adopt radical measures and even to contemplate liberating its slaves.

Revolutionary ruptures usually follow in the wake of popular movements driven by powerful radicalizing ideas leading to war. The dislocation of the defeated society's social and political structures opens the way for major change. The abolitionist drive and hardening Southern resistance produced the conflict in America. Its outcome, the defeat of the South, opened the way for restructuring class relations in the former Confederacy.[47] The Northern war aims projected comprehensive social change for the defeated South. Radicals believed that liberating the slaves meant overthrowing the ruling oligarchy and using newly enfranchised blacks to deter the return of the old ruling class.

Though the Civil War left the South prostrate and opened the way for revolution, the North did not seize the opportunity to carry out major changes in society. Once the war was over, the radical impulse that people's war generated dwindled, and there were no effective radical mass parties to continue the struggle. This reopened opportunities for the traditional political elites to return to the conventional parliamentary politics of brokering compromises. By 1877, it culminated in the reimposition of the previous racist governments.

During the war, a core of politically aware Northern soldiers contrived to see the conflict in radical terms. Major L. Horney with the 10th Missouri (U.S.) voiced the revolutionary trend: "I believe in all great Revolutions and it is no longer possible to shut our eyes to the fact that there is not only a great Revolution and Rebellion going on in the Southern States but that a great revolution at the North is working Boiling surging and threatening vast changes in our social and political System."[48] Conservatives like Horney feared the changes the war was generating. If the war continued much longer, it would irrevocably alter both warring societies. Neither victor nor vanquished would recognize the society they had gone off to preserve. Northern liberal individualism had unleashed the abolitionist crusade against the South. At the same time, it was generating antimonopoly and anticorporate egalitarian sentiments among the troops.[49] A groundswell was rising from the ranks, castigating wealthy classes and profiteers. Robert W. Henry, another conservative Democrat, protested that the cause had been hijacked: "So things have gone on for two years and yet the blinded Bigots of Abolition Cry still for the blood of brave Northern sons and children of the South Flee the *torch* and *sword* to be carried over the fields of the South to let loose and, free negroes to *devastate* and *murder*. . . . Our cause today is not what it was in 1861. It has merged from the restoration of the Union into the Abolition . . . and building up Tyranny Bastilles and despotism."[50] A Southerner living in Ohio lamented: "Most people here has the Niger on the Brain & they don think, Preach or Pray, for any thing else."[51]

How extensive was the support for emancipation among the politically articulate troops? Seventy-one percent of the North's soldiers favored freeing the blacks and enlisting them in the war effort. Even among the few Southern soldiers who discussed the idea of arming blacks, opinion divided evenly over the issue. In the Northern armies, the soldiers from the Northwest were the more numerous and stronger advocates of freeing and arming blacks than their comrades from the East. Seventy-five percent of the westerners supported the idea, but only 60 percent of the eastern troops shared this view.[52] Again, the difference may be attributable to the higher level of political conflict between western radicals and Copperheads. It enlivened the political awareness of the soldiers and radicalized their outlook.

The Union soldiers advanced many reasons for supporting emancipation, using their political perception to justify their devotion to the cause. The most frequent reasons were: outrage against the planter class after seeing slavery firsthand; foreign policy advantages gained by liberating the slaves; the need to increase the North's manpower pool and, conversely, reduce the manpower accessible to the South; and, finally, the need to carry out a revolution by abolishing Southern slavocracy.

When Northerners came into contact with slavery, their opposition to the institution grew.[53] Adoniram Judson Withrow of the 25th Iowa described an encounter with the slave system in Mississippi that revolutionized his political attitude: upon learning that slaveowners were hiding their slaves in the cane breaks in Mississippi, the 25th dispatched a detachment of volunteers to find them and extend to them the army's protection: "In about an hour they returned with 27 of the most wretched looking creatures I beheld, all women and children half starved, filthy looking objectives. Some of them had on nothing but a coarse cotton shirt reaching only down to their knees, neither hat or bonnet, shoes or stockings. They had been in the swamp two days with nothing to eat and nothing to shelter them from the cold and chilling blast. . . . I must acknowledge I felt a slight moisture about the eyes looking at them, and a thirst in my heart for vengeance when I looked upon the master." The detachment of liberators sought out the owner and forced him to divulge the whereabouts of his other slaves. "After some *persuasion* [the slave owner] went along and about a mile in the woods and cane they found two men chained to a tree, with their hands and wrists swollen enormously from the galling chains. They forced the *master* to liberate the *slave with* the threat that if it was not done *instantly* they would hang him higher than Haman." Moved by the plight of these wretched people, the Iowans shared their rations with them. One of the Union soldiers resolved: "If we never do anything more than the rescuing of [these] . . . slaves I think we will be paid for the toil we have undergone so far."[54]

Troops' letters began to include moral injunctions against slavery. It was astounding, wrote Humphrey Hughes Hood, that "men pretending to be christians can tollerate an institution leading to such results."[55] Seeing slavery firsthand sharpened soldiers' political awareness. It made Lyman W. Ayer a convert to emancipation. He realized that the Democrats' contention that slaves led an idyllic existence in Dixie was false. The harsh reality was that slavery was an abomination. It was a myth that a benevolent relationship existed between master and slave and that slaves were so well treated that they would not flee if they could. "Though the years of bondage may have in a measure *weakened* that universal love of freedom common to all men, it is still strong enough to cause very many of them to run the greatest risks to secure it. And I have yet to see that one that wishes to return or that does not prefer even the very imperfect freedom they enjoy with the army to slavery. We have two blacksmiths (colored) which have been with us about nine months and there are no two men in the battery that have been of more service to it than these two."[56]

After coming into contact with slavery, Union soldiers turned to examining slave society and the planter class that ruled it. This regime had generated an arrogant ruling class whose ideas were alien to a democratic society. Chaplain William J. Gibson of the 45th Pennsylvania Volunteers observed that by its very nature, Southern society had bred racism and inhumanity. "The whole system," he wrote, "is to drive the negroes to the lowest point of degradation and consequently to lessen their estimate of them as human beings. I am not sure that they have not persuaded themselves that the negroes do not belong to the human species at all."[57] Robert Hubbard, a surgeon with the 17th Connecticut, wrote deprecatingly of a rusticating slaveowning grandee who prevailed in a rural Virginia backwater. The *hobereau* was "named Mount & the surrounding [area was] dignified by the name 'Mountville'. He is the owner of 800 acres of land and sundry Negroes of various sizes & colors many of them better looking than the master."[58]

Foreign-policy considerations were another reason for supporting emancipation. Emancipation would mobilize popular support in Europe, and ordinary people in those countries would restrain their aristocratic regimes from aiding the South.[59] World opinion would no longer give countenance to slavery. The entire Christian world condemned it. It was "too much against what is morally right according to the Scriptures."[60]

Manpower needs were also an important incentive for emancipating the slaves of the rebellious states. In this view, the fight against slavery had nothing to do with morality; the North had to muster more men to win the war while reducing the South's labor supply.[61] Many soldiers concluded that emancipation was the only way to secure victory.[62] From Lake Providence, Louisiana, an Iowan explained that he hated the idea of "freeing the infurnal woolys but if we [cannot] whip [the South] any other way then I say free them."[63] A soldier with the 95th Pennsylvania concurred. Joshua W. Haas did not care "if the Niggers eat the Whites or the Whites kill the Niggers, just so that the War be ended." But Haas cautioned that the "Proclamation will not go even as far as our bullets go."[64] In truth, the Emancipation Proclamation's impact far outranged the Union soldiers' bullets. It was a revolutionary blow at the very innards of the enemy society. Emancipation awakened a fifth column that would undermine enemy capability. Jasper Barney understood the significance of the slavery question as early as fall 1862, when he told a friend the war "never will come to a Close while the negroes is left wheare they are to rais suplies fore the rebel army." Barney reckoned, "if we take a way the main root of Evil and confiscate all their property they will have nothing to fight fore."[65] Emancipation unleashed a revolutionary wind that preceded the army's progress. Soldiers realized that the Emancipation Proclamation was like a "flea in a nigger's ear"[66] and that no matter what the government intended, blacks in the South would arm themselves at the first opportunity and would never accept enslavement. This was revolution.[67]

Finally, emancipation became a Union war aim because the war sharply focused attention on the key cause of the conflict and the key means for ending it decisively; that key was emancipation. The war made abolition explicit and tangible because the North's politically aware soldiers came to realize that it would hasten victory and moralize the purpose of the war as realistic purposes and idealistic ends coincided.

The radicalization process accelerated as the North's troops began to scrutinize Southern society and its ruling class, which they blamed for the war. Northern soldiers realized that Southern rulers relied on slavery to maintain their influence. Many soldiers reasoned that emancipation would destroy the source of the landed aristocracy's wealth and power. This reasoning coincided with a legal argument that justified punishing the entire planter class. Northern soldiers argued that they were chastising the Southern ruling class because it had committed treason against the United States. As early as ancient Rome, the response to treason was to confiscate a traitor's property. For this reason, a negotiated peace was unacceptable. Myron Underwood, an Iowa soldier, argued that the Union could not negotiate with criminals. It was, he believed, equivalent to plea bargaining with a criminal's friends for the malefactor's freedom even after the jury had handed down a guilty verdict.[68] Moderation may have been acceptable in conventional political life, but this was a national emergency with fundamental moral and legal issues at stake. Compromise with traitors was out of the question. The 61st Illinois Infantry, a regiment that already had seen heavy fighting at Shiloh, voted a resolution that maintained that it "utterly repudiate[d] and condemn[ed] all compromise with a nation of criminals." A resolution of the 62d Illinois warned the Democrat-dominated Illinois legislature that any negotiations would be deemed treasonous.[69]

Many Northern soldiers saw the war only as a punitive expedition. They did not consider the political or economic consequences arising from ruining an entire class. Few men imagined emancipation's egalitarian implications. Rarer were the soldiers who thought ahead to the idea that blacks would get the right to vote. There were, however, some politically aware soldiers who thought about the impact that emancipation would have on Southern society. They believed freeing the slaves would transform Southern political and economic life. Simultaneously, it would strengthen democracy in the North. There were some who saw a chance to reform Northern society and make it more liberal and egalitarian. Religious and secular arguments combined to drive the revolutionary impulse of the radical reform elements in the Union army. Among soldiers who argued for revolution on moral and religious grounds were some who believed that guilt extended to the North as well. Radical reform in the North and revolution in the South had to proceed in tandem to redeem the whole country. The South had sinned against God by practicing slavery and the North had sinned by condoning it. The Civil War was divine retribution for the evil that had festered in the nation's soul since independence. William R. Rapson, 1st Battalion,

50th New York Engineers, echoed his comrades' religious redemptive outlook when he explained why he opposed slavery: "I dont think we will [ever] be blest as a nation until slavery is put-down."[70] "We are a nation," wrote 7th Wisconsin Cavalry Captain J. Newman Kirkpatrick, that "boasted our freedom and at the same time have been holding millions of human beings at the South in bondage and now if God ever punished a nation for anything, he is punishing the whole United States."[71] It was time for the whole society, both North and South, to reconsecrate itself to conform to divine strictures and reembark on its historic mission as beacon of democracy in the world. Robert Hubbard, a surgeon with the 17th Connecticut Infantry, proclaimed to his wife: "This Cause SHALL be fought through and the results will be a glorious renovation of this entire government so that a temple of political freedom, of greater beauty and grandeur than the world has yet seen will be the result."[72]

Colonel Thomas Wentworth Higginson, commanding black troops in South Carolina, also saw emancipation as a means of moral revitalization:

> The only revolutions in this world that bless mankind with a blaze of glory, are the *radical* revolutions, that tear in pieces the selfish interests of the hour.
>
> The only cures that are worth anything, are *radical*. Who would have any other cure for his disease than one that is radical. Hence I believe the more *sudden* and *complete* the change from Slavery to Freedom, the better for all parties concerned.... Any half-way freedom will partake of the combined evils of Slavery and unbridled license.[73]

Millennial issues spurred politically motivated soldiers to persevere during the dark days of the war. Sergeant George Fowle, 39th Massachusetts Infantry, was "glad more than ever that I enlisted sence I have read the President's Proclamation because I think the fight is freedom or slavery. I thank God I have the priverlidge of doing what I can do to proclaim freedom to all men, white or black. I have not been sorry a moment that I have enlisted."[74] Men like Fowle rejoiced in their role as historical agents for grand ideals. Robert Gooding, encamped at Murfreesboro with the 59th Illinois Infantry, expressed a similar view: "It is freedom and liberty we [are] proclaiming to the world[.] I want all to Participate[.] I want both Small and great Black and White to enjoy."[75] White Americans would have to accept equality with blacks, argued John Hiller, a radical second lieutenant with the 2d Cavalry of the Missouri State Militia (U.S.). Hiller saw no objection to equality: "If the black man has been endowed with the ability to elevate himself to the high position which will place him on a level with the white race, I say let him come up."[76]

News of the Emancipation Proclamation, however, unleashed "universal disgust" among Massachusetts Democrats like Henry Livermore Abbott of the 20th Regiment. Officers resigned. Lincoln's name was greeted with groans, and Jefferson Davis was cheered.[77] Many soldiers vowed never to fight alongside black troops.[78] In Wisconsin, German and Irish militia companies disbanded to avoid fighting to free slaves.[79] These men had many political reasons for opposing emancipation. Some argued that abolition would generate divisions in the North and weaken its resolve to continue the war.[80]

Conservatives opposed emancipation because it was at cross-purposes with their ideas about war aims and the type of war that they wanted to wage. They did not believe that the war was being fought between two different societies with different values. Contrary to the radical view, they believed it was between two parts of the same polity. It was a war between political factions, not between peoples. Political brokering had temporarily failed, but if negotiations resumed, some sort of mutually acceptable arrangement still could be salvaged. This could only be possible if the status quo ante bellum were reinstated. A revolutionary aim such as emancipation would nullify any chance of settling the issue because the South would react to radical war aims with desperate resistance, and the region never could be conquered. Even Lincoln's 10 percent support requirement to set up a pro-Union government was possible only in Louisiana, warned Second Lieutenant Peter Eltinge of the 156th New York at Baton Rouge.[81] Attitudes had hardened elsewhere in the South.

Many in the army would not accept such radical aims. The pro-Democrat 109th Illinois Infantry from Little Egypt was operating near Holly Springs, Mississippi, when the Emancipation Proclamation was issued. The outfit mutinied and its men were arrested. Recruits' letters poured out denouncing the war: "The country . . . must know that this war . . . is a war of revenge and fanaticism." The war was run like a "John Brown raid on an extended scale" to free slaves.[82] The purpose was unconstitutional. Moreover, emancipation precluded any chance of finding a compromise settlement. But the war would never be settled by fighting; only negotiation would resolve the problems between the two sections. It was up to politicians in Washington, not soldiers in the army, to end the conflict. D. A. Kreiling of the 13th Indiana had been a moderate Republican, but now he parted ways with the administration: "I never did think it was right to free the niggers in this country nor never will," and if the abolitionists wanted to free the slaves, let them do it by themselves.[83] Democratic soldiers challenged the radicals' idea of an egalitarian community expiating its sins in war. As conservatives, they doubted the feasibility of a revolutionary revitalization. Richard R. Puffer, serving in Mississippi with the 8th Illinois, cautioned people back home against expecting a new Jerusalem to arise after the war: "The question in my mind is will the people of the north like or treat [blacks] any better than their southern brethren." Puffer believed that the freedmen would be just as cruelly exploited in the North as they had been in the South.[84]

Besides political motivations for opposing emancipation, soldiers also expressed emotional reasons. Racism infused the American civic culture with bigotry and hypocrisy. Americans avoided facing these blights on their soul by claiming historical exceptionalism. Arthur B. Carpenter refused to believe that freedmen could be equal to whites. Carpenter typified many white soldiers when he ridiculed a freedmen's meeting in North Carolina: "Several specimens of the ebony hued and thick liped race held forth in spasmodic effusions of negro eloquence and logic. . . . I was so disgusted that I have had a sour stomac ever since, and I fear I shall have to take an emetic."[85]

The South accurately perceived that it was fighting a Northern army carrying out a revolutionary war. Colonel Thomas Jefferson Green, formerly in command of the 2d Battalion, North Carolina Troops, used his vantage as prisoner of war on Johnson Island to explain the U.S. war aims. The North, he concluded, would smash the rebellion and then tyrannize the South: "To accomplish this design, they declare that it is both the right and the duty of Congress to confiscate the property of our people, both real and personal, and to apportion it among their soldiers and freedmen (slaves whom they liberated); they propose to take the arms of the whites and put them in the hands of the negroes; they propose to extend the right of suffrage to the blacks; while among the whites, it is to be restricted to those who have been hostile to their country throughout the war."[86]

The South was right in assuming that ultimately the North was going to ban slavery. In 1860 the South appeared to be reacting impulsively to Lincoln's election. When the secessionist banner was unfurled, it seemed that reason had ceased. Yet the South's response was founded on a prescient assessment of the issue. In reality, the Confederacy knew war could have been averted. Southerners went to war to protect slavery, because they correctly perceived that it was ultimately the central issue at stake. To have waited would have weakened the South's hand in Congress as new states entered the Union. Confederates understood that the government was no longer based on old North-South duality. Now trilateralism had come to the fore with the rise of the West. The West opposed slavery, and slave labor was the defining feature of the South's economic, social, and political system. The South would not be the South without slavery. To destroy slavery would have destroyed the class relations and the power of the oligarchy that characterized the political and economic system. Many politically aware Southern troops knew this fact. Some were sophisticated enough to know that Northern victory would jeopardize their status in the social order by throwing them into direct competition with cheap, unskilled, black labor. Despite its revolutionary rhetoric borrowed from 1776, the Southern army was fighting desperately to stave off revolution. Yet it is ironic that the war forced the South onto a radical path.

The South was fighting to maintain its slaveholding oligarchy, but it was using a people's army to defend such reactionary interests. The inherent contradiction of using an army composed of ordinary citizens—who for the most part did not own slaves—to fight for the wealthy slaveowners grew apparent by 1863. National survival demanded new war aims that would jettison slavery to save independence, which meant arming blacks to fill the depleted ranks of the Confederate army. It was not a new idea: the Lower South had organized units of free blacks early in the war. There were Native Guard units in both New Orleans and Mobile. Enlisting blacks would retain the loyalty of the middle caste of black freemen and also might show slaves that their fellow blacks supported the Confederacy.[87] Extending military service to the enslaved part of the black population and promising them manumission gained momentum after the North proclaimed emancipation and began to enlist contrabands. The justification for organizing Confederate regiments of freed slaves was that it would teach a lesson to Northern "nigger lovers." The North would see that emancipation was not having its desired effect; it could not turn the blacks against the South.[88]

Arming and emancipating slaves had both political and military advantages for the South. Some slaveowners were willing to acquiesce because they assumed that the freed slaves could not constitute a threat to power if they remained poor and disenfranchised. Planters like J. H. Stringfellow believed that even if black soldiers gained freedom in exchange for enlisting, the slaveholding class could maintain its supremacy by withholding the franchise and land from the former slaves. The white rulers could continue to control blacks politically and economically.[89] From a strictly military point of view, it was better to use the blacks for the Southern cause than let the North use them.[90] And in terms of war aims, better that the South should survive with half a loaf than perish trying to preserve both independence and slavery.[91] Southern republicanism was founded on these interdependent war aims. Slavery, after all, defined Southern republicanism; without it the sagacious rule by a slaveowning leisure class would be impossible. Paradoxically, however, while the North was combining slavery and Union together, by considering emancipation the South was separating slavery from independence and eliminating the defining trait of the polity for which secession initially had occurred.

The military entered the picture in February 1864, when General Patrick Cleburne and other divisional and brigade officers called for emancipating blacks who agreed to serve in the Confederate army. The leaders argued that this action would take away the North's moral advantage and put the South on the moral high ground. But the idea raised concerns among Generals Joseph E. Johnston and Patton Anderson, who called the whole idea "monstrous" and "revolting." [92] Fearing dissension in the army, President Jefferson Davis shelved the idea and forbade further discussion among the officers. Cleburne, meanwhile, never again received a promotion before he died at Franklin. [93]

As defeat piled on defeat and retreat followed retreat, the idea reemerged, but this time in diluted form. In February 1864, Davis called for purchasing forty thousand slaves as military laborers, with eventual manumission after the war. The Confederate Congress procrastinated, however, perhaps under the impression that the public would not support the plan. [94] During the winter of 1865, Davis came to the realization that the blacks would have to be armed and organized even though it would entail arming as many as three hundred thousand men. Another million or more relatives of the black enlistees would also have to be freed, which would assuredly undermine slavery among the other 2.5 million slaves. [95] Lee supported the idea by then, even though he feared that it would undermine the class system. He reasoned that if the South did not arm former slaves, the invading Northerners could unleash the blacks against the South, a far worse alternative. [96] Lee's position earned him the enmity of the hard-liners, who denounced him as a "hereditary federalist." [97] Though the measure passed on March 13, 1865, it was too late for the South to mobilize blacks in any number. A few were reported on the Richmond front in late March and April, though they never were organized at regimental level. [98] One historian claims that some black Confederate units even saw action against General Philip H. Sheridan, while others were spotted in the retreat to Appomattox. [99]

By early summer 1863, some Southern troops were considering the idea of manumission and were willing to entertain the idea of arming the blacks. Lieutenant Colonel Theodore Gillard Trimmier of the 41st Alabama surveyed the grim political and military conjuncture facing the South after the repulse at Gettysburg and the surrender of Vicksburg: "The institution of slavery will I think soon be a dead letter. Congress will put the negro in the service. General Lee says it is necessary and they will do what he recommends." He went on to explain that "the soldiers are willing and anxious to see the negro put in the field. They have suffered untold hardships and are getting tired of the war, they are disgusted or disheartened at the conduct of the men at home.... Congress ought to put all in the service and close this thing at once." [100] By 1864 and especially in 1865, Southern soldiers came to support the idea. Some had doubts about the blacks' fighting capability and relegated them to service in home-guard battalions. [101] But desperate times called for desperate measures, and most officers and men grudgingly embraced the idea of armed blacks in front-line outfits. Joseph Robert Davis's brigade near Petersburg voted resolutions supporting the idea and calling on the Confederate Congress to enact the necessary legislation. Everything, they argued, had to be subordinated to the cause of Southern independence—even slavery.

The 15th Alabama backed the idea, too, and it called some congressmen "very tender-footed" on the question. The 15th's colonel also claimed that the 4th and 44th Alabama shared his men's views. They were willing to take black recruits to bring the regiment back up to strength as long as the organization could be preserved and its honor sustained. Even regiments like the 56th Virginia, with a large portion of soldiers from slaveholding families, gave their reluctant assent to the idea. Virginia's 3d Cavalry Regiment, which would be presumed to have the cavalier aristocracy in its ranks, equally endorsed the necessity.[102] Even Bratton's Brigade from South Carolina, the bastion of secession and slavery, voted a resolution acquiescing to arm the blacks.[103] Charles L. Anthony, 10th Battalion, Virginia Artillery, contemplated the South's dilemma as his world began to come apart. Opinion was moving toward enlisting the slaves, but could it be carried out? A Southern soldier explained that the idea raised a dilemma for the South: "Shall we give them their freedom if they fight for it? Who has condemned negro soldiery more than us? Shall we place them along with veterans of our land? Who has condemned equality between the white and black stronger than us? Or shall we make them equal participants with us in our national deliberations? . . . I believe it will be done. Present necessity I believe will compel us to conscribe him and place him in the field as a soldier. We will regret to see it done. But anything rather than subjugation."[104]

A Kentucky general conceded to his son, who was serving with the 4th Tennessee: "what we need now is men to fill up our thinned ranks, & the Yankees have taught us that Negroes make good soldiers." Besides, he argued, "if we don't free them[,] the Yankees will."[105] Captain Joseph Branch O'Bryan, commanding Company B, 1st Tennessee Infantry, expressed the same sense of resignation. He was willing to assent to the idea for "the public good." Moreover, he believed, "we can certainly live without negroes [labor] better than with Yankees."[106] Seeing black Confederate troops—perhaps a labor battalion—go into trenches at Petersburg, Samuel Sublet, Company G, 11th Virginia Infantry, reacted with wry irony: "The South is doing what [Lincoln] has been trying to get them to do all of the time."[107] Thus, the war was imposing the same democratic dynamic on the South as it was on the North.

As the war dragged on and the plight of the Confederacy grew desperate, war aims ceased to be vague ideals. They gained substance and precision. Meanwhile, rumors of peace proposals and peace delegations intensified the soldiers' political interest in the outcome of the war. The men in the ranks tried to understand what the war aims would entail. The list of demands expanded or contracted with the fortunes of war. Following federal reverses in December 1862, rumors circulated in Confederate camps that the Europeans would soon impose mediation. Napoleon III of France would back his mediation offer with a threat to intervene. Stories circulated that former conservative Whigs and Democrats would call for a national convention to amend the Constitution. This meeting would acknowledge the South's right to secede until 1869 or 1873, thereby giving both sides plenty of time to settle on peace terms in an orderly manner.[108] Some former Whigs and Democrats thought that Montgomery Blair would lead conservatives in the Lincoln cabinet in a push for a negotiated peace. Others expected a more straightforward peace initiative. Lieutenant George R. Elliott, a Missouri Confederate, thought the North would consent to an agreement that would include Southern independence, a customs union, free navigation on the Mississippi, and a mutual commitment to maintain the Monroe Doctrine.[109]

When the situation deteriorated, the Southern soldiers' demands for a settlement became desperate. They began to see the war as an unmitigated national disaster. Its costs far outweighed the importance of any of the government's proclaimed war aims. A soldiers' petition from the Second Corps of the Army of Northern Virginia pleaded with President Davis to show flexibility during the Hampton Roads, Virginia, peace contacts: "We pray you to strive every way in your power to settle our troubles by arbitration. Let the sword have no more bloody work to do. If nothing but reunion can be had, let it come, lest worse [a] fate befall us."[110]

Others, however, remained defiant. Captain Lewis Henry Webb, with Battery A, 13th North Carolina Light Artillery, mistrusted those who called for negotiations. He would arrest, out of hand, any Northern self-appointed peace commissioners coming south to see if they could "turn a penny." He went on to declare: "If I had the management of them[,] I think I would speedily end such occurans by hanging the next . . . North Western Peace Democrat—or confreres of Abe Lincoln who has not come openly & honestly, accredited by his Movement to meet a like commissioner on our behalf." He believed that the Yankees' truce was personally dishonorable and a collective humiliation for the South by calling for abolition, confiscation, and unconditional submission to military rule and to Northern masters for a pardon for participating in the rebellion. Webb opposed any dealings with Lincoln's "mephistopheles," Secretary of State William Henry Seward, and believed harsh Union peace terms would rekindle Southern determination to resist.[111] Surgeon John Hendricks Kinyoun, 28th North Carolina Troops, concluded that there was no alternative to fighting on. He believed that the South could never accept "terms so oppressive, so insulting, so disgraceful as proposed by the Northern government." Even if Richmond fell, Kinyoun reasoned, it would be impossible for the North to occupy and control such a vast territory.[112]

Southerners rejected Northern peace terms because they were dishonorable.[113] The North demanded prior conditions, thereby forcing the South to renounce its claims to sovereign status. The Southerners could not abide being branded treasonous outlaws. For its part, the North would not negotiate as an equal with a criminal government. Given these contradictory perceptions, the peace efforts became a dialogue of the deaf. The only concrete results of the peace rumors was that they accelerated the desertion rate already hemorrhaging the Confederate army.[114] Louisiana gunner James B. Walton summed up the problem of negotiating a peace: "The South will have nothing Short of Independence & recognition. And the North demands unconditional subjugation & the ultimate abolition of Slavery."[115] Texan Robert Franklin Bunting compared the situation to the British refusal to negotiate on equal terms with the American colonists, who also refused to accept a pardon because it implied submission.[116] Consequently, the Southern soldiers overwhelmingly doubted that a peace could be negotiated. The war would define its own peace, just as it had defined its own aims. Peace would be imposed over the corpses of the vanquished, not negotiated at the table. No one controlled the war anymore, and no one controlled the peace. Two-thirds of the Confederate soldiers believed that the peace feelers were futile.[117] By February 1865 peace negotiations were a moot point: the Confederate citizen-soldiers were "tiard" of the war and were ready to accept reentry into the Union.[118]

The Northern conception of an honorable peace was freighted with moral and political assumptions. There would be no negotiations and no concessions to traitors. The Southern rebels were "armed theives and murderers whos sworn design is to destroy the government . . . and pollute the air of our native homes," wrote R. M. Lyons of Ohio.[119] Even in the darkest days of the war, in December 1862, 22d Iowa Sergeant Fred M. Clarke summed up his attitude about peace, declaring: "I wan peace, but Nary Compromise."[120] When Sherman negotiated lenient terms with Johnston, grumbling arose from the ranks. Surgeon B. F. Moulton of the 9th U.S. Colored Troops feared that conservative generals like Sherman would subvert radical peace terms. "What a dark cloud Sherman has cast over his career," Moulton told his father. "He seemed to want to take the proceedings of the President, Congress & everything into his own hands and make peace a very easy thing for the Johnnies."[121]

Politically aware soldiers of the Union army were conducting a punitive war against traitors, and many felt no compassion for the South in its dying convulsions. "Let all traitors learn that they have got to bow before the government they have abused," wrote Corporal Abial Hall Edwards.[122] Most men cared little about postwar policy toward the South. They sought only to get home as soon as possible and forget the war. They were not interested in reconstruction. If anything, they wanted only to reconstruct their lives. Men like Robert J. Baird, Company K, 152d Ohio Volunteer Infantry, realized that the "three best years of my life are gone." He wondered whether he could adapt to civilian life.[123] Others, like David Seibert, wanted to "reconstruct" their financial situations. Seibert was planning investments and new enterprises for when he would return home. He authorized his father to purchase twenty-five shares of the Lebanon [Pennsylvania] Oil and Mining Company for him.[124]

Yet there were some soldiers who did take an interest in postwar policy. Among these men, 86.7 percent advocated a hard reconstruction policy. They were not prepared to return to the status quo ante bellum. There had to be proportionality between the war's cost in lives and its outcome. The results of the conflict had to be commensurate with the huge effort that the entire nation had expended. The peace had to have world historical dimensions; it had to signify a new plateau reached in the progress of republicanism and democracy. The bloody pilgrimage had to lead to the New Jerusalem. The South must be reconstructed, made anew. Meanwhile, the North had to renew its devotion to its founding principles. The cathartic revolutionary impact of the war had to bring change in both halves of the country. It should revitalize both sections by reaffirming patriotic and republican values forgotten since the American Revolution. Northern veterans also wanted to settle accounts with disloyal unpatriotic elements that had opposed or hindered the war effort. They would revitalize democracy in the North by purging the body politic of these traitors. Zerah Coston Monks had campaigned in the eastern theater of operations with the 155th Pennsylvania Volunteers and was returning to Ohio to rejoin his family. While he waited for transportation home, Monks castigated the Copperheads. He was eager for "reckoning up old accounts." He warned: "there will be less traitor's talk or more cracked heads" when he got back.[125]

The most politically articulate federal soldiers called for a revolutionary upheaval in the South. Henry Clinton Forbes of the 7th Illinois demanded nothing less than the "Yankeeizing of the South," driving out "the old Aristocrat Stock, to transplant a sturdier and honester race."[126] Only by remaking the South to resemble the North could the two societies meld together again. Chaplain William J. Gibson of the 45th Pennsylvania Volunteer Infantry echoed the same theme. He also believed that measures had to be taken to change the civic culture of the South. The North had to destroy the planter class that had dominated Southern politics and culture. This class, by its very nature, was warlike because it lacked any useful skills for civilian life. It could only find outlet in politics, war, and rebellion. It was a parasitic class whose values were in contradiction to middle-class republican virtues prevailing in the North. Preserving the Southern aristocracy would forever cause new frictions between the two civic cultures. Furthermore, the lower classes in the South were "toadies" to the planter oligarchy.[127] Slave catchers and others low down on the Southern social pyramid were hardly the yeomanry on which to found a democratic republican revival. From Memphis, Colonel Edward Prince, the commander of the 7th Illinois Cavalry, advised Governor Richard Yates to "banish every man woman & child beyond the limits of the U.S. whose sympathies are not with the United States." Prince argued that the North should apply "the sword and torch" to extirpate all traces of slavocracy.[128]

These sentiments in the army strengthened the hand of radical political leaders, who sought to eliminate the Southern aristocracy's source of wealth. They drafted reconstruction constitutions that canceled all debts owed to anyone who had aided the rebellion. They changed the distribution of wealth to favor poor farmers. Reconstruction abolished the aristocracy's political power by disenfranchising the military and political leadership and barring them from holding public office.[129]

The defeated Southerners saw a dark horizon before them as they surrendered their weapons. Sergeant Major John William Green of the 9th Kentucky Infantry (C.S.A.) heard rumors of the impending defeat on May 4. He devoutly prayed that a cask of whisky would materialize so that he could go into the woods "and die drunk & bury all my sorrows."[130] Others could not bring themselves to believe that the cause for which they had sacrificed so much was truly dead. Even as the curtain was coming down on the Confederacy and federal armies were ranging almost at will over their land, John Joyes Jr. of Byrnes's Horse Artillery still hoped that "the cloud's silver lining will soon dispel the darkness and leave us a future."[131]

When news reached Texas that finally confirmed the end, Confederates were shaken to their depths. To Peter Newport Bragg it seemed like the very ground had shifted under his feet: "To realize the fact of a sudden [upheaval] without any premonitory warning, that the independence of our country is gone, almost without hope, was a shock I was little prepared for, and one that I should not have allowed myself to submit to had the news come in any other manner, than officially from Department Headquarters."[132] Elbridge Gerry Littlejohn, 10th Texas Cavalry, awaited the end in Cuba Station, Alabama, and rendered a heartbroken cry: "Oh! My Country! My Country! What a deplorable condition Thou art in; what future destiny awaits thee I can't tell. . . . No longer will [we] be a free people, no longer have our rights, but must submit to the cruel relentless yoke of Yankee Tyranny. . . . Thrice happy are they whose bodies bleach the plains of Shiloh, Manassas, Murfreesboro, and Chickamauga."[133]

After the men absorbed the initial shock of defeat, concerns for the future began to creep into their writings.[134] The more articulate soldiers also assessed the reasons for the failure of their cause. Francis Warrington Dawson, ordnance officer on General James Longstreet's staff, believed that "the great fault lay with the People who were . . . never half in earnest."[135] Others blamed the Confederacy's political leadership. Titus Pomponius Bibb composed a lengthy bill of particulars against the Davis administration. The South had gone to war believing that cotton would be a trump card. The need for cotton would bring support from the European powers. But, alas, "the war came, and Cotton was no King." And the political leadership of the Confederacy "cared for nothing but itself and its own success in plunder & aggrandizement." And in the end the Confederacy was "a falsehood and a farce" whose government

> destroyed its solemn [promise to protect] . . . State Sovereignty by the Conscript Act and Slavery itself by the Negro Soldier bill. Thus Jeff Davis became master of both white and black and his flatterers told him he should be King in Dixie. All principle was gone, the plausible pretext of Secession was gone and the naked vile villainous scheme of mean men was revealed to all. The army gave way of its own accord and by force of arms and the Davis Dynasty died. Suddenly ridiculously and "all over" like the widow Wilkins Pig. "When it lived, it lived in clover, and when it died it died all over."[136]

Bibb resigned himself to the defeat and called on the South to come to terms with its destiny and accept "the results of the war as the judgment of Heaven upon our appeals to arms."[137] Bibb's resignation exemplified most Southern soldiers' reaction to defeat. Like Bibb and Dawson, a strong majority of Southerners—61 percent—acknowledged the end of the Confederacy with total acceptance. Partly this reaction was an acknowledgment of the obvious. The South was so badly defeated that there was no choice but submission. Yet Southerners were also culturally predisposed to defeat. The South's pietism made its soldiers more politically passive than their Northern counterparts. Religious pietism led Dixie's defenders to portray themselves as subject to God's will and as victims of history. Northerners, by contrast, tended to see themselves agents of history. God and history had tested them. The South had failed to measure up morally and now would have to submit. The South's soldiers, despite all their élan on the battlefield, came closer to what Gabriel A. Almond and Sidney Verba have called a passive "subject" civic culture, in contrast to the "participant" culture of the North.[138] Reflecting Southern troops' reversion to religious resignation, Robert David Jamison spoke of God's "chastening hand."[139] While Northern troops sang of "Jubilo" and "Glory Road," the Southerners spoke of the "hand of Providence."[140] According to a Tennessee Confederate, all was divinely preordained because "the Lord will not send us more than He giveth grace to bear."[141] "I hate [defeat] very much . . . but it is the will for the Lord," conceded another rebel.[142] In the end, the Southern soldier could only submit and put his "confidence in the goodness of God."[143]

Succumbing to defeat, the Southern troops' first act of submission was to take the oath of loyalty to the Union. Most felt that emigration was an unacceptable alternative, and they believed continued resistance was doomed to failure. There was no choice but to take the oath. They did so in overwhelming numbers. Captain Francis Atherton Boyle of the 38th Regiment of North Carolina Troops, a prisoner of war, recorded that all but one hundred of the six thousand enlisted men in his camp swore loyalty to the Union, while 1,680 of 2,000 officers affirmed their loyalty to the North.[144] Even before the surrender, in February, John Hampden Chamberlayne sold off his slaves while there was still a market for them. Like others, Chamberlayne was reconciled to the idea that he would have to yield to the federals.[145] Colonel James B. Walton of Louisiana's Washington Artillery summed up the views of many survivors of the war: "The war is at an end, four years of the best of my life have been lost. Oceans of blood has been shed, thousands of lives sacrificed, all, all for nothing, . . . [leaving] the country embittered, distracted, ruined, & in prospect nothing but anarchy and tyranny. . . . But by gones must be by gones. All I want is to be permitted to return to my pursuits & for the remainder of my days labor for the good of those whose love is all I have left."[146]

Only a minority reacted defiantly to the prospect of the collapse of organized resistance. Most of these men were officers and were more politically articulate. Almost twice as many officers as enlistees—62 percent to 38 percent—vowed never to yield and live under Yankee dominion.[147] Based in Mobile with the 1st Tennessee Regiment, Joseph Branch O'Bryan believed "we are not yet whipped. They may succeed in scattering our armies & issue their proclamation of peace. . . . [But] it will *never* be healthy for a Yankee to take a house in the O.S. [Old South]."[148] Richard H. Bacot swore to continue the fight as a guerrilla: "I say fight Yankeedom forever, if we have to Bushwhack & live in the swamps."[149] After organized resistance collapsed, other defiant Confederates decided to emigrate. Rather than submit to Yankee rule, Captain Elijah P. Petty of Walker's Texas Rangers decided to flee to Brazil, Argentina, or Hawaii. Petty would "beg my bread and drag my family out of the country in poverty and rags, . . . [and would swear] my children to eternal hostility to the Yankee race."[150]

Guerrilla warfare was not an unrealistic strategy. During the war, partisan units had caused serious problems for the invaders, obliging them to retain a third of their forces for garrison duty. It would have been difficult for the Union troops to occupy such a vast area after the conventional war ended. But a guerrilla war could have turned into a racial conflict if the North had mobilized the ex-slaves to fight. Such a war would force the federal government to deploy regulars to prop up their black political allies. Soon, Southern diehards believed, the Northern public would begin to demand that the troops return home in response to growing political dissension. The policy would ultimately force the North to abandon its political and military surrogates in the occupied areas, argued Clement S. Watson, a Southerner.[151]

Nonetheless, a guerrilla strategy had drawbacks for the South. Richard E. Beringer holds that reverting to guerrilla warfare had significant, perhaps revolutionary, implications for Dixie's stratified class system, undermining the power of the ruling class.[152] Guerrilla warfare would have taken the war out of the hands of the South's traditional elites and turned it over to the ordinary people. Furthermore, according to Beringer, the South lacked one of the chief elements for conducting a successful guerrilla war: a strong enough sense of national identity to sustain such a protracted and costly struggle. Most Confederate soldiers were not prepared to sacrifice home and family to continue to resist for national independence.[153]

Ultimately, such effective partisan warfare never occurred. The only guerrilla fighting remained essentially banditry driven by racism (the Ku Klux Klan) or greed (Jesse James and the like). Part of the reason why no effective guerrilla movement emerged may be the nature of the Southern society, which was stratified and had a powerful conservative class governing the polity. Its leaders had no interest in supporting a guerrilla war that they would not be able to control. If groups arising from the people were successful, they would displace the Southern aristocracy. Worse yet, partisan actions would engender a more severe repressive policy against the South. The upper classes' property would be hostage to Northern reprisals. Better for the wealthy class to yield and eventually collaborate with the occupier and keep its economic power intact and regain hegemony in Southern politics. Watson's prediction of Northern dissension leading to withdrawal proved all too true by 1877. The plan to carry out a revolution in the South was abandoned, and with it ended the revolutionary ideas of the politically motivated citizen-soldiers who had fought to bring those ideas to fruition. Yet Alfred Patton, a Missouri Confederate who fled his home, was right when he predicted that it would take three hundred years before the "memory of the deep wrongs shall pass away."[154]

5 Leaders and Politics

POLITICAL AFFAIRS AT HOME, ABROAD,
AND BEHIND ENEMY LINES

Politically enlightened citizen-soldiers understood that victory could be won only if the Northern people remained resolute and chose effective leaders. To vanquish the South, the North would have to be prepared to undertake a protracted brutal struggle to grind down enemy morale by disrupting its economic and political life. Finally, the more informed soldiers realized that conquest could be hindered, even prevented, if the South could secure help from abroad. The war had ramifications that extended beyond American society's military capabilities. The outcome hinged on relations with other great powers. Foreign governments had a stake in the outcome. They would follow events and could exert pressure on their governments' relations with the belligerents.

Among the questions relating to U.S. affairs was the quality of its political leadership. The national political leadership was a frequent topic in politically motivated soldiers' correspondence. Confidence in the political leadership is a mainstay of morale in an army of citizen-soldiers. The volunteer needs assurance that he is being wisely led. When he offers his life for the republic, he does not want his leaders to squander that precious gift foolishly. During the second half of the war, 62 percent of Union troops voiced confidence in their political leaders, compared to only 32 percent of Confederates. Defeats and retreats in the West corroded the Southern soldiers' confidence in the national government. Many held it responsible for ineffective theater commanders in Arkansas and Mississippi. Rebels blamed Richmond for retaining generals such as Theophilus Hunter Holmes in the trans-Mississippi and Braxton Bragg in Tennessee, suspecting incompetence and cronyism in Richmond. The soldiers reproached Richmond for inadequate supplies, poor intertheater coordination, and general failure to husband and deploy the armies effectively. Confederate troops also castigated their political leaders for putting personal ambition and faction ahead of the national welfare. Many believed that the government was in the hands of an oligarchy, a regime devoted to bestowing privileges on the few while conferring only obligations on the many. This attitude contrasted sharply with that of the Union citizen-soldiers, who, though they criticized profiteers on occasion, generally assumed that their government worked for the general interest.

The soldiers in gray showed no mercy in accusing the Confederate leadership.[1] Jefferson Davis and his cronies were butchering the army "by gross criminal incapacity," raged Colonel Laurence Massillon Keitt of South Carolina just before he died at Cold Harbor. They were murderous cretins, killing the men and the national cause by their stupidity, fumed Keitt. Keitt damned the South's inability to define a revolutionary vocation and to be governed by such mediocrities. Unlike Robespierre, Danton, and Saint-Just, Davis and his "poor creatures" in the cabinet were revolutionaries only by the consequences of their inept policies, policies that were causing discontent and bread riots in Charleston and Richmond.[2] The rank and file shared Keitt's opinions. Sergeant Edwin H. Fay held the view that any other army would long ago have risen against such an incompetent government.[3] Cajun Jacques Alfred Charbonnet, with a cavalry outfit, avidly fantasized about the fools in Richmond doing the fighting themselves. The idea probably brought joy to many soldiers.[4]

Specifically, the troops blamed the national government and the state authorities for thinking more of partisan and local interests instead of coordinating policy to defend the country as a whole. Self-serving provincialism and petty political bickering among political leaders disgusted the volunteers, and their sentiments were reinforced by polemical writers in the highly partisan press. Colonel Keitt laid down his broadside paper to lament: "I hear that Toombs is on the stump in Georgia, and is arraigning Davis in a terrible manner. I have always feared the divisions which I saw would spring up among us. You cannot have liaison, connection, unity among a planting community. Too many revolutions have shipwrecked upon internecine divisions."[5] Deep divergences also appeared over peace terms, and calls for peace from the Southern opposition eroded the troops' morale. Major William Johnson Pegram of Purcell's Battery demanded that Tennessee's pro-Unionist congressman, Henry Stuart Foote, be silenced. His "jabbering" was dividing the country.[6]

Complaints about factionalism in the Confederate Congress found echo among soldiers as the polemics of the partisan press pulled the soldiers into the political maelstrom. Keitt decried political gridlock between the Confederate Senate and the presidency.[7] Senators indulged in "fine recreation" instead of addressing the important issues, bemoaned another Confederate.[8] When the citizen-soldiers visited their new national capital, they went away convinced that their political leadership was ineffective. Felix G. Buchanan of the 1st Tennessee Regiment got leave between campaigns to visit Richmond, where he attended a session of the national legislature: "I had the pleasure of seeing most of our *great* men, and heared short speechs from a few of them. Our congress is composed for the most part of fine intelligent looking men, but that is all I can say in their behalf. Or I am not a good judge of such things consequently ought not to grumble, but I must say that I do not think that that body reflects much honor upon our government."[9] By 1863 ordinary soldiers of the South were scoffing at Henry St. Paul's florid philippics in the *Mobile Register.* St. Paul exhorted the people to trust Congress to "steer their ship over the stormy seas of revolution."[10]

The citizen-soldiers in the South's armed forces also were dismayed when Davis insisted on keeping failed army leaders like Bragg. Such political and military decisions directly affected their chances of survival if Bragg had led them into more disasters. But Joseph E. Johnston's removal in the middle of the Atlanta campaign caused universal indignation and reinforced the belief that Richmond did not know what it was doing.[11] The rank and file held the view that it was wiser to sacrifice Atlanta than to lose the beloved commander of the Army of Tennessee. William Johnson Pegram was among the few who did not share this view. Nevertheless, he railed against Davis for favoring Bragg over Lee. He concluded: "No man who would sacrifice a general, & thereby the good of the cause to his prejudice, can be a patriot."[12] Fay shared Pegram's doubts about Davis's military leadership. He attributed the Confederate president's ineptitude to his preoccupation with the eastern theater. Davis mistakenly overrated the importance of eastern cities, and he overlooked the significance of important strategic places like Vicksburg.[13]

The soldiers' political interest gradually extended to economic affairs when they related these problems to the overall war effort and blamed the government for the steady decline in buying power at home and the supply shortages at the front. Tampering with money and taking goods in lieu of taxes outraged upper-class officers like Keitt. "Rude interference with property," he muttered, "is full of danger. You may repeal the Habeas Corpus, and men will grumble, . . . but touch the corncrib and they will fight. Women may give up their butter and eggs, as well as their sons, to the needs of the country: but men are apt to give up the child and hold the granary."[14] As the war progressed, it sharpened the men's awareness of political and economic inequality, for though the rank and file may have shared the upper-class disapproval of such confiscatory measures, they nonetheless believed that the wealthy classes were not bearing their fair share of the economic burden. Private James C. Zimmerman of the 57th North Carolina Regiment complained that the government was taking taxes and commandeering everything from the poor while the rich got off lightly. He enjoined his wife not to send produce to the front; the officers feasted on it while her husband starved on half rations. The taxes were going only into the pockets of corrupt officials and speculators.[15]

The rising awareness of injustice emerged as soldiers railed against the Confederate government's conscription policy.[16] The legislation allowed special exemptions for the planter class to oversee their slaves. Other upper-class gentlemen's sons got state militia assignments to avoid combat. James C. Zimmerman wondered why local men did not come out and help with the fighting: "All they care for is to keep the poor men run away from home and they lay at home feesting upon the good thing of the land laying in their good beds and sheltered from all the cold and rain while we poor soldiers are forced away from home and dare not return."[17]

The politically informed Southern soldiers often ignored or had little interest in discerning the complexity and diversity within the South's leadership. After the disappointments of 1863, they turned their frustration and disappointment against perceived ruling-class privileges and the oligarchical nature of the polity. "During revolutions, the cream always rises to the top, and that's why, God seldom blesses revolutions," wrote Charbonnet.[18] He was expressing the conservative's distrust of the revolutionary process. He, like some other politically articulate Southern soldiers, saw the war coming full circle. It started as a popular uprising against Northern tyranny but eventually would end with the establishment of another tyranny when the planter oligarchy consolidated its powers. The planter class, argued Francis Warrington Dawson, was willing to sacrifice its sons but never its blacks. Its economic interest superseded the nation's interest. It would never agree to free the slaves to fight for the South.[19] Serving with a Texas regiment in Arkansas, Corporal Jonathan Thomas Knight watched the planter class confirm Dawson's distrust as it scurried to hide its slaves instead of taking up arms to drive back the invader.[20] The Southern rank and file blamed the fire-eaters of the planter class for getting the country into the war and then shirking their duty. The planter class was the core of the secession movement, but it was reluctant to part with its wealth to help the cause. Knight complained that many planters refused to accept Confederate money from Southern troops trying to buy food.[21] Theophilus Perry branded the wealthy slaveowners "miserable dogs" who would not fight yet had the effrontery to question why soldiers were on leave. The rich were aware of the soldiers' resentment, which is why wealthy planters and their political allies opposed soldiers running for office.[22]

The Union troops also grumbled about their political leaders, but complaints were comparatively few. One reason Union support for its political leadership was twice as high as the Confederates' confidence was President Abraham Lincoln's stewardship. By contrast to Jefferson Davis's patrician bearing, the men believed Lincoln to be one of them; they felt he was a fellow soldier who had enlisted in the cause. They shared Lincoln's ideas about winning the war. They admired Lincoln's determination to wage relentless war against the South.[23] Lincoln had proven himself a "good and faithful soldier" who could "take charge of the Ship of State" and therefore deserved four more years in office, declared 22d Iowa Quartermaster Sergeant John Walter Lee, with Sherman's army.[24] Eastern soldiers expressed a similar attitude. Edward Griswold of Connecticut's 1st Battery of Light Artillery at Chaffin's Bluff registered his support for Lincoln: "Day before yesterday the Connecticut troops had an oppertunity to vote for President, and I had the privelege of doint the best deeds of my life by casting my vote to sustain one of the best governments the world has ever known and to do my part in crushing rebellion, treason, oppression, & wickedness of all kinds."[25] The soldiers were politically sophisticated enough by 1864 to be able to distinguish George B. McClellan's military achievements from his political views. McClellan was no longer the darling of the army. The men in the ranks believed that McClellan, Lincoln's opponent in the 1864 election, was a hypocrite, a liar, and a traitor for running on a Democratic peace platform.[26]

The 1864 election signaled the empowerment of ordinary people to decide the country's fate. The political struggle was a counterpart to the people's involvement in the war. The citizenry fought with ballots and bayonets, simultaneously mobilizing its battalions to the front and to the polls, all the while sensing, perhaps for the first time in the nation's history, its power to decide the course of events. In 1864 the people had become increasingly politically involved. They were now aware that they could decide the course of the war in the field by their decision in the presidential election.[27]

The 1863 elections had shown a shift in the political winds favoring the Republicans. That year's fall contest revealed that the Democratic Party, largely controlled by Clement Laird Vallandigham's peace faction, was losing the ground it had gained in 1862. Vallandigham's total in the race for the Ohio governorship was 11 percent below the Democratic margin of 1862. The "thinking bayonets" in the victorious Union armies and their supporters at home were taking back ground lost two years earlier in the political arena. Lincoln and the Republicans were so encouraged by these results that they launched their reconstruction policy the month after the 1863 election results came in, proclaiming confidently that any state could set up a "loyal" government with the approval of only 10 percent of those who had cast their ballots in 1860.[28]

There was also little chance that the Democratic Party could ever rise beyond second place if it continued to accept Confederate survival. Soldiers and civilians reasonably concluded that Democratic victory was synonymous with Confederate independence, the perpetuation of slavery, and the dissolution of the Union.[29] Thus, buoyed by the 1863 results and having gained the support of the prowar Democratic faction, the Republican Party entered the 1864 election with important political cards in hand. Its leader, Lincoln, had become a shrewd political strategist during his first term, and he badly wanted a second term.[30]

Lincoln had little to fear from opponents in his party. Though Salmon P. Chase's name had been bandied about by the radical unconditionals because the former secretary of the treasury seemed more radical and because he had an extensive patronage system in the party, Chase had withdrawn his nomination after Lincoln had arranged to include endorsements from Ohio, Chase's own state. John C. Frémont, the original Republican standard-bearer in 1856, elicited some interest, but he had too many enemies. Germans and abolitionists had supported him, and they organized a meeting in October 1863, but he had little organization. Though the abolitionists were divided, most preferred to stay with Lincoln, who seemed more reliable than the stormy Frémont. Another alternative candidate could have been Benjamin F. Butler, a War Democrat representing the other side Republican-Union coalition, but he had little strength in the Republican organization.[31]

For all of these reasons, Lincoln easily won the nomination at the Baltimore convention in June, and he also was able to impose his ideas on the party's platform. The platform was adroitly formulated. It encouraged the radicals by calling for an implacable war until there was an unconditional surrender, thus precluding any talk of an armistice and negotiation with the Confederates. The platform also tried to please radicals by supporting abolition and the use of black troops. The Joint Committee on the Conduct of the War and leaders like Senator Benjamin Wade had been pressuring Lincoln on these issues. Earlier, however, Lincoln had opposed the radical-sponsored Wade-Davis bill, which would have imposed more severe standards for rebel states to reenter the Union and would have provided for more effective protection for ex-slaves. In fact, the unconditionals were not sure of Lincoln's commitment to the cause. They remembered that he had offered to step aside for Peace Democrat Horatio Seymour in 1862, and they believed that the Emancipation Proclamation was not radical enough because it did not free the slaves immediately and unleash a servile insurrection against the enemy. The radicals also were not confident that Lincoln would energetically implement reconstruction policy, which they believed should remain in the hands of Congress. At the same time, Lincoln pleased moderate Republicans and War Democrats by selecting a pro-Union Southern Democrat, Andrew Johnson of Tennessee, as his vice presidential candidate.[32]

The Republican Party's political fortunes also were favored by the conservatives' failure to coalesce. A coalition of Democrats and former Whigs might have thwarted the Republican strategy, but this endeavor failed. Instead, the conservatives divided their loyalty among moderate Republicans, Unionist Democrats, and Peace Democrats.[33]

The Peace Democrats ran former Army of the Potomac commander McClellan for president and nominated George H. Pendleton of Ohio as vice president. They were an odd couple. While McClellan supported the war, Pendleton was from the Vallandigham antiwar wing of the party, although he lacked Vallandigham's rhetorical excesses. Nevertheless, the plank in the Democratic Party platform declaring the war a failure and implying an armistice preceding a negotiated peace as soon as possible proved unpopular outside the convention hall. This plank opened Democrats to accusations of treason. The Republican press claimed that the Democratic Party was being manipulated by Richmond's agents and had ties with treasonous secret societies in the North. These themes frequently appeared in the soldiers' correspondence. Ultimately, as John A. Rawley contends, the 1864 election was a referendum on Lincoln, on his conduct of the war, on party unity, on war aims and on emancipation, and ultimately on the definition of American nationality.[34]

The men in the ranks supported leaders for their vigorous prosecution of the war.[35] Democrats who advocated peace had little to offer. Their policy depended on events outside their control. It was a policy predicated on Union misfortunes. Short of a major military reversal or foreign intervention, the best the Peace Democrats could do was to snipe at the administration from the sidelines while waiting for an opening. With this strategy, however, the Peace Democrats appeared to wish for the nation's defeat, because negotiation and compromise could only be activated if there were disaster.

Colonel John L. Mcnaugh lamented the lack of a George Washington among the present generation of leaders to steer the country through its trials and tribulations. Instead, all the Union had was an "anecdote personified as President." Lincoln, Mcnaugh believed, was preventing peace by his relentless war policy. The concurrence of abolitionist support at home and demands for an all-out war in the army only hardened Southern resistance and prevented negotiated peace between equals.[36] Major Henry Livermore Abbott, who served with the Democrat-dominated 20th Massachusetts Infantry, wrote venomous letters against Lincoln while waiting impatiently for election day to come so the country could kick out the government.[37] Another Bay State Democrat, a major with the 18th Regiment, deemed anyone a fool who would risk body and soul for such a blundering, homicidal, and perfidious concern as the Lincoln government.[38] Lincoln's opponents even turned their scorn on the president's wife. Observing the president and First Lady during a spring visit to the Army of the Potomac,

Robert Hubbard, another New Englander, likened Mary Todd Lincoln's expressiveness to an "unbaked loaf of bread."[39]

The Democratic soldiers' bill of particulars against the Lincoln administration not only condemned emancipation and arming the blacks but also censured the president for suspending the writ of habeas corpus. Major Abbott warned that there was no way to hold off the drift to "Russian despotism," where any dissent would be considered treasonous. Democratic soldiers, moreover, opposed recruiting "foreign mercenaries" like "Dutch boors, Maccaronis, and Frogatecs."[40] They added Lincoln's choice of generals like Ambrose E. Burnside to the list of their complaints. Burnside's winter campaign had accomplished nothing other than making a "graveyard of Virginia."[41] Such defeats convinced Democrats that the Lincoln administration would not win a second mandate.

In general, citizen-soldiers seized the chance to participate in state and national elections as a way of reaffirming their status as citizens and distinguishing themselves from regulars and mercenaries. As mentioned earlier, Maine showed that it valued its citizen-soldiers more than regulars, according its citizen-soldiers the right to vote in the field but denying that right to the Maine men serving with regular outfits. The militiaman was a citizen first and soldier second.[42] His military duty arose from political decisions in which he had participated by exercising his franchise. W. H. Sanders, a surgeon with the 11th Alabama, explained the significance of the right to vote in a people's army: "One matter upon which we all felt considerable interest and which we hope may receive proper attention, and that is in allowing the Army to vote. . . . Nothing is more natural than that we should desire to have a voice in their settlement." It would be "unfair" to conclude a peace without consulting the soldiers.[43] Soldiers vigorously petitioned for their enfranchisement in states like Illinois, where the legislature had gone Democratic in 1862 and had blocked Governor Richard Yates's efforts to enfranchise the men in the field.[44]

The soldier came to understand that the war had a political dimension as he fought with ballot in one hand and musket in the other. He was waging a war against two enemies. He was wielding sword and musket against the enemy in the field while using the ballot against traitors in the rear. After casting his vote for Lincoln, a soldier wrote: "The day of the greatest battle & I believe the greatest victory . . . has been fought and I know won today."[45] The political war was waged in many ways. Soldiers attended meetings, drafted petitions, and voted resolutions supporting or opposing candidates.

Southerners as well as Northerners participated in election campaigns. Colonel W. A. Owen of the 53d North Carolina Troops authorized his men to send regimental delegates to a political convention to thwart the rising peace move-

Union soldiers lining up to vote in the field during the 1864 presidential election. The poll illustrates the importance of politics in the people's armies of the American Civil War. Alfred H. Guernsey and Henry M. Alden, *Harper's Pictorial History of the Great Rebellion* (Chicago: McDonnell Bros., 1868), 2:668.

ment in North Carolina.[46] In the South, the system was oligarchical: the wealthy portion of the population dominated the political process. In North Carolina and similar states, the dominant class was the people who owned twenty or more slaves and who expanded their economic activity beyond the plantation to investment, commerce, and industry. Constituting 15 to 20 percent of the population, these people formed a cohesive nucleus of power holders through their contacts in business and government. The majority of the population were small farmers, mechanics and artisans, and landless laborers living in isolated communities whose franchise was limited to certain state and county offices. For example, property qualifications restricted those of modest means to voting only for members of the lower house of the legislature and for the sheriff, while the gentry could elect senators and justices of the peace—those who governed the county. Also, overrepresentation of electoral districts in tidewater areas gave a disproportionate number of legislative seats to the wealthier class.[47]

Despite the oligarchical distribution of political and economic power in the South, the common people had gained political importance since the Jacksonian era. The "rail splitter" class of small farmers were drawn into the political arena by the elites, who sought votes. The number of small farmers made them important in the protodemocracy of the planter-dominated ante bellum South. Flattered by the elite's political solicitation, hating blacks, and, in some cases, aspiring to slaveownership, these whites of modest economic circumstances gained a sense of political empowerment. This sense of political relevance had been fostered by the upper class's political flattery and by the development the yeomanry's own sense of self-reliance and social competence, which they nurtured in the isolated frontier environment where they had learned to settle affairs with neighbors and establish community standards on their own with little outside involvement.[48]

The most important form of political participation, however, was voting. Petitioning for the right to vote in the field, Hoosier gunner William Inwood declared that it was the "imperative duty" of every Indiana soldier to defeat the Democratic Party's peace platform in the coming election.[49] The election ritual had a symbolic significance that transcended even the outcome of the vote. Voting in the field affirmed the army's status as a deliberative body that was actively participating in political life; it was not a passive instrument of the government, like the old professional army. This symbolic difference is reflected in the soldiers' letters and diaries as they carefully recorded electoral returns. Elections were solemn political festivals that affirmed republican government.[50] Marching through Georgia, far from any polling station, and unable to send home the results of the regimental vote, the 17th Ohio Volunteer Infantry nonetheless held a straw vote, and one soldier's diary reported that no votes were cast for McClellan.[51] Even prisoners of war performed the election-day ritual to reaffirm their status as citizens. From a South Carolina prison camp, Sergeant Henry H. Stone, Company I, 11th Massachusetts Infantry, recorded the proceedings: "A day of great fun here. All voted this morning at roll call. There are polls established for the purpose of voting by means of black and red beans: black for A. Lin. and red for Mc."[52] Though Stone never gave the results, George Marion Shearer of the 17th Iowa, a prisoner at Camp Lawton, Georgia, reported that his regiment voted for Lincoln, 213 to 16.[53]

Election and straw-poll results boosted morale, especially among men languishing in prison camps. John W. Northrop reported the effect of Lincoln's victory on the men incarcerated in a Confederate prison:

I saw that stooping figure of Thompson's approaching & he was singing "Ulysees leads the Van" and clapping his hands in glee. He was coming to tell me news him not being so merry for months. "North, North! I have rich news, Lincoln carried every State but three. The Copperheads are beat out of sight & old Seymour of N.Y. was drove down without splashing. Fenton is elected Governor by from 30,000 to 50,000. Bully! bully!

bully! North! I told you we'll beat [them]. . . . Glory to God! It is the greatest triumph the world ever saw, The moral sentiment of the North is truly
in the ascendant. The victory is won!" Shouts pealed thro' the musky air
& satisfaction beamed on faces that had not smiled for weeks."[54]

Soldiers reported how keenly their units' had supported the cause by voting for
Lincoln. They conveyed their unit's political zeal for the cause as if they were reporting the outcome of a battle.[55]

As the fortunes of war turned in their favor, Republicans advocated voting in
the field. Republicans were aware of soldiers' rising political consciousness and
radicalization and realized that the soldiers were their strongest political allies.
Most states in the North provided for soldier voting.[56] The administration became certain that the people's army would not support the professional officer-
corps candidate, McClellan, but only the states had the authority to decide if and
how the soldiers would exercise the franchise.[57] Two methods prevailed: ballot
boxes taken to the camps by state election commissioners and "proxy voting,"
in which the state authorized the soldier to write down his choice and send it
to a reliable friend or relation, who would cast the vote in the home precinct.
One flaw in conducting the poll in the field was that officers could influence the
voting. They verified the eligibility of the participants, supervised the voting,
sorted the ballots, and proclaimed the results, thus enabling them to manipulate
the election at every stage of the process. Maine's handling of soldier voting was
typical. Its law provided for three ranking officers to supervise all aspects of the
election in every battery, battalion, and company from the state.[58] To reduce
officer influence, some states appointed civilian commissioners to conduct the
poll. Iowa was among the states that had effective means of preventing officers
from tampering with the voting process. The Republican-dominated Iowa legislature authorized the State Census Board to appoint one commissioner for
each regiment. The commissioners received poll books from the secretary of
state that were delivered to commanding officers. Then soldiers selected election judges, who prepared and manned the ballot boxes.[59] Connecticut's legislation excluded officers entirely. The state sent commissioners to distribute, collect, and return ballots to town clerks. In most states, however, officers retained
a major role in the process.[60]

Republicans accused Democrats of election fraud. Both sides claimed a shortage of tickets. When men were away from their units, they often were disenfranchised. In other cases, officers sabotaged elections by moving their units closer
to the front, beyond the control of election commissioners. Commanders would
argue that an election hampered fighting efficiency.[61] Sometimes the enemy was
more cooperative than the officers. Simon Bennage of Company E, 76th Penn-

sylvania, reported that the Confederates assisted Union polling by stilling their guns until the votes were in under the mistaken belief that doing so would ensure a Democratic victory.[62]

While states usually authorized voting in the field in national elections, voting in state and local elections sometimes had a residency requirement under which votes could only be cast at township meetings.[63] Soldiers returning home to vote often faced residency challenges and other impediments. Returning soldiers carried orders that they were on special duty, which allowed them to carry their arms to ward off anyone who tried to prevent them from exercising their right to vote.[64]

In Illinois, the Democratic legislature blocked legislation authorizing voting.[65] Company commander Stedman Hatch thought it a searing humiliation that Illinois soldiers were not allowed to vote. How was it possible that the very men who were mortgaging their lives for their country's survival were denied the right to cast a ballot?[66] Hatch vowed that this injustice would be remembered when the soldiers returned. Meanwhile, the disenfranchised soldiers nevertheless conducted straw votes to make their views known and reaffirm their status as citizens.[67] Washington did all it could to see that Union soldiers had a chance to vote. Generals received telegrams from the capital urging them to spare as many men as they could to vote in those states that did not authorize absentee voting, and in response, Republican General Joseph Hooker ordered all men furloughed to go home and vote.[68] Military authorities even emptied hospitals and cleared soldier homes of ambulatory patients so that the men could go home to vote. Men streamed out of camps and hospitals, forming convoys of soldier voters and causing congestion on railroad lines.[69] In the camps of Pennsylvania troops, it was rumored that fifteen thousand soldiers were crowding the "election express" to vote in state elections.[70]

In the 1864 U.S. presidential election, the country overwhelmingly supported Lincoln, as did its soldiers. Sergeant John Walter Lee rightly foresaw that there would be a Republican sweep: "[In] this army (as it is with all others) 'Old Abe' has the preference. his majority will be large in the army. McClellan lost friends by accepting the nomination on such a platform as that Chicago convention got up."[71] Some soldiers voted more than once. William Foster admitted that he voted for Lincoln and "exerted myself a little to obtain more of the same kind [of ballots]."[72] In other cases, the pro-Lincoln rank and file exerted peer pressure on suspected Democrats. Edward Griswold, serving in a Connecticut battery, noted that McClellan voters could be spotted by their discomfiture at the polls because they appeared ashamed to look directly at their comrades.[73] After the vote, Ohio soldier Carlos Parsons Lyman remarked that McClellan votes were at a "big discount."[74] In fact, American electors gave Lincoln a comfortable majority. The soldier vote was only significant in the outcome in Indiana, Maryland, New Jersey, New York, Oregon, and Pennsylvania.[75] The soldier vote could have been more influential in states with strong Democratic Parties. In those states, however, Democrats were in a position to block enfranchising legislation; they knew soldier sentiment tended to be pro-Republican.[76]

Soldiers voiced many reasons for supporting Lincoln over McClellan. They believed Lincoln's administration was committed to bringing the war to a speedy and decisive close. They were politically sophisticated enough to become disappointed with McClellan for allowing noted Copperheads like Vallandigham to influence the party platform. They also questioned McClellan's loyalty because of his willingness to share the ticket with Pendleton, a notorious Copperhead. Because McClellan had made such concessions, they realized that he really represented the peace-at-any-price faction of the Democratic Party, whose platform contradicted McClellan's vow never to sign an armistice that acknowledged Southern separation. The platform, in effect, supported a negotiated peace and rejected the soldiers' demand for unconditional surrender. Corporal Samuel Augustus Wildman, 25th Ohio Volunteer Infantry, represented many soldiers' reactions to McClellan and the Chicago platform: "I think 'Little Mac' will lose some friends in this company if he accepts the nomination on that platform and runs for the Presidential chair by the side of so notorious a copperhead as Pendleton. One of our Sergeants who was a warm supporter of George B. before the nomination has expressed his intention . . . of not voting at all under present circumstances."[77]

This peace-at-any-price platform made soldiers determined to throw out Democratic traitors and reject their "evil designs."[78] McClellan was parting ways with the men who had followed him across Virginia for two years. He "won't amount to much after this," concluded one of his former soldiers.[79]

From the Little Rock General Hospital, Luther Short of the 43d Indiana wrote: "I wan Abraham to handle the rains until this rebellion is crushed and the Old Flag waves proudly over this land again. I think to elect any other man than Old Abraham wil only prolong the war." Short, a keen political observer, realized that the military situation would affect the outcome of the election. He understood that the rebels would do everything in their power to hold off the Union armies to undermine support for Lincoln. They would do their utmost to hold Atlanta and, if possible, even threaten Washington.[80] Peace could not be negotiated, it had to be won.[81] The increasingly politicized soldiers were alert to the fact that a vote for McClellan was really a vote prolonging the war.[82]

Samuel Storrow of Massachusetts was acutely aware of the momentous issues that would be determined by the election. It was union or disintegration, honor or dishonor, prosperity or misery, freedom or slavery. In this national deliberation, the choice was between Lincoln and victory for the holiest of causes and McClellan and defeat and disgrace.[83] In the eyes of many of the Union's politically motivated soldiers, the election of 1864 was a contest between good and evil. The Civil War had polarized politics, forcing old Whigs to ally with the Democrats in a conservative counterrevolutionary coalition to oppose the Republicans by late 1862 to early 1863. There was no middle ground for the conservative Unionists' August 1863 centrist convention at Rochester, which failed to garner much support.[84] There was no room for a moderate conservative party anymore; there were either Copperheads or radicals. The 1864 election campaign polarized the issues. Even though McClellan did not support negotiated peace, many soldiers judged him by the company he kept—his sharing the ticket with Pendleton and the Democratic platform. The soldiers saw the contest as a struggle between two diametrically opposed parties: one for a negotiated peace and the other for the South's unconditional surrender and abolition.

In the Confederate army, soldiers had the right to vote by proxy in North Carolina, Tennessee, Alabama, Georgia, Florida, Missouri, and Virginia, with Virginia's troops voting as early as May 1861 in the state's secession referendum.[85] There were, however, no presidential elections because the Confederate constitution provided for a six-year presidential term. There were congressional elections and vociferous contests at the state level, particularly in North Carolina, where popular opposition to the war party was strong.[86]

There was growing fear that the liberty of the citizens and soldiers of North Carolina was being eroded by the increasing military power of the authorities in Richmond, specifically in implementing conscription. Davis was demanding complete control over recruitment, which would undermine local government and individual liberties. Many people feared that they were on the road to military despotism. The fears were underscored by the Confederate government's revocation of habeas corpus after October 1862. The threat of arbitrary arrest left no one's person or property safe. There were almost one hundred protest meetings across the state in July and August 1863. They raised questions about the independence of the judiciary and complained that North Carolinians were being oppressed and treated unfairly.[87] Like the Copperheads in the North, William W. Holden's *Raleigh Standard* called for a peace convention of states to negotiate an end to the war.[88] Zebulon Baird Vance, however, believed that North Carolina had to fight to the bitter end. He feared that if the state went its separate way, it would open itself to Union army occupation and a harsh Northern reconstruction policy. It would also risk Confederate invasion to reinstate Virginia's communications with the rest of the South. After the twin defeats at Gettysburg and Vicksburg, unrest mounted, and in September 1863 mobs fought in the streets of Raleigh. Vance ultimately carried the day, defeating

Holden 44,856 to 12,647 in the race for the governorship.[89] Holden, however, drew support from a deep well of discontent. His conservative party attracted much of its backing from poorer classes, who saw their rents rising at hyper-inflationary rates of 500 and 600 percent in 1863. Food prices also soared; the cost of a barrel of flour had risen from seven dollars to fifty dollars.[90] Conscription and taxes in kind on farm products weighed heavily on the poor farmers and generated marauders whose activities made entire counties so dangerous that Confederate troops dared not venture there.[91]

News of the political discontent at home reached the North Carolina troops' camps. The Tar Heel troops denounced the Holdenites, and entire regiments held political conventions and drew up petitions censuring Holden or sent delegates to help Vance's election campaign.[92] Sergeant James W. Biddle, with the 1st North Carolina Cavalry, summed up the soldiers' attitude when he vowed: "Most all of them . . . speak of Holden and his party in the bitterest terms, and declare that if N.C. is carried by Holden . . . they will no longer acknowledge her as a State of their nativity. Ware almost ashamed of N.C. even now and hate what we were once proud to be called 'Tar heel.'"[93]

In Arkansas, Unionist sentiment was strongest in the northern part of the state—for example, in the Pine Bluff area, with its large number of small farmers. But there were also reports of staunch loyalists in Sebastian County, around Fort Smith, and in Logan and Yell Counties, as well as in Clark County in the southwestern part of the state. In the Ouachitas, loyalists even raised a Union regiment. Union support came from unconditional Unionists, people who opposed secession, and those who had been forced into exile or hiding. There were secret Union sympathizers who awaited their chance to rise up. There were opportunists who supported whatever side seemed to be winning, and by 1862, it appeared to be the North. Finally, there were disenchanted secessionists who were angry at Confederate demands on their sons and their wealth. Conscription, the debasement of Confederate currency, and confiscatory taxes alienated large parts of the population.[94]

Even in the Deep South, there was pro-Union sentiment. In northwest Alabama, requisitions, conscription, and inflation kindled resentment against the government in Montgomery. Dissidence became open as the federal forces moved up the Tennessee River in April 1862. Support for the Union cooled, however, when more ardent occupying forces in northern Alabama, like those led by Colonel John Basil Turchin and his 19th Illinois, sacked Athens while other Union units carried out reprisal raids, burning houses and destroying livestock.[95] In East Tennessee, bridge burning and a smoldering insurgency ready to break into open rebellion at the approach of Union forces created a climate of fear and repression. Confederate military tribunals were hard at work disposing of hundreds of dissidents and "conspirators." The repression drove many Unionists into Kentucky, where they joined the federal formations who were preparing to invade Tennessee. Local militia were unreliable for maintaining the Confederate government's imperium. Failing all else, Richmond had to resort to declaring its own lands in Tennessee "enemy territory," thus suspending all civil rights and turning the area over to the heavy hand of the military occupiers.[96]

North Carolinians felt they were fighting a political war at home and a real war at the front, a sentiment echoed among Northern soldiers. The citizen-soldiers' two-front war led to a popular pun: a Confederate was an armed Democrat, and a Democrat was an unarmed Confederate.[97] In countries engaged in desperate conflicts, fear of treachery always emerges. Yet in earlier centuries, when kingdoms fought dynastic struggles with professional armies, dissidents seldom gained a foothold among these troops. Professional forces had few ties to society and were usually apolitical. For this reason, in monarchical Europe dissent usually centered in a small camarilla of court schemers.

A change came with the rise of people's armies, which were recruited from the entire population. Thus, the entire populace had a stake in the conflict, and large parts of the population could become disaffected. To maintain broad support among the citizenry, the political elites had to convince the people and their soldiers that the war was justifiable and that the authorities' war aims and policies were appropriate. There was always the risk that dissent might grow. If it did, it would not be confined to the ruling class. In a democracy fighting a people's war, dissent would extend beyond a court clique to large segments of the population, who could seriously hinder or even sabotage the war effort. The soldiers were acutely aware of the effect of any disaffection among the people. The soldiers feared treachery and called for stern measures against dissenters. Lewis B. Blackford, with the 1st Engineers at Wilmington, North Carolina, excoriated profiteers and disloyal elements who were "whining grumblers," wishing to "receive absolution from Father Abraham while they may have their purses and their precious necks." Blockade-running had corrupted the entrepreneurial class in Wilmington: "They are lost to every consideration of patriotism, of honor, and even honesty. [W]ith them it is one breakneck race to accumulate money in foreign lands so they may be ready to run when the time comes."[98]

The American Civil War generated waves of popular excitement that radicalized citizens and soldiers. Collective panics arose, alleging Copperhead plots to seize a local arsenal, county seat, or even state capital (Springfield, Illinois, was a case in point). In the South, rumors of abolitionist conspiracies to unleash servile insurrections spread like wildfire across the countryside. The American Civil War knew *la grande peur,* as did the French in their revolution and in their civil war against the Vendéens and the Chouans in 1793–94. Only firmly held political beliefs could harness the home front and the army to pull together in the war. Yet there were large parts of the community who opposed war in both the North and the South.

The loyalty question was a frequent political topic among soldiers, with Union troops almost twice as concerned with the loyalty issue as the Confederates.[99] This phenomenon is paradoxical because the Confederates had far more serious problems with dissident elements than the North did. Irredentists and draft evaders challenged the Confederacy's authority in western North Carolina, northwest Virginia (West Virginia), northern Arkansas, northern Alabama, and eastern Tennessee. Throughout the South, dissent arose over military issues such as the draft more often than over political questions. There were no presidential elections in which a peace candidate might have focused attention on political questions, in contrast to the North. When disloyalty entered the political arena, it remained a local or state matter, like the Holden gubernatorial candidacy. Southern state governments expended considerable military resources on keeping communications open. They mobilized forces to chase deserters and draft evaders in areas like the estuaries of the North Carolina coast or the state's western mountains.

In the North, dissent focused on political issues. Returning from the war, Illinois soldier William B. Birkley lamented that besides being disabled by the war, he had to suffer the "Bite of theas Copperheads."[100] The loyalty question was most intense in Northwest states like Illinois: northwestern troops raised the loyalty issue a third more frequently than their counterparts in the east.[101] Peace Democrats had a strong foothold in Illinois and Indiana, and they also had Southern irredentist settlers in the Illinois region of Little Egypt. Indiana had pro-Southern areas in the hill country between Martinsville and the Ohio River. The Democratic Party had important successes in the Ohio, Indiana, and Illinois legislative elections of 1862 and fielded a serious challenge in the 1863 Ohio gubernatorial race. And in 1864, the peace party, hoping to capitalize on earlier local successes in 1862 and 1863 with McClellan, challenged Lincoln's Unionist coalition. The Democrats' decision generated venomous diatribes against disloyal elements at home and in the army. "History will stigmatize [the Copperheads'] children as the descendants of traitors," vowed Indiana Colonel James R. Slack.[102]

The troops' indictment of the peace party supporters included several charges. Soldiers complained that many of their fellow citizens were evading military service. The Copperheads, wrote Matthew R. Perry from the trenches around Atlanta, "don't care a dam what kind of peace is agreed so [long as] they will get cleared of the draft." Such "cowardly . . . sons of bitches" would only fight the war in a "lager beer saloon."[103] In Illinois, farmers dared not hire blacks to replace their sons at the front, while Copperheads demonstrated against the draft and openly cheered for Jeff Davis.[104] On the Southern side, John Francis Shaffner, a surgeon with a North Carolina regiment, warned friends at home that Holdenite machinations were spreading "pernicious teachings" among the men and encouraging desertion. "The blood of hundreds of fellow-citizens, cries at his door for retributive vengeance, and he will yet meet with the reward due to treason."[105]

The soldiers in the field blamed disloyal elements for undermining the country's political unity. Union troops railed against the Copperheads' "constant *hissing* at the Administration,"[106] which raised doubts among the people and undermined the country's resolve. These dissenting ideas even reached the army and threatened morale: Andrew Bush, with the 97th Indiana in Tennessee, deplored treasonous content in letters to soldiers from Indiana Copperheads.[107] The letters were so blatantly traitorous that they sounded like Jefferson Davis himself was writing to the men. Some Copperheads advised the men to desert rather than fight for emancipation, while others even called on soldiers to turn their arms against the government.[108]

Besides blaming dissidents, soldiers in the South also believed speculators were undermining morale as prices soared and shortages spread in 1863. Manning the guns at Fort Fisher, Macon Bonner cursed the "speculators and extortioners, the thousand percent men, who are coining their fortunes out of the sweat and agony of the war and like vultures stabbing their bills into the vitals of the country." They would get their just desserts after the war, like the Tories four score years earlier.[109] Merchants and speculators of every ilk were hampering the war effort by gouging soldiers' families.[110] There would be no statute of limitations for their crimes: returning veterans would settle the profiteers' accounts in a different coin.[111]

The men in the ranks also accused dissidents of aiding and abetting the enemy by giving information and sustenance to opposing forces.[112] Worse yet, some comrades were traitors. Except for Company K, which was made of "sound corn," the entire 109th Illinois was suspected of disloyalty. There were reports that the regiment had met with enemy civilians in Holly Springs, Mississippi, and asked them to contact the nearest Confederate forces to arrange the regiment's parole. Other rumors held that the regiment had been too zealous in returning contrabands to their owners and that its soldiers wanted no part of a "war of revenge and fanaticism." Regulars had to disarm the suspect Illinois unit and march it away under guard.[113] Fears of disloyalty among the soldiers from notorious Copperhead regions extended to other regiments, like the 131st Illinois from Shawneetown in Little Egypt, which was also rumored to be unreliable.[114] There were fears of disloyalty in other states' regiments. "Dellona" wrote to his hometown newspaper in Wisconsin accusing his state's 33d regiment of being infiltrated by Copperheads.[115] In other cases, the problem was limited to a small nest of Copperheads. Levi A. Ross thought that there were no more than forty unreliable individuals among the 330 men in his 86th Illinois, but these few traitors were spreading their venom.[116] The quartermaster of the 94th Ohio Volunteer Infantry was said to have been seen reading a disloyal newspaper that was subverting regimental morale.[117]

To lower morale, Copperheads seized on every defeat or mistaken policy to criticize the government. They "worked up a bad feeling in our ranks," complained a Hoosier soldier.[118] Samuel Storrow reported on the insidious activities of Copperheads in his Massachusetts regiment. He was horrified by the treasonous talk in the ranks. The men boldly advanced the conviction that the war was useless, that the Union could never be restored, and that all the blood and misery were for naught. He feared that such ideas were making headway among the men.[119]

The soldiers suspected anyone who voiced the mildest doubts about the cause. Such talk, they believed, would strengthen the enemy's will and prolong the war. It weakened their comrades' resolve and caused heavier losses by reducing the unit's effectiveness. Those who undermined the unit's morale were "infernal god allmighty god damn Butternut Sons of Bitches."[120] There was no place for dissent and division when the nation's very existence was at stake. "All who are not for us are against us," wrote a North Carolinian.[121] Worse yet, any appearance of division within the North's army could trigger French or British armed mediation.[122]

There were moral reasons for the implacable anger against dissenters. Lack of support was a blot on the honor of the army, the country, and the cause. The "slime of deserters and traitors" was disfiguring Southern society, wrote Texas Captain Elijah P. Petty.[123] Northerner William H. Philips was embarrassed to be identified with his regiment, the 118th Ohio Volunteer Infantry, when a third of its men voted for Vallandigham. The worst traitors in the unit were in Company G, from Hancock, and Company K, from Lima. Philips was mortified when other regiments jeered and booed the 118th.[124]

The frustration against disloyalty at home and at the front found many outlets. When the enemy invaded their home states, some soldiers were maliciously pleased in knowing that the enemy sympathizers were having their goods seized and destroyed by the opponent whose cause they had been supporting. There were also tangential political benefits reaped from the Confederate invasions of the North, which would get rid of profiteers who wanted to drag out the war for their own ends. When Lee invaded Pennsylvania, Northern troops rejoiced;

they hoped the Confederate depredations would bring retribution against the state's large Copperhead faction. Federal troops exulted at seeing "the gauntness of war penetrate Pennsylvania and New York to wake them up and stimulate them to do their duty," wrote 11th U.S. Infantry Major James W. Ames on the eve of Lee's invasion.[125] Oscar Cram, 11th Massachusetts Infantry, would not mind if Lee had "gone to Phila & burnt half the city[,] then the *Pesky* Copperheads would begin to open their eyes & this thing would be closed up."[126] Carlos Parsons Lyman regretted that General John Hunt Morgan's raiders had been captured so soon after they crossed the river into Ohio. The raid, he speculated, might have cut voter support for Vallandigham in the coming gubernatorial election.[127] Lee's second invasion drew cheers from soldiers who thought Pennsylvania Copperheads would get their just desserts.[128] Levi A. Ross believed an invasion of the North would energize the United States: "The boys . . . feel glad that Lee is making a raid into Pa. for we think it will arouse the *'stay at homes'* from their apathy to a sense of duty which they owe to their Country & themselves." Ross maintained that these Confederate incursions would add a "little smell of gun powder & good taste of bitter realities of *war*" to the Copperhead banquet. It would have "a salutary effect upon their treason loving souls."[129]

The soldiers also called on their state governments to rigorously apply conscription laws, especially against disloyal elements. It would silence dissenters and simultaneously provide replacements for depleted units. "I would like to have some copperheads with us just for them to dodge bullets." Referring to Morgan's raid, Bergun H. Brown wrote: "I suppose some of the cowards have been dancing to the music of 'John Morgan got your mule.'"[130]

Other soldiers thought that anyone who was politically unreliable should be ostracized. John W. Baldwin told his wife that he intended to end his relationship with anyone who intended to vote for Vallandigham.[131] Whenever the tides of war turned, there was a chorus rising from the ranks calling for a purge of all disloyal elements as the men vented their frustration. After months of defeats, William Foster, encamped at Martinsburg, West Virginia, grew angry when he heard of the carping against the war back home. He wrote an explosive letter blaming civilian society for leaving the army in the lurch: "I have felt badly ever since the Autumn [1862] Elections. I think the southern element manifested itself at that time. If the coming Congress cripples the Army and makes it necessary to conclude a disgraceful peace, and the army is sent home to reflect over their disasters, defeats, slain comrades. . . . If they do this, there will be, in the mouths of some 500,000 men but one word—*retribution*."[132]

The same bitterness resonated from the Confederate ranks. "I would walk a weary mile to see [Holden's] body hanging food for birds," a North Carolinian said of his state's peace candidate for governor. "Submissionists" were a blot on the Confederacy's future and merited death for their treachery.[133] Colonel John F. Sale of the 12th Virginia Infantry swore that he and his men had already selected the lampposts they would use for gibbets. There would be a price on every traitor's head if Sale had his way. He swore that blacks would come in for particular treatment for helping the Yankees.[134]

Union soldiers like John H. Burrill echoed their Confederate enemies' vows to exact revenge when they got home. Burrill "wished to God about 10,000 of the copperheads of the North could be hung."[135] The Union soldiers promised they would give the country a good "scouring out" when they got home.[136] Corporal David Goodrich James had had his baptism of fire with the 16th Wisconsin at Shiloh and was subsequently languishing at Lake Providence, Louisiana, with plenty of time to dwell on his anger. He pledged that he would "hang every Cussed one of the traitors as quick as you would kill snake." The whole 16th was eagerly waiting for the war to end to return and clean out the filth with their bayonets.[137]

Some officers seized on the soldiers' anger against Copperheads and channeled it to support the radicals at home. Brigadier General Mason Brayman wrote to Governor Yates of Illinois that "the Soldiers of Illinois are in earnest. . . . He holds the remedy in his own hands and will apply it when the cartridge box gives way to the ballot-box."[138] When a Copperhead challenged a prowar speaker in Olney, Illinois, soldiers set upon the heckler. Only when they had virtually beaten the man to death did officers pull them away.[139] When rumors circulated of a Copperhead plot to assassinate Yates, Lieutenant Colonel James Drish of the 122d Illinois proposed that Grant detach units to return to Illinois to kill "Every Copperhead in the State." Drish assured the governor of his men's political reliability. Yates, he claimed, was "the Idol of the Soldiers, they love him next to their wives."[140] Brigadier John McAuley Palmer also offered troops to Yates to crush the opposition. He advocated a coup d'état against the Democrat-dominated Illinois legislature. He thought he could organize two or three thousand reliable men on leave in Illinois to crush the Democrats, subsequently using the unit to ferret out all treasonous elements in the state.[141] A Hoosier sergeant with the 10th Regiment concurred with his Illinois neighbors. Indiana also was paralyzed by a Democrat-dominated legislature. The sergeant called on Governor Oliver P. Morton to "hang the last one of them or Send them to the army & we will do the work for them."[142]

The men also persecuted the dissidents within their ranks.[143] To prevent treasonous ideas from circulating, Iowa Governor Samuel Gordon Kirkwood asked officers to intercept any Copperhead letters. George S. Richardson of the

6th Iowa Regiment agreed and took part in the purge. He thought it his duty to ferret out disloyal elements, and he urged his kinfolk to do the same at home.[144]

Soldiers doubted that their parent society shared their political zeal. They believed that the war corrupted society. Profiteering, opportunism, and cowardice were signs of a general moral decline. Civic virtue and moral righteousness had yielded to greed and fear. The soldier-patriot looked over his shoulder toward home and saw snivelling cowards trying to avoid induction. These people would accept peace at any price, even if at the expense of their honor.[145] "Nearly all [back home] are submissionists," lamented an Army of Northern Virginia engineer. They all "seem to be more despondent here than in any county. . . . How can they think of union or Submission[?] I can not conceive. they talk about union when the blood of the best sons of the Confederacy has already tinged on the land . . . with human gore—when so many thousand of Virginia's best and noblest sons have voluntarily give up their lives for Liberty & Independence."[146] George W. Grubbs, serving with the 42d U.S. Colored Troops, shared his enemy's resentment against his parent society. While Copperheads at home skulked, his black troops in Chattanooga were firing off an enthusiastic thirty-gun salute and holding a public reading of the Declaration of Independence.[147]

Besides their concern about morale at home, politically motivated soldiers scrutinized conditions on the other side to see if the enemy society's will to fight was holding firm. In a people's war, the morale of the opposing populace was as important as the spirit of the opposing army. "Slavery is dad in this state, and the masters all begin to see it. They begin to bring their slave here and get a receipt for him," noted Edward J. Bartlett, writing from Tennessee and describing what he believed was the first sign of declining morale among the Confederate ruling class.[148] The state of affairs in the enemy camp was a frequent theme in soldiers' correspondence, acquiring an urgency as the war dragged on. Troops on both sides—but especially Confederates—desperately wondered which side's resolve would crack first. The South's soldiers vainly tried to hold off the North's overpowering onslaught and anxiously looked north to see if there were any signs of faltering Union resolve. The Confederates showed almost three times more interest in political and economic conditions in the North as their Union opponents exhibited toward Southern society (27.8 percent to 10.1 percent).[149] Rebels anxiously sought signs of weakening enemy resolve, hoping that the Northern tide was about to recede. They realized that their arms alone could not hold off the Yankee host; victory also depended on the North's will to fight.

Politically motivated soldiers were keen observers of the situation behind enemy lines. Many soldiers innately understood that there were various dimensions to the enemy's power, ranging from political and morale sources to material ones. Soldiers relied on three sources of information about the state of affairs in the enemy camp: their own impressions, newspaper reports from home and from the enemy press, and exchange of news with prisoners and pickets.[150] Probably the most accessible source available to the soldiers was enemy newspapers. Serving in the Petersburg lines with the 1st Company of Louisiana's Washington Artillery, Paul Grima avidly followed the 1864 election in the Yankee press. He hoped that the outcome would favor the South's cause. "Things are heating up North according to their papers," wrote Grima. "The Democratic party is about to erupt in an explosion that will long be heard. The resulting Democratic victory will put us in an advantageous position."[151]

Soldiers were aware of the tangible and the intangible sources of enemy power. Tangible sources were elements they could readily measure: population, industrial output, number of soldiers, and so forth. Intangible power sources were less easily quantified, like leadership and morale. Enemy morale was the most important of the soldiers' intangible indicators of the enemy's fighting capacity. Each side sought information on the subject. When the enemy was inactive or when deserters came in at higher than usual rates, it indicated that morale was falling. Arthur B. Carpenter, who served with a regular outfit besieging Atlanta, told of rumors that the rebel troops were losing heart: "Yesterday in front of the Brigade on our left the rebel pickets were ordered to fire on our pickets who were advancing, they fired a volley of *blank cartridges* then dropped their muskets and ran into our line. Such facts indicate strongly that they are in a state of demoralization."[152] On the other side, Southerners followed reports in the Northern press that many Union soldiers were refusing to reenlist. Those who returned from the front after their enlistments expired were becoming "missionaries" for the peace faction. They would "assist in inducing the Northern people to [reach the] right conclusions in the elections," hoped a North Carolinian.[153]

The wild card in the unpredictable outcome of the 1864 election was the situation at the front. Sherman's or Grant's defeat could upset the political advantage. The battles along the Rapidan reduced confidence in "Unconditional Surrender" Grant. The radicals were beginning to complain. The call for a new draft also weakened Lincoln's chances during the summer.[154] Republicans feared that events at the front could cause Lincoln's downfall, especially with the Democrats running a warrior candidate. Rebel soldiers perceived that their efforts on the battlefield could affect the result. They were as much participants in the electoral campaign as their Northern counterparts, and the Confederates sensed an opportunity to determine the outcome of the election and the war.

Southerners also eagerly watched for signs of popular disenchantment with the Lincoln administration, including evidence of an emerging peace movement. One of the chief indicators of enemy resolve was the progress of the peace party in the opposing side's election campaigns. A Mississippi prisoner of war witnessed the political atmosphere in the North during the 1864 election. He noted a rise in antiwar sentiment: "Things are said now, on the stump of every public occasion, that one year ago, would have banished, or imprisoned any man daring to utter such sentiments. Indeed, fifteen months ago, Mr. Vallandigham, the great main-stay, & present backspring of the peace Democracy of Yankee-dom, was banished from the United States, for the expression of much less treason, than the merest of his followers now spouts defiantly." [155]

The Confederates fervently hoped that the Democrats would carry the day. Better a Lee be vanquished in the field than a Democrat be defeated in the elections. [156] Politically articulate Confederate soldiers followed the 1864 presidential election in the North from the Chicago Democratic convention onward. McClellan's nomination, however, did not convince some Confederates that he would bring peace. His prowar stance and his service in the army suggested that he would not be any more conciliatory than Lincoln. The Confederates also were perplexed by the contradiction between McClellan's prowar stand and Pendleton's links to the peace wing of the party. Private J. D. Sprake of the 8th Kentucky Cavalry (C.S.A.) astutely observed that the Democratic platform was merely an election ploy when he declared that "the platform according to my thinking means anything you want." [157] Some, like Colonel James B. Walton of the Washington Artillery, thought the platform was the defining element of the party's war policy because it was a peace platform that would force McClellan to accept terms with the Confederates if he won the election. [158] Other sophisticated Southern soldiers not only doubted that the Chicago convention decisions would have much bearing on the fate of the Confederate cause but also feared that the ambiguity of the Democratic platform might create illusory hopes in the South. A McClellan victory might dampen Southern soldiers' zeal and lessen their reliance on their own military prowess; they would instead rely on events in the North to save their cause. In addition, the Democrats might make generous peace offers calling for a mild reconstruction policy, yet the South still would have to yield its demands for independence and open itself to the conqueror anyway. [159]

Whatever the Democratic Party might do if it won the 1864 election was secondary to a strong peace party's impact on the North's ability to act decisively. Perhaps, some Confederates thought, if the elections brought political paralysis and anarchy, it would force the North to ease its pressure on the South. [160] A Confederate reading accounts from the Northern press, hoped that the U.S. election would unleash a wave of anger that would explode into riots and destruction in "their sinful land," thereby destroying the North's ability to wage war against the South. The Union would be paralyzed, fighting against itself.[161] Texas gunner James Postell Douglas thought that the Republicans might not be as unified as many assumed. Moderate Republicans might bolt their party and rally to the Democrats.[162]

The Confederates correctly perceived that the 1864 presidential election in the North could create many opportunities as well as many dangers for the South. Much depended on how the South conducted its war policy; its strategy should seek to influence the election. If General John Bell Hood's Army of Tennessee could hold off Sherman's legions at Atlanta while Lee held the Union soldiers off at Petersburg, Northern morale might plummet and favor a peace candidate. Confederate hopes for the Democrats also rose when General Jubal Early led his corps north to threaten Washington during the 1864 summer. They hoped that Early's actions would demoralize the North and strengthen the peace party.[163]

Some politically prescient Confederates nonetheless thought that the South's success on the battlefield would have little or no effect on the Northern election. A Confederate with Purcell's Virginia Battery contended that no Democratic candidate could defeat Lincoln.[164] "The election will . . . be all one way," concurred another Confederate.[165] Northern pickets told Captain William Biggs of Company A, 17th North Carolina Troops, that it looked like a Lincoln victory. At any rate, thought Biggs, "it will make but little difference to us who those people see fit to elect for in my humble opinion it is *War* with either, and we had just as well make up our minds to that fact, however disagreeable it may be."[166] Junius Newport Bragg shared this view, concluding that Republicans and Democrats were united in one basic aim, restoration of the Union. With such an objective, whoever won the election would still mean war.[167]

Lincoln's victory in 1864 certified that the struggle would continue to its ultimate paroxysm. "Abraham Lincoln being elected for four years again, I safely congratulate myself four more years of service," Bragg resignedly wrote.[168] Lincoln's victory would mean an even more implacable war. Lincoln would draft more whites and would organize more black battalions.[169] With a Republican electoral victory, all-out war would "probably hold high carnival during another term of four years," wrote a North Carolina surgeon.[170]

Not all were despondent after Lincoln's electoral victory. Even in January 1865, Felix Pierre Poché still hoped for a miracle before Lincoln could be inaugurated. Even if the Democratic Party were too divided to stop Lincoln in Congress, perhaps McClellan and other conservative generals might carry out a coup d'état.[171]

While Confederates closely followed the Northern elections as an indicator of the Unionists' resolution, Union soldiers tracked other intangible components affecting the enemy's morale. They perceived the seeds of Confederate weakness in the very nature of its society, whose culture was characterized by "shiftlessness and decay" because of its proximity to "niggerdom." Thus, Southern society did not have the fortitude to carry on for long.[172] An Illinois officer serving with a Missouri cavalry outfit at Little Rock displayed this outlook when he remarked: "Every day I become more & more disgusted with this moral desolation which seems every where. . . . Men & women—married & unmarried—black & white seek only to gratify their sensual desires, & it matters little whether or not there is a commingling of the races. . . . I do not believe there is more than one woman in a thousand in the whole Southern Confederacy who is virtuous, & they are universally libertines."[173] Northerners believed the South was incapable of disciplined collective action because Southern society lacked the moral stamina to sustain a long conflict. It was not a self-controlled citizenry, and thus it could not govern itself effectively and maintain its resolve for a high purpose. Its people were too sensuous and impulsive, lacking civic virtue and personal discipline. In Northerners' eyes, Southerners lacked republican virtues.[174] In the meantime, the "rich nabobs" who controlled the Southern slavocracy stayed in power and lorded over the rest of the population, which was too ignorant to be aware of the inequalities. This was a society where poor whites were doing the fighting without realizing that they were hardly better off than the slaves.[175] Northern soldiers hoped, however, that reverses in the field eventually would cause cracks between the ruling class and the poor. Northern troops waited impatiently for these fissures to appear; when they did, they would herald the collapse of slavocracy.

The South also believed that the North's population lacked unity of purpose. Regional tensions appeared to confirm that belief. When the Emancipation Proclamation went into effect, rumors circulated among Confederate troops that the northwestern states would soon secede. Union deserters were bringing welcome news that western troops would refuse to fight for the "Niggers and that the Western Troops intends to com over to our Side," according to William S. Woods of the 20th Alabama at Vicksburg.[176] Southern troops pounced on reports from prisoners and on news culled from the press. "The news from Yankeedom becomes more and more favorable," wrote a North Carolinian. "I almost believe the disintegration is progressing. . . . The erection of a third independent Empire appears now an irresistible consequence. May that consummation speedily ensue, for then we shall have peace on *our own* terms, however exacting."[177] Robert Franklin Bunting, a chaplain in the 8th Texas Cavalry, thought that the Northwest would secede, yet he opposed including any Northwest states in the Confederacy because they would bring in abolitionists.[178]

Besides the soldiers' appraisal of the military capabilities of their own officers, discussed in chapter 3, the troops also turned their attention to the quality of the enemy's military leadership, another intangible component that entered the citizen-soldier's assessment of the enemy's military capabilities. Frequent changes in commanders suggested that the North was unable to use its army effectively and that it was losing faith in its military leadership. After the Union reverse at Fredericksburg, a Tennessean wrote: "General Burnsides has been superseded by Genl Jo Hooker, fighting Jo as the Yankees call him. . . . But judging from his testimony [before Congress], . . . I can not believe that he is much military man."[179] When Hooker was forced to resign a few months later, the Southern troops speculated about the next likely candidate for dismissal.[180] When John C. Pemberton's loss of Vicksburg resulted in Grant's promotion, Louisiana trooper Edwin H. Fay figured that Grant was inept but very lucky.[181] Even when Grant bottled up Lee in Petersburg a year later, the Confederates continued to believe that Grant's campaign was a failure. He had not achieved a decisive victory, and his large losses would ultimately undermine Washington's confidence in him.[182]

There were also more tangible sources of evidence of the enemy's strength. Many realized that a country's economic capability was the key to success in a people's war. The chief gauge of the economy's strength and an indicator of the progress of the war was the value of a country's currency. Major Charles Jackson Paine, an officer with the 33d Massachusetts Regiment, observed that the war only would last as long as the currency maintained its value.[183] On the other side, Lieutenant Charles E. Denoon, 41st Virginia Infantry, also appraised the tie between the political situation and his country's economic predicament: "Gold sells at auction for $17 Dollars. Green backs are selling at the Brokers for $11. That is a nice state of affairs under President Davis."[184] Rebel soldiers were aware of the corrosive effect that military reverses were having on the value of their money. Dan Scully, serving with the Confederates in northern Louisiana, read reports of Lee's retreat with increasing dismay in May 1864, and Scully presciently recorded in his diary that the end was near and ominously predicted that money would tumble. Citing Louis XIV, Scully observed that "the last guinea will win." If the Confederates were losing confidence in their currency, they were also losing faith in their cause.[185] Viewing the South's predicament from the other side, Sergeant Daniel Gookin, 17th Maine Infantry, summed up the link between the military and the financial situation in the South when he joyfully reported: "Two big days, Richmond gone up, and gold has gone down."[186] Soldiers on both sides commented on economic problems in enemy society and they noted supply shortages in the enemy camp.[187] The strength of the currency was as much an indicator of morale as was the number of enemy captured. When gold went up in New York in early 1863 and again in 1864, Confederates believed that it showed that the Northern bankers were losing heart. Confederates desperately hoped that bankers and foreign investors who had invested in U.S. bonds would withdraw support and cut off funds, causing a financial collapse and an end to the war.[188] Southerners tracked the price of gold as an indicator of popular confidence in the government. When the pro-peace Vallandigham campaigned against Lincoln in 1864, Sergeant James W. Albright, serving with the guns of the 12th Virginia Battery at Petersburg, saw it as a sign of disaffection in the North: "Vallandigham boldly defies his enemies—Chase has resigned . . . gold 225 [to] 265, showing great excitement."[189] A Mississippian noted that McClellan's fortunes moved in tandem with the price of the yellow metal.[190]

Finally, politically minded soldiers watched to see if their opponents were having problems filling their ranks. Serving at Vicksburg, Daniel P. Wade was getting tired of the war by March 1863. Still, he believed the North would give in before the South did because conscription would alienate the Northwest and divide the Union.[191] This hope seemed to be coming to pass as Northern newspapers reported that the draft was not bringing in enough men.[192] Confederates, moreover, thought that the situation would worsen when three hundred thousand Union soldiers' enlistments expired.[193] Southern troops also noted rising markets for bounties, indicating manpower shortages and declining morale in the North.[194] The draft riots in New York confirmed the assumption that the North's population was unwilling to continue the war.[195]

Soldiers became more aware of international politics as the war continued. Politically motivated Southern soldiers hoped that foreign intervention would accelerate the North's demoralization. This possibility received extensive newspaper coverage in both the North and the South. Some Union troops were looking over their shoulders to gauge the chances that England or France might step in and prevent the North from crushing the rebellion. Sergeant William R. Rapson crossed from Canada to Ogdensburg, New York, to enlist with the 50th New York Engineers, while his fellow Canadians were generally gloating over Union defeats and the Canadian press was overwhelmingly supporting the South. Rapson reproached his compatriots for supporting a slavocracy because of Canada's jealousy toward the United States. He wrote to his brother: "You as a Loyal Subject of John Bull[,] ou[gh]t to be proud that i am doing my best to put down the rebellion[.] but this is not so with John Bull he has helped Rebs all he can against us giving them Municians of War vesels in fact everything. . . . Every way he can give the Union a blow he does his best. . . . well all i care about John Bull you can stick in your eye."[196] Most Unionists thought foreign intervention unlikely, however. Furthermore, by 1864 few believed it would make much difference. The

Confederates, with far more at stake and more desperate to reverse their declining fortunes, showed more interest in getting European help, with 57 percent of all comments on this topic coming from Southerners even though they comprised only 40 percent of the data set.[197]

Southern and Union soldiers were concerned with three primary questions about foreign involvement: What interests were at stake for the European powers? What was the likelihood that they would intervene? And finally, what effect would foreign intervention have on the war? Still trusting in King Cotton's rule, the rebels believed that France and England had to intervene to alleviate the South's economic distress.[198] The Confederates also thought France would interfere because it was committed to its proxy, a Habsburg princeling whom Napoleon III had forcibly enthroned in Mexico.[199] In addition, England and France had imperial prospects in Latin America and thought that the Monroe Doctrine thwarted those interests. Union soldiers saw British hostility as the same old enemy that had fought the republic in 1776 and 1812. American democracy's historical foe was again supporting its enemies, backing the Southern slavocracy. British hostility was an enduring factor in American foreign relations.[200] Only the working people of Britain and France restrained the ruling aristocracy from interfering more actively against the United States.

Fears of Anglo-French intervention grew following reports in the Copperhead press that a bargain had been struck between Napoleon III and the rebels. The rumor indicated that the South would make minimal slavery reforms and put the Confederacy in a more favorable light for European public opinion, opening the way for recognition. In exchange, Napoleon III would get a free hand in Mexico and French warships would break the Union blockade. Dormant Know-Nothing sentiments soon reawakened as rumors pointed to a Franco-Confederate axis under the patronage of the Catholic Church. After all, Napoleon III was an ally of the French Catholic Church in its struggle against liberals. Catholic and Napoleonic interests coincided in Mexico; the church feared Benito Juarez's revolutionary secularism and Napoleon III needed the church to legitimate his proxy regime in Mexico against popular opposition. Republicans and Protestants noted that the Catholic Church was a notorious ally of the Copperheads. Some Northern soldiers believed that the New York riots by Irish Catholics confirmed the church's hidden hand at work. Catholics in France and in the United States were enemies of the Lincoln administration. This axis had emerged among New Orleans Cajuns and Creoles who had appealed to France to send its fleet to liberate them from the Protestant Yankees.[201]

There was some foundation to these conjectures. In June 1863 French troops marched into Mexico City and French General E. F. Forey set up a handpicked provisional government. There were also rumors that France had designs on

Texas. They were given credence by Edward Everett, special adviser to the State Department. Stories circulated of a French plan to create an independent league under French tutelage of Texas, New Mexico, California, the northern states of Mexico, and possibly Louisiana.[202]

Foreign intervention seemed most likely by spring and early summer 1863, after the Union defeats of the preceding year. Henry Mortimer Favrot, soldiering with the 4th Louisiana Infantry, thought the war had reached a promising new conjunction. There was rising opposition in the North that was reflected by Vallandigham's rumored arrest. Additionally, there were reports that U.S. warships were searching neutral shipping to try to plug the holes in the blockade. Finally, there was the Confederate victory at Chancellorsville. Together they presented a unique opportunity for Anglo-French intervention.[203] Mississippi trooper Isaac Newton Brownlow shared these views. He believed the war was almost won when newspapers were reporting that the British had sent the U.S. ambassador home and were ordering one hundred warships to take to sea against the Yankees. France was preparing to take action, too. Brownlow assumed that in the event of Grant's failure to take Vicksburg, France would impose armed mediation and an end to the war.[204] Napoleon III had been trying to persuade Austria to support France, Spain, and Great Britain in the endeavor since summer 1862, but the Austrians remained recalcitrant.[205] Confederate Robert Patrick also avidly followed the dispatches from London, reporting that members of the British cabinet were calling on Lord Palmerston to recognize the South. British political leaders could now count on their people's support as well as support in the North for British mediation. Intervention might even help the Lincoln government save face.[206]

However, by July 1863, the tone of the letters changed. Disappointment set in among the Southern troops at events that transpired abroad. Correspondence and diaries reported a change in momentum in London.[207] The English were increasingly unlikely to support the South, leaving it in the lurch. Southern soldiers angrily concluded that the British were driven by cowardly self-interest. Yet Jacques Alfred Charbonnet, a New Orleans Creole, still pinned his hopes on France, the "champion of generous ideals." Charbonnet hoped his Gallic motherland and "master of the world by its genius, will rise soon" and come to the aid of the South. The North feared war with France. Unionists must realize that fighting "against France is like fighting against God."[208] Most Confederates, however, turned their angry disappointment against all Europeans. When Captain Elias Davis, 8th Alabama, settled into winter quarters and prepared for yet another year of war, he blamed all the foreign powers for the South's plight: "Those Governments have not sent armies to invade our country: but they consented to a blockade of our Ports in violation to international law: shutting us in from communication with the world: confining us to our resources to fight vastly superior numbers, backed by the almost united world." [209] Fellow Confederate Peter M. Wright, Company B, 58th Virginia Infantry, saw things the same way as Davis. As far as Wright was concerned, the Confederates had to reconcile themselves to the notion that they were fighting the whole world. Instead of helping the South, Southern soldiers believed that Britain was sending its unemployed to serve as mercenaries in the Northern army. [210]

On the other side, a surgeon in the 117th Illinois infantry concluded that the British would never intervene because European bankers were lending money to the North and not to the South, a clear indicator of British and French ideas about which side to support. Even when Union hopes were dim in winter 1863, Surgeon Humphrey Hughes Hood remained sanguine, noting a report that Britain believed the North would win and that Treasury Secretary Salmon P. Chase supposedly had received a European consortium loan offer of one hundred million dollars, a loan that could not have been made without Britain's approval. [211]

What effect would intervention have had? Some Confederates overestimated French and British power. Neither country had shown much military effectiveness in the Crimean operations. Few Confederates commented on this fact, but the small number who did tended to overrate the capabilities of the British and French empires. C. Fackler, riding with General Nathan Bedford Forrest, believed that French military prowess was such that it could end the war in a matter of days. [212] Other Southern soldiers doubted the two European powers could tilt the balance. [213] Even if the French sent a minister to Richmond and Franco-British fleets opened the South's ports, they probably would not provide ground forces to back the Southern army. The South would still have to do its own fighting and rely on its own resources. [214] A gunner with Purcell's Virginia Battery agreed that the South would have to fight its own fight. The South needed European help in 1862, but by 1863 the South had the upper hand and could dispense with help from abroad. [215] But Charles Woodward Hutson, manning a South Carolina battery, doubted that the South could dispense with European help. Even if the South won the war, the North would remain a dangerous opponent and would never acquiesce in its defeat or live in peace with the South. A victorious Confederacy would need continued European support to protect it from Northern revanchism. [216]

For their part, Northern soldiers doubted that European intervention could decide the outcome of the war. Union troops were sure they could defeat any combination of powers after July 1863. The real danger was that European powers would strengthen their hold along the nation's borders. England held British North America, while the French threatened from Mexico, where Napoleon III had installed a puppet government. "The interference of the French Emperor with affairs on this continent must be stopped," wrote a lieutenant of the 19th U.S. Infantry. Napoleon III "will have to withdraw from Mexico or fight[.] [I]f he chooses to engage in that costly luxury, he will find us prepared to meet him. I imagine now that we are a considerable fighting nation and can take a set too with most any body."[217] An Iowa trooper voiced the same confrontational tone. Not fearing the Great Powers, he called on Washington to defy Britain with an ultimatum demanding that "the business of fitting out confederate cruisers in British ports must be stopped or our cruisers will destroy them in the ports. The only result that I can see which will result from this is that the British ministry will very gracefully reced[e] from their position & apologize for what has been done."[218] An Illinois infantry lieutenant colonel even welcomed European intervention. Like Secretary of State William H. Seward, James F. Drish thought intervention would "bring the South back and Kill off the sectional prejudice and firmly reunite them in a national war to save the whole country and submission & subjugation wil be forgot and the rebs will be good Union Men before they know it."[219]

While some Southern troops hoped desperately for foreign intervention as the curtain came down on the Confederacy, others hoped that Lincoln's assassination would rekindle the war's dying embers. Virginia trooper Rawleigh William Downman thought the Yankees now would take a harder line toward the South. The war would be reanimated, and the French and British would intervene, giving the South another chance to survive.[220]

After the South's defeat, however, whatever residue of pity there was in the North for the vanquished rebels evaporated when a megalomaniacal Southern fanatic assassinated the president. Confederate troops anxiously wondered what political repercussions would follow for themselves and their families. "The sad fate of President Lincoln affects us greatly," wrote a North Carolina prisoner of war, "but though I trust we all feel proper abhorrence for the deed the principal cause of our feeling the matter strongly is the question of how it will effect us."[221] Most believed that Lincoln's death boded ill for the South. "Our officers all regard the death of Mr. L. as a sad blow to our future for we [are] fully impressed with the belief that his policy would be lenient," Lieutenant John Joyes Jr., with Byrne's Horse Artillery, recorded in his diary.[222] Another Confederate made a corresponding assessment, declaring that he feared that the "Vice President is a much worse man." Andrew Johnson, he believed, would implement a harsher occupation policy.[223]

Confederate fears that the Union soldiers would seek revenge seemed justified. The killing radicalized Northern soldiers, leading a soldier in the 22d Iowa to declare: "Every soldier now goes in for having revenge and . . . exterminat[ing] every traitor."[224] Many of Lincoln's followers vowed vengeance against the Confederates and their Copperhead sympathizers. "The soldiers want to hang every man in the South," vowed a Worcester, Massachusetts, infantry-man.[225] When the telegraph brought the news of the president's death to the 1st Vermont Artillery, Sondus W. Haskell evoked his comrades' anger at Lincoln's death: "the soldiers think if they could get hold of the Man that shot him his hide wold been full of [more] bulletts than [holes] in a strainer."[226] A captain in the 41st Ohio described the impact of the news: "You can have no idea what a gloom it cast over the countenance of all. For some time the men were so affected they could not speak. Then commenced walking about with clenched fists swearing that they would have revenge. A large majority of them voluntarily took the most solemn oath that if during their lives any one in their presence ever [intimated] that they were pleased on account of Lincoln's death, they would die instantly. The rebels who fall into our hands will have no mercy done them."[227] The colonel of the 125th Ohio Volunteer Infantry approved of Union troops shoot-ing Nashvillians who openly rejoiced at Lincoln's murder.[228]

What effect, soldiers asked, would the loss have on the political situation? Most answered that the loss would strengthen the hand of the radicals. Johnson would not be as conciliatory as Lincoln would have been toward the defeated South. Now there would be no mercy for the South.[229] Most soldiers heartily concurred with the idea that the Union now should show no mercy. "Such kind-ness as the President has shown the Rebels I hope will never be shown them again," a Maine corporal insisted. "Let them suffer for their fiendish deeds. . . . The Rebels probably think that they saved them selves when Lincoln was as-sassinated but they have hurt them selves."[230] B. F. Moulton, a New York sur-geon serving with the U.S. Colored Troops, surveyed the political aftermath of Lincoln's death: "The South has murdered their best friend."[231]

The assassination also envenomed attitudes toward Copperheads. John Wilkes Booth, after all, had lived in the North. "I never felt so ugly and indignant since this war began," a Pennsylvanian told a comrade. "I think it was done by northern traitors, and I cannot bear to have a copperhead speak to me these times."[232] Fearing for their lives, Copperheads maintained a low profile. One re-ported: "I was scared out of my wits when Lincoln was killed. They were wild, said all rebels, Copperheads, Democrats, should be hung. We all marched to Church next day with solemn faces. [We] found the whole inside draped in black. . . . The preacher, a puke of [a] union refugee from Tenn. was so overcome he could not speak for crying." The writer added, however, that he hoped Booth had escaped.[233]

After expressing grief and anger, Union soldiers tried to come to terms with the loss. Many reflected on their commander in chief's leadership. They wrote his political obituary appraising his role in saving the Union and freeing the slaves. "We have lost a father & a protector," lamented an Ohioan who had been in the service since Shiloh. Like the New York surgeon, the Ohio soldier believed that "the world has lost a patriot and the Rebels have lost their best friend."[234] As a leader, Lincoln ranked alongside George Washington. "Geo. Washington will always be considered the father, and Abraham Lincoln the savior of this great republic."[235] Another Ohio volunteer praised the dead president for directing the war with "an energy & sagacity & devotedness to his country's weal."[236] A fellow Ohioan lamented that the "world has lost a patriot but heaven has received an angel."[237]

The chapter has surveyed the soldiers' views about their national political leaders, political issues, elections, foreign affairs, and the situation at home. Confederates frequently expressed critical opinions of their political leaders, accusing them of cronyism, petty bickering, and poor judgment in selecting generals. Some Southerners also resented the national government's increasing power as it desperately mobilized men and resources for the war. Confederate troops especially resented policies that undermined individual liberty or favored the wealthy class over the ordinary soldier. They railed against requisition of poor farmers' crops in lieu of taxes, a policy that left the soldiers' families hungry; conscription laws that favored the rich; and the repeal of habeas corpus, which gave the military judiciary powers that threatened freedom and property and ultimately the yeoman of the slave-based republic.

The 1864 U.S. presidential election crystallized issues for the Northern troops. It sharpened the Union troops' political awareness by tying decisions at home to the outcome of the war at the front, which enhanced the citizen-soldiers' political perspicacity. The election pointed out the tie between political and military affairs in a people's war and brought the realization that the troops' were playing a decisive role in the conflict both at home and at the front; armed with ballot and bayonet, they believed that they were expanding freedom and democracy. For this reason, the election ritual of voting in the field symbolized the citizen-soldier's critical role in the war as part of an army of thinking bayonets. Inspired by this outlook, soldiers overwhelmingly supported Lincoln even though the Democrats ran the father of the Army of the Potomac, who had been beloved by his men. But the sharpened political awareness of the soldiers in 1864 distinguished McClellan's military role from the platform of the party he represented. Most soldiers realized there was little likelihood of winning the kind of peace for which they were fighting if the Democrats were elected with their platform's plank calling the war a failure and thereby implying acceptance of Confederate survival. This policy would put the Union on the slippery slope to an armistice, a negotiated peace, and the perpetuation of slavery. Union soldiers rightly suspected that a Democratic victory was synonymous with dissolution of the Union if the South could survive as a political entity.

Southern soldiers were equally aware of their stake in the 1864 election, and they also understood the interdependence between events in the political arena and the evolving situation at the front. Civilian morale at home and the lack of steadfastness behind their lines would undermine morale in the army. In North Carolina this issue came to the fore in local, state, and congressional elections. Paradoxically, Southern soldiers like the North Carolinians feared threats to their own liberties yet saw no inconsistency when they denounced traitors at home and called on the government to take exceptional measures against dissenters. Northern troops also castigated political opponents at home. Both armies generated surges of popular anger against dissenters and clamored against treason at home. Because of this chorus of denunciations from the front, the entire society was politicized by dividing everyone into two political camps: traitors and patriots. There was no room for apolitical people. Everyone had to take a political stand. This attitude among the citizen-soldiers drove the political process at home as the war parties in the North and the South waged election campaigns against treachery at home. People were forced to define their places at one pole or the other of the political spectrum, if only to identify friends from enemies and to know why they were being judged traitors or patriots by neighbors and kin.

6 The Caesarist Impulse

POLITICAL RELIABILITY AND THE OFFICER CORPS

Civil War soldiers looked to their officers to help them control their fear, encourage them in attack, make them as safe as possible in defense, and set an example as virtuous citizens of the fighting republic. They wanted their commanders to show appropriate zeal for the cause. The traditional commanders' persona of "heroic captain" exhibited by George B. McClellan and Robert E. Lee came to share place with another persona of command that was more suitable for a commander leading citizen-soldiers. This persona was epitomized most clearly by Ulysses S. Grant's style of leadership. Even though Grant was a professional soldier, his demeanor portrayed an unheroic but effective leader who shared the average citizen's modest attributes, maintained an ordinary civilian's bearing even in uniform, and exhibited the same political values as his citizen-soldiers. The men judged officers not only on the basis of traditional military virtues but also on their political outlook. Thus, the officer in the people's armies of the Civil War had to maintain the confidence of the citizen-soldiers serving in his command, and he had to insure that the political authorities had confidence in him as an instrument of the republic. Chapter 3 discusses how the rank and file scrutinized their officers' military ability and made sure they made their opinions felt whenever they could vote for officers. Chapter 5 shows how the troops also made their views known about fellow soldiers whose political loyalty was uncertain. This chapter will examine the political dimension of the officers' status, specifically the activities of the rank and file and civilians in monitoring the political attitude of military leadership; conversely, this chapter will examine the role that officers played in indoctrinating the troops and assuring the appropriate political climate in their commands.[1]

Republicanism had transformed the relationship between the ordinary soldier and the state. The philosophers of the Enlightenment distrusted large standing armies. The Founding Fathers shared this attitude. They feared antidemocratic tendencies among professional officers leading long-service soldiers who no longer had roots in civil society. The Founders preferred a very small professional army that could not threaten civil institutions. They intended to thwart any Caesarist tendencies among the regular officers by filling out the army with citizen militia whenever a national emergency arose. Citizen-soldiers would restrain professional officers' political interference, because militiamen shared the same civilian values as the parent society. They would thwart any professional officers who might undermine democratic ideals by challenging war aims that the civilian leadership defined.[2]

The democratic ideas of the American and French Revolutions ushered in another dimension to the command relationship. It brought a political component into relations between officers and the rank and file. Ordinary soldiers and commanders alike were judged on their political reliability as much as their military effectiveness. Monitoring political reliability in the people's armies during the American Civil War was a concern shared by the rank and file and the officer corps. Ordinary soldiers and officers monitored each other's political attitudes. Officers began to watch for any signs of disloyalty in the ranks to prevent such attitudes from undermining morale among their men. They maintained political orthodoxy in the ranks. The officers in the citizen armies also monitored elections in the field to ascertain their men's political attitude (as will be discussed more extensively later in the chapter).[3] Officers scrutinized each other's behavior for signs of disaffection or lack of zeal in fighting for the country's war aims. Volunteer officers often were more radical than regular officers. Like their counterparts in the French revolutionary armies, volunteer officers were civilians immersed in the life and politics of their communities. Many came from the professions. They were teachers, lawyers, journalists, and officials and tended to take a more active role in politics than did regular officers. Some believed that their responsibilities as officers and leaders included taking steps to assure that their fellow officers and their men shared a sense of common purpose in order to raise morale and increase cohesion.

For their part, politically motivated enlisted men eyed their superiors for signs of disloyalty. Private William Hamilton of the Pennsylvania Reserve reported on the attitude of its Democrat-dominated officer corps when Governor Andrew Gregg Curtin visited the army. Curtin was a staunch Republican and a strong advocate of vigorous prosecution of the war. He was a stalwart ally of Lincoln, and the Republican Party in turn extolled him as the "soldier's friend." When Curtin reviewed the Pennsylvania troops and made a presentation to General George Gordon Meade in September 1863, Private Hamilton noted that the Democratic officers played down the affair and left the concourse to reduce the political impact of Curtin's visit. Hamilton advised the governor that certain officers tried to keep Curtin away from the rank and file.[4]

The new political dimension of the people's armies provoked tensions between volunteers and regular officers. Differences between the organizational culture of a regular army of long-service soldiers and a people's army of short-service troops fostered political tensions. The regular army had been a repository of deference, hierarchy, and unquestioning obedience. Discipline more than political convictions guided the professional officers' attitude toward enlisted men.[5] This situation changed with the rise of people's armies. The new recruits brought with them the democratic, egalitarian, and individualist values of civilian life. Traditional military values such as submission and conformity had never been highly regarded in a liberal democracy. Contrary to regulars, short-service militia volunteers resented the blind discipline of the regulars and never acknowledged the army's control of every facet of their life in the military. Civil society had never been as intrusive; it had tolerated diversity of dress and behavior, and the citizen-soldiers expected the same permissiveness in the army. While democratic society postulated equality among its citizens, military tradition assumed inequality between ranks.[6] Soldiers in people's armies, like the English Levellers of the seventeenth century, the French Revolution's troops in the eighteenth century, the American recruits in the Civil War, and even the GIs of World War II, never exchanged their civilian traditions for military values.[7]

Officers commanding men in the new institutional culture of a people's army could not entirely rely on coercion and professional incentives to the same degree as regular armies had done. Officers had to invoke political motivators to gain obedience and sustain morale. They relied on war aims of millennial proportions to mobilize society and inspire its soldiers. It was struggle for the highest good and against the worst evil. "The Beast would be overthrown and Babylon laid waste," to bring the "true Kingdom of Heaven on Earth," proclaimed Cromwell's Puritans. The troops believed that democracy had to temper military authority. A soldier in the English parliamentary army explained that when he enlisted he retained his status as a free citizen of the republic and distinguished himself from a common mercenary. "If we had not a right to the kingdom, we were mercenary soldiers," he declared. The radical Leveller Gerrard Winstanley defined the distinction between citizens in a people's army and professional soldiers: "The wars fought by 'kingly' armies were merely 'to destroy the laws of common freedom; and . . . enslave both the land and the people, [but] commonwealth armies'" fought for the common good.[8] American Civil War soldiers shared this outlook as they started their military pilgrimage on the road to national salvation. They too were fighting to advance millennial ideas like republican government, democracy, and freedom. By infusing the army with the parent society's aspirations, officers increased cohesion and enhanced morale.

Citizen volunteers expected officers to share the same political convictions.

The officers had to pass muster as competent military commanders and loyal political leaders who had to exhibit patriotic devotion to the sacred endeavor. With true revolutionary rhetoric, an Alabamian lauded not only the technical competence of his officers in the state's 18th Regiment but also their patriotic devotion: "the field officers, feeling the great responsibility which rests upon them as the defenders of the best cause that ever enkindled the pure fires of patriotism in manly breasts, . . . leave no stone unturned in the pursuit of theoretical and practical knowledge of their profession."[9] Such views appeared in the French revolutionary armies as well. Cobb describes how French troops refused to even be called soldiers, referring to themselves as "révolutionnaires" or "sansculottes," defining themselves by their social class.[10]

Long-service troops are less likely to share the citizen volunteers' millennialist image of war because the war did not hold the same significant place in regular officers' lives as it did for volunteer militia. The volunteers joined the colors for the highest of reasons, to play a role on history's stage. They were part of the broader movement of historical change in which the army was an instrument for attaining great historical objectives and could be sacrificed for high purpose. Professional soldiers often did not share these priorities; for them, the army was an institution central to their lives. It provided them with a career, defined their identity, and was the source of their livelihood. Though wars brought changes, regulars wanted their beloved army to emerge intact so that it could fight again in subsequent conflicts. For this reasons, regulars refused to sacrifice the army for costly maximalist ends.

Tensions over the nature and purposes of the war arose between professional and volunteer officers. Volunteers saw the army as an instrument of political change. The volunteers had no particular attachment to the army. Their careers were not embedded in the military: the army was only an instrument, the "sword of the republic," to hew down its enemies. If it was dulled or destroyed in the process, it made no difference as long as it achieved its political purpose. Unlike McClellan and other professionals, citizen-soldiers did not believe the army had an intrinsic value in itself. Though revolutionary rhetoric did not always prevent fraternization with the enemy during the war, the men were quite willing to carry out hard-war policies and destroy civilian property when so ordered. The war depersonalized and demonized the enemy host as a threat to the soldiers' most cherished political beliefs. If an all-out war was the only way to bring a rapid victory and get the citizens in arms back home, then the army should pay the price.

The volunteers' apocalyptic image of war created enormous social energy, and the huge social forces unleashed in a people's war required commensurate aims, aims that can only come through total victory. The war became a struggle against evil; no quarter asked, none given. There was a divine or ideological purpose in which the army's preservation counted little compared to the historic ideals that were at stake in the struggle. Many regular officers like McClellan feared such tendencies in a people's army. He advocated a war for limited negotiable ends using the fastidious tactics that stressed maneuver to reduce casualties and keep the army intact.

Differences between the revolutionary aims of the volunteers and the conservative outlook of many regular officers added to the distrust between the two groups, especially in the North, where many volunteers had doubts about the loyalty of the regular officers. Too many professionals had betrayed their country to fight for the South. Their flight to join the South was the historical equivalent of the French officers who joined the émigré forces.[11] Both the French revolutionary army and the Union army in the American Civil War had reason to harbor suspicions about regular officers. In both cases, the governments took measures to counter the rise of Caesarism among conservative officers. Citizen-soldiers demanded that the army share the same democratic values as its parent society.[12] By maintaining the primacy of civic values, society could restrain Bonapartist tendencies in the officer corps. Local recruitment also tightened the bonds between civil society and the army and assured officers' political reliability. Local newspapers monitored their regiments' morale and reported on the political attitudes and effectiveness of the militia officers. Military reverses generated political unrest in the army. "If we only had a man possessed of the Genius of Bonaparte and the Purity of Washington, I should be glad to see him act as Dictator," an Illinois surgeon wrote in the dismal months of defeat.[13] Disappointments in 1861 and 1862 aroused Caesarist tendencies among Union officers like John Ames as the idea of a military takeover gained ground in some quarters of the corps.[14] Back home, "treason walk[ed] unblushingly," and Copperheads dominated the political arena, while "honest men [were] in fear," complained one officer. He believed the country yearned for "the strong arm of despotism" to set things straight.[15] Early 1863 was the nadir for the Union cause; a political ally of Congressman Elihu B. Washburne reported on the gloomy situation: "*Our friends* are filled with foreboding and gloomy apprehensions . . . all confidence is lost in the Administration." The writer wished a strong man like General Benjamin Butler would seize power.[16] Conservatives in the ranks believed that after the defeats of 1862 and the failure to take Vicksburg in winter 1863, the war was at a stalemate, and the Emancipation Proclamation made things worse because it would strengthen the South's resolve. An Illinois soldier wrote:

> I believe that there are many officers high in command that will join any movement to overthrow the government & the sooner the volcano breakes

fourth & spends its force the sooner we shall have peace & quiet. I would be sorry indeed to see the praries of Ill[inois] become the theater of war but one way to avoid it & that is for the Administration to throw off that radical influence which has ruled it for the last 8 months. I am sure the army will not sustain it & we all know that the great central states pronounced against it last fall. . . . The last act . . . of Congress . . . was the negro soldier bill [which] was in my opinion the last nale in their coffin.[17]

The same ideas circulated among Southern officers when the situation at the front deteriorated. Calls for dictatorship and suspension of habeas corpus rang out. There was talk of throwing out Jefferson Davis and putting in General Robert E. Lee. Some in command believed that only Lee could alleviate the sufferings of the army.[18]

Reports of unrest among the regular officers in the Union army began to filter back to the civil authorities. The *Cleveland Herald* carried an editorial accusing Brigadier Generals Truman Seymour and William Babcock Hazen of lacking zeal. They were politically suspicious because they had spent part of their careers in the South. The *Herald*'s editorial asserted that "almost every Regular Army officer [was] an opponent of emancipation."[19]

Many ordinary soldiers shared the people's distrust of the regular officer corps, harboring suspicions that the regular officers did not endorse a hard-war policy. Radicals suspected professional officers of having hierarchical, elitist attitudes that were inimical to the ethos of an army of citizens.[20] Professional officers were deemed politically out of step with the administration. Officers in both armies were less supportive of the government than the rank and file, with 60 percent of enlisted men backing their political leaders but only 46 percent of officers holding a favorable view of the administration.[21]

Caesarism is latent in a citizen army. Officers argued that when the parent society broke its covenant with the army and grew weary of the war, the army had the right to intervene to reimpose order and restore civic virtue.[22] Events like the draft riots reinforced the conviction among some officers that society and its politicians were deserting the army and forsaking patriotic obligations.[23]

Disputes between the army and political leaders over war aims also generated Caesarist tendencies. The first wave of opposition came from Democrats in the army, who rejected the Second Confiscation Act in July 1862. The Emancipation Proclamation heightened discontent and many officers threatened to resign.[24] There was talk of a coup d'état.

Officers in both armies resented the way that the political leaders were conducting the war, but a comparison of Union and Confederate attitudes indicated that the Confederate officer corps was more critical of its political leaders than the Union officers. Sixty-three percent of the rebel officers were critical of the way the government was conducting the war, compared to half of the Union leaders.[25] The difference, however, is not surprising since the Confederates were losing the war and they were lashing out at the political leadership.

A colonel in the 68th Ohio Volunteer Infantry could have spoken for either side's officers when he wrote darkly that the army had become the politicians' "foot ball." He went on to declare there was no chance of success until Lincoln and his loathsome advisors were all done in.[26] Officers blamed civil authorities for meddling in military affairs. When Joseph Hooker took command, one officer hoped that the general would have a free hand in conducting the war. The army's commanders had been thwarted by the political leadership, which was imposing a political agenda at the expense of military objectives. The generals should be freed to conduct the war as they saw fit.[27] Democratic enlisted men shared these views. A Pennsylvania private reported that privates and noncommissioned officers in his outfit overwhelmingly believed that peace would come only when McClellan drove the politicians out of Washington.[28]

There were Bonapartist tendencies pulling the Southern officer corps leftward, including Confederate officers who did not believe Southern republicanism was founded on slavery. They opposed the conservative domination of the government and the determination to twin maintenance of slavery with Southern independence. These officers believed that slavery should be sacrificed for national survival. They hoped that the high command would join in exerting pressure on the civilian authorities. On the other hand, Bonapartism in the Union army came from the right. The emancipation issue generated a conservative backlash in the federal army in 1863.

Freeing the slaves caused new reverberations in the Southern army the following year, when some officers advanced the idea of salvaging Southern independence while giving up slavery. A severe manpower shortage in 1864–65 brought the emancipation issue to a head. The idea of arming the Confederacy's blacks was not new. It had already been broached when Louisiana used a regiment of free blacks to defend New Orleans. Tennessee enacted legislation to enlist free Negroes between fifteen and fifty years of age. In fall 1863 the Alabama legislature also considered using slaves more effectively.[29]

In 1864, Major General Patrick R. Cleburne and a group of field-grade officers in Joseph E. Johnston's army drafted a proposal calling on Richmond to free slaves and enlist them in the Confederate army.[30] The Cleburne proposals had revolutionary implications for the South. The officers realized that the North's radical strategy of liberating the slaves was beginning to work by furnishing manpower to the North while the South lacked that source of labor and replacements for the war effort. Also, slaves who did not go north constituted a fifth column, providing the North with information and material aid and obliging the Confederacy to disperse its forces in garrisons across the country to prevent a servile insurrection. If these blacks were freed, they might serve the South as wagoners, nurses, and cooks while liberating whites for service in the field. The Confederacy also could dispense with many of its garrisons at home and could use those troops at the front. Besides, Cleburne argued, blacks could be good soldiers. The Helots had fought well for Sparta, galley slaves rowed bravely at Lepanto, and the blacks of Santo Domingo had defeated the French. Further, freeing the slaves would induce the European powers to recognize the South. Moreover, it would create political divisions in the North between Democrats and Republicans in the 1864 election. Finally, it would give the South a cause that would be meaningful to the citizen-soldier. He would be fighting for liberty instead of protecting the property of the slaveowning aristocracy. Cleburne and his fellow officers also called on the Confederacy to democratize the war by ending the use of substitutes and denying exemptions. Heretofore, these policies favored the wealthy while causing ill feelings among the ranks.[31]

Higher-ranking Confederates refused to sign the younger officers' proposal.[32] President Davis was not favorable to the idea either, but with the situation deteriorating in 1864 he raised the issue again in his annual message to Congress. Davis recommended using black labor on military works. Congress passed an act on February 14, 1864, permitting the army to mobilize black labor battalions.[33] But Davis never acceded to freeing and arming the slave population. Accepting the Cleburne proposal refuted the South's main war aim, argued a brigadier general. He, like most of the high command, opposed the idea.[34]

Conservative opponents argued that freeing and arming the slaves would be a repudiation of the Southern republic's racialist character and thus would abdicate the reason for which the South had seceded and fought. As noted earlier, the much postponed measure was finally enacted on March 13, 1865. The Confederate Congress had fiddled while Rome burned, and it was too late to implement the legislation extensively. The measure only had grudging support among the political leaders in Richmond and had the proviso that no more than 25 percent of the slaves of any state could be emancipated for military service, and emancipation was left to each state.[35]

The officer corps in both armies became increasingly divided on political issues. In the South, there were commanders like Cleburne who supported freeing slaves. In the North, conservative McClellan supporters in the Army of the Potomac opposed Republican generals like Hooker. Officers were being drawn into the political arena, lobbying Congress, and corresponding directly with the radical and opposition leaders about presidential leadership. Then Major John Keys, brother of one of McClellan's staff officers, was among those who went too far. When Keys declared that Lincoln was purposely dragging out the war by calling for emancipation, the administration immediately dismissed him.[36] Later, the McClellan candidacy of 1864 generated more political turmoil in the ranks. By seeking office on a peace ticket, McClellan parted with most of his soldiers. Sergeant Day Elmore of the 36th Illinois vowed: "If George B. McClellan be elected & acts as his 'Chicago Platform' directs . . . then will we the 'soldiers' take the *rains* of this government in our own hands and 'go on with the war' until that dear old flag . . . floating from every house top and all the lesser *buildings* in the so called 'Corn fed' States."[37]

Elmore was aware of the officers' conservative penchant; many officers resigned and campaigned against emancipation. Colonel Thomas J. Whipple denounced the war and ran as a peace candidate in New Hampshire. Though military involvement never became a serious threat to either government, it reflected a significant and important political change during the last half of the war. Politics had become militarized. Military defeats and perceived political ineptitude created a vacuum that sucked the army into politics. Civilian leaders seemed more intent on partisan bickering among themselves than on addressing the issues, according to Robert Steele of the 23d Wisconsin Infantry. Steele condemned both parties and all politicians: "There are a great many in the diferant political partyes in the north who think mor of puting down their opposing party than they do of puting down the Rebelion. . . . For proof of this look at the rangling and gangling in Congress each one thing his the only polesy."[38]

Prowar Southerners urged officers to quit the front and fight the war in the political arena to check the rising peace movement.[39] While Whipple of the 2d New Hampshire Infantry Regiment resigned to campaign for the Peace Democrats, Colonel Michael T. Donohue of the 19th New Hampshire Infantry gave up his command to campaign for the War Democrats.[40] The Iowa gubernatorial election pitted a Democrat and hero of Shiloh, General James M. Tuttle, against Colonel W. M. Stone of the 22d Iowa, a Lincoln defender.[41] The 1864 election in Wisconsin yielded an even larger crop of colonel candidates.[42] Antiwar opposition grew in 1864, and the Republicans began to consider casting Lincoln aside and replacing him with a military hero like Grant or William S. Rosecrans.[43] Whenever a war hero took the political field, the Lincoln administration countered with its own war hero candidate.[44] Republican political leaders often turned to politically reliable Democratic generals like John Alexander Logan for support. The administration pulled him out of the siege of Atlanta to fight another type of campaign, the 1864 election. He was more important to the cause at home than he was at the front.[45]

The problem of checking Caesarist proclivities and imposing political orthodoxy on the officer corps was particularly acute in the North. The Joint Committee on the Conduct of the War monitored the actions of the highest generals, making its displeasure known whenever a commander overstepped the bounds regarding high policy. The most important case occurred late in the war, when General William Tecumseh Sherman made unauthorized political concessions to General Joseph E. Johnston during the truce negotiations. Both men were old-line conservative generals, and both feared a guerrilla movement might arise if the terms were too draconian. Conservative upper-class Southern leaders feared they would not be able to control Southern society if there were a popular resistance movement after the armistice. For his part, Sherman did not mention abolishing slavery in the surrender terms, which rang political alarms in Congress and led to an inquiry by the joint committee.[46]

Making sure that the army carried out the objectives of its parent society required that the political leadership, the citizenry, and ordinary soldiers monitor officers' political attitudes to root out disloyal elements. When, for example, the Lincoln administration announced lenient conditions for the readmission of Arkansas and Louisiana, fears arose in the Confederate army, leading to rumors that officers from those states might betray the Richmond government and "kiss the rod and go back" into the Union.[47] The Confederacy also apprehended leftist Locofocoist tendencies among some officers, because left-wing former Democrats among the officers believed that the Confederate government was fighting the war on the backs of the poor.[48]

On the other side, the Union army buzzed with denunciations of officers deemed too soft on the war.[49] For example, rumors spread that the administration would fire General Meade because he had allegedly prevented soldiers from voting for Lincoln.[50] Soldiers accused Democratic officers of persecuting their men for backing the Republican candidates. Pro-Republican soldiers complained that Democrats dominated the army so that whenever someone denounced disloyal Democratic officers, he found himself under arrest.[51]

When the war went badly, the generals' political reliability came under even sharper scrutiny. A North Carolina soldier warned home that there were numerous officers who opposed Governor Zebulon Baird Vance and were sympathetic to dissidents who were calling for a negotiated peace and Union.[52] However, the North's army was subject to more political tensions than the Southern army because the North had more hard choices to make than the South. Being invaded and having lost the initiative to the North, the South's options depended largely on Northern actions. When the North begin to dominate the battlefield in late summer 1863 and adopted emancipation, the South had only two alternatives: surrender and occupation or a fight to the finish. Only if the North changed war aims or was fought to a stalemate could the South hope to negotiate a peace. By contrast, the North could choose between two war aims. It could adopt limited goals that would restore the Union and hold the slavery question in abeyance for later negotiation, or it could adopt a radical policy for emancipation and unconditional surrender. Also, the North held national presidential elections during the war, which heated up the national debate on war aims. In the South, where Davis never had to run for reelection, the political issues came up only in state and congressional elections, making it more difficult for the opposition to consolidate its forces nationally.

The Union officers became an important political nexus for a national opposition movement. The officer corps was one of the most conservative institutions in the country; most of the regulars, especially the generals, were Democrats. Soon civilians were muttering that the generals were not in earnest, that they were not fighting the war hard enough, and that many regular officers were not motivated by high ideals. The regulars were fighting the war routinely and often did not believe wholeheartedly in the cause.[53] "We have hopes," wrote a resident of Mount Carroll, Illinois, in 1863, "that a better lot of Generals are in the field now, and that there won't be quite so much 'strategy' after this. If this cursed Rebellion don't get some crushing blows soon. The *once* United North may get to be like 'The Kingdom divided against itself.'"[54] Radicals contended that if the government purged the army of its conservative officers, it would fight more zealously.[55]

Republican officers complained that more than 80 percent of the brigadiers and major generals were Democrats. Republican commanders suspected their Democratic colleagues; General Hooker believed that Democratic officers in his army sought his failure and sabotaged his command.[56] Public demand for a purge reached a crescendo in early 1863. The present Democrat-dominated high command was getting nowhere. "Why are the true Generals—Frémont, Hunter, Butler, Lane & others kept back," asked one of Senator Benjamin F. Wade's radical constituents, while General Abner Doubleday believed he and other Republicans would never advance in the army because it was dominated by too many proslavery officers.[57] One of Senator Lyman Trumbull's constituents complained: "We are becoming sick of the policy that retains in command . . . bitter and uncompromising political enemies of the president, and men who if not in direct sympathy with the Rebellion desire to bring down the administration, and bring into contempt all Republicans. . . . Halleck [Henry Wager Halleck], Meyers [Montgomery C. Meigs?], [George Henry] Thomas desire the utter overthrow of Mr. Lincoln's administration."[58] Not even General Grant's reputation spared him from suspicions of being a Democrat. Rumors circulated that he had allowed himself to be misled by Southern sympathizers in his command.[59]

The atmosphere of suspicion and rumors of a purge prompted Quartermaster General Montgomery C. Meigs to lament to Senator Henry C. Wilson that "no service seems to be sufficient to protect the public officers from suspicion. So many men formerly reverenced by the public have broken the oath . . . that many have lost all confidence in the usual pledges of character & position." He also complained that the Senators were making unfounded accusations against officers. If they had any substantiation for these charges, Meigs wrote, let there be a full public inquiry to shed light on the situation.[60]

Yet accusations of disloyalty in the high command continued to circulate. Major General Samuel B. Curtis, commanding in Missouri, called on the Senate to "sift the wheat from the chaff and approve only true loyal men such as will make the [Emancipation] proclamation felt in Dixie not in the Moon."[61] When the administration expanded the number of major generalships and brigadier generalships in early 1863, the Republicans were finally able to help their candidates gain promotions. Republicans supported the careers of hard-war generals like Carl Schurz, Franz Sigel, Julius Stahel, James Samuel Wadsworth, and David Hunter.[62] For some radicals, this was still not enough. The executive branch had not shown sufficient zeal in weeding out politically unreliable generals. General Benjamin Butler floated the constitutionally dubious idea of giving Congress control over all appointments to check conservative Bonapartist tendencies in the army.[63]

In response to rising suspicions that the army and the officer corps did not share the same ideas on the war as the people, national and state governments began to vet prospective appointees for political reliability. For example, Ohio created local military committees to help the state's adjutant general weed out undesirable elements in militia companies. The military committees and sheriffs oversaw the selection of officers and vouched for their political reliability to the adjutant general, and when the local military committee was itself suspect, the Union League added its views on appointments.[64] In St. Louis, for example, the city's committee of public safety monitored even high officers and forced some to resign.[65] The branches of the Union League also had considerable influence in verifying officers' political credentials, publicly accusing those whose loyalty it deemed suspect.[66]

Military competence was not enough for commissions or for promotions; candidates also needed support from ordinary townspeople and comrades. When Captain J. M. Sindley sought a promotion to major in the 19th Indiana of the Iron Brigade, fellow officers questioned his loyalty. He had to ask his men to write to Governor Oliver Morton denying he had ever uttered any statements against the Republican administration.[67] Letters attesting to the aspirant's "good character," affirming that he had "from the beginning been an active and warm supporter of the government," poured into governors' and adjutants general's offices. A typical letter of recommendation concerned an officer seeking command of a battery, declaring that the man in question was "A good honest young man and has taken proper grounds in the union cause although raised to hate republicans as a Democrat from the old Virginia school of States rights men & the brothers and cousin has in one or two instance Volunteered and deserted their flag. So that we can see that it takes a good deal of nerve to leave friends who oppose the country in what they call abolitian *war* and stand against and be denounced by old party friends."[68] Correspondents sometimes argued that a particular appointment had political advantages, by putting the Copperheads of the area in their place.[69] In Illinois, residents of Stoneport sent a petition to the governor supporting the candidacy of Jacob P. Stucker for colonel of a new regiment; the petition declared that he was a "Patriotic Lover of Liberty indorsing the [Emancipation] proclamation."[70]

Politics increasingly permeated the appointment process.[71] When requesting appointments, candidates vowed that they were sound on abolition and detested the Copperheads. They swore that they had been the "blackest of Republicans" from the earliest and that they had never voted for anyone but Republicans or Whigs. They added that they were all ready to "push forward the good work" of the government and rid the country of slavery.[72]

Meanwhile, vicious denunciations flooded in. For example, a suspected Whig might have a dim future in the Confederate army.[73] Confederate officers, like General John C. Pemberton, who came from the Northern states also were suspected by their soldiers and fellow officers. Confederate soldiers believed officers of Northern origin were "pusilanimous, & treacherous" and never should be given high positions.[74] And officers who had the misfortune of being born in pro-Union areas of the South, like Buncombe County, North Carolina, were accused of treachery.[75] A letter from a North Carolinian warned of disloyalty among militia officers serving in a pro-Union area called Dunn's Rock:

We have a nest of traitors—Union reconstruction I may say Lincoln men in these mountains—simple, ignorant men, who are led astray from their loyalty by a set of political demagogues who are preaching resistance to the laws of the State, and the confederacy. . . . Foremost is the arch traitor, the renegade, south Carolinian, and broken down grumbler, Genl Jones, whose lackey boot lick is the cowardly sneak and contempable dog Col. Galloway Duckworth of the 107 Regt N C Militia—Yes sir at a recent Union re-construction, Lincoln meeting composed of the Col and his staff, the valiant (god saw the mark) Colonel endorsed all the treason uttered by the said Jones, thereby committing perjury.[76]

Suspicions in the Confederate officer corps intensified when the Cleburne proposals began to circulate. General W. H. T. Walker congratulated Braxton Bragg for quashing the move and requested the names of the conspirators in the treasonous cabal.[77]

There were suspicions in the Union army as well; Union soldiers accused their officers of being "Copperhead[s] of the most venomous stamp."[78] When Napoleon Bonaparte Buford sought a major generalcy, a fellow brigadier denounced Buford to a congressman. Buford had come under fire for holding aristocratic views "at variance with our republican institutions."[79] Reports accused General Grant of authorizing the Copperhead *Chicago Times* to circulate in his camps. "This shows *pretty plainly*," declared an informer, "which way his political sentiments run."[80] Army informers told radical senators like Benjamin F. Wade that General Lorenzo Thomas had appointed pro-secessionists to his staff. "We fear," wrote a Republican officer, "that many military revelations to the rebels of our movements are leakages from his office."[81]

Letters crossed governors' desks questioning the reliability even of lowly militia captains. One was suspected because he had voted the Bell-Everett ticket in 1860.[82] Another young officer was denounced because his wife was an Arkansan.[83] Yet another officer, this one a member of General John A. McClernand's staff, was blamed for marrying into a "strong secesh family." The letter also reported that the officer had been spotted visiting "one of the holes of the Knights [of the Golden Circle]." Worse yet, he was seen emerging from that meeting with a satchel in his hand that must have contained letters and documents destined for the South.[84] In Indiana, informers claimed Copperhead militia officers were in cahoots with the Knights of the Golden Circle, plotting the downfall of the republic.[85]

An officer had to be very careful about what he said in public; informers were everywhere, as Captain Charles Devereux of the 19th Massachusetts learned to his dismay. One informant, probably affiliated with the Union League, denounced him to Governor John A. Andrew:

> I went into the store of Wm. Burbeck in Salem on Sat. last and there had my feelings outraged by the treasonable language of Mr. Devereaux [sic] who I understand holds a Capt.' Commission. . . . Some of his statements were like the following: He would not fight for the good of a negroe? It would discourage enlistments if the army was to fight for negroes. These remarks refered to the emancipation proclamation. He hoped to God that every man in the army of the Potomac would come home if they were to fight for negroes. He taunted us with the want of success of the union armies and asked exultingly if that looked as if [God] was on our side. He

said that the army's ranks could not be filled after the present men's time was out because the people would not enlist and a draft if ordered could not be enforced even in Massachusetts.[86]

Secretary of War Edwin Stanton's spies were soon ferreting out suspect officers. One of his agents, John A. Hawke, reported a conversation between high officers in a Washington hotel:

> Being informed by Mr. Perkins that you wish me to reduce to writing certain remarks made, touching the Rebels and the Rebelion, by Col. Thomas, at present Actng. Qr. Mr. Genl. I proceed to state as follows: About the middle of June last in Room No. 28 in Winder's Building, in presence of Capt. Lowry, Dr. Finkle and myself. Col. Thomas stated that the present war was brought on by the North not minding its own business—by its constant agitation of the slavery question—that the Rebelion could not be crushed now than it was at the beginning & that if our institutions had to be either all slave or all free as was said, then by God, he was in favor of having them all slave.

The informer went on to relate the comments of the other people involved in the treasonous conversation:

> Dr. Finkle laughing, said now Col. that didn't come from the heart—He replied. yes by God it did come from the heart; and as for the slaves it would make no difference whether they were crowded into fifteen states or scattered over the whole of them—He was very animated and spoke with great warmth—The idea of crushing the Rebellion he treated with bitter scorn, and was very decided and emphatic in repeating that it could never be done.

The spy went on to report that Colonel Thomas had interjected that the Confederates were not responsible for the war and that he did "not have much confidence in the Abolitionist policies." Colonel Thomas "preferred that the war be ended by accepting the inevitability of separation." Another participant at the meeting, "Dr. Finkle" had a "questionable past." He had been around the wrong people: "he is an old War Department clerk from the days of Jeff Davis's tenure. Finkle was also a Democrat."[87]

Stanton also distrusted New York Governor Horatio Seymour, a Democrat, and he suspected General Charles Sanford, who headed the New York state militia. Their response to the draft riots of July 1863 excited Stanton's distrust.[88] Stanton's greatest enemy was McClellan. Stanton had received reports questioning McClellan's political reliability in 1863.[89] With the 1864 election approaching, the Union League proved an important ally in Stanton's campaign against his archenemy. The Union League circulated stories raising questions about McClellan's loyalty. A league letter accused the general of sympathizing with the South and aiding the Confederacy during the operations around Richmond in 1862. It alleged that while in retreat down the peninsula, McClellan had sanctioned the burial of rifles for the Confederates. A league informant also accused him of allowing two hundred wagons and teams to fall into the hands of the advancing Confederates on the peninsula. The informant went as far as alleging that McClellan had offered his services to the South at the outbreak of the war. Such scurrilous gossip proved timely during the election.[90] Other abolitionists held that McClellan was a traitor for not showing enough zeal in prosecuting the war. The defeat at Second Manassas generated ugly rumors claiming: "While [General John] Pope was struggling with the Enemy for the relief of the Army of the Potomac, the traitor Commander of the Army . . . [delayed] withdrawal as much as possible."[91] These accusations provided powerful political ammunition against the candidate in 1864.

In this venomous environment, officers were constantly looking over their shoulders for fear of being denounced. A Massachusetts Democrat serving in Virginia asked his father to keep his letters criticizing the administration secret because "it might cost me [my] commission."[92] When one of his statements to the press might have been construed to be disloyal, Brigadier General John G. Barnard, chief engineer in charge of the defenses of Washington, a particularly sensitive position, hastily pledged his loyalty to the administration in a letter to Stanton. In the letter, Barnard vowed that he was in fact a strenuous defender of the government. Stanton, nonetheless, admonished the general, saying that his statements to the press contradicted his avowals of loyalty and aided "assailants of the President."[93] Others did not get off as lightly. An assistant surgeon who had volunteered for service with an Illinois regiment was arrested twice for disloyalty before finally being dismissed from the service without ever finding out the charges.[94]

There were investigations churning away at every level in the North. At the top was the Joint Committee on the Conduct of the War, whose members intended to make the officer corps realize that the army was now a political instrument in which the people intended to take a direct hand. There would be no more tolerance of superannuated incompetents, many of whom were Democrats whose devotion to the cause was doubtful anyway. The McClellans, Hallecks, Buells, Porters, and Nelsons would have to be replaced by zealous, politically motivated generals who would fight the kind of war that the people wanted.[95]

After its inquiry into the Ball's Bluff affair leading to the nocturnal arrest of General Charles P. Stone in February 1862,[96] the committee turned its attention to the situation in the high command in Missouri. Conditions had become so envenomed that the matter reached the Joint Committee on the Conduct of the War, whose investigation found that

> the superior officers of the federal troops in the State [of Missouri], in many instances, sympathize with the rebels, especially upon the subject of slavery; and they have directed their policy so as to protect, as far as possible, those entertaining disloyal sentiments. There is reason to believe that they have used the troops under their command to prevent the escape of slaves. . . . There is reason to believe that they have pursued a systematic course of persecution of the soldiers under their command, who are known to entertain radical sentiments, and by means of packed court-martials have secured convictions upon frivolous charges, upon which unusually severe sentences have been pronounced and confirmed.[97]

Missouri loyalists had accused General Egbert B. Brown of the district of harboring proslavery views.[98] Missouri Unionists accused other federal officers of making contacts with Copperhead societies and of sending information to Confederate General Nathan Bedford Forrest.[99] When John C. Frémont agreed to head a radical ticket that would have split the Republican vote, charges suddenly surfaced accusing him of being in the pay of the Confederacy. The accusations smeared Frémont and undermined his candidacy. They also assured that the Lincoln-Johnson Union ticket would have no competition for the antislavery vote.[100]

The Joint Committee on the Conduct of the War also carried out an investigation of proslavery General Jefferson C. Davis, who commanded Sherman's XIV Corps during the march through Georgia. Davis ordered a bridge over the Buck River burned after his corps crossed, leaving a column of black refugees stranded on the other side, at the mercy of pursuing Confederates.[101] One of his officers witnessed the horrifying scene. When cries arose that the rebels were coming, the contrabands became terrified; they dashed to the river and plunged in, trying to scramble to safety. Some managed to swim across, others were swept away screaming. At first the troops were stupefied by the disaster unfolding before their eyes, and they began throwing whatever could float to the foundering men, women, and children. No one ever determined how many perished, but the soldiers seethed with anger over Davis's callous action. He had not a spark of humanity, according to a chaplain of the 58th Indiana who witnessed the event.[102] Another accuser suspected Davis of harboring Copperhead sympathies and denounced him to the Joint Committee on the Conduct of the War.[103]

With the spies and investigations came the courts-martial. Though few of the cases before the courts-martial involved political loyalty, there were enough of them to intimidate military officers, who learned to hold their peace because even private conversations were reported. Courts often tried officers for merely espousing unacceptable political views, even though they never translated those ideas into disloyal actions. At times, the army's zeal to prosecute officers who questioned the administration's war aims was purely vindictive. General William Brindle, a Buchanan Democrat from Kansas, was arrested a year after leaving the army.[104] A lowly Kentucky lieutenant was arrested for motivating his resignation with "sentiments which only a traitor and enemy of his country could harbor."[105]

The military authorities used several charges to prosecute suspected officers: uttering treasonable or disloyal language, conduct unbecoming an officer, and finally using disrespectful language about political leaders. When emancipation aroused the anger of the conservatives, many denounced the administration and were charged with making treasonable or disloyal utterances. "God damn the Government; let her go to hell, and I'll be found in the ranks fighting her," declared General James G. Spears.[106] Lieutenant Edward H. Underhill vowed that his commission in Battery A, 1st New York Artillery, did not come from that "damned Lincoln-Nigger Government" and said he would not fight for it.[107] An Ohio lieutenant was hauled before a court for denouncing the conflict as a "damned Abolition War." He had flaunted his views by wearing a butternut emblem to show his hostility to the Lincoln administration.[108] A Minnesotan was dismissed for saying that the war was a "damned rotten concern."[109] A second lieutenant with the 1st New York Mounted Rifles who wished aloud for the South's success wound up in prison for the duration of the war.[110] Captain A. R. P. Tancray, 10th Tennessee Cavalry (U.S.), was more fortunate—he was only cashiered after declaring that "the Northern sons of bitches that were put in command of Tennesseans ought to be killed."[111]

Another charge commonly used against suspect officers was conduct prejudicial to an officer and gentleman. This accusation also involved statements that were deemed disloyal to the government. There was, for example, the Illinois lieutenant who declared: "This Government of the United States is a God damned rotten, worthless concern: all the officers of it may kiss my ass."[112]

A third charge related to political loyalty was officers' use of language disrespectful to their superiors. When a letter of congratulation from the Ohio legislature to General Rosecrans for his victory at Murfreesboro was read aloud to the troops, a colonel promised to give Rosecrans any gift he could imagine if the general could make him "believe any such stuff." The colonel in question did not help his cause when he declared, "Abe Lincoln's Nigger Proclamation will damn him to eternity," and said future generations would curse him for fighting a war to benefit the blacks. He ended his diatribe by declaring that Vallandigham's arrest was politically motivated and that "the d——d nigger is at the bottom of the whole affair." The colonel was dismissed.[113]

Officers also had to be careful about what they wrote in their personal letters. For example, Lieutenant J. M. Garland of the 42d New York Volunteers sent a letter to a friend denouncing the government, and because the letter did not have sufficient postage it remained at the post office, where it was opened. The postal service reported its contents to the army. The army brought charges against the unfortunate lieutenant, accusing the officer of expressing "a feeling toward the Administration and toward the rebels which seems to be in complete conflict with the duties imposed upon him by the sword he wears." Garland had written: "The Administration have at last shown their hands, and that their principles and their hearts are blacker than the 'niggers' they are fighting for," and he wrote that the Emancipation Proclamation was "as unconstitutional as it was unjust." He too was dismissed.[114]

Some officers went beyond words by carrying out treasonous acts. Punishment for such acts was swift and brutal. Two regular officers were apprehended spying for the Confederacy near Franklin, Tennessee, and were summarily tried and hanged that same night from spikes hammered into a nearby tree.[115]

While the rank and file and civilian authorities watched the officer corps for any signs of disaffection, the officers also exercised vigilance over their men's political attitudes. Many volunteer officers had been active in local politics before joining the army. They continued their political activity in the military, canvassing the troops to identify and rid the army of political opponents. An Indiana officer with the Iron Brigade held that there was no place in his regiment for any Copperheads.[116] Officers were especially vigilant about politically pernicious tendencies among the men during elections. For example, leaders monitored regiments from New York, where Democrats ran the government and the election machinery was suspect. The New York state law of April 1864 required that votes in the field be authenticated by New York state commissioned officers, who also were to help soldiers when they reported to their commanders to cast ballots. Some of Democratic Governor Horatio Seymour's appointees took a more "active" role by forging soldiers' signatures on ballots. The officers were caught and charged with "conduct prejudicial to the military service." Others tried to induce soldiers to vote for the administration when they came to collect the ballots.[117] Conversely, Republicans believed that Democratic officers commanding pro-Republican regiments prevented their men from voting.[118]

Officers played a political role in the citizen armies in many ways. They monitored the political ideas of their men as well as silencing and punishing those suspected of disloyalty. They restricted and censored reading material, and they organized petitions favoring the administration. They brought in speakers to indoctrinate the troops. They also were in charge of conducting voting in the field and in that role canvassed soldiers for the government.[119] They took their units' political pulse as elections approached; for example, the 44th North Carolina held a meeting to gauge the pro-Holden sentiment among the men and to see if the regiment would actively support the Vance administration. The regiment voted on a resolution condemning the pro-peace Holdenites during the gubernatorial campaign.[120] On the Union side, officers nervously sent estimates of the number of votes they could marshal for pro-Lincoln candidates.[121] With Vicksburg not taken and Lee victorious in early 1863, Republican governors like Andrew G. Curtin of Pennsylvania no doubt found solace in political reports like the one from Colonel James L. Selfridge of the 46th Pennsylvania Volunteers: the colonel assured Curtin that "every officer and man in the Regiment is your friend and admirer" and could be relied on in an election.[122] At Benton Barracks in St. Louis, officers of the 122d Illinois Infantry counted the number of Copperhead badges that the troops pinned on their uniforms. The officers only dared tear the badges off after Vicksburg had fallen and the Union army had repulsed Lee at Gettysburg.[123]

Just as officers were subject to court-martial for political disloyalty, ordinary soldiers were punished when they voiced inappropriate political views or were suspected of being members of subversive organizations such as the Knights of the Golden Circle.[124] Brigadier General G. K. Warren presided over a court-martial at the headquarters of the Left Grand Division of the Army of the Potomac that convicted Sergeant William B. Gillespie of Company H, 28th New York Infantry, of writing a disloyal newspaper article in which he denounced Congress and the president for enacting the Emancipation Proclamation. Gillespie declared that it would cause many to desert. He added sarcastically that the newly freed blacks should all be "shipped to Washington that their Massa Linkum and Cabinet might give them a hearty welcome."[125] The military authorities also tried a saddler in the 18th Pennsylvania Cavalry who was charged with "disloyal conduct" for declaring that if he got to Richmond, he would immediately head for Liverpool, England, to "ship in the Alabama," a Confederate raider.[126]

It is difficult to assess the impact of the trials. Though I have only discussed general courts-martial in two armies, the same types of trials must have been taking place in other armies, and other types of purges must have been occurring at a lower command level. The number of arrested officers probably never came near to the 13,535 civilian arrests alleged in Mark E. Neely Jr.'s *The Fate of Liberty*. However numerous, the trials and dismissals must have silenced those who feared for their advancement. The charges came under military jurisdiction and obviated constitutional issues that arose regarding the administration's revocation of habeas corpus and the use of military commissions to try civilians in the North, nonmilitary personnel in its armies, and rebellious whites in the South.[127]

Like their officers, the soldiers had to take care with their mail, which they complained was being censored by the officers themselves.[128] Union soldiers complained that their mail was opened and their access to newspapers and magazines was restricted by "narrow-minded Republican officers acting as censors."[129] There were also political leaders and officers who advocated censoring the mail and the press. Senator Justin Smith Morrill wanted to counteract the influence of newspapers that were too critical of the administration. He considered a proposal from the governor of Vermont that called on the army to authorize sutlers to sell only the *New York Herald*.[130] General Sherman shared the disapproval of hostile newspapers in his camps.[131] Officers often acted on their own to confiscate, destroy, or forbid antiadministration newspapers in the Union army.[132] One celebrated case of censorship involved General Stephen Augustus Hurlbut, who banned the Copperhead *Chicago Times*. A fellow officer agreed with Hurlbut's decision; why, he asked, should the country spend millions of dollars and hundreds of thousands of lives to crush the rebellion yet give free reign to treason and treachery in the press?[133] In another incident, General Grant silenced the *Memphis Bulletin* when it called for paving the city's streets with the skulls of the occupying army.[134] Soldier correspondents who earned a few dollars for each letter to a newspaper had to make sure that their officers were kept unaware. They resorted to pseudonyms to avoid detection.[135]

Officers indoctrinated their men by distributing political tracts and by drafting resolutions supporting candidates or the Emancipation Proclamation.[136] During the siege of Vicksburg, an Iowa soldier described how he was called out on parade to declare his support for the administration. The officers read a resolution backing emancipation and called on the men to endorse it. In one case, when a quarter of the men refused, the colonel ordered them to step forward. The men who backed the resolution were marched past the recalcitrant troops, who emitted groans of disapproval.[137] When the 109th Illinois contingent was placed under arrest for opposing emancipation, officers in sister units from Illinois hastily drafted resolutions supporting administration policy to show that the state remained behind President Lincoln and Governor Yates.[138] After drawing up a resolution supporting emancipation, one colonel told his men that he would shoot anyone who refused to sign it.[139] Officers also drafted pro-emancipation resolutions in the eastern regiments. They called on the 17th Connecticut to give three boisterous cheers for the government and three sorrowful groans for the Copperheads.[140] And anyone who circulated pro-Democrat petitions would find himself under arrest.[141]

To further indoctrinate soldiers, officers marched their men to political rallies to hear speakers like radical leader Jim Lane of Kansas.[142] When speakers were not available, editors like Joseph Medill of the Republican *Chicago Tribune* shipped tens of thousands of copies of his proadministration paper to the men at the front. Medill made a determined effort to undermine McClellan's presidential candidacy in the 1864 election.[143] George Putnam's Loyal Publications Society distributed tens of thousands of copies of loyal newspapers and more than fifteen thousand political pamphlets to the men of the Army of the Potomac.[144] Officers and politicians also relied on the zealous efforts of army chaplains to orient the political attitudes of the troops; preventing political deviancy was like saving souls. Chaplains furthered God's work by circulating political reading material among the troops, with the officers themselves lending a hand in the indoctrination process by giving speeches in support of emancipation and condemning those who grumbled about fighting to free the slaves.[145]

Finally, officers were responsible for supervising voting in the field by each regiment, battalion, battery, or company. They checked the voting eligibility of each soldier-citizen. They sorted and counted the results, and they declared the results.[146] Some states, like Missouri's Union government, allowed soldiers to vote viva voce, while others permitted the officers to collect the ballots publicly. This placed the officers in the position of influence over their soldiers.[147] Officers who managed to muster a large percentage for Lincoln congratulated themselves on their success in getting the men to vote the right way.[148] Officers in the 6th Massachusetts ran the vote like Boston ward heelers by getting their men to vote several times during the gubernatorial election of October 1864.[149] Others made sure that Democratic ballots never reached the troops.[150] Some officers prevented state election commissioners from gaining access to the troops. They disenfranchised their men by claiming that their units were too close to the enemy and an election would be too disruptive.[151] Such actions aroused complaints that soon reached home. The men resented officers who infringed on the free exercise of their rights as citizens, but none of the complaints apparently led to courts-martial.[152]

In a people's war being fought with citizen-soldiers in which politics is central to defining the cause and motivating soldiers, officers had to share their men's beliefs. If their loyalty was doubtful, they could not only undermine their men's morale but also weaken the bonds between society and its army by fostering the idea that the army was a thing apart from its civilian society and was not bound by the same political decisions as the rest of society. Once the rupture occurred, civil society and the army would begin to define different war aims and see a different stake in the outcome. Finally, there would be contrary ideas about when to end the war. For example, conservative professional officers feared that all-out war would destroy the army if it was fought to achieve radical purposes such as ending slavery. The enemy would resist more bitterly and the cost of victory would be prohibitive. The army's institutional value outweighed the extreme purposes advanced by the Northern radicals. Better an early negotiated peace than a wholesale destruction of the officer corps in a war of attrition. The society and its citizen-soldiers warily watched over the officer corps for the emergence of such attitudes. At the same time however, the officers monitored their men's political sentiments. The officers played an important part in motivating their troops by overseeing attitudes and by influencing their men's political views, but they were also essential in helping develop a fighting style peculiar to a mass army of citizens, which will be examined in detail in the next chapter.

7 The "Hard War"

FIGHTING STYLE OF PEOPLE'S ARMIES

In Leo Tolstoy's *War and Peace,* just before the battle of Borodino, a Russian officer, Prince Andrew Bolkonski, explains how wars should be fought in the new era of people's armies. The prince despises the way the foreign professionals commanding Russia's armies are conducting the war. Bolkonski argues that a war between peoples is not a gentlemen's affair. Professionals sanitize war, trying to turn it into a ritual of strategic maneuvers meant to limit losses because foreign officers do not have a stake in the struggle like the average Russian soldiers who do the real fighting. The professional soldiers reduce war to a pirouette of intricate maneuvers conducted according to the conventions of dandified chivalry. Bolkonski claims that if he were in charge of the Russian army, he would make war so terrible that none would ever resort to it again. There would be no negotiations or diplomatic niceties between professionals. Like the citizen-soldiers of the American Civil War, Bolkonski demands merciless all-out war, war fought until one people is completely overwhelmed. Professionals, he claims, only play at war, while ordinary people do the fighting and pay with their lives. Ordinary soldiers fight with the full knowledge that it will be a merciless struggle. War must never be fought the way professionals conduct it—as an idle pastime.[1] Implicit in Tolstoy's view of war, expressed by the character Bolkonski, was the assumption that wars between peoples could only be justified if great issues were at stake. The people's survival and the defense of universal political principles were the only legitimate purposes that justified slaughter on such a scale. Once the people took up arms, the conflict could never be limited. The ruling elites risked losing control when they unleashed the massive forces of a people's war. The war's dynamic could lead to revolutionary changes in the camps, which in turn threatened the status of ruling groups.

The conservative professional officer and the upper class have been wary of using people's armies, whose "armed hordes" of citizen-soldiers could destabilize society.[2] In a war fought by volunteer militia, there are no limits to the violence against the enemy and its collateral effect on the victorious society.[3] During the Civil War, conservatives correctly perceived the tie between the country's radical war aims and the ferocity of the conflict. If the war aims called for the total defeat and the overthrow of the enemy regime, then the adversary's resistance would be as unrelenting.

Political changes were as important as technology in making war more lethal. The predemocratic, eighteenth-century professional armies used a fighting style that produced high casualties among regulars—for example, 33 percent at Malplaquet in 1703—but seldom affected civilians. European regular armies were more cosmopolitan, including mercenary contingents of foreign troops. For example, the French kings used Swiss mercenaries and the British used Germans from Hesse. This policy reduced the savagery associated with interethnic conflicts. Wars between polyglot armies of professionals sanitized the fighting. Conservative military and political leaders preferred to fight wars with regular troops and professional officers, because such armies would limit the intensity of the violence and prevent any political spillover into society that might threaten the political status quo. Besides, the leaders argued, regulars were better trained and more disciplined and more able thus to fire volleys precisely on command and maneuver and fight in compact, disciplined formations. This too limited collateral damage and unnecessary casualties. Finally, warfare in the eighteenth century was less destructive because of the rational spirit of the age. True to the character of the time, warfare was conducted according to the principles of professional military science, with violence fastidiously controlled to reduce collateral destruction.

By contrast, war in the romantic revolutionary era was driven by popular emotions and fought by large formations of inexperienced short-service troops, causing boundless violence. It was no longer a game of skill played by professionals or a sparring match between generals. Now it was a contest of brute force driven by the popular passions that no leader dared oppose or could even control.[4] Unleashed by these forces, human conflict took on a dynamic of its own. Wars fought by people's armies now advanced politically idealistic goals and maximalist war aims.[5] In the eighteenth century, professional soldiers and conservative politicians had tried to rationalize and tame war. They perceived war as a scientific endeavor and tried to isolate it from popular passion.[6] Democracy and its citizens' armies removed this partition between popular passion and war. Karl von Clausewitz, an officer during the Napoleonic invasion of Russia and a military theorist, was among the first to be aware of this change. He knew that modern armies would have to motivate large numbers of citizen-soldiers with grand ideals, and he realized such passionate war could never be tamed and conducted fastidiously or "scientifically."[7]

Peoples' armies thus fought war differently from the professional armies of the eighteenth century. Strategy and tactics were driven by popular passion and political imperatives.[8] By 1864, Civil War strategy and tactics had become increasingly politicized. Campaigns were tailored to political needs. War was conducted not only to gain specific military objectives, but also to influence opinion at home and demoralize the enemy. Union political and military leaders perceived that taking Atlanta and Richmond was strategically important, but the two cities were also politically essential for Lincoln's reelection.[9] Tactics were not only politicized but more brutal. For example, after Ulysses S. Grant's repulse at Cold Harbor, he refused to request a truce to collect his wounded. Grant may have realized that a truce would signify a Union defeat, thus jeopardizing home-front morale and weakening Republican electoral prospects. Conversely, Robert E. Lee allowed the wounded to languish under his guns in the June sun, showing the Northern public the horrors and futility of continuing the war and the folly of supporting the Lincoln administration. Confederate President Jefferson Davis also let political imperatives dictate strategy when he responded to public impatience over the never-ending retreat to Atlanta by firing Joseph E. Johnston and ending Johnston's professional-style war of maneuver that yielded so much ground to the invader. The people demanded action, not maneuvers. In Johnston's stead, Davis appointed General John Bell Hood to attack the enemy relentlessly in the hope of driving William Tecumseh Sherman from the national soil by waging the type of hard war the people were demanding.

The more politically articulate the soldiers, the more they demanded a pitiless war. They realized that this was a new type of struggle for high political—even revolutionary—purposes in which the entire citizenry had a direct stake. Such soldiers were almost four times as likely to call for war without mercy.[10] They devoted more reflection to the issues at stake. They believed that unrestricted war could overcome the enemy.[11] Lieutenant Francis F. Audsley, Company F, 71st Missouri State Militia (U.S.), participated in the forced removal of the pro-Confederate population in Jackson, Cass, Bates, and Vernon Counties in Missouri in 1863. It was late fall, and the harvest had been taken in, so the land was completely barren. Bereft of food, the people were driven from their homes. Yet Audsley felt no pity for their plight. The rebels deserved what they got.[12] The volunteers were in earnest, and they wanted the war conducted without pity.

Mark Grimsley has already shown how this policy evolved from conciliation to a war against civilian morale and the South's economy. This assessment does not challenge Grimsley's contention that much of the destruction was carried out for military necessity and that the high-command sought to control the havoc. Directed devastation would best characterize the high-command policy in the South in 1864–65.[13] But the soldiers were not always aware of such subtleties, and they found it hard to carry out the repression according to a refined scale of graduated brutality with differing codes of conduct for different elements of the population and different levels of destruction for different types of property. Besides, company-grade officers, who had to actually carry out the devastation, could not easily control their men once they were set loose on the countryside. When the high command began to carry out what were called "extreme repressive measures," the men saw this as an authorization to intensify the scope of the violence to the entire society without taking the time to quibble over degrees and proportionality.

The purpose of my research is to examine soldier attitudes and not to examine Northern occupation policy. What is of concern is the attitude of the soldiers toward the new hard-war policy during the second half of the war. A clear change occurred in the attitude in the rank and file. Grimsley contends that the Northern troops generally supported a conciliatory policy toward the South, at least in the early stages of the war.[14] But this work argues—and the overwhelming majority of politically aware soldiers' comments during the second half of the war support this view—that the rank and file became fierce proponents of hard war after 1862. They did not show much patience with the high command's and political leaders' ideas about proportionality of destruction or their ideas that the demolition must be strategic and not gratuitous. Stephen V. Ash points out that the rank and file had little patience with the legal niceties of martial law and the constitutional status of the occupied states. Once an area was occupied, there were few guidelines about occupation policy for company-grade officers. They improvised as best they could, and they and their troops often reacted harshly when they were insulted and humiliated by the citizenry.[15] The corroding relationship between the army and enemy civilians made soldiers eager participants in the hard-war measures. The soldiers saw the war as a struggle of moral absolutes. Charles Royster has argued that the war became brutal because political and military leaders began to implement their own rhetoric about making the South pay for its misdeeds, punishing the miscreant secessionists and slaveholders, and razing the society to the ground. Royster points out that Southern commanders like Stonewall Jackson voiced the same apocalyptic vision.[16] Combined with the enormous scope and dynamic of the war, this vision escalated its destructiveness. Even if the level of devastation and brutality never equaled the Spanish campaigns in the Netherlands in the sixteenth century, they represented a heretofore unknown level of ferocity.[17]

The same attitude emerged on the other side. Peter Newport Bragg at Arkansas Post called for a war of annihilation, a war by poison or powder until the "vermin" were exterminated or driven from the land.[18] Regiments framed resolutions calling for all-out war; they wanted the war prosecuted zealously until the enemy was annihilated.[19] There was no place for political compromise or military half-measures. Conservatism and compromise were not appropriate policies for a people's war. For the citizen-soldiers, one social order could only exist to the exclusion of the other: slavery or freedom, victory or oppression. Northern Democrats had to accept unrestricted war. They had to support maximalist war aims, including abolition.[20] Fighting, not negotiation, was the only way to settle the matter. The men demanded an end to the professional officers' strategic finessing. Congress responded by creating the Joint Committee on the Conduct of the War to oversee the professionals' conduct.[21]

When they talked about a hard war, the soldiers meant that the war had to be fought relentlessly. To forge the instrument for fighting a hard war, they demanded full-scale national mobilization and a thorough purge of all disloyal elements. In the Northern army, politically aware soldiers also advocated a merciless occupation policy to root out the remaining seeds of rebellion and resolve the political and social questions once and for all. In addition, they called for unconditional surrender terms and no prisoner exchanges, realizing that the total war would only end when one side or the other was drained of its manpower pool. Nor should quarter be given or asked.[22] Prisoners were slaughtered by both irregulars and regular troops. One of the most notorious atrocities occurred at Centralia, Missouri, where Confederate guerrilla leader Bill Anderson killed Union prisoners. Another ignominious affair happened at Fort Pillow in Tennessee, where Nathan Bedford Forrest's command massacred black Unionists. Whether Forrest encouraged the murder of the soldiers is secondary to the negrophobia that prevailed among the Southern troops. Arming blacks confirmed deep-seated Confederate fears of a servile rebellion.

Total war is a multifaceted concept. First, it signifies a certain type of behavior toward noncombatants, specifically, making war on civilians as well as soldiers. Second, the conqueror has a new type of war aim entailing major internal changes in the enemy's society. Third, the scope of the war is different than that of limited wars, because it requires more comprehensive mobilization of the citizenry and the society's productive capacity for the war effort. And finally, it involves a new kind of soldier, the citizen-soldier, who must be politically motivated to believe that the cause merits a personal commitment and brutality. The American conflict conformed in some degree to all four criteria.

First, noncombatants were frequently victims in this conflict. Warfare, according to the total-war doctrine, need not be limited to purely military targets. Nor do reprisals against the enemy have to be proportionate to the violence of enemy actions. Violence can be unrestrained to bring down the whole society and thereby devastate not only a society's instrument of war—its army—but also its ability to forge the tools of war. Philip H. Sheridan, Sherman, and Grant all foraged to sustain their armies. They also destroyed the enemy's productive capacity and communications network as necessary. But they went further in their carrying the war to the citizen's door. Traditionally, only open resistance justified reprisals against civilians. However, political objectives as much as military purposes motivated Union severity. Political opposition and not just military resistance triggered harsh measures, because the North wanted to undermine the enemy's will to resist and compel the Southerners to acquiesce in the new political order. Like all revolutionary armies, the Northern army predicated its repressive violence not only on civilian armed resistance but also on the citizenry's political defiance. Driving out all politically unreliable people, specifically those who refused the loyalty oath, was the corollary of this policy.

Mark E. Neely Jr. has argued that Union commanders sought to restrain their men's depredations to military targets, though one can only wonder how wide the gap was between the desires of generals and the actions of their agents at the company and squad levels. This is one of the reasons Neely questions whether it was a total war. For example, he also asserts that Sherman's objectives in Georgia remained essentially military.[23] But even if his objectives were strictly military, war on such scale imposed a dynamic of its own. The trail of destruction and mayhem in the wake of such large armies was considerable. The sheer logistical needs of massive armies meant that the war leeched enormous amounts of wealth from the civilian population and caused considerable collateral destruction when it cut a swath through Georgia. Merely giving receipts for confiscated goods did not change the significance of such actions.[24] The generals' putative intent was one thing; the actual consequences, however, were another.

Second, total war signifies that the conqueror's objectives extend beyond limited military or territorial ends. The objectives are revolutionary because they are directed to bringing about major internal changes—"reconstruction"—of the enemy's society. The war is not limited to negotiable settlement involving mutual incremental adjustments. Lincoln's peace terms, proclaimed July 9, 1864, coupled abolition with restoration of the Union. As soon as emancipation was proclaimed, abolition became the focus of the conflict, because the logic of this aim entailed that the economy that underpinned the power of the Southern ruling class and the class relations that it fostered would be undermined.

Third, such a revolutionary purpose could only steel the opponent's resolve to resist to the bitter end, which in turn obliged both sides to fight ever more fiercely and muster far more resources to overcome the adversary. Both societies had to resort to conscription to mobilize the entire male citizenry and new taxes, and the Confederate government even seized its citizens' property. The magnitude of the effort was enormous, and the losses sustained in the American Civil War have never been matched. If this was not a total war, it was the nearest America has ever come to it.

Fourth, the American Civil War resembled a total war because of the nature of the soldiers who manned its armies. Since the French Revolution, total wars have been fought by citizen-soldiers, many of whom were politically motivated to enlist. The backbone of these armies is the politicized soldiers, and they tend to see the war in simple binary terms: as a struggle between good and evil. In this Manichean struggle, incremental and negotiated change are pointless. Good must prevail; compromise with evil is an anathema. Total war means total commitment, total defeat of the enemy, and total reconstruction of his society, according to the politically aware warrior.

Neely correctly observed that the American Civil War was not a total war when compared to the Second World War.[25] I contend, however, that it was a total war by definition because the four components that characterize such a conflict appeared simultaneously in this struggle through the intent and actions of the soldiers.

A people's war also meant war against civilians and their society. Combatants felt no qualms about indiscriminate blockades and sieges that starved noncombatants. Wisconsin army surgeon Robert Mitchell Jr. supported blockading the Arkansas River, even if it meant starving loyal elements along with pro-Confederate Arkansans.[26] The armies directed violence against noncombatants. They bombarded towns. They robbed the population. They confiscated food, and they burned stores.[27] Ohio Major DeWitt Clinton Loudon opposed handling the rebels with kid gloves. He argued that a sterner policy would bring rebels to heel that much more quickly.[28] Lieutenant Colonel Harvey Graham, 22d Iowa Infantry, concurred. He maintained that unrestricted depredations and population removals were the only way to end the war expeditiously: "They are going to confiscate all these plantations and get all the negro women and old darky men that are not fit to go into the service to [start] raising grain and other things to feed the Army and drive all the white families outside of our lines that is what suits me."[29] Congress responded in early summer 1862, when it voted to arm ex-slaves and confiscate rebel property.[30]

Unrestricted war signified enlisting the entire community in the war effort, requiring a rigorous political orthodoxy to assure that the community provided disciplined support for the war effort. It also meant mobilizing the whole male population through strict enforcement of the draft. The men heartily approved of this policy. Anyone who could chew hardtack should shoulder a musket.[31]

A corollary of a people's war was a stern occupation policy that relied on a political triage of the vanquished population by political category: those who subscribed to the victor's political worldview and those who did not. This meant persecuting anyone who stood in the way of the conquering forces. John W. Baldwin of the 74th Ohio served in Tennessee and unhesitatingly backed the high command's decision to arrest any women suspected of Confederate sympathies.[32]

Grant's public acclaim for demanding unconditional surrender and the inclusion of abolition alongside restoration of the Union as the twin war aims of the North augured the new type of war. The enemy had to prostrate themselves so that their society would be malleable for imposing a new political order. Ordinary soldiers would not tolerate generals who arranged cozy surrender terms with their West Point friends; these arrangements might leave the enemy with the dignity and means to resist. The enemy army had to be destroyed and its society's social structures razed. Only total victory could ensure that the sacrifices made would yield lasting results.

Why did the citizen-soldiers advocate unlimited war? Moral and political principles were among the reasons. Unionists believed that the Confederacy incarnated evil. Its citizenry were traitors who deserved to be punished. This was not merely a war of conquest but a punitive expedition against a wayward people who were guilty of a collective crime. A resolution of the officers of the 82d Illinois characterized this punitive outlook. The sixth article declared: "We hope and wish, that this rebellion may soon be suppressed, but *only* by force of arms, and that then the traitors in the north as well as the leaders of the rebellion in the south, may not evade their just punishment."[33]

Along with their destructive revolutionary zeal, politically articulate citizen-soldiers brought along many skills into the army. People's armies were able to devise new tactics and new weaponry because there were people from all walks of life in the ranks and they had a variety of tactical and technical ideas.[34] Both the French revolutionary forces and the American Civil War armies tried new devices such as a balloon corps, flamethrowers, gas shells, submarines, and compass-guided targeting. Enhanced signaling capabilities and the use of telegraphic contact with corps headquarters improved command and control of the large people's armies.[35] In addition, people's wars made extensive use of irregular troops as guerrilla units. The name originated in the Peninsular campaign against Napoleon, whose Spanish opponents were called *guerrilleros*. The use of light infantry or mounted infantry for rapid movement was a further innovation of revolutionary people's wars. The French revolutionary armies and later the American Civil War forces used ever larger masses of *tirailleurs* (skirmishers) fighting in loose formations.[36] They also served as foragers and pillagers to destroy the enemy economy and civilian morale.[37] American Civil War armies also used *tirailleurs* and other types of mobile advance forces to contact fifth

The "hard war" waged by the South. Confederate guerrilla raid in a western town, probably in Missouri. *Harper's Weekly,* September 27, 1862.

columns operating behind enemy lines and spreading their political doctrines and harassing the enemy's rear.[38] For example, the radical Senator Benjamin F. Wade advocated a revolutionary fighting style similar to Saint-Just's when he demanded that blacks become the North's revolutionary fifth column, creating fears of servile insurrection behind Southern lines.[39]

The volunteers developed a special style of attack. They advanced in swarms rushing from cover to cover. Soldier-citizens were more adept than regulars at using such tactics, which required greater individual initiative to seize advantageous terrain and to operate more independently. Soldiers in people's armies also had a different image of war. While the professional officer corps had a cavalryman's peripheral outlook, relying on dash and maneuver to seize an important point and check the enemy, citizen-soldiers saw war from an infantryman's perspective—from the center of the melee. They pictured war as an irrational phenomenon, a swirl of uncontrolled forces and unregulated violence. There was no planned order of elaborate enveloping movements; sophisticated maneuvers dissolved after the enemy's first volley. The battle became a brutish contest between two collective wills.[40] It was the infantryman's mass over the professional officer's war maneuver.[41] Only overwhelming forces could overcome the enemy because the citizen army lacked skills to use combined arms effectively or to make intricate coordinated movements. The armies were too ungainly to exploit breakthroughs, and they could seldom win decisive victories.[42] Technology also affected the tactics of the American Civil War's armies. As the accuracy, range of weapons, and intensity of fire increased, complex maneuvers with compact masses became increasingly costly. The citizen-soldiers and officers relied on looser formations to reduce casualties, often with entire regiments operating as skirmishers. Finally, the broken and wooded terrain of many American battlefields made it difficult to operate with large compact columns or lines. Early battles like Shiloh exemplify these points.[43]

Regular officers held a dim view of short-service troops for making war so costly and for resorting to unorthodox improvisations that made command and control difficult and war even more unpredictable.[44] Yet such eccentric tactics sometimes worked. At Chattanooga, an army of farmers, villagers, and clerks had little knowledge of orderly advances and the need to protect flanks; nevertheless, they rushed the heights overlooking the besieged city and kept going until the enemy was driven down the other side. They succeeded in carrying off an operation that the regular officers thought imprudent.[45]

As the Chattanooga case illustrates, people's armies did not rigidly follow tactical doctrine. Their volunteer officers encouraged them to operate independently, leaving more initiative to subalterns and allowing freedom to improvise as the situation might require.[46] Such tactics were often chosen out of necessity, because the armies were fighting in broken terrain and lacked an experienced staff to maintain command and control.[47] Besides, the citizen-soldiers did not take readily to fighting in highly disciplined formations; they retained the self-reliant habits nurtured in civilian life. At the same time, the volunteers easily took to fighting as independent detachments, as exemplified by the 53d Ohio Volunteer Infantry, which broke and ran during the initial Confederate onslaught at Shiloh but whose elements fought on as independent companies or attached themselves to other units.[48]

Cavalry became adept at fighting as infantry, advancing ahead of columns to seize strategic crossroads and hold them until the rest of the army arrived. Meanwhile, infantry learned to improvise defensive positions with an unorthodox assortment of material, including cotton bales, crushed sugarcane, grapevines, and felled trees for their gabions, fascines, and parapets.[49] Infantry also quickly modified their tactics to suit new weapons, such as the repeating rifle. For example, General John T. Wilder's brigade fired off a volley at Confederates at Chickamauga and then feinted reloading. The enemy, seeing an opportunity to make an advance, exposed themselves to six more volleys at short range.[50]

People's armies in the American Civil War, like their counterparts in the French Revolution, saw their war as an apocalyptic struggle of good against evil, which in turn affected tactics. The soldier-citizens believed that their moral superiority and enthusiasm would compensate for tactical ineffectiveness. French revolutionary people's armies relied on élan instead of sophisticated maneuvers. People's armies went to war armed with romantic myths. Though use of the *arme blanche* in frontal assaults was costly, the cold steel of the righteous bayonets of the republic was supposed to hasten the enemy's path to eternity. According to French revolutionary commanders like Meunier, Houchard, Desjardin, and political leaders like Collot d'Herbois, the pike and bayonet were the way to prove the tactical and moral superiority of the citizen-soldier over the professional soldier.

Not surprisingly, different fighting styles strained relations between regulars and volunteers in people's armies.[51] One Union officer said that the regulars of the 15th U.S. Infantry "are a great nuisance. They cultivate *contempt* for all volunteers . . . and this is true not only of the officers . . . but of the men also. The men though treated like dogs by their officers, appear to hold themselves as vastly the superiors of all volunteers. A Regular *Private,* in their estimation outranks anything less than a commissioned Staff officer while a non-commissioned Reg. officer is the equal of a volunteer Colonel."[52]

Another attribute of the people's army's fighting style was its propensity to make war against the citizenry. Here again, politics influenced the way the armies fought because the citizen-soldier perceived the Civil War as a conflict between peoples pursuing mutually exclusive political objectives; thus it could not be a limited war over a few territorial adjustments, like eighteenth-century dynastic conflicts. Instead, it was a war of ideas and principles, not territory; it was a war against an evil people, against Gomorrah, where God could not find ten innocent men.

Conservatives like George B. McClellan could have cited the example of democratic Athens to justify their abhorrence of people's war. Athens sent a punitive expedition against the Melians during the Peloponnesian Wars. The Athenians massacred most of the population and destroyed the city in the name of their righteous arrogance. Conservatives argued that only an elite professional force would maintain proportionality between ends and means, but both the French Revolution and American Civil War were fought by troops armed with moral absolutes.[53] Both the French and American armies perceived their wars as crusades against evil, and both used punitive violence against the civilian population. Lee pillaged Pennsylvania and Sherman plundered Georgia. While the high command's professionals tried to justify the punitive nature of campaigns against the populace by claiming that they deprived the enemy of economic resources, the rank and file did not resort to such sophistry. Union troops believed they were punishing a traitorous population. The North was inflicting retribution against a criminalized enemy. Meanwhile, Southern troops believed that they were carrying out reprisals for the Northern enemy's unjustifiable depredations in their homeland.[54]

Clausewitz attributed violence against noncombatants to the changing purpose of war as entire peoples fought each other. A people's war turned into a test of resolution. By 1863–64, the armies and their leaders realized that occupying enemy territory would not bring victory if the enemy's will to resist remained firm. A new political and economic dimension was added to the conflict. Union forces confiscated slaves and plundered and destroyed the South to break the enemy's will to fight, confirming Clausewitz's theory of modern war against the whole society.[55]

While the people's armies and their irregular auxiliaries proved enthusiastic plunderers, they also showed that they were good fighters. There are several measures of combat effectiveness: desertion rates, numbers of active surrenders and passive surrenders, successes in routine defense, gaining objectives in an attack, and number of tenacious defenses.[56] Results vary according to the measures that are used for evaluating the American Civil War's armies. By 1864, the American armies had nearly reached professional European proficiency. The improvement showed in Emory Upton's assault at Spottsylvania and George Thomas's offensive at Nashville.[57] Improved effectiveness also can be seen by comparing casualty ratios of killed to missing and wounded during an early engagement, such as Shiloh in 1862, with those of the attacks at Atlanta in mid-1864. At Shiloh the ratio was 1,754 killed to 2,885 wounded and missing, yielding a ratio of .604. At Atlanta there were 4,423 killed versus 4,442 wounded and missing, yielding a ratio of .995, a 40 percent improvement.[58]

European military historians were surprised by the ferocity of the fighting in the American Civil War. They attributed it to the power of political ideals. Fanaticism characterized the bloody fighting in a civil war, sniffed Jock Haswell, a British military historian.[59] But this monocausal explanation is inadequate. At least five factors coincided to make the American Civil War armies fight fiercely: the irrational romanticism of the revolutionary era, the size of the armies, the armies' military ineptitude during the early part of the conflict, the ideological hatred that the war unleashed, and the maximalist and mutually exclusive war aims that each side advanced.

Attitudinal factors—the romantic nationalism and idealism of the age—played an extremely important role in defining people's armies' fighting style. War became romantic theater, an ideological morality play where the combatants embarked on glory road to carry out a morally cathartic drama. Release came through the paroxysm of total war. Men marched off to the sound of the *Marseillaise,* reciting Goethe's poems calling for national liberation, or singing "Jubilo."[60] Death was sanitized as an appropriate conclusion to war's drama.[61] The morality play ended with evil opponent vanquished and right restored. Such a romantic image of war generated powerful enthusiasm in the first great encounters of the Civil War at Shiloh and during the Seven Days' battles. Bravery in the early stages of the war was theatrical and choreographed by the popular press and in pulp novels.

Democracy and universal military service increased the size of the armies, but they also increased the number of casualties. The democratic revolutions put a ballot and a musket in each hand. The industrial revolution made it possible to arm a large force with standard equipment. It was easier and more efficient to arm large armies composed of short-service troops once industry became mechanized to produce large quantities of crude but reliable muzzle-loaders. Besides, prevailing opinion held that only professionals could be trained to use complex repeating breech-loaders; such weapons were hard to maintain and thus more appropriate for trained professionals.[62] The same assumption prevailed when it came to smoothbore muzzle-loaded artillery versus breech-loaded rifled cannons.[63]

People's armies were hastily mobilized in response to a national emergency, and they did not have time for adequate training. Nor were there enough experienced officers to command them. These deficiencies made for long wars and brutal indecisive battles. As the war dragged on, it grew more barbaric. Discipline grew lax when the armies ventured deeper into hostile territory. "Bummers" fought "partisan rangers" and local militia in a war without mercy. Unrestricted war brutalized combatants.[64]

Political convictions justified ruthless depredations in enemy territory. Political hatred served as an important motivator leading to demands that only unconditional surrender was acceptable against organized collective evil.[65] Zealous hostility swept the land and intensified the calls for unrelenting war. The drums beat with an inexorable tempo, impatiently demanding that the army close quickly with the enemy and vanquish him. The public demanded results. Generals were under heavy public and political pressure to devise a way to bring rapid resolution of the issue, making the struggle more costly as it lurched from one indecisive outcome to the next.

The last element that affected the nature of the people's armies' fighting style was the maximalist war aims, requiring total victory and unconditional surrender. Such goals were so threatening to enemy society that they hardened its soldiers' resolve. Clausewitz foresaw that a nation's very existence was at stake, as war became a zero-sum contest for survival or subjugation.[66] The enemy threatened everything of value; victory was worth any cost. Maximalist war aims based on such moral absolutism intensified people's wars. The soldiers recorded their hatred and displayed callous indifference to the foe's plight. Confederates nurtured implacable hostility toward the Northern invaders. The Yankees were threatening their homes and their way of life. Confederates vowed to kill Northerners without compunction. Reflecting a morally intransigent view of the war, Southerners swore never to make peace with the invader. They would go to any length to keep the Northerners away from their homeland and from destroying their way of life by imposing racial equality, which they believed would lead to miscegenation.[67]

For their part, Northern troops came to see the war as struggle between two mutually exclusive political systems. By 1863 it was a war between freedom and slavery, between democracy and oligarchy. There was no room for a middle ground. "We are all Abolitionists, unless we are copperheads," wrote an Illinois officer.[68] It was a struggle against the South's institutionalized wickedness; it was a war against an evil society that treated human beings like chattel. The South would have to expiate its sins. Northern soldiers perceived themselves as God's instrument of retribution.[69] Seeing slavery firsthand confirmed the righteousness of the Union cause and substantiated the belief that slavery was inherently evil. The system of servitude not only persecuted blacks but also brutalized the South's whites by turning them into a nation of callous murderers. A Pennsylvanian at Beaufort, South Carolina, saw a slaveowner appear in camp to demand return of his seven slaves. When the contrabands refused to accompany their owner, he drew his revolver and shot five of them with no more compunction than if he were butchering livestock.[70] Such occurrences convinced many Unionists that slaves had to be freed to fight against their masters. Moral high purpose justified all-out war, while the willingness to use extreme brutality confirmed the combatants' resolve. The revolutionary citizen-soldier possessed the earnestness that Prince Bolkonski had advocated in *War and Peace*. The citizen did not take up arms lightly, but when he did, it was for high principle. When the North went to war, it fought the war like John Brown's raid on a massive scale. By 1863 people's war had become an unrestricted war of retribution against the Southern racist aristocracy and for redemption and liberation for the slaves.[71] Two-thirds of the most politically cognizant Union soldiers favored emancipation, more than double the level of support exhibited by all 613 of the Union soldiers in my sample. The higher the level of political sophistication, the more radical the outlook.[72]

For the Union's politically articulate soldiers, brutality was morally therapeutic and politically enlightening. Brutality was the instrument for expiating the South's sins according to the lights of the Old Testament. The army was the agent of God's apocalyptic vision as it meted out punishment for a people's collective guilt. During the American Civil War, the enemy's guilt was politically defined. Newspaper editors, pamphleteers, and political leaders invoked revolutionary ideologies instead of divine will to mobilize their warriors for a punitive war of "just retribution for [the South's] manifold crimes," wrote an Illinois soldier during Sherman's march.[73] It was an unrestricted war that was fought relentlessly until "the instigators of the accursed & hell begotten treason lie low in their graves."[74] The implacable nature of the war was exemplified by the Union soldiers who hastily inscribed this epitaph on a Confederate grave: "two Johnnys, a worning to all traters caught in arms."[75] The North's soldiers were fighting criminals, outlaws, and traitors who did not qualify for treatment according to the laws of war. They were to be killed and their property confiscated.[76] Myron Underwood, serving with the 12th Iowa, pledged to "kill evry trator that I can."[77]

Brutality was seen as an instrument for spreading democracy and freedom in the South. No doubt much of the talk of politically therapeutic violence to destroy slavocracy in the South was only rhetoric. Yet the drumbeat of this theme in the press and among the radical leaders came to justify brutal measures and morally absolved soldiers of any excesses they may have committed. Studies of brutality in World War II have shown that if repeated often enough and loudly enough, words do often lead to deeds. Like the Red Cavalry of Isaac Babel's short stories about the Russian Civil War,[78] the Union army used extreme violence as an instrument to bring political enlightenment to the benighted South:

> The demoralization, the drunkenness, and the violence of Southern life; the unthriftiness and the hopeless poverty of its laboring white population; the "skeleton that sat at the feast" of every planter, in the fearful shape of *Insurrection;* the recklessness of the young; the hardiness of heart, and bitter ambition of the old, which any one could observe in Southern life; the sensitiveness that winced from the least touch of censure on the sore of their political body . . . all showed that the Southern mind and heart were utterly subverted, corrupted, and turned to froth, to "bitterness and gall."[79]

And when starved and humiliated foes filed out of the fortifications of Vicksburg, a captain in the Wisconsin infantry immediately began to politically indoctrinate the prisoners by ordering his men to read them the Declaration of Independence.[80]

The North's merciless war radicalized its Southern enemies as well, envenoming them against the Northern host.[81] Confederates demonized the enemy too, accusing the North of "wilful crimes" and promising "chastisement" for its deeds.[82] There would never be any peace with the "detestable vagabonds" who destroyed the Southern land.[83] By 1863 some Southern soldiers could no longer bring themselves to socialize with Union troops during informal truces.[84] Passing a rudimentary Northerner's grave, a Louisianan expressed grim satisfaction in knowing the grave would wash away with the next summer storm. When he encountered wounded men in blue, he heartlessly referred to them as "singular looking object[s]."[85] Black prisoners were treated with exceptional brutality; any black troops that fell into Southern hands were killed.[86] For example, a Confederate cavalry unit tied black teamsters to their wagons and burned them alive.[87]

Soldiers on both sides hardened their hearts.[88] When he encountered hostile Southern civilians who called his unit "Yankee sons of bitches," a Wisconsin cavalry sergeant declared he would as soon shoot unarmed civilians as kill a "mad dog." Meanwhile, he was grimly pleased that his occupation force had the enemy's women and cotton.[89] Union soldiers had little empathy for starving Confederate civilians, pitilessly shooing them away from their camps.[90] Southerners reciprocated with equal brutality, flogging a woman slave who had cooked them dog stew instead of pork or diverting themselves at Port Hudson by using wounded and dead in no-man's-land for target practice.[91]

There was no room for compassion in this righteous war between irreconcilable creeds. Even members of the same family turned on each other. Soldiers changed their names rather than share them with traitorous brothers.[92] An Iowa soldier vowed that if his brother turned traitor he would not lift a finger to save his sibling's life. "I am ready for any sacrifice. . . . I am in Earnest," he warned.[93] As the war went on, the increasing savagery of the fighting and growing brutality of the combatants became apparent. Confederate Captain Frank M. Myers described the trench warfare that was hardening his soul. When Union troops, their courage fortified with liquor, were trapped in a captured trench line because they were too drunk to climb back out, Myers's 35th Virginia Cavalry relentlessly bayoneted them by the hundreds. The Virginian exclaimed that "nothing has done me so much good for a long time as seeing the thousands of dead yankees strewed over the country." Myers added: "It does me good to the toes of my boots any time to see a dead yank and you can imagine how much good it does to look at miles of them."[94]

William Foster of the 126th Ohio Volunteer Infantry saw inhibitions restraining the army's cruelty dissipate as the troops plunged deeper into the South. The Ohioan exclaimed that if he were a Southerner, he too would join a guerrilla band to get revenge.[95] Southern people did exactly that. They unleashed guerrilla war against their Northern tormentors and local dissidents. When Confederate General Sterling Price invaded Missouri, he ordered guerrillas like "Bloody Bill" Anderson to carry out depredations in conjunction with his advance. During the campaign, Anderson murdered Union captives in Centralia.[96] "Bushwhackers" had the run of the land, robbing neighbors, killing black troops, and hanging political adversaries.[97] Union forces responded with extreme repressive measures. They shot guerrillas like "wild beasts," adding humiliation to cruelty by making Confederate guerrillas die naked.[98]

Popular hatred characterized the Civil War as artillery shelled ambulance trains and pro-Unionist bodies draped the trees along the roads of East Tennessee and North Carolina.[99] Union troops told Confederate captives to draw lots to see who would be shot in reprisal for atrocities.[100] When General Nathaniel Bedford Forrest captured Union troops whom he suspected of burning homes, he tied them together and threw them into an inferno.[101] After a successful attack during the battles around Atlanta, Southern troops, flush with victory and liquor, went on a howling rampage, cursing and abusing their Union prisoners. Even the Confederate officers participated in the melee; one drew his sword and slashed and hacked a captive while others shot and bayoneted prisoners who straggled.[102] This was not an isolated incident. Escaped Union prisoners accused General Joseph Wheeler of shooting captives as a reprisal for Sherman's plundering in Georgia and the Carolinas.[103] Exchanged Union prisoners brought in reports that General Forrest also had shot straggling Union prisoners and ordered his columns to trample any blue coat who fell exhausted in front of his column.[104] Partisan rangers were particularly cruel. They killed a wounded Union general being evacuated.[105] Confederate soldiers applauded reports that Mosby's raiders hanged thirty Union prisoners.[106] Union troops also abused and murdered captured Confederates. When General Sherman came upon rebel mines blocking his line of march, he organized chain gangs of Confederate prisoners, with preference given to officers, to pull heavily loaded wagons ahead of his columns.[107]

The Confederates reserved special treatment for captured black troops. The Fort Pillow massacre was the most notorious incident. The battle was particularly savage because Tennessee Unionists and black gunners were defending the fort. Major General Forrest, a notorious racist, commanded a large part of the Confederate attacking force; when the assault was over, the number of blacks killed was far out of proportion to the number of whites killed. Only 58 of the original 262 Negro troops were able to surrender unharmed.[108] The federal authorities and the army swore vengeance. "Kill all thats my doctren," wrote a sergeant in the 10th Indiana.[109] Fighting became more desperate and merciless.[110] Sherman, a conservative, had opposed the use of black troops because he feared as the war took a revolutionary turn, it would embitter the fighting. He warned Secretary of War Edwin H. Stanton that Fort Pillow would lead to more atrocities. The U.S. Colored Troops vowed retaliation, which in turn would cascade into a chain of barbarous reprisals, according to Sherman.[111]

Confederates refused to give quarter to black troops who tried to surrender at Milliken's Bend in June 1863 and mutilated, beat, and executed black prisoners in Kansas.[112] After the Battle of Poison Spring in Arkansas in April 1864, Southern troops slaughtered four hundred prisoners from the 1st Kansas Colored Volunteers. The Confederate brutality included driving captured Union wagons over the bodies of dead and wounded blacks, and Southern troops boasting of crushing "nigger heads." Even after the prisoners were dead, their bodies were desecrated. They were scalped, stripped, and buried to the waist as their own grave markers. Confederates blamed Choctaw allies for the horrors, but the Southerners were in command and could be held responsible for condoning the atrocities. General John Sappington Marmaduke, who headed the Confederate force, as well as his fellow officers never admitted to the butchery.[113] Confederates also bayoneted hospitalized black troops in Virginia.[114] In the trans-Mississippi theater, Confederate troops were reported to have handed over 480 black prisoners to the tender mercies of their Choctaw allies.[115] An orderly sergeant in Company D, 2d U.S. Colored Cavalry, testified that he had seen Confederates hang black prisoners who had been captured at Plymouth, North Carolina, in 1864. Confederates took still others, stripped them, lined them up naked facing the river, and shot them. The rebel troops dragged some by the neck through the town throughout the night and then killed them, too.[116]

There were also atrocities against black troops on the Richmond-Petersburg front. Firing was more intense against trenches with black troops.[117] Union officials accused the Confederates of using black prisoners of war to toil under fire on the works of Fort Gilmer.[118] Worse yet, a full-scale massacre occurred during the Battle of the Crater. Black troops in Brigadier General Edward Ferrero's division formed the second wave. They were to exploit the gap after troops detonated a mine under the Confederate trenches. But the black troops could not scale the sides of the crater. Rebels seized the advantage and shot and bayoneted the troops despite their efforts to surrender. "This was perfectly right," wrote a Confederate participant, adding, "I have always wished the enemy would bring some negroes against this army. I am convinced . . . that it has a splendid effect on our men."[119]

With politically and racially inspired brutality against enemy soldiers came atrocities against the civilian population.[120] "Gut and destroy as you go and let the Niggers run" became the watchword of the Union's invading columns.[121] At first, when Union officers opened an area to plunder, the conservative high command bitterly opposed the "gut and destroy" policy. When Colonel Ivan Turchin, commanding the 19th Illinois, opened Athens, Alabama, to plunder for two hours, regulars like General Carlos Buell were outraged. Buell ordered Turchin court-martialed; instead, the Republican administration promoted Turchin to brigadier, and his admirers presented him with a sword. By 1863 the

The results of a Confederate "hard war" during an incursion into Pennsylvania in September 1864. Chambersburg's main street after its destruction. Alfred H. Guernsey and Henry M. Alden, *Harper's Pictorial History of the Great Rebellion* (Chicago: McDonnell Bros., 1868), 2:709.

war against the citizenry was in full swing. Brigadier General Frank Blair Jr., commanding a federal force in the Yazoo Delta in the spring and summer of 1863 destroyed more than one million bushels of corn and other commodities in the area.[122]

Union commanders routinely reported results of the "extreme repressive measures" against the civilian population of the South. They tallied the number of barns destroyed, they recorded how many mills burned, they reported how many crops were set afire, and they numbered the livestock driven off. A report from Major General Philip H. Sheridan in the Shenandoah Valley informed Grant that after the troops finished, there would be "little in it for man or beast" to subsist on between Winchester and Staunton.[123] Union generals ordered details to destroy "every house, store, and out-building" except churches or property belonging to known Union sympathizers. The Shenandoah was turned into a "barren waste."[124] The Union troops were zealous about their work. Not only did they destroy crops, homes, barns, and railroads, but they also bombarded civilian targets, burned and sacked towns, and even set fire to institutions of higher learning, like the College of William and Mary. They also pillaged public libraries and destroyed Confederate soldiers' homes.[125]

Whether by reprisal or by order, Confederates committed their share of destruction, plundering and burning Chambersburg, Pennsylvania, and carrying out merciless operations against the dissident population in East Tennessee.[126]

By 1864, the campaign of systematic brutality and pillage against Southern homes began to achieve its purpose. Confederate home-front morale was declining. The Southern society's ability to provide for its army was withering.

The first indications of this decline appeared in the trans-Mississippi, where the depredations had been going on the longest. The governors of the area held a conference at which Texas delegates suggested a separate peace. Arkansas considered a scorched-earth policy after moving its entire population west, leaving guerrillas behind to harass the invaders.[127]

Combatants in a people's war used extreme measures to undermine enemy civilian morale while raising their own society's spirit and destroying enemy resources. Violence had a strategic and a political purpose by tailoring strategy and tactics to political considerations. Even if, for example, an objective were militarily infeasible and even reckless, the political benefits from gaining such an objective might have outweighed the military costs. Major General Nathaniel Prentiss Banks's Red River expedition, for instance, may have been militarily ill advised, but it served a useful political purpose for the Lincoln administration, which no doubt had heard the talk of a separate peace in Texas.[128] If Banks had reached his objective, he might have prodded Texas back into the Union.

Shoring up home-front support for the army and the government's war aims meant advancing the war's high idealistic purpose. Fighting to free East Tennessee from Confederate oppression may not have been militarily significant, but it generated moral enthusiasm and strong popular support. There was much sympathy in the North for the loyal East Tennesseans, who had resisted secession and had sent many regiments to fight on the Union side. Union soldiers were moved by their plight. In Memphis, a Missouri federal watched Tennessee refugees waiting in the rain on the Memphis levee for transport north. They had lost everything and had nowhere to go; the children were ill and the whole miserable lot verged on death. Nearby, he observed another pitiful sight, wounded soldiers lying on the open decks of a steamer. Both the refugees and the wounded were sunk so deep in their misery that they could not muster groans or lamentations. "When shall these horors sease?" the soldier asked himself disconsolately.[129]

While Major General Buell never came to grips with the political and emotional dimensions of the struggle,[130] citizen-soldiers almost innately comprehended the political advantages of certain objectives. For example, they not only understood Vicksburg's military significance but also appreciated the economic benefits of opening the Mississippi to commerce from the Northwest to the Gulf. They also realized that the economic benefits would undercut support for Copperheads in the Northwest.[131]

Selecting politically significant objectives also bolstered morale by focusing anger against the enemy.[132] Liberating regions where dissent was strong and where the occupier had used a heavy hand highlighted the oppressive nature of the enemy's government. It generated popular hatred and kindled support for retribution. East Tennessee, western Virginia, and portions of Missouri were such regions. They had loyalist movements providing fruitful ground for fifth-column operations. Conversely, Southerners lamented the plight of Maryland, Missouri, and Kentucky under the Union's yoke. Even deep in the South, the Union's amphibious operations in Florida had political aims, seeking to prepare the ground for installing a reconstruction government similar to those in Louisiana and Arkansas.[133]

Military strategy was also politicized in order to generate electoral support for the war party. Politically articulate soldiers among the rank and file comprehended this dimension of strategy in the war. For example, Confederates hoped that the approaching election in the North would stay Grant's hand and save Petersburg in fall 1864. A member of Purcell's Battery believed that Grant would put off further offensive operations until after the presidential elections because a costly defeat might jeopardize Lincoln's chances.[134] Other Confederates drew different political conclusions. When the enemy launched assaults against Richmond in November 1864, Confederates reckoned that Lincoln needed successes to improve his electoral chances. Southerners realized that if Lee could beat Grant in the field, McClellan could defeat Lincoln in the election and open the way for a negotiated peace.[135] Confederates in Atlanta also perceived the political stakes of the Union siege. Republicans needed a victory to win the election, and Confederates believed that a Lincoln electoral victory would mean four more years of war.[136] Illinois sergeant Day Elmore saw a close tie between the conduct of the war and Hood's offensive in Tennessee, which Elmore believed was more to help McClellan's electoral prospects in the North than to recapture Nashville. Hood was simply electioneering for McClellan.[137] Confederates knew that they had to hold onto as much territory as possible. Even if this strategy was militarily faulty, it was politically astute because it would strengthen the North's peace party.[138] Soldiers understood why a successful invasion of the border region, such as Lee's autumn 1862 incursion into Maryland or Bragg's invasion of Kentucky, coincided with congressional elections. They hoped that James Longstreet's 1863 fall offensive would affect Lincoln's political fortunes and help Clement L. Vallandigham, the Democratic peace candidate in the Ohio gubernatorial election.[139] Union soldiers also reckoned that Hood's desperate attacks around Atlanta strove to deprive Lincoln of a prize he needed to win support for a second mandate.[140] When the offensive failed and Hood moved north to invade Tennessee, one of his men still saw political benefits arising: "If we ar just sucesfull in this move I think it will shorten the war to a great extent. It will defeat Linkhon alection."[141]

Destroying the enemy's capability to wage war was another political dimension of the fighting style of people's armies. The war against the enemy society relegated civilians to combatant status when it served political or economic purposes.[142] As early as 1862, civilians were subjected to new levels of privation. Inspired by Secretary of War Stanton, Major General John Pope signed a general order calling on the Army of the Potomac to live off the country and to carry out reprisals against the civilian population living within a five-mile radius of rebel acts of sabotage. The order further commanded that all civilians be rounded up in the army's zone of operations and be told to take the oath. Those who resisted would be pushed through the lines to burden the Southern economy and disrupt its social structure.[143] Though such orders were generally ignored early in the war, in later stages, armies lived off the country and drove people from their homes, as in Missouri, for political reasons like refusing to take the loyalty oath.

The idea of waging total war by making enemy society a target dismayed leaders like McClellan, Buell, and Meade, but in 1863 military and political necessity prevailed over chivalry. Targeting society was the only way to subdue a large hostile population and undercut its ability to sustain its army. Soldiers and civilians were ahead of the high command on this question. They were quicker to advocate a no-holds-barred fight. By early 1863, soldiers like Robert Gooding, a Missouri Unionist who had enlisted in the 59th Illinois, believed that only a war of annihilation would bring the South to its knees. Only confiscating rebel property would force them to submit. Furthermore, such a merciless war would serve a domestic political purpose by discouraging dissenters. After the war, Gooding advocated turning the army against the Copperheads in the North.[144] The public added its pressure for all-out war. Newspapers and public rallies called for a war of retribution and expressed impatience with military delay and overscrupulous generals.[145]

Scorched-earth campaigns during the French Civil War in the Vendée in 1794, in Spain in 1808, in Russia in 1812, and during the American Civil War denied provisions to an enemy army when the invader was in the heart of enemy territory and beyond his supply bases. A systemic scorched-earth policy denuded certain counties of Missouri, the Shenandoah Valley, and other areas of food and fodder.[146] The North also tried to seize parts of the South to glean manpower. Confiscating slaves deprived the South of much-needed labor.[147] Union cavalry was soon raiding slaveholding areas to liberate the black population and bring them north. Such raids also forced the South to spread its soldiers among many garrisons to protect slaveowners' interests.[148] The strategy took a revolutionary turn when Sherman issued Special Field Order 15 in January 1865, which directed his troops to seize lands in Georgia and South Carolina from white opponents of the administration and to repopulate the area with pro-Union poor whites and freed slaves. This measure would take away the ruling class's economic power and provide a social and economic bulwark against any efforts to undo Reconstruction.[149]

Finally, the North also tried to undermine enemy morale by targeting population centers. The Union navy bombarded Charleston, the army shelled Atlanta, and batteries fired on Petersburg. The Yankees were the "most God-forsaken wretches on the face of the earth" for making war on the civilian population, exclaimed a rebel soldier as the shells shrieked overhead.[150] The Union appeared to have adopted a policy of *schrecklichkeit* to terrorize and demoralize the people. Confederate soldiers eagerly anticipated the opportunity to take the war to the Yankee populace. Said a Virginia artilleryman: "I am jubilant at the idea of getting into Maryland again & may the God of Battles give us strength to maintain our ground when we get there & to show the vile Yankees there & in Pennsylvania what War is. I believe the only way to end the war is to carry it into the enemy's country. There is one thing certain—I intend to live well when I get up there among those rich *Pennsylvania Dutch.*"[151]

Both sides realized that the outcome of the war depended as much on the enemy society's morale as it did on its army's military success at the front. The home front was the last and most important political dimension in the war between people's armies. The Civil War in America never reached the scope and intensity of violence against the civilian population that occurred in European people's wars in the nineteenth and twentieth centuries. However, in all these people's wars, the same trends appeared. Armies warred on civilian populations, politics often dictated strategy, and the warring parties destroyed the other sides' industrial capabilities. As the Civil War progressed, the heated rhetoric influenced the behavior of the more politicized soldiers. Soldiers were following the editorials exhorting them to show no mercy to the enemy. This study tabulated the responses of 294 highly politicized soldiers who commented on the way the war was being fought and found that they were twice as likely (33 percent to 16 percent) as all 1,013 soldiers in the sample to call for a hard war. The soldiers quoted here show how some of the more politicized soldiers were receptive to this angry public discourse, and, on occasion, they took their generals' utterances at their word. They applied their orders to live off the land and punish the evil enemy with zeal, and they vented their anger against hostile citizens, believing that all these actions could be condoned for political reasons.

8 The War against Dissidents

THE HOME FRONT AND ITS SOLDIERS

Marshal Bugeaud, a veteran of Napoleon's campaigns, underestimated the importance of home ties. He maintained that strong attachments to their homes would prevent the army from making recruits into truly effective soldiers. He advocated, like most regulars, that the soldier should be severed from his community so that he could more easily internalize the military ethos. Recruited locally, citizen-soldiers in the American Civil War relied more closely on the home front to sustain morale than did regular troops. Short-service troops did not have as much time to develop strong ties to their units and to foster the type of regimental pride that motivated professional armies; consequently, citizen armies went to war carrying home-grown political beliefs with them, and they relied heavily on their parent society to keep up their spirits. The soldiers were aware that their conduct at the front was being watched back home. Word was getting back to the people of their community through reports from soldier correspondents and men on leave. Wanting to return to live and work among his friends, neighbors, and kinfolk, the Civil War soldier feared returning with a blemished reputation. Even when the distance grew between the citizen-soldier and his community, it was due less to the soldiers' detachment from the homefolk than to the perception that the people back home had lost respect for their men. Like Australia's locally recruited army fighting at Gallipoli in 1915, officers in the American armies of the Civil War were known to report home the names of men who had shirked their duty in an engagement.[1]

The New Model Army of the English Civil War was the seventeenth-century precursor of the people's armies in the American Civil War.[2] The words of one of its soldiers set forth the importance of a citizen army's interest in political issues, particularly war aims: "We are not a mercenary army, hired to serve any arbitrary power of the state but called forth and conjured by the several declarations of Parliament, to defence of our own people's just rights and liberties. . . .

We think we have as much right to demand and desire to see a happy settlement, as we have to . . . the common interest of the soldiers."[3]

Political relations between the civilian society and its soldiers became a tacit social contract.[4] The contractual relationship between society and its soldiers first emerged during the French Revolution, when a group of officers wrote: "Every French citizen is born free. In becoming a soldier he sacrifices his liberty, and possibly his life, for the freedom of all, for the safety of their lives and property, and for the glory of the country. From that moment the country contracts obligations toward him and these obligations bear on his personal existence and the consideration that is due him."[5] The Jacobin government in the French Revolution showed concern for the welfare of its soldiers and their families. It made sure to reward them for their sacrifices. In February 1793 the National Convention set aside émigré property valued at 400 million livres for pensions, bonuses, and family allowances.[6] The same contractual obligation existed in the American Civil War. Local governments aided soldiers' families. County commissioners provided one dollar a week for each soldier's family.[7] The soldiers expected their communities to stand by them and their loved ones, and when local funds were not forthcoming or when county commissioners cut support payments, the troops branded the officials Copperheads and traitors. The men demanded that the government induct the commissioners into the army, where the troops would show them no mercy.[8] When Confederate General Gideon J. Pillow learned that his men were complaining that the local authorities were not providing for their families, Pillow threatened to furlough his men for winter.[9]

The men at the front also counted on their home communities to share the sacrifices. Soldiers who had just defended Pennsylvanians at Gettysburg were outraged when its inhabitants gouged troops fifty cents for a loaf of bread.[10] Arkansas soldiers grew angry at reports that their people were refusing to accept Confederate money. Yet these same people paid bounties for their soldiers' lives with Confederate specie.[11]

Citizen-soldiers' reputations were hostage to their parent community. Their regiments were the progeny of the hometowns; like most eighteenth- and nineteenth-century manpower systems, the units were recruited locally. An Illinois soldier promised he would send "a list of all the names of the men and officers of Co. G, 48th O.V.I. and what they are doing and who has deserted . . . exposing them to the public."[12] The tradition was defined in the country's most important public documents.[13] The Virginia Declaration of Rights, Article 5 of the Articles of Confederation, and Article 2 of the U.S. Constitution of 1787 proclaimed that citizen-soldiers organized in militia companies would protect the country in a national crisis. Communities often made singular efforts to mobilize their youth, especially at the outset of the war; for example, Arkansas, with its population of only 324,000, managed to muster twenty regiments in the first four months of the war.[14]

Communities used an array of social pressures and inducements to prod youth into the ranks when patriotism alone did not suffice. "It was simply intolerable to think that I could stay at home, among the girls, and be pointed at by the soldier boys as a stay-at-home," recalled Leander Stillwell before joining the 61st Illinois Infantry.[15] Local business leaders even funded units at their personal expense; a wealthy New Orleans merchant named Querouze organized and equipped the Orleans Guard (designated the 13th Louisiana).[16] This was a major expense; an infantry unit cost more than forty thousand dollars to pay and equip for three months.[17]

The local recruitment system was the only rapid way for organizing and motivating short-service troops. Lacking national cadres in the beginning of the war, the country had to rely on local ties to hold the men together until their military experience forged other bonds.[18] The role of local communities in recruitment declined in the twentieth century as more of the mobilization process was taken over by the national authorities.[19]

Equally important was the supporting role that the community provided to the front in services and material for the troops in the field.[20] A government that was too poor or stingy to clothe its soldiers did not deserve to win the war, in the opinion of an Arkansan citizen-soldier.[21] When society failed in its duty, so did its army. Arkansas was among the first southern states to experience difficulties providing for its militiamen and their families. Prices skyrocketed when transportation down the Mississippi was blocked. Harvests also were poor because of labor shortages. County governments lacked the revenues to alleviate the plight of the soldiers' dependents; making matters worse, price controls on farm products impoverished rural families.[22] Local provisioning became too burdensome for many small communities in the South. The army responded by confiscating supplies. It seized poor farm families' meager stocks in lieu of taxes. These draconian exactions eroded support for the Confederate government.

Towns also provided their troops succor on the battlefield. After the battle at Shiloh, communities chartered steamers with medical personnel and supplies to help the army. Unfortunately, resources were not used efficiently. Cities and towns often gave priority to their own troops. Fortunate was the wounded man who was taken in another state's hospital.[23]

A third obligation that fell upon the home front was to sustain army morale and bolster the soldiers' commitment to the cause. Communities continued to nurture a sense of civic duty among their citizens in the field, reaffirming the citizen-soldier's responsibility even after he left home. Communities were concerned that their men not lose the values that had underpinned their lives before they joined up.[24] Second Lieutenant John W. Baldwin, from an Ohio farming family, illustrated the community's moral nurturing role. He assured his wife, Gussie, that he would not let the army corrode his character now that he had "gone a soldiering." He pledged that he was comporting himself like a good Christian, just as he had at home. He also promised his wife that he would never take a "partnership" with anyone else. He told her she could check with his neighbors serving under him in the same company to prove that he was following the straight and narrow path.[25]

Military sociologists have cogently argued that a military organization must instill the parent society's values in order to maintain morale.[26] In open societies like the Confederacy and the United States, much of the indoctrination was instilled by local means. The army did not need a national system for assuring the men's political motivation.[27]

The last and most important role that the home front had in supporting its army was to indoctrinate its soldiers to fight zealously for the cause. The Roundhead forces in the English Civil War were among the first people's armies to systematically indoctrinate their troops. Parliament dispatched preachers to minister to the troops. Oliver Cromwell devoted as much time to selecting preachers to motivate his troops as he did to finding good officers. He was convinced that a people's army that prayed well also fought well.[28] Later, the new secular fighting faiths in the eighteenth and nineteenth century had civil agents instead of preachers. The French revolutionary government sent *représentants-en-mission* to spread its ideas, while in the American Civil War state and local authorities sent delegations to the camps to speak to the troops or to distribute pamphlets and provide politically reliable newspapers.[29]

Friends, neighbors, family members, and even children had to share the army's devotion to the cause and its hatred for the enemy. Colonel Laurence Massillon Keitt of the 20th South Carolina Regiment wanted his children to be brought up to hate the North, telling a friend shortly before dying at Cold Harbor: "I teach my children daily to hate the Yankees; I tell them of noble kindred slain, point to all the maimed that throng the streets and their gallant cousins— alas, life long cripples—and say, My, children, the Yankees did this."[30]

The community had to control groups and individuals who wavered in their support for the cause because the army demanded strong repressive measures against dissenters and "croakers," who were blamed for compromising the war effort.[31] Communities at war develop "an observation-and-reporting system" to eradicate politically deviant groups and impose correct social and political attitudes.[32] The soldiers feared that the community would ostracize them if they failed to show courage at the front.[33] For its part, if society did not support the ideals for which its soldiers were fighting, its bonds with the army frayed and ultimately broke, sending morale plummeting. Since a people's army relied on its parent society for moral support, when backing failed to materialize, the army too felt betrayed and orphaned from the parent society. The army's efforts seemed unappreciated and its cause misunderstood.[34] If the political leadership tolerated dissent and partisan bickering, politicians would have to answer to the army. "If this army dont all die in the service," wrote an Ohio soldier, "there is one thing mighty certain. There are some men now riding high horses in the offices & councils of the country who will catch particular hell when the war is over."[35] In their dealings with the parent society, soldiers put great store in assurances that their communities were standing by their obligation to the army and the cause. Soldiers like the Texan serving in the trans-Mississippi theater welcomed reassuring letters affirming that people were as unyielding as the army. "You know or outh to know," wrote a soldier's friend, "that I never believed a word of the Peace Arrangement." He agreed that Lincoln's true aim remained the same: "murder, devastation, desolation and subjugation" of the South.[36]

The army needed society's reaffirmation of its commitment to the cause, which meant that civilians could not tolerate political dissent. A soldier explained to his friends at home how they could identify traitors: they were those who criticized the administration, who harped on the constitutionality of emergency measures, who criticized the governing leader, or who opposed conscription.[37] The soldiers reasoned that when a democracy mobilized its army, the army embodied the community's general will. Thus, civil society had to emulate the army and maintain moral and political discipline. The army demanded political conformity at home. Soldiers expected the same disciplined cohesion among people back home as prevailed in the army because only unity would bring victory.

Imposing political conformity was easier in mid-nineteenth-century America than in modern America. For one thing, the country was ethnically and culturally more homogeneous. Moreover, both the North's and the South's populations lived mainly in small towns, where it was easier to impose social cohesion by relying on a neighbor observing and reporting. There was little private space in the small-town America of the Civil War. Everyone knew their neighbors and who they met in church, at festivals, or at election rallies. In a small tightly knit community with a dense network of relationships, it was easy to monitor inappropriate attitudes and suspicious conduct.

The army expected local leaders and opinion makers to bolster morale and generate strong support for the war back home. Soldiers read local newspapers and chastised any editor who lacked the requisite patriotic zeal.[38] They followed political events at home and read their leaders' speeches.[39] Troops also sought

War against the dissidents on the home front. Mob attacking a Massachusetts editor who expressed sympathy for the South. Paul F. Motteley and T. Campbell-Copeland, ed., *Frank Leslie's The Soldier in Our Civil War* (New York: Stanley Bradley Publishing Co., 1895), 145.

news from home on the political attitudes of friends and relatives. "I am sorry that you found the Washington relatives so disloyal," wrote a Connecticut surgeon, "for I think they are to be pitied for the narrow views they take of our government and institutions. It is really ludicrous to see the shifts the Northern traitors are driven to in trying to manage popular opinion."[40]

The soldiers also demanded that society prove its dedication to the cause by furnishing enough replacements to fill gaps in the ranks. They railed against the rich who hid behind exemption laws or who could afford two thousand dollars for substitutes.[41] One Unionist chided those who were avoiding military service: "Are they afraid of a little danger of hardship? If they are, they are not fit to be called *free Americans.* I would hate to have people think I was afraid of Rebel bullets and if the young men at home are not willing to take their part of the danger. . . . They need not cry 'Nigger War' to shirk their responsibility."[42]

Both the army and the citizenry rejected those who shirked their duties, expecting units to do their duty and never bring disgrace on their communities. When a captain in the 17th Connecticut behaved dishonorably at the battle of Chancellorsville, the rank and file drove him out of the army and told him that they hoped that "the folks at home would treat him as such."[43] The men in the ranks also reported thieves and deserters to the people back home, calling on their communities to help track miscreants down and flog them for betraying their comrades and fellow townsmen. Citizen-soldiers who would not fight for their hearths ought not have any. Malingerers and draft dodgers merited only a prison cell.[44]

While purging their ranks of men who were derelict in their civic and military duty, soldiers also turned to the community to drive out the disloyal elements at home. Dissenters undermined morale in the army. They spread defeatism and incited desertion. A petition by North Carolina troops in the Army of Northern Virginia demanded that the community take action against traitors: "We believe that the spirit of discontent among our soldiers owes its birth and growth to the influences of those of our citizens at home, who by evil causes and by fear have been made to despair of the success of our cause, and are constantly, while the soldiers are on furlough and through the mails, instilling into them opinions which too often culminate in desertions. We are led to this conclusion by letters frequently intercepted addressed to those who have deserted."[45]

Morale, North and South, declined in 1863, and the armies received reports of disaffection and despair. In the North, the Copperheads were becoming more vocal. Clement L. Vallandigham's allies demanded a prisoner exchange with the South: Lincoln for Vallandigham.[46] Opponents of the war alleged that the abolitionists were ready to let ten white men be killed to free one black. It had become a war "for the niger and not for the Constitution and the Union."[47] There were reports reaching the troops that the Democrats were sabotaging the draft. Their families wrote of night-rider depredations, and fear pervaded communities along the Ohio River and the Missouri. Meanwhile, letters to Southern soldiers spoke of shortages and civilian disaffection.[48]

The troops demanded that the people back home bolster their courage and take stern measures against backsliders. Copperheads in Pennsylvania should be crushed; otherwise, Lee could invade and gain succor from the disaffected population. Soldiers asked why civilians were not curbing such traitorous activities. Why did people not round up traitors and shoot them?[49] "Is a drop of Blood left" in the veins of the men back home to confront these traitors? If not, "let the women help," wrote a Wisconsin corporal serving in Louisiana.[50] The army had enough on its hands fighting traitors on the battlefield; it was up to the men back home to stamp out their traitors. Soldiers also did not believe that the government should allow "every Fop Editor of a penny Sheet" to slander the government.[51] The rank and file reproached Richmond and Washington for restraining the military from dealing more forcefully with political opponents. For example, Union soldiers believed that Lincoln made a bad mistake when he revoked General Ambrose Burnside's order. As commander of the Department of the Ohio, Burnside had suppressed the *Chicago Times* for publishing anti-administration editorials. Siding with the radicals, the soldiers and their families also demanded that Vallandigham be imprisoned or shot. Deporting him south would leave him free to spread Copperhead venom. Lincoln's failure to adopt a sterner repressive policy opened the way for Vallandigham to run for governor in Ohio. In a letter to New York Governor Horatio Seymour from the U.S. gunboat *Exchange,* moored at Cincinnati, Vallandigham claimed that his arrest and deportation would backfire on Lincoln. They would not keep him from issuing statements from the South or from continuing his campaign for a negotiated peace.[52] The troops wanted stronger measures against William W. Holden and Vallandigham and lesser traitors. Whenever the people back home heard a "traitor letting loose his sympathizing slang, they should *bust his crust,*" wrote an irate Iowa captain.[53]

The people back home responded to the soldiers' demands for remorseless prosecution of political dissidents. They echoed calls that all "treasonable sheets" be confiscated and their writers and editors be arrested, and they called for special military tribunals or commissions to impose summary justice against all those who were not wholeheartedly behind the war.[54] During the 1863 Northern elections, soldiers petitioned to help the people at home by bringing their ballots to fight the Copperhead "polecats." In Missouri, where the Copperhead threat was palpable, Democrats and soldiers walked to the polls with their sidearms at hand.[55]

Whether they voted at home or in the field, the troops exercised political influence over their communities. Soldiers demanded that communities show no tolerance of dissidents. They wanted their families and neighbors to wage their own wars against political opponents at home. Citizen-soldiers were transforming politics into a war where the political opposition was likened to the enemy in the field, redefining politics at home. Before the war, conflicts were settled through parliamentary methods, with equally legitimate politicians brokering benefits and adjusting differences through negotiation and compromise. Peacetime politics assumed the legitimacy of each party in the competitive bargaining process. Neither political party could be disqualified and excluded. But the process eroded and finally collapsed in the war's embittered political atmosphere. With the onset of the people's war, politics became an uncompromising struggle between implacable protagonists bent on eradicating their treasonous opponents. Such adversaries did not merit the constitutional protection that governed peacetime parliamentary politics. The terminology was no longer political but military. It was a "war" against "traitors" who were "allies" of the "enemy." The ballot was a "political bullet." A war at home thus paralleled the war at the front. In either case, the enemy was the same; he was a traitor, not a political competitor.

A resolution by Iowa officers and noncommissioned officers reflected the militarized view of politics:

> Resolved,—That . . . WE regret to be compelled to acknowledge that there are traitors upon [Iowa's] soil, and that we hold in greater contempt a cowardly traitor in our rear than we do a manly foe in our front who dares to meet us upon the battle field. That it is the duty of all loyal men to avoid and despise all enemies to our Govt. as [our] Fathers did Benedict Arnold. Resolved that in this crisis there can be but two classes of men "Patriots and Traitors" and as defenders of our flag and Govt.; we will now & hereafter refuse to support, sustain or fellowship with any man who in this great struggle is not emphatically and truly loyal.[56]

"Dad, I am in sober earnest," wrote an Iowa infantryman, "when I say now that you must be careful. Don't waiver in your devotion. . . . Load your gun and strike the traitor before you have to sacrifice one atom of principle. Do they call you an abolitionist? . . . Watch who the sympathizers are and put their names in black and white so that we can settle with them when we come home if it can not be paid to them before."[57] A Wisconsin soldier serving near Lake Providence, Louisiana, gave voice to a similar sentiment. He too believed that the opponents of the war should be excluded from politics. They had no right to have access to the political arena. Opponents of the war were traitors, they should be shot, not debated. "Is there no grit left [in] the inhabitants or be they afraid to use their Shotguns and Riffles . . . [and] hang every Cussed one of the traitors as quick as you would kill a snake?" asked a soldier.[58] "The longer I stay in the Army the worse I feel toward [the Copperheads]," wrote an Iowan, adding that "they have no rights *But to be hung.*"[59] War Democrats also took an uncompromising attitude toward dissidents. An enlistee in the 18th Wisconsin wrote categorically: "If a man is not fer his country these times he had not outh to be allowed to live in it."[60] Soldier pressure for fighting a political war against treason at home radicalized politics. By early 1863 a climate of fear and foreboding pervaded both belligerent societies. Denunciations poured into the offices of adjutants general, governors, and provost marshals.

In the South, entire classes of people were deemed unreliable. There were of course blacks, but people also believed the Irish were of doubtful loyalty.[61] As in the North, political dissenters were singled out for denunciation. For example, when salt output seemed too low at Confederate Point, near Wilmington, North Carolina, Governor Zebulon Baird Vance received letters accusing some of the workers of harboring Holdenite sympathies.[62] Informers also charged that certain individuals were seeking deferments with false claims.[63] Letters accused others of making defeatist statements and undermining morale. A Mr. P——allegedly told some soldiers that they were "whipped & if the soldiers were to all leave & come home the war would end."[64] The targets of these charges scrambled to prove their political reliability to the local authorities. "Recently I learned that some insidious sneaking Scoundrel had written a letter to Gen Clark assailing me in a most false & slanderous manner impeaching my loyalty as a Southern man and insisting that I should forthwith be deprived of the government contract which myself & Son have to furnish wagons," wrote a frightened businessman who probably had outbid a politically connected competitor.[65]

In the North, informers denounced alleged traitors whose sons had fled to Canada.[66] State authorities received lists of disloyal individuals. People informed on "evil advisers" who were in control of local militia companies and were discouraging enlistments. There were allegations that neighbors encouraged soldiers to desert or harbored deserters and draft evaders.[67] Above all, people listened in on neighbors' conversations and reported them to the authorities.[68]

People throughout the country believed that traitors were everywhere and were mobilizing. Copperheads accused Republican Governor John Andrew of Massachusetts of being an enemy of the country and ally of blacks against whites.[69] "Many of your beloved brethren in color,—I mean the niggers, for I believe you are half nigger your self[,]—have seriously died [at the Crater] before Petersburg," chortled an anonymous opponent who signed his venomous letter "Not a Nager."[70] There were rumors alleging organized conspiracies. Confederate prisoners in Ohio were supposedly conspiring with the Knights of the Golden Cross to mount an insurrection in the Northwest and then escape south.[71] In Illinois, "desperate men," many of them from Missouri, were rumored to be preparing an uprising that was to break out during a Confederate invasion.[72] In Indiana, Colonel James G. Jones, acting assistant provost marshal general, sent an alarming report claiming that the Sons of Liberty and other groups were plotting to seize power to prevent Lincoln from being reelected.[73]

Opposition in the North and in the South went beyond rumors. Some opponents of the war did enter into conspiracies and engage in resistance activities. Sometimes the resistance was only passive. In North Carolina, for example, reports told of entire counties signing the Union oath.[74] However, the most feared group in the South were the blacks. Authorities dreaded that blacks might make common cause with poor farmers, deserters, and draft evaders who were hiding in remote parts of the country. A petition from inhabitants of Columbia, South

Carolina, warned the government that an insurrection was afoot and called for extreme repressive measures:

> We the undersigned respectfully call to your attention the names of
> —— as persons who are dangerous to the Community, subversive of all
> discipline among our slaves and hostile to our government.
>
> They have been for many years engaged in trading with and harbor-
> ing slaves. But have conducted their illegal acts with so much cunning that
> it has been as yet impossible to convict them. They have been guilty of
> breaches of the peace. And there have been buildings burnt, the firing of
> which almost the universal opinion of the Community attributes to them.

The petition went on to accuse these elements of avoiding military service and voicing opposition to conscription. The people discussed were generally "hostile to the Government" and would incite a servile insurrection. The petitioners frantically urged the executive council to dispatch armed forces to take whatever measures were necessary.[75]

Political coercion was particularly severe in the South, where class cleavages were deeper, because it coincided with racist economic and political structures. Slavery was the most divisive issue among Confederates. Fears of a servile insurrection and resistance by the poor farmers and mechanics reached paranoic dimensions as the economic situation worsened. It was not only a racial demarcation line but also a social and economic one. The rich, who overwhelmingly supported the war, feared that the servile population would flee north and return as Union soldiers. They also dreaded a populist alliance of blacks and poor classes like the Irish that would foster a populist uprising to challenge the ruling group.[76] The blacks, the poorest and most oppressed, had the greatest reason to desire a Northern victory, though the poor white population, which bore the burden of fighting the war, also had ample cause to question spilling their blood to save slavery for the rich.[77]

These latent common interests shared by blacks, deserters, draft evaders, and poor whites materialized along the coastal waterways of North Carolina. There a jacquerie broke out, pitting poor whites against the rich planter class in Gates, Perqimans, Bertie, and Hertford Counties.[78] The poor organized roving bands called buffaloes in the Roanoke-Chowan River region.[79] The marauders used federal bases along Albemarle Sound as far up as Edenton, North Carolina, and even threatened Weldon and the railroad link connecting North Carolina to Petersburg and Richmond. Rising misery and new defeats swelled the rebels' numbers with draft evaders, escaped slaves, and deserters. As the lower class grew restive, they began a social war within the Civil War. At first, the buffaloes operated in company-sized units. They fought off Confederate enrollment officers and soldiers and attacked large planters. When overwhelming forces arrived, the buffaloes withdrew to the shoreline under the protection of the guns of federal warships. In March 1863 Raleigh sent the 42d North Carolina Troops to suppress the uprising. They burned out many buffalo bases and forced the rebels to flee to the safety of federal warships. But the buffaloes were back in operation the following year, this time at regimental level with regular federal officers seconded to their organizations. With better training and leadership, they drove back the North Carolina partisan rangers who had been sent to hold them in check.[80]

There were also large-scale uprisings in the Appalachian region of the South. There, draft evaders, deserters, and poor farmers organized armed bands to drive off enrollment officers and tax collectors.[81] As with the buffaloes of the North Carolina coast, the North sent money and organizers to help the fifth columns. North Carolina led the Confederacy in the number of deserters at large.[82] The internal social war became extremely bitter, fostering personal vendettas that continued for generations in the South. A member of a Unionist partisan organization challenged local authorities to enter his territory:

> If you ever hunt for us a gin i will put lead in yo god dam your hell fire soll. yo have give people orders to shoot us down when they find us and if yo dont take your orders back i will Shoot yo. If Such men as yo are is Christians of heaven i want to know who is the hippocrite of hell. we have never done yo any harms for yo to hunt for us we will give yo something to hunt for here after. her after when any body Sees us i will know where to watch for you the Secessions neddent to begrudge what we Steel for we are the United States Regulars.... When the Yankees Comes we will go and Show them Some Secess to kill.[83]

In Madison County, North Carolina, which was known for its pro-Union sympathies, the 64th North Carolina Troops conducted punitive raids. They hanged old men and boys suspected of guerrilla activities in a state-sponsored terror campaign.[84]

There was internal war in the Northern states too. Radicals and Copperheads took their fight from the parliamentary hemicycle and the ballot box into the streets. Prowar mobs attacked Copperheads. Troops on leave or assigned duty at home also lent a hand against dissidents. Political rallies turned into fights; politics was transformed into often violent collective actions against traitorous opponents. When Unionists held a pole-raising in Summerville, Illinois, Copperheads countered with their own demonstration to draw away attendance from the Union festival. "I say kill every one of them [Copperheads]," raged the sister of a Union soldier.[85] Usually such inflammatory words ended there, but in some cases things did get out of hand. Demonstrations turned violent and heated words led to blows, even if there was no official policy to arrest or silence every would-be opponent. There was no political dialogue with Peace Democrats. They were enemies who had to be silenced. Their newspapers were purveyors of treason. They were the voice of evil.

Much of the Northern opposition arose in response to the conscription laws. There were draft riots in the large metropolitan centers of the Northeast; in the Northwest, armed bands also posed a serious threat to enforcement of conscription laws. In October 1862 mobs took to the streets of Port Washington, near Milwaukee, Wisconsin, and drove off the draft commissioner and destroyed enrollment records.[86] The next month, another uprising broke out in Wisconsin, where Belgian farmers marched, scythes in hand, on Green Bay. In Washington County, Germans descended on West Bend to attack the draft commissioner. Catholic Luxemburgers denounced Protestant bankers for exploiting the poor and sending them to fight an unpopular war. The governor of Wisconsin had to suspend the draft after Milwaukeeans threatened open rebellion.[87]

In Illinois, reports stated that five hundred Copperheads had tried to rescue some deserters but loyal forces finally drove them off.[88] Copperhead saboteurs were cutting rail lines. They were stealing horses and pillaging farmers around Whitehall. There were reports of two thousand night-riding partisans in the area, leading Unionists to ask for artillery to overcome the resistance.[89] Brigadier General Jacob Ammen, commanding the District of Illinois, warned Governor Richard Yates that the draft could not be implemented without five regiments to back up local militia.[90] Concerned by the reports, Yates requested reliable regiments to suppress the unrest.[91] But after the 1862 elections, the Peace Democrats controlled the Illinois legislature, and they bruited that they intended to confer the Republican governor's military powers on a Democrat-controlled legislative committee. In response, Republicans contemplated breaking up the legislature with a few reliable regiments.[92] Meanwhile, in Missouri in 1863, bushwacker activity drove out pro-Union families: many went north to Iowa.[93] Reports of clandestine arms shipments from Illinois Copperheads to their allies in Missouri further troubled federal authorities.[94]

In this climate of internal war, the bayonet replaced the ballot in politically hostile sections of the North. There were calls for mass removals of dissidents, which paralleled large scale evictions heretofore only perpetrated against non-white populations like the Cherokee. "Not a chicken, nor a hog nor a cow . . . would be left" in suspect areas. Anyone who refused to enlist in the Union army should be driven south.[95]

Republicans also called for a purge of the bureaucracy to oust suspected officials.[96] Treason seemed to be rife in Washington, leading to demands that heads roll. The army proposed creating a special regiment to back up the administration's purge.[97] Congress set up the Potter Committee to investigate the federal bureaucracy. Ultimately, the committee charged more than five hundred employees with disloyalty.[98] It also required that new appointments, even paymasters, postmasters, and provost marshals, be vetted for their political reliability.[99]

Such fear and repression transformed political life. Soldiers were radicalized by the war, and they in turn radicalized politics at home by calling for force in place of debate and compromise. They wanted to make war on dissenters: "Oh! to be there [fighting the draft rioters in New York] with the second brigade of regulars," exclaimed a major from Massachusetts. "I never saw men choke with rage before, as we do here on receipt of this news. Glory and brightness and good news from everywhere, except in our rear, in our own nest, from the north! the luxury of firing into the crowd, of bayoneting rascals, men women and children, of piling up the dead bodies as we have seen them here [at Gettysburg], is what we sigh for now. . . . We have no scruples left about killing a few thousand of such vile Copperheads." [100] The metaphor of war divided the political arena into loyal citizens and traitors. There could be no compromise or negotiation between them. The war narrowed the scope of permissible discourse. For the soldiers and their supporters back home, only those who approved of a hard war and unconditional war aims were deemed legitimate political participants. All others were unreliable at best and traitors at worst; either way, they were to be excluded from the public arena.

The political leadership responded with proposals for a tougher line. There was talk of creating a secret organization of Republican members of Congress to discuss repressive policy. This secret committee would be composed only of the most reliable members of Congress and would correspond with secret affiliates at the state and county levels. It would vigilantly monitor newspapers' editorial policy and would oversee a uncompromising purge of treasonous elements: "One thing the Republican members ought to know—that all *conciliation* or *truckling* to Democrats or border State Unionists is lost on them—you never gain a vote by such a course—they are no part of the government & ought not to have a voice in its destruction." [101] Both the North and South deported some dissenters while silencing others.[102] Assistant U.S. Adjutant General E. D. Townsend told Major General Samuel Peter Heintzelman, commanding the Department of Washington, to deport all inhabitants in pro-Confederate Alexandria, Virginia.[103]

Political repression had several purposes: political intimidation during elections, military coercion against draft evaders and deserters, annihilation of regional dissident movements, and economic coercion through taxes and confiscations. The secessionist government was a jerry-built construct founded on slavery and separatism and thus felt less secure than Lincoln's administration. The Southern landed aristocracy had translated its wealth into political power. It held key local and state offices and it possessed a network that it could use to exclude opponents from the political process. Ipso facto, the elites dominated the instruments of social control, like sheriffs' offices, courts, and election commissions.[104] Meanwhile, the South's poor not only lost many of their kin in battle but also lost out economically. In 1863 land rents rose 500 to 600 percent, and food prices soared at the same rate. Soldiers' pay did not keep up with rising living costs. As the incomes of the lower classes fell behind, there was talk of revolution.[105] There were arrests for "using treasonable language," while President Jefferson Davis called for suspension of habeas corpus.[106] Confederate units like the 45th Virginia Infantry waged war on civilians instead of Yankees. Its soldiers charged dissidents with being "dangerous to the Southern Confederacy" and producing "mischief."[107]

Southern repression intensified when Lincoln issued the Emancipation Proclamation. The war became a revolutionary conflict directed at the South's social fabric. The Confederacy's fear of servile insurrection grew real. In Virginia there were reports of free slaves organizing secret meetings and refusing to work. The authorities increased their vigilance and forbade any meetings by blacks after nine o'clock.[108] Politics took a radical repressive direction in Arkansas, where Harris Flanagin and the hard-liners drove Governor Massie Rector out of office after limiting his term to two years. Flanagin and the conservative legislature imposed draconian conscription legislation that required every able-bodied man to take up arms and patrol the roads for escaped slaves and draft evaders. Military authorities imposed martial law and instituted an internal passport system in Arkansas.[109]

Federal and state authorities feared dissidents would rise up to challenge their power. Governor Oliver P. Morton, who had lost control of the legislature of Indiana to Peace Democrats, apprehended upheavals in the Northwest, New York, and Pennsylvania. These states might open negotiations with the South while excluding abolitionist New England.[110]

Confederate military authorities in Richmond threatened to silence opposition newspapers, though they never actually carried out the threats. The provost marshal in the Confederate capital, Brigadier General John Henry Winder, threatened to shut down the *Richmond Whig*.[111] Such measures intimidated other publishers. There was no room for fence-sitters in this struggle. Each society demanded absolute loyalty to the cause. Winder even suspected that Quakers were a "set of damned traitors."[112] In Raleigh, North Carolina, soldiers attacked the *Standard,* a pro-Holden paper.[113]

In the North, the military also closed newspapers and attacked opponents of the administration. For example, angry servicemen broke up a McClellan election rally in St. Louis.[114] Soldiers also fought Copperheads in South English, Iowa, and attacked Peace Democrats in Canton, Ohio, and Lewiston, Illinois.[115] In Albany, New York, the men of the 5th Wisconsin Infantry of the Iron Brigade broke up a demonstration against the Lincoln administration.[116]

Soldiers were generally more radical than the citizenry, and they were easily induced to attack dissident newspapers like Samuel Medary's Columbus, Ohio, *Crisis,* a pro-Vallandigham sheet that War Democrats like Joseph A. Wright of Indiana and Andrew Johnson of Tennessee considered a thorn in their side.[117] Even the ambulatory wounded at the military hospital at Keokuk, Iowa, lent a hand against disloyal people when they stormed the offices of the *Constitution-Democrat,* wrecked its press, and threw its type out the window. The *Dubuque Herald* also was shut down. In addition, soldier mobs attacked the Mahoning, Ohio, *Sentinel,* the Lancaster *Ohio Eagle,* the Dayton, Ohio, *Empire,* the Fremont, Ohio, *Messenger,* and the Chester, Illinois, *Picket Guard.* In most cases of mob action, however, the newspapers were operating as soon as their staff cleared the debris and repaired the damage. In Greenville, Ohio, Democrats got a taste of the new militarized politics when bands of soldiers attacked them and wrecked their offices.[118] When General Ambrose Burnside shut the *Chicago Times* down and sent soldiers to occupy the premises, the outcry that followed this deed, which occurred just after Vallandigham was arrested, obliged Lincoln to rescind Burnside's order.[119] The *Times*'s editor, Wilbur D. Storey, responded with force by backing his paper's editorial policy content with loaded muskets and steam hoses.[120] Allan Nevins estimated that approximately three hundred newspapers were closed at any one time during the last year and a half of the war.[121]

Military authorities also instituted grand-jury investigations of the most influential New York Copperhead newspapers. They knew that the major eastern dailies' stories were picked up by the local press. By refusing to give some big dailies access to the mails, authorities also could silence smaller newspapers. They also arrested publishers and editors.[122]

The army helped organize these campaigns of political repression. The state adjutants general set up local military committees to serve as conduits between military headquarters and townships and counties. These committees helped seek out disloyal officers, as previously discussed, and the army also used them against civilian opponents of the government.[123] The administration twinned suspension of habeas corpus with military contingencies, claiming it needed to thwart efforts to hinder conscription. Lincoln could countenance draft dodging by ordinary citizens, but he was outraged by resistance by opinion leaders such as politicians and publishers.[124]

The provost marshals in the North and South intensified interference in local politics in conjunction with their efforts to protect enrollment officers and suppress opposition to the draft. They set up networks of informers to keep them apprised of the political situation in their districts.[125] In Arkansas, martial law went so far as to authorize provost marshals to grant or refuse permission to travel outside the state.[126] Provost marshals were backed up by cavalry detachments, by men from the invalid corps, and by local militia. They cast a wide net, hauling in political prisoners with the usual catch of deserters and draft evaders.[127] The South's provost marshals were particularly zealous. They began making arrests almost at will. Secretary of War James Alexander Seddon finally had to call on General Dabney H. Maury, who commanded the District of the Gulf, to restrain his provost marshals' activities.[128]

The military also intervened in politics by appointing election judges and requiring voters take an oath of loyalty. Troops also ostensibly "guarded" polling stations during elections to keep so-called traitors from voting.[129] General Lew Wallace deployed troops in Baltimore in 1864 to intimidate Democratic voters, and Lincoln carried Baltimore by a ratio of five to one.[130] Military authorities helped the administration by censoring newspaper stories.[131] Soldiers arrested judges and members of national and state legislatures for criticizing the government.[132]

With their new political power, the military authorities began to issue a spate of draconian orders against political opponents. There was, for example, Burnside's General Order no. 38 announcing that any declaration of sympathy for the enemy would no longer be condoned.[133] In Missouri, the Headquarters of the District of the Border at Kansas City issued General Order no. 10 empowering the army to seize any politically suspect persons for forced labor. It set in motion the forced removal of women and children from districts where there was guerrilla activity. Moreover, the August 18, 1863, order dictated that all blacksmith shops, furnaces, and fixtures be destroyed to deprive the guerrillas of weapons.[134] Finally, the acting assistant adjutant general ordered that all people not certified loyal to the government be deported and their property seized or destroyed.[135]

The North established military commissions to implement new repressive policies against political opposition. They were special military courts to purge the nation of dissidents.[136] Their work was supervised by Joseph Holt, the army judge advocate general, and James P. Fry, the provost marshal general.[137] Holt did his best to set clear guidelines and limit the excesses of the military commissions. Nevertheless, it was difficult to oversee the actions of hundreds of these tribunals. Generally, the commissions dealt with cases involving civilians or in some cases sutlers, teamsters, and other contractors who were working for the army. Military personnel, however, were subject to courts-martial.[138] The military commissions wielded considerable power, arresting anyone who challenged their authority.[139] For example, when civilians declared that the Lincoln's assassination was a "great and glorious" event, they were arrested, hauled before a commission, and sentenced to imprisonment.[140] The army also silenced opponents by charging them with hampering military operations, encouraging draft evasion, or generally discouraging the troops by making public statements against the war.[141] In the South, the number of arrested Northern sympathizers strained Virginia's prisons.[142]

It is difficult to assess whether this situation was typical. More than four thousand persons were brought for trial before military commissions: is this typical of a democracy or of a repressive government bent on silencing the opposition to its policy? Mark E. Neely Jr. makes the point that most of the work of the military commissions occurred in the border areas and in occupied states against violations of the loyalty oath, guerrillas, horse thieves, and bridge burners. Thus, the commissions were part of the war. They were not usually directed at civil society in the North. Neely estimates that only 5 percent of the trials by military commissions occurred in the North.[143] Nevertheless, this phenomenon indicates yet another oppressive trend. Military repression against civilians was spilling over the Mason-Dixon line and affecting the political process in the North.

Conscription was another military measure that was used against some opponents. Soldiers had long demanded that the conscription law be used to draft dissidents because all those who supported the administration's policies had long ago volunteered. An Indiana sergeant was "jubilant over the conscription bill. . . . I think it will Bring in Some butternuts if we can get them in our reg. I think we can find something far them to Do besize Staying back at home howling about this War."[144] The high command agreed that conscription could be used to break up the Copperhead movement.[145] The army deemed anyone trying to escape conscription suspect and liable to summary execution. Confederate recruiters penetrated the pine woods of north Louisiana in search of deserters and draft evaders, shooting one before the eyes of his wife and children. They burned houses and farms and drove widows and orphans onto the road.[146] In North Carolina, troops searching for draft evaders and political dissidents tortured their wives for information. Soldiers suspended one unfortunate woman from a tree by her thumbs after they had tied her arms behind her back.[147] Other Southern dissenters were beaten as they slowly strangled, hanging from trees.[148] The new militarized politics had no room for debate. No one really can know the extent of torture. Military torture of civilians was not reported unless complaints reached other authorities, as in the case of a British national who had been arrested for desertion and suspended by his wrists. Foreign nationals arrested as bounty jumpers were subjected to "violent cold shower baths."[149] Yet it must be conceded that such measures were far less severe than some of the punishments inflicted on soldiers for lesser offenses. But the very fact that torture occurred was a disturbing trend in civil society.

This repressive policy against dissidents required new organizations to carry out the repression. The regular army in the field could not spare enough manpower to undertake the repression. New paramilitary organizations composed of administration supporters took the field in the battle against politically disaffected elements. These political soldiers were to fight the war at home while the men in the regular forces fought the enemy at the front. The irregulars were often motivated as much by their aversion to going to the front as they were by the desire to protect the cause at home.

In the Confederacy, some states organized partisan rangers for detached duty to chase draft evaders and deserters and to quell dissident activities in pro-Union counties. Like the notorious patrollers, they were supposed to hunt escaped slaves and carry out reprisals against political dissidents.[150] In some states, service with these poorly trained mounted bands had the added advantage of allowing members to keep "enemy" property they seized, though all arms were to be handed over to the state authorities.[151] These irregular forces quickly became a scourge for poor farming families in the Appalachian counties. Some jettisoned all patriotic pretense. They became privateers, robbing trains and smuggling people and goods through the lines.[152]

Paramilitary groups bastinaded, hanged, pillaged, and burned their way across the pro-Union districts of the Confederacy.[153] Loyal Confederates began to complain: "Those guerrilla bands of ours that swarm around Memphis I think caused those people who live around there an immense deal of trouble, whilst they are doing the cause scarcely any good at all. If they were all compelled to join the regular army and to quit prowling all over the country, when they do just about as much harm as the enemy could possible do, it would strengthen our army at other important points and do us much more real service."[154] The pillaging became so extensive that some of their own leaders rejected such methods. From Glasgow, Missouri, even William Clarke Quantrill, who had committed his share of atrocities against political dissidents in places like Lawrence, Kansas, complained to his nominal commander, General Sterling Price, that "Bloody Bill" Anderson had to be brought under army control. He called for investigation of a recent incident in which Anderson's band had massacred defenseless soldiers. "Anderson is a terror to every Southern man in our country and should not be at large," he declared.[155]

During the high tide of the Confederacy in 1863, when John Hunt Morgan's forces moved into Indiana and Lee drove into Pennsylvania, the North feared that Copperheads might unleash an uprising in conjunction with an invasion. "I have never felt more hopeless of the Union," lamented a Union officer.[156] "We deem it our duty to inform you," wrote a pro-Union resident of Illinois, "that we consider ourselves in great danger from invasion. The Rebels having made such progress in Indiana and we are in as equally great danger here. For there are plenty of men among us who would give them assistance and [cheer] their coming with joy. . . . We must take measure of ourselves. We can find the men, can you furnish arms?"[157]

The Union responded by creating new organizations for exerting social control; among such instruments of repression, the Union Leagues were the most conspicuous. They first arose in the Midwest, where the political threat was the most serious.[158] They had several responsibilities, including vetting the state military committees' loyalty (the committees, in turn, were verifying the loyalty of officers).[159] The Union Leagues were semisecret organizations of politically reliable men who reported on administration opponents. The South organized a Confederate League in November 1861, before the North created theirs, but the Southern organization appears to have been an apolitical benevolent society to help soldiers and their families.[160] One Union League founder in Illinois claimed that there were fifty thousand members in Illinois by late 1863 and seven hundred thousand nationwide by 1864.[161] If the league's auxiliary groups, such as the Strong Bands, National Union Associations, and the Women's Loyal Leagues were included, membership numbered almost one million.[162] The leagues formed a national network stretching from the Mississippi Valley to the Atlantic states. They held conventions and maintained contacts with national and state governments.[163] Though they were ostensibly nonpartisan, their members tended to be hard-line radicals who agreed with the politically articulate extreme elements in the army. They shared the politically motivated soldiers' belief in waging an implacable struggle at home and an unrestricted war at the front. Union Leaguers were often from upper-class families who supported Lincoln. They were men of personal probity and public virtue who traditionally conducted civic and business affairs. They believed that dissenters were not only dangerous for their disloyalty but also were the vanguard for popular unrest.[164]

The leagues served as repressive auxiliaries of the government by staging rallies in support of it. They were its "Cromwel[l]ean mace that scattered the traitors," breaking opposition demonstrations, attacking Copperhead newspapers, and demanding that suspect officeholders be ferreted out.[165] They took to the streets to track down deserters, draft evaders, and other political troublemakers.[166] During elections, they canvassed voters, recruited speakers, conducted smear campaigns against opposition candidates, watched the polls, distributed campaign literature, and in general intimidated Democrats who opposed the war.[167]

The authorities sanctioned the leagues' actions and provided them with support and encouragement.[168] Some, like Iowa Governor Samuel Jordan Kirkwood, recruited his personal bodyguard from the Union League, trusting it more than the army.[169] The federal authorities also sponsored Union League paramilitary organizations in conquered regions of the South. In Memphis, Union Leaguers helped purge the area of disloyal elements. The city boasted thirteen hundred members with several hundred Union soldiers serving as "honorary" members.[170] There were efforts to set up a paramilitary League at Fort Smith, Arkansas, to fight the "demon secesh who call themselves partisan rangers . . . The most outrageous pack of Villains this side of Perdition."[171]

The North also established its equivalent of the South's partisan rangers. The Unionists used vigilante groups and local militia companies to subdue opponents. For example, in Missouri there was the enrolled militia. General John M. Schofield organized these units in 1862. Each member brought his own arms and horse. There were—at least on paper—eighty-five regiments and independent companies. They were a poorly led hodgepodge of pro-Unionist Missourians. The bands not only fought guerrillas but also harassed disloyal elements and terrorized pro-Confederate families.[172] Across the Mississippi River in southern Illinois, there were many pro-Confederate counties where loyal citizens were in "poor fix." They beseeched the state government for arms.[173] Illinois loyalists demanded authority to organize home-guard outfits to "help put down this accursed rebellion" for "father Abraham." The companies offered to administer the loyalty oath to neighbors and fight the disloyal elements in their towns.[174] Part of the problem was that neither Lincoln nor his opponents had a clear idea of what constituted disloyalty. There also was no agreement on how to draw the line between the right of a government at war to take measures it deemed necessary to assure its survival and the right of citizens to be secure in their homes and their possessions and to exercise their freedom in the public forum. Notwithstanding *Ex Parte Milligan,* where the U.S. Supreme Court answered the question by declaring that military trials could not displace civilian jurisdiction, the issue has never been completely resolved and perhaps never will be.[175]

The people's war had come full circle. Society had mobilized and politicized the army to fight the great struggle and bring revolution to the enemy. Now the war and the army were changing the society too. Military and paramilitary repression turned the political arena into another battlefield on which political enemies at home were crushed. War, as Prince Bolkonski advocated in *War and Peace,* now was fought relentlessly, pitilessly. It was fought by the entire society and within the society. It was fought to its bloody conclusion by a people's army whose soldiers were in earnest so that never again would arms be taken up lightly. The motivation of the politicized citizen-soldiers, their apocalyptic political vision, their pressure on officers to adhere to the prevailing political orthodoxy, and their willingness to fight a hard war while demanding that the parent society show the same zeal fused and interacted to unleash the trends explored in the preceding pages.

Abbreviations

AFS	*Armed Forces and Society*
AHC	Arkansas History Commission
AHR	*American Historical Review*
AJCP	*American Journal of Community Psychology*
AJPS	*American Journal of Political Science*
AlaDAH	Alabama Department of Archives and History
AOP G & CMO	Army of the Potomac General and Court Martial Orders
APSR	*American Political Science Review*
CHS	Chicago Historical Society
Confed. GO	Confederate States of America General Orders
CW Correspondence	Civil War Correspondence. Letters, Diaries, and Journals on Microform.
CWH	*Civil War History*
CWLC	Civil War Letters Collection
CWMC	Civil War Miscellaneous Collection
CWTIC	Civil War Times Illustrated Collection
DOC GO	Department of the Cumberland General Orders
DUL	Duke University Library
GCMO	War Department. General Court-Martial Orders
HCWRTC	Harrisburg Civil War Round Table Collection
HNOC	Historic New Orleans Collection
IllSA	Illinois State Archives
IllSHL	Illinois State Historical Library
Ind. Adj. Gen. Corres.	Indiana Adjutant General Correspondence

Ind. Adj. Gen. Rec.	Indiana Adjutant General Recommendations
IndHS	Indiana Historical Society
IndSA	Commission of Public Records. Indiana State Archives
IndSHL	Indiana State Historical Library
LC	Library of Congress
LHA Coll.	Louisiana Historical Association Collection
LLC	Lewis Leigh Collection
MC	Eleanor S. Brockenbrough Library, Museum of the Confederacy
MDAH	Mississippi Department of Archives and History
MHS	Massachusetts Historical Society
MSA	Massachusetts State Archives
MVHR	*Mississippi Valley Historical Review*
NA	National Archives
NCSA	North Carolina State Archives
OHS	Ohio Historical Society
OR	*The War of the Rebellion: A Compilation of the Official Records of the Union and Confederate Armies*
SHC	Southern Historical Collection
SHSIa-DM	State Historical Society of Iowa-Des Moines
SHSIa-IC	State Historical Society of Iowa-Iowa City
SHSW	State Historical Society of Wisconsin
TFC	The Filson Club
TSLA	Tennessee State Library and Archives
TUL	Howard-Tilton Memorial Library, Tulane University
UIaL	University of Iowa Library, Iowa City
UNC	University of North Carolina
USAMHI	U.S. Army Military History Institute
VHS	Virginia Historical Society
VSLA	Virginia State Library and Archives
WDGO	War Department. General Orders
WHMC	Western Historical Manuscript Collection
WRHS	Western Reserve Historical Society
YUL	Sterling Memorial Library, Yale University

Notes

CHAPTER 1: The Sword of the Republic

1. George Green Shackelford, *George Wythe Randolph and the Confederate Elite,* (Athens: University of Georgia Press, 1988), 92–96.

2. John Baynes's description of the 2d Scottish Rifles is particularly interesting in his book *Morale: A Study of Men and Courage* (London: Cassell, 1967). A more general description of prerevolutionary Europe's armies appears in chapters 2 and 3 of Geoffrey Best's *War and Society in Revolutionary Europe, 1770–1870* (New York: Oxford University Press, 1986).

3. Maurice Faivre, *Les Nations armées* (Paris: Economica, 1988), 6.

4. E. R. Kellogg, Recollections, USAMHI.

5. Jean-Paul Bertaud, *The Army of the French Revolution* (Princeton: Princeton University Press, 1988), 168.

6. John Ellis, *Armies in Revolution* (New York: Oxford University Press, 1974), 2, 238.

7. Eliot Cohen, *Citizens and Soldiers* (Ithaca: Cornell University Press, 1985), 50.

8. Martin Crawford, "Confederate Volunteering and Enlistment in Ashe County, North Carolina," *CWH* 37 (March 1991): 38; Thomas R. Kemp, "Community and War: The Civil War Experience of Two New Hampshire Towns," in *Toward a Social History of the American Civil War: Exploratory Essays,* ed. Maris A. Vinovskis (New York: Cambridge University Press, 1990), 37.

9. Allan Nevins, *The War for the Union,* vol. 1, *The Improvised War, 1861–1862,* (New York: Charles Scribner's Sons, 1959), 77.

10. John R. Galvin, *The Minute Men* (New York: Pergamon-Brassey's, 1989), ix–x, 3.

11. Richard E. Beringer et al., *Why the South Lost the Civil War* (Athens: University of Georgia Press, 1986), 453.

12. Robert S. Chamberlain, "The Northern State Militia," *CWH* 4 (June 1958): 106–10, 115.

13. Faivre, *Les Nations armées,* 21.

14. Ibid., 23–24.

15. Michael Barton, review of *We Need Men: The Union Draft in the Civil War*, by James W. Geary, *AHR* 97 (December 1992): 1598.

16. James M. McPherson, *Battle Cry of Freedom* (New York: Oxford University Press, 1988), 601; Allan Nevins, *The War for the Union*, vol. 2, *The War Becomes Revolution, 1862–1863* (New York: Charles Scribner's Sons, 1960), 465; Allan Nevins, *The War for the Union*, vol. 3, *The Organized War, 1863–1864* (New York: Charles Scribner's Sons, 1971), 126–27.

17. Hugh C. Earnhart, "Commutation: Democratic or Undemocratic?" *CWH* 12 (June 1966):138; also see Eugene Murdock, "Was It a 'Poor Man's Fight'?" *CWH* 10 (September 1964): 245.

18. James W. Geary, "Civil War Conscription in the North: A Historiographical Overview," *CWH* 32 (September 1986): 213–16, 221, 226; Emily J. Harris, "Sons and Soldiers: Deerfield, Massachusetts, and the Civil War," *CWH* 30 (June 1984):157, 161, 163; Kemp, "Community and War," 45.

19. Eugene C. Murdock, *One Million Men: The Civil War Draft in the North* (Madison: State Historical Society of Wisconsin, 1971), 186.

20. M. I. Finley, *Politics in the Ancient World* (1983; reprint, New York: Cambridge University Press, 1984), 19.

21. Jean-Jacques Rousseau, *On the Origin of Inequality* (Chicago: Encyclopaedia Britannica–Great Books, 1952), 325.

22. Crawford, "Confederate Volunteering and Enlistment in Ashe County, North Carolina," 43.

23. Richard N. Current, *The History of Wisconsin*, vol. 2, *The Civil War Era, 1848–1873* (Madison: SHSW, 1976), 306.

24. John A. Lynn, *Bayonets of the Republic: Motivation and Tactics in the Army of Revolutionary France* (Chicago: University of Illinois Press, 1984), 65–66; Earl J. Hess, *Liberty, Virtue, and Progress: Northerners and Their War for the Union* (New York: New York University Press, 1988), 60.

25. Josiah Benton, *Voting in the Field* (Boston: privately published, 1915), 125.

26. Charles A. Cotton, "Commitment in Military Systems," in *Legitimacy and Commitment in the Military*, ed. Thomas C. Wyatt and Reuven Gal (Westport, Conn.: Greenwood Press, 1990), 52.

27. Robert A. Dahl, *Modern Political Analysis*. 4th ed. (Englewood Cliffs, N.J.: Prentice-Hall, 1984), 8–12; Mark O. Dickerson and Thomas Flanagan, *An Introduction to Government and Politics: A Conceptual Approach* (Toronto: Methuen, 1982), 13.

28. Karl von Clausewitz, *War, Politics and Power: Selections from "On War" and "I Believe and Profess,"* ed. and trans. Edward M. Collins (1833; reprint, Chicago: Gateway, 1962), 169.

29. Wilson S. Miller to father, January 19, 1864, Wilson S. Miller Letters, Federal Collection, TSLA.

30. Erastus Winter Hewett Ellis to Lazarus Noble, June 6, 1863, Ind. Adj. Gen. Corres., IndSA.

31. Dean Sprague, *Freedom under Lincoln* (Boston: Houghton Mifflin, 1965), 163; Alexander Howard Meneely, *The War Department, 1861* (New York: AMS Press, 1970), 154; Kemp, "Community and War," 37.

32. McPherson, *Battle Cry of Freedom,* 326.

33. Joseph T. Glatthaar, *Forged in Battle* (New York: Meridian Books, 1991), 55.

34. Donald L. Lang, "Values: The Ultimate Determinants of Commitment and Legitimacy," in *Legitimacy and Commitment in the Military,* ed. Thomas C. Wyatt and Reuven Gal (Westport, Conn.: Greenwood Press, 1990), 21.

35. Cotton, "Commitment in Military Systems," 52; Omer Bartov, *Hitler's Army* (New York: Oxford University Press, 1991), 10.

36. Lang, "Values," 23.

37. James H. Meteer to Professor Mills, April 18, 1864, Caleb Mills Papers, IndHS.

38. Henry Thweatt Owen to Harriet, July 18, 1863, Henry Thweatt Owen Papers, VHS.

39. Edgar A. Walters Memoir, HCWRTC, USAMHI.

40. T. Harry Williams, "Voters in Blue: The Citizen Soldiers of the Civil War," *MVHR* 31 (September 1944): 198.

41. Faivre, *Les Nations armées,* 13.

42. William H. T. Walker to Braxton Bragg, March 8, 1864, William P. Palmer Collection, WRHS.

43. James Hughes to Oliver P. Morton, December 16, 1864, Ind. Adj. Gen. Rec., IndSA.

44. Katherine Chorley, *Armies and the Art of Revolution* (London: Faber and Faber, 1943), 242.

45. McPherson, *Battle Cry of Freedom,* 65; Barton, review of *We Need Men: The Union Draft in the Civil War,* 1599; Phillip Shaw Paludan, *"The People's Contest": The Union and Civil War, 1861–1865* (New York: Harper and Row, 1988), 177–78.

46. Regarding community ties in the American Civil War, see Reid Mitchell, "The Northern Soldier and His Community," in *Toward a Social History of the American Civil War: Exploratory Essays,* ed. Maris A. Vinovskis (New York: Cambridge University Press, 1990), 80.

47. Ibid., 80, 82.

48. Lizzie to George, May 10, 1861, and January 16, 1862, George to Lizzie, March 24, 1862, George Smith Avery Letters, CHS; also see Sara Billings to brother Levi, September 21, 1864, Sara Billings Letters, SHSW.

49. Louicy Ann May Eberhart, Reminiscences, IllSHL.

50. Mitchell, "The Northern Soldier and His Community," 84.

51. Reid Mitchell, *Civil War Soldiers* (New York: Viking Penguin, 1988): 64–66; also see Mitchell, "The Northern Soldier and His Community," 88–89.

52. Theda Skocpol, *States and Social Revolutions* (New York: Cambridge University Press, 1979).

53. Edwin Leigh, *Literacy in the United States,* annual report of the Commissioner of

Education, prepared for the Secretary of the Interior, U.S. Congress, 41st Cong., 3d sess., 1870, Executive Document 1, pt. 4 (Serial 1450), 468.

Literacy is not the only indicator of political awareness. Soldiers also expressed their political views orally. The campfire, the country store, the tavern, and the public meeting were as important as newspapers, letters, or diaries for expressing political views. Thus, illiterate soldiers could have participated as actively in political discussions as their literate comrades.

CHAPTER 2: *"Les armées délibérantes"*

1. James Jones, himself a regular with the 25th Division in World War II, described how such motivations flashed through the mind of a regular noncommissioned officer during an infantry attack on Guadalcanal in *The Thin Red Line* (1962; reprint, New York: Avon Books, 1975), 243.

2. James Horrocks, *My Dear Parents: The Civil War Seen by an English Union Soldier,* ed. A. S. Lewis (New York: Harcourt Brace Jovanovich, 1982), 67.

3. John Vestal Hadley to Mary [Hill], November 29, 1863, Lilly Library, Indiana University, Bloomington.

4. Henry W. Gay to father, September 20, 1863, Henry W. Gay Letters, CWMC, USAMHI.

5. Polybius, *Histories,* trans. W. R. Paton (London: Cambridge University Press, 1954), 1:257.

6. Plato, *Laws* (Chicago: Encyclopaedia Brittanica–Great Books, 1952), 1:630.

7. Edward Gibbon, *The Decline and Fall of the Roman Empire* (New York: Modern Library, n.d.), 1:541.

8. Niccolo Machiavelli, *Discourses* (New York: Penguin, 1987), 292.

9. Finley, *Politics in the Ancient World,* 13.

10. Robert Franklin Bunting to the editor of the *Telegraph,* August 11, 1863, Robert Franklin Bunting Letters (transcript), TSLA.

11. Charles H. Firth, *Cromwell's Army* (London: Methuen, 1962), 347; Hess, *Liberty, Virtue, and Progress,* 58.

12. John W. Northrop Diary of Prison Life (transcript), November 8, 1864, WRHS.

13. Hess, *Liberty, Virtue, and Progress,* 10.

14. Aristotle. *Nicomachean Ethics* (Chicago: Encyclopaedia Brittanica–Great Books, 1952), 3.8.1116.

15. Hiram Howe Civil War Diaries, SHSIa-IC.

16. Lord Charles Moran, *The Anatomy of Courage* (1945; reprint, London: Constable, 1966), 160.

17. Gerald F. Linderman, *Embattled Courage* (New York: Free Press, 1987), 20–23.

18. Demosthenes, *Harangues,* book 2 (Paris: Société d'Edition "Les Belles Lettres," 1955), "Third Philippic."

19. Machiavelli, *Discourses,* 292.

20. Michael Walzer, *Obligation: Essays on Disobedience, War, and Citizenship* (Cambridge: Harvard University Press, 1970), 77.

21. Thomas W. Hardin to wife [Kate], March 7, 1863, Hardin Family Letters, AHC.

22. William Ward Orme Scrapbook with aphorisms, William Ward Orme Papers, IllSHL.

23. Hess, *Liberty, Virtue, and Progress,* 13; Mitchell, *Civil War Soldiers,* 3–4.

24. Thomas Stuart Garnett to wife, April 5, 1863, Thomas Stuart Garnett Letters (typescript), VSLA.

25. Walzer, *Obligation,* 77.

26. George S. Avery to Lizzie [Little], February 23, 1863, George Smith Avery Letters, CHS.

27. Harvey Graham to wife, March 14, 1863, Dr. Graeme O'Geran Collection, SHSIa-DM; also see George A. Brockway Diary, January 21, 1864, SHSIa-DM.

28. Walzer *Obligation,* 91–93.

29. Ibid., 94.

30. Elijah P. Petty to wife, March 13, 1863, in *Journey to Pleasant Hill: The Civil War Letters of Captain Elijah P. Petty, Walker's Texas Division CSA,* ed. Norman D. Brown (San Antonio: University of Texas Institute of Texan Culture, 1982); also see William Hamilton to parents, n.d., William Hamilton Letters, LC.

31. John H. Burrill to parents, December 18, 1863, John H. Burrill Letters (typescript), CWTIC, USAMHI; David Logan Houser to Malvina, May 21, 1863, David Logan Houser Letters, SHSIa-IC.

32. Ellis, *Armies in Revolution,* 86.

33. Jean-Jacques Rousseau, *On Political Economy* (Chicago: Encyclopaedia Brittanica–Great Books, 1952), 324; also see Simon Schama, *Citizen: A Chronicle of the French Revolution* (New York: Alfred A. Knopf, 1989), 161.

34. Mitchell, "The Northern Soldier and His Community," 80.

35. "Six Rules," Benjamin Hieronymous Diary (typescript), IllSHL; also see Maxims at end of Nelson Purdum Diary, 1863, OHS.

36. Bertaud, *The Army of the French Revolution,* 215; W. J. Reader, *At Duty's Call* (Manchester, England: Manchester University Press, 1988), 78; John Springhall, *Youth, Empire, and Society* (London: Croom Helm, 1977), 71.

37. Day Elmore to parents, February 3, 1864, Lucian B. Case Papers, CHS.

38. Thomas S. Taylor to [sons Johnie and Billie], July 20, 1863, Thomas S. Taylor Letters, CWLC, AlaDAH.

39. Ephraim S. Holloway to wife, January 28, 1863, Ephraim S. Holloway Letters, OHS.

40. Frederick Wildman to son, Samuel Augustus Wildman, March 22, 1864, Wildman Family Papers, OHS.

41. Jesse B. Connelly Diary, May 5, 1863, IndHS.

42. Henry Clinton Forbes to "Fransanna," August 16, 1861, Henry Clinton Forbes Letters, OHS.

43. Benjamin F. Ashenfelter to mother, September 1, 1863, Benjamin F. Ashenfelter Letters, HCWRTC, USAMHI.

44. John W. Baldwin to [wife] Gussie, December 13, 1863, John W. Baldwin Correspondence, OHS.

45. Nathaniel L. Parmeter Diary (typescript), December 18, 1863, OHS.

46. George Phifer Erwin to mother, October 8, 1863, George Phifer Erwin Papers, SHC, UNC.

47. Dewitt Clinton Loudon to Hannah, May 25, 1864, Dewitt Clinton Loudon Papers, OHS.

48. Frederick J. Manning and David H. Marlowe, "The Legitimation of Combat for the Soldier," in *Legitimacy and Commitment in the Military,* ed. Thomas Wyatt and Reuven Gal (Westport, Conn.: Greenwood Press, 1990), 68, 70.

49. Theodor W. Adorno et al., *The Authoritarian Personality* (New York: Harper and Row, 1950), 221–41; Hans J. Eysenck, *The Psychology of Politics* (London: Routledge and K. Paul, 1954), 170–98; Rupert T. Wilkinson, *The Broken Rebel* (New York: Harper and Row, 1972), 282–86.

50. Jean H. Baker, *Affairs of Party: The Political Culture of Northern Democrats in the Mid-Nineteenth Century* (Ithaca: Cornell University Press, 1983), 28–29, 72–74, 80–83, 90, 94, 106–7.

51. Ibid., 29–32, 45, 60.

52. David Brion Davis, ed. *Antebellum American Culture* (Boston: D. C. Heath, 1979), 43.

53. Lydia Maria Francis Child, *The Mother's Book* (1831; reprint, Old Saybrook, Conn.: Applewood Books, 1992), 22, 25, 30.

54. Lawrence A. Cremin, ed. *The Republic and the School: Horace Mann on the Education of the Free Men* (New York: Teachers College, Columbia University, 1957), 16.

55. Anne C. Rose, *Victorian America and the Civil War* (New York: Cambridge University Press, 1992), 21.

56. John Joyes Jr. Diary, November 14, 1864, TFC.

57. David Kaser, *Books and Libraries in Camp and Battle* (Westport, Conn.: Greenwood Press, 1984), 8.

58. Ibid., 3, 16.

59. Cremin, *The Republic and the School,* 7.

60. Ibid., 7–8, 50–51.

61. Ibid., 90.

62. Hess, *Liberty, Virtue, and Progress,* 13.

63. Ibid.

64. Dolores P. Sullivan, *William Holmes McGuffey: Schoolmaster of the Nation* (Rutherford, N.J.: Fairleigh Dickinson University Press, 1994), 149–50.

65. Ibid., 153–54.

66. Ibid., 157.

67. Fred Arthur Bailey, *Class and Tennessee's Confederate Generation* (Chapel Hill: University of North Carolina Press, 1987), 46.

68. Rose, *Victorian America and the Civil War,* 222–23.

69. Ibid., 196–97.

70. Ibid., 197–98.

71. John Blair Diary, March 13, April 9 and 22, 1863, Confederate Collection, TSLA.

72. Kaser, *Books and Libraries in Camp and Battle,* 14–15, 26–29, 47, 78, 80.

73. Rose, *Victorian America and the Civil War,* 200.

74. Kaser, *Books and Libraries in Camp and Battle,* 5.

75. William H. Bradbury to wife, February 17 and 28, 1864, William H. Bradbury Correspondence, LC.

76. *South Western Baptist* (Tuskegee, Ala.), February 27, 1862.

77. *Memphis Daily Appeal,* February 20, 1862; permission for use given by the *Commercial Appeal,* Memphis, Tenn.

78. *Memphis Daily Appeal,* March 1, 1862.

79. Joseph Allan Frank and George Reaves, *"Seeing the Elephant": Raw Recruits at the Battle of Shiloh* (Westport, Conn.: Greenwood Press, 1989), 18–19, 117.

80. Ibid., 137.

81. William Goodrich James to father, September 25, [1864], David Goodrich James Collection, SHSW.

82. Dahl, *Modern Political Analysis,* 8–12; Max Weber, *The Theory of Political Organization* (1947; reprint, New York: Free Press, 1964); Harold D. Lasswell and Abraham Kaplan, *Power and Society: A Framework for Political Inquiry* (New Haven: Yale University Press, 1950); Bertrand de Jouvenel, *The Pure Theory of Politics* (New Haven: Yale University Press, 1963), 30; Dickerson and Flanagan, *An Introduction to Government and Politics,* 13.

83. Clausewitz, *War, Politics and Power,* 169.

84. Dickerson and Flanagan, *An Introduction to Government and Politics,* 90.

85. Robert C. Luskin, "Measuring Political Sophistication," *AJPS* 31 (November 1987): 862. Also see Jacques Van Doorn, "Ideology and the Military," in *On Military Ideology,* ed. Jacques Van Doorn and Morris Janowitz (Rotterdam, Holland: Rotterdam University Press, 1971).

86. Amos A. Jordan Jr. "Troop Information and Indoctrination," in *Handbook of Military Institutions,* ed. Roger W. Little (Beverly Hills, Calif.: Sage Publications, 1971), 354–56. Other pertinent works are: Luskin, "Measuring Political Sophistication," 856–57, 864; Eric R. A. N. Smith, "The Levels of Conceptualization: False Measures of Ideological Sophistication," *APSR* 74 (September 1980): 685–86, which posits that the least politically sophisticated people are those who are unable to conceptualize their situation into broader relationships.

87. Corrected chi square $= 1.38$, df $= 1$; however, there was a 24 percent probability of chance in these findings. Phi, however, only yielded .037, which suggests no directional relationship between nationality and political sophistication.

88. McPherson, *Battle Cry of Freedom,* 689; also see Nevins, *The War for the Union,* 3:64.

89. Corrected chi square yielded 6.39 and .19 respectively, with df $= 3$ and 4 respec-

tively, but with the caveat of a high probability of error that ranged from 17 to 24 percent, it also yielded a weak measure of association, Cramer's V = .98.

90. Corrected chi Square = 22.793, with df = 1, probability of chance = 0, and phi = .15 yielded a noncommittal measure of association between the two factors.

91. James M. McPherson, *What They Fought For, 1861–1865* (Baton Rouge: Louisiana State University Press, 1994), 35.

92. Corrected chi square = 31.94, df = 1, probability of error = 0; again, phi was a weak .18.

93. Luskin, "Measuring Political Sophistication," 861, 867. Also see Lowdnes F. Stephens, "Political Socialization of the American Soldier," *AFS* 31 (Summer 1983): 615–16.

94. Corrected chi square = 0, df = 1, probability of chance is total; therefore, the cross-tabulation is not reliable.

95. Corrected chi square = 1.56, df = 1, probability of chance 21 percent, and phi yielded only .06.

96. Corrected chi square = 33.91, df = 1, probability of chance = 0, and phi was an indeterminate .18.

97. Corrected chi square = 4.06, df = 1, probability of chance .04, and phi .149.

98. Gabriel A. Almond and Sidney Verba, *The Civic Culture: Political Attitudes and Democracy in Five Nations* (Boston: Little, Brown and Co., 1965). Also see Douglas Madsen, "Political Self-Efficacy Tested," *APSR* 81 (June 1987): 572; Marc A. Zimmerman and Julian Rappaport, "Citizen Participation, Perceived Control, and Psychological Empowerment," *AJCP* 16 (1988): 725–39.

99. Letter of Captain F. D. Stone, 11th Regiment, stated that the resolutions were drawn up by officers then read to the regiment for adoption. No mention of any debate or opposition was made. Not one soldier apparently questioned any of it (E. B. Quiner Papers: Correspondence of the Wisconsin Volunteers, 1861–63, reel 3, vol. 9, p. 77, SHSW).

100. Paludan, "*The People's Contest*," 156–57. It is difficult to compare a sense of political effectiveness with the South's enlistment rate, because the Confederacy enacted a draft law very early in the war.

101. Ibid., 11.

102. Alexis de Tocqueville, *Democracy in America* (New York: Alfred A. Knopf, 1980), 1:191–98; Paludan, "*The People's Contest*," 30–31.

103. Humphrey Hughes Hood to wife, February 18, 1863, Humphrey Hughes Hood Correspondence, IllSHL.

104. Corrected chi Square was 21.37, with df = 1, probability of chance = 0, and phi only .15.

105. Philip H. Powers to wife, February 21, 1864, Philip H. Powers Letters, LLC, USAMHI.

106. Constantine Hege to parents, August 2, 1863, Constantine A. Hege Letters, LLC, USAMHI.

107. Beringer et al., *Why the South Lost the Civil War*, 369.

108. Corrected chi square $= 22.80$, df $= 1$, probability of chance $= 0$, and phi $= .15$ shows no strong association.

109. Corrected chi square $= 15.28$, df $= 1$, probability of chance $= 0$, phi $= .19$, suggesting no strong association.

110. Corrected chi square $= 37.46$, df $= 1$, probability of chance $= 0$, and phi $= .12$ reveals no strong association.

111. This number is near the 7.6 percent of 841 Wisconsin soldiers who scored highly on all three measures of political awareness in the previous study.

CHAPTER 3: The Strategic Picture

1. L. F. Davis to father and mother, April 1862, Thomas O. Moore Collection, SHSW.

2. James W. Albright Diary (typescript), June 14, 1864, SHC, UNC.

3. A. A. Johnson to father, May 21, 1863, A. A. Johnson Civil War Letters, AHC.

4. Corrected chi square $= 12.63$, df $= 1$, probability of chance $= 0$; phi scored an insignificant .11.

5. Junius Newport Bragg, *Letters of a Confederate Surgeon, 1861–1865*, ed. T. J. Gaughan (Camden, Ark.: Gaughan, 1960), 153–54.

6. Joseph Kohout to family, June 4, 1863, Joseph Kohout Letters, UIaL.

7. Elias Davis to wife, April 7, 1864, Elias Davis Papers, SHC, UNC.

8. Junius Newport Bragg to Josephine, February 14, 1864, in *Letters of a Confederate Surgeon.*

9. Henry Clinton Forbes to sister, January 20, 1863, Henry Clinton Forbes Letters, OHS.

10. William Biggs to sister, July 6, 1864, Asa Biggs Papers, DUL.

11. James Postell Douglas to wife, May 20, 1864, in *Douglas's Texas Battery, CSA,* ed. and comp. Lucia Rutherford (Tyler, Tex.: Smith County Historical Society, 1966).

12. Edwin W. Bearse to mother, September 23, 1864, Edwin W. Bearse Correspondence, MHS.

13. Humphrey Hughes Hood to wife, September 16, 1864, Humphrey Hughes Hood Correspondence, IllSHL.

14. John A. Hooper to wife, August 11, 1864, John A. Hooper Letters (transcript), SHC, UNC.

15. Martin Malone Gash to sister, February 8, 1863, Martin Malone Gash Papers, NCSA.

16. Robert Patrick, *Reluctant Rebel,* ed. F. Jay Taylor (Baton Rouge: Louisiana State University Press, 1959), 178.

17. Benjamin F. Ashenfelter to mother, January 28, 1863, Benjamin F. Ashenfelter Letters (photocopies), HCWRTC, USAMHI.

18. This statistic has the caveat that the corrected chi square $= 8.64$, df $= 7$, with a probability of chance $= .28$ for the western Confederates; the measure of association was also weak, Cramer's V $= .38$; eastern Confederate troops also did not yield conclu-

sive results: corrected chi square was only 2.39, df $= 3$, with a probability of chance $=$ .495, while Cramer's V $= .21$.

19. Here again, the statistical measures are too weak to give much weight to the findings. For eastern troops, the corrected chi square only registered 8.72, df $= 7$, probability of chance $= .27$, but Cramer's V yielded a more respectable .45 in registering the impact of the regional factor on the soldiers' attitudes toward their generals; among western troops, the results were inconclusive as well, with corrected chi square $= 6.71$, df $= 6$, probability of chance .35, and Cramer's V only .24.

20. Macon Bonner to wife, April 10, 1863, Macon Bonner Papers, SHC, UNC; Zerah Coston Monks to Hattie Rohrer, January 13, 1863, Monks Family Papers, WRHS.

21. George M. Barnard Jr. to father, June 15, 1864, George M. Barnard Papers, CW Correspondence, reel 17, MHS; Burton H. Bristol to cousin Case, November 6, 1864, Lucian B. Case Papers, CHS.

22. George H. Fifer to family, September 14, 1863. Joseph Wilson Fifer Letters, IllSHL.

23. James W. Albright Diary (typescript), June 20, 1864, SHC, UNC.

24. Henry Livermore Abbott to father, July 6, 1863, in *Fallen Leaves,* ed. Robert Garth Scott (Kent, Ohio: Kent State University Press, 1991).

25. James W. Ames to mother, July 19, 1863, John W. Ames Letters (typescript), LLC, USAMHI.

26. Henry Livermore Abbott to father, January 27, 1863, in *Fallen Leaves.*

27. Henry Livermore Abbott to father, May [7], 1863, in ibid.

28. James W. Albright Diary (typescript), September 6, 1863, SHC, UNC.

29. James W. Ames to Fisher, August 2, 1863, John W. Ames Letters (typescript), LLC, USAMHI.

30. George M. Barnard Jr. to father, March 28, 1863, George M. Barnard Papers, CW Correspondence, reel 17, MHS.

31. Robert Hubbard to wife, December 16, 1863, Robert Hubbard Papers (typescript), Civil War Manuscripts Collection, YUL.

32. Joseph Kohout to family, February 4, 1863, Joseph Kohout Letters, UIaL.

33. John H. Burrill to parents, March 21, 1864, John H. Burrill Letters (typescript), CWTIC, USAMHI; James W. Ames to mother, July 19, 1863, John W. Ames Letters (typescript), LLC, USAMHI.

34. Henry Livermore Abbott to father, January 22, 1863, in *Fallen Leaves.*

35. Henry Livermore Abbott to father, May 5, 1863, in ibid.; Nathan Hayward to father, May 12, 1863, William P. Palmer Collection, WRHS; Henry Bruce Scott to Lizzie, May 4, 1863, Henry Bruce Scott Papers (typescript), MHS.

36. William Hamilton to Boyd, June 21, 1863, William Hamilton Letters, LC.

37. Henry Livermore Abbott to father, July 27, 1863, in *Fallen Leaves;* George M. Barnard Jr. to father, July 7, 1863, George M. Barnard Papers, CW Correspondence, reel 17, MHS; George T. Gill to brother John, July 5, 1863, Gill Family Papers, Civil War Manuscripts Collection, YUL.

38. John W. Baldwin to Gussie, November 1, 1863, James W. Baldwin Correspondence, OHS.

39. Emerson Opdycke to wife, October 21, 1863, Emerson Opdycke Papers, OHS.

40. *Jonesboro (Illinois) Gazette,* April 18, 1863.

41. George M. Barnard Jr. to father, June 15 and July 1, 1864, George M. Barnard Papers, CW Correspondence, reel 17, MHS.

42. Daniel Bishard to brother, July 20, 1864, Daniel Bishard Letters, SHSIa-DM.

43. James Austin Connolly Journal (typescript), December 15, 1864, James Austin Connolly Papers, IllSHL.

44. Humphrey Hughes Hood to wife, September 24, 1864, Humphrey Hughes Hood Correspondence, IllSHL.

45. Patrick, *Reluctant Rebel,* 194.

46. Larry J. Daniel, *Soldiering in the Army of the Tennessee* (Chapel Hill: University of North Carolina Press, 1991), 101, 129, 131–32.

47. C. Fackler to sister, March 26, 1863, C. Fackler Letters (typescript), DUL. For other soldiers' attitudes about Bragg, see Judith Lee Hallock, *Braxton Bragg and Confederate Defeat* (Tuscaloosa: University of Alabama Press, 1991), 2:21, 25.

48. Edwin H. Fay to wife, July 10, 1863, in *"This Infernal War": The Confederate Letters of Sgt. Edwin H. Fay,* ed. Bell I. Wiley (Austin: University of Texas Press, 1958).

49. John W. Harris to George, October 13 and November 11, 1863, John W. Harris Letters, Confederate Collection, TSLA.

50. Joseph Branch O'Bryan to sister, July 9, 1863, Joseph Branch O'Bryan Papers, TSLA.

51. Lunsford Pitt Yandell Jr. to [Frank], October 17, 1863, Yandell Family Papers, TFC.

52. Joseph Branch O'Bryan to sister, July 13, 1864, Joseph Branch O'Bryan Papers, TSLA.

53. John A. Johnson to Ella, June 1, 1864, John A. Johnson Letters (transcript), SHC, UNC.

54. Gary W. Gallagher, "Lee's Army Has Not Lost Any of Its Prestige," in *The Third Day at Gettysburg and Beyond,* ed. Gary W. Gallagher (Chapel Hill: University of North Carolina Press, 1994), 2–3.

55. Ibid., 10–11.

56. James E. Green Diary, July 3, 1863, James E. Green Papers (typescript), SHC, UNC.

57. Franklin Gaillard to Maria, July 17, 1863, Franklin Gaillard Letters (typescript), SHC, UNC.

58. Henry Clinton Forbes to sister Flavilla, August 18, 1862, Henry Clinton Forbes Letters, OHS.

59. Corrected chi square = 3.0, df = 1, probability of chance = .08, and phi a weak .05.

60. Samuel Storrow to parents, January 22, 1863, Samuel Storrow Papers, CW Correspondence, reel 9, MHS; also see Robert Gooding to brother, May 19, 1863, Robert Gooding Collection, WHMC.

61. Elias Davis to wife, May 23 and July 8, 1863, Elias Davis Papers, SHC, UNC; J. Kelly Bennette Diary (typescript), July 30, 1863, SHC, UNC.

62. Charles Jackson Paine to father, January 28, 1863, Charles Jackson Paine Letters, MHS.

63. Wilbur Fisk to Editor Freeman, September 25, 1863, Wilbur Fisk Letters, CWTIC, USAMHI; also see David C. Gamble to Governor Richard Yates, August 25, 1863, Yates Family Papers, IllSHL.

64. Jasper Barney to [J. Dinsmore], October 24, 1862, J. Dinsmore Collection, IllSHL.

65. Charles Jackson Paine to father, February 12, 1863, Charles Jackson Paine Letters, MHS.

66. Francis F. Audsley to wife Harriet, May 12, 1865, Francis F. Audsley Letters, WHMC.

67. McPherson, *Battle Cry of Freedom*, 716–17; "Peace to Be Enduring Must Be Conquered," Republican Congressional Committee draft of a position paper outlining its war aims for the 1864 election campaign, William P. Palmer Collection, WRHS.

68. James C. Zimmerman to wife, May 23, 1863, James C. Zimmerman Papers, DUL.

69. Corrected chi square $= .126$, df $= 1$, probability of chance a very high $= .72$, and phi a weak $= .039$.

70. Voleny G. Barbour to Lucian B. Case, November 16, 1864, Lucian B. Case Papers, CHS.

71. Andrew R. Linscott to father, September 2, 1864, Andrew R. Linscott Correspondence, CW Correspondence, MHS.

72. John H. Burrill to parents, September 13, 1863, John H. Burrill Letters (typescript), CWTIC, USAMHI; Peter Eltinge to parents, March 29, 1863, Eltinge-Lord Family Papers, DUL; Benjamin F. Ashenfelter to father Churchman, August 23, 1863, Benjamin F. Ashenfelter Letters (photocopies), HCWRTC, USAMHI.

73. John H. Stibbs to father, March 4, 1863, Stibbs Family Papers, TUL.

74. Tilmon D. Kyger to sister Sarah, October 8, 1864, Tilmon D. Kyger Letters, IllSHL.

75. Benjamin F. Ashenfelter to father Churchman, August 12, 1863, Benjamin F. Ashenfelter Letters (photocopies), HCWRTC, USAMHI.

76. Albert Burton Moore, *Conscription and Conflict in the Confederacy* (New York: Hillary Publishers, 1963); James W. Geary, *We Need Men: The Union Draft in the Civil War* (Dekalb: Northern Illinois University Press, 1991); Nevins, *The War for the Union*, 2:64, 464–65; 3:8; McPherson, *Battle Cry of Freedom*, 31, 56; Barton, review of *We Need Men: The Union Draft in the Civil War*, 1598; Kemp, "Community and War," 51–57; Current, *The History of Wisconsin*, 2:10–11, 334–35.

77. Current, *The History of Wisconsin*, 2:317.

78. Nevins, *The War for the Union*, 3:120.

79. McPherson, *Battle Cry of Freedom*, 57.

80. Nevins, *The War for the Union*, 2:465.

81. Ibid., 3:127.

82. Kemp, "Community and War," 52.

83. Moore, *Conscription and Conflict in the Confederacy*, 3, 5, 29–30.

84. Company A, 18th Indiana, Protest Letter, IndSHL.

85. D. Vanankem to Charles E. Haverly, September 18, 1863, Charles E. Haverly Letters, SHSIa-DM.

86. Henry Metzger to father, December 5, 1864, Henry C. Metzger Correspondence (photocopies), HCWRTC, USAMHI.

87. Theodore Lyman III to [wife], October 18, 1864, Lyman Family Papers, MHS.

88. Voleny G. Barbour to cousin, April 10, 1864, Lucian B. Case Papers, CHS.

89. John H. Burrill to parents, December 5, 1863, John H. Burrill Letters (typescript), CWTIC, USAMHI.

90. William Pedrick to father and mother, January 6, 1863, Benjamin Pedrick Papers, DUL; also see James W. Ames to mother, July 19, 1863, Milton C. Arthur to sister, December 10, 1863, John W. Ames Letters (typescript), LLC, USAMHI.

91. James A. Garfield to Emerson Opdycke, March 30, 1865, Emerson Opdycke Papers, OHS.

92. Voleny G. Barbour to Lucian B. Case, November 16, 1863, Lucian B. Case Papers, CHS.

93. Burton H. Bristol to Lucian B. Case, October 12, 1864, Lucian B. Case Papers, CHS; Humphrey Hughes Hood to wife, February 24, 1863, Humphrey Hughes Hood Correspondence, IllSHL.

94. Samuel M. Scott to Governor Harris Flanagin, April 27, 1863, Kie Oldham Papers, AHC.

95. James W. Biddle to father, January 3, 1864, Samuel Simpson Biddle Papers, DUL; Burton H. Bristol to Lucian B. Case, September 16, 1864, Lucian B. Case Papers, CHS; Watkins Kearns Diary (photocopy), December 10, 1863, VHS.

96. *Free South,* February 7, 1863; Glatthaar, *Forged in Battle,* 7; Christopher Dell, *Lincoln and the War Democrats* (Rutherford, N.J.: Fairleigh Dickinson University Press, 1975), 213. Even the South took some tentative steps in this direction; see McPherson, *Battle Cry of Freedom,* 837.

97. Corrected chi square = 1.502, df = 1, probability of chance = .22, and phi an insignificant .10.

98. Isaac Plumb to unknown, January 11, 1863, CWMC, USAMHI; also see Cyrus F. Boyd, *The Civil War Diary of Cyrus F. Boyd: Fifteenth Iowa Infantry, 1861–1863,* ed. Mildred Throne (Iowa City: State Historical Society of Iowa, 1953), 63.

99. George D. Bellows to Richard Yates, May 14, 1863, Yates Family Papers, IllSHL; William W. Jones to sister, January 27, 1863, William W. Jones Letters, TUL.

100. John Lynch to A. Kitchell, February 15, 1863, Yates Family Papers, IllSHL.

101. I. Gillespie to John McAuley Palmer, December 28, 1863, Yates Family Papers, IllSHL.

102. Felix Pierre Poché, January 22, 1865, in *A Louisiana Confederate: Diary of Felix Poché,* ed. Edwin C. Bearss (Natchitoches: Louisiana Studies Institute, Northwestern State University, 1972); also see John Hampden Chamberlayne to sister, March 29, 1865, John Hampden Chamberlayne Papers, VHS.

103. Samuel F. Richards to Lewis, August 31, 1863, Samuel F. Richards Letter, CWTIC, USAMHI.

104. Michael Guinan to sister Eliza, September 18, 1863, Michael Guinan Letters, Williams Research Center, HNOC.

105. Caleb Hadley Beale to uncle, February 7, 1863, Caleb Hadley Beale Correspondence, Civil War Correspondence, MHS.

106. Alonzo G. Rich to father, July 31, 1864, Alonzo G. Rich Letter, CWMC, USAMHI.

107. Humphrey Hughes Hood to wife, April 16, 1863, Humphrey Hughes Hood Correspondence, IllSHL.

108. Byron M. McClain to brother, February 21, 1864, Byron M. McClain Correspondence, UIaL.

109. Issashar Davis to friend William, August 8, 1863, Oscar Faulkner and Holt Family Papers, SHSIa-DM.

110. Samuel Storrow to parents, April 6 and 13, 1863, Samuel Storrow Papers, CW Correspondence, reel 9, MHS.

111. R. S. Webb to cousin Jennie, August 13, 1864, Webb Family Papers, SHC, UNC.

112. William Biggs to father, July 14, 1864, Asa Biggs Papers, DUL.

CHAPTER 4: Fighting for the Right

1. Seymour Drescher, David Sabean, and Allan Sharlin, eds., *Political Symbolism in Modern Europe: Essays in Honor of George L. Mosse* (New Brunswick, N.J.: Transaction Books, 1982), 2–5.

2. John William Green Diary (transcript), December 22, 1864, TFC.

3. Frederick F. Bowen to Charlie, October 15, 1864, Frederick F. Bowen Papers, VHS; Elijah P. Petty to wife, January 10, 1863, in *Journey to Pleasant Hill;* John C. Dinsmore to wife, November 5, 1863, J. Dinsmore Collection, IllSHL; George Phifer Erwin to mother, April 2, [1863], George Phifer Erwin Papers, SHC, UNC; John I. Faller to sister, June 25, 1863, John I. Faller Correspondence (transcript), HCWRTC, USAMHI; W. D. Wildman to [Miss Greggs], February 8, 1863, Wildman Family Papers, OHS; Luther Furney to friend Case, November 28, 1864, Lucian B. Case Papers, CHS; Levi A. Ross to parents, November 3, 1863, Levi A. Ross Diary (typescript) and Letters, IllSHL; George W. Bailey, *A Private Chapter of the War (1861–1865)* (St. Louis: G. I. Jones and Co., 1880), 10, 20; William Peel Diary, February 4 and April 8, 1864, MDAH; Thomas Hopkins Deavenport Diary, April 28, 1864, Confederate Collection, TSLA; David C. Gamble to Richard Yates, April 25, 1863, Yates Family Papers, IllSHL; McPherson, *What They Fought For,* 26, 42.

4. David Logan Houser to Malvina, August 14, 1863, David Logan Houser Letters, SHSIa-IC.

5. McPherson, *What They Fought For,* 26, 42.

6. Corrected chi square = 3.33, df = 1, probability of chance .07, phi a weak .20.

7. John W. Northrop Diary of Prison Life (transcript), May 6–7, 1864, WRHS; also see Joseph Bloomfield Osborn to parents, [November] 1863, Joseph Bloomfield Osborn Correspondence, LC.

8. Robert W. Henry to wife, June 3, 1864, Robert W. Henry Letters, SHSIa-IC.

9. Voleny G. Barbour to friend Case, August 14, 1863, Lucian B. Case Papers, CHS; also see Oscar O. Cram to Ellen, February 3, 1865, Oscar Cram Letters, CWMC, USAMHI.

10. E. B. Quiner Papers: Correspondence of the Wisconsin Volunteers (microfilm), reel 5, vol. 9, p. 124, SHSW.

11. Marcus Hefner to parents, July 19, 1863, Marcus Hefner Papers, NCSA; also see W. H. Horton to sister, November 30, 1864, W. H. Horton Letters, SHC, UNC; Randall C. Jimmerson, *The Private Civil War* (Baton Rouge: Louisiana State University Press, 1988), 198.

12. Macon Bonner to wife, January 12, 1863, Macon Bonner Papers, SHC, UNC.

13. Anonymous Commissary Sergeant to aunt, April 8, 1864, Federal Collection, TSLA.

14. Stuart McConnell, *Glorious Contentment: The Grand Army of the Republic, 1865–1900* (Chapel Hill: University of North Carolina Press, 1992), 183, 187, 215, 222.

15. John N. Strayer to Susan Greggs, March 23, 1863, Virginia Southwood Collection, WHMC.

16. Alfred Pirtle to father, January 30, 1863, Alfred Pirtle Civil War Letters, TFC.

17. William H. Philips to wife Hattie, September 13, 1864, Philips Collection, OHS.

18. Caleb Mills to son, December 2, 1864, Caleb Mills Papers, IndHS; Benjamin F. Ashenfelter to mother, September 1, 1863, Benjamin F. Ashenfelter Letters (photocopies), HCWRTC, USAMHI; William H. Church to Ella, September 3, 1864, William H. Church Papers, SHSW.

19. "Q.M." to Alice Grisham, May 29, 1862, Civil War Correspondence, MDAH.

20. James W. Biddle to sister Rosa, December 7, 1863, Samuel Simpson Biddle Papers, DUL; Edgar Ashton to sister, December 6, 1863, Cocke Family Papers, VHS Poché, January 22, 1865, in *A Louisiana Confederate;* Andrew H. Kay to brother, January 17, 1865, Baylor Family Papers, VHS; Obed William Carr Diary (transcript), January 1, 1862, DUL; James M. Little to friend [Mitchell], July 13, 1864, David L. Mitchell Letters, CWLC, AlaDAH.

21. William Foster to Kate, February 4, 1863, William Foster Papers, WRHS; also see *Free South,* February 7, 1863; and Mitchell, *Civil War Soldiers,* 13.

22. John Wesley Marshall Journal (typescript), July 31, 1863, OHS.

23. Henry Fleck Memoirs, 13, HCWRTC, USAMHI; also see Hess, *Liberty, Virtue, and Progress,* 3.

24. Michael Kammen, *A Machine That Would Go of Itself: The Constitution in American Culture* (New York: Alfred A. Knopf, 1987), 16, 115.

25. Levi A. Ross Diary, political testament [1864], Levi A. Ross Diary (typescript) and Letters, IllSHL.

26. Robert Franklin Bunting to the editor of the *Telegraph,* August 11, 1863, Robert Franklin Bunting Letters (transcript), TSLA.

27. Samuel Storrow to parents, January 22, 1863, Samuel Storrow Papers, CW Correspondence, reel 9, MHS.

28. Hess, *Liberty, Virtue, and Progress,* 96.

29. Peyton McCrary, "The Party of Revolution: Republican Ideas about Politics and Social Change, 1862–1867," *CWH* 30 (December 1984):330–31.

30. McPherson, *Battle Cry of Freedom,* 494–96.

31. McCrary, "The Party of Revolution," 337.

32. Hess, *Liberty, Virtue, and Progress,* 81.

33. McCrary, "The Party of Revolution," 338–39, 341.

34. McPherson, *Battle Cry of Freedom,* 495.

35. Hess, *Liberty, Virtue, and Progress,* 99.

36. McPherson, *Battle Cry of Freedom,* 495.

37. Ibid., 354.

38. Hess, *Liberty, Virtue, and Progress,* 98.

39. Paludan, "*The People's Contest,*" 201–2, 209.

40. McPherson, *Battle Cry of Freedom,* 496.

41. Paludan, "*The People's Contest,*" 236, 248.

42. McPherson, *Battle Cry of Freedom,* 769.

43. McCrary, "The Party of Revolution," 343.

44. Nevins, *The War for the Union,* 2:240.

45. Eugene Marshall Diary (transcript), July 10, 1863, DUL; also see Harvey Graham to wife and children, January 10, 1864, Dr. Graeme O'Geran Collection, SHSIa-DM.

46. Dell, *Lincoln and the War Democrats,* 287.

47. This definition incorporates the ideas of Samuel Huntington, *Political Order in Changing Societies* (New Haven: Yale University Press, 1969); Theda Skocpol's *States and Social Revolutions;* and a survey article of the literature on the topic by François Chazel, "Les ruptures révolutionnaires," in *Traité de Science Politique,* ed. Madeleine Gravitz and Jean Leca (Paris: Presses Universitaires de France, 1985).

48. L. Horney to John Courts Bagby, April 10, 1863, John Courts Bagby Collection, IllSHL.

49. See for example, a letter from a soldier in the 13th Wisconsin, E. B. Quiner Papers: Correspondence of the Wisconsin Volunteers (microfilm), reel 5, vol. 9, p. 124, SHSW; Eric Foner, *Politics and Ideology in the Age of the Civil War* (New York: Oxford University Press, 1980), 24.

50. Robert W. Henry to wife, April 4, 1863, Robert W. Henry Letters, SHSIa-IC; also see Hess, *Liberty, Virtue, and Progress,* 1.

51. George F. Elliott to Elizabeth Elliott, April 21, 1864, Collins D. Elliott Papers, TSLA.

52. Corrected chi square = 2.115, df = 1, probability of chance = .15, phi a weak .13; also see McPherson, *What They Fought For,* 64, 67.

53. Edward J. Bartlett to Martha, November 19, 1863, Edward J. Bartlett Papers, CW Correspondence, reel 1, MHS; Warren Goodale to children, December 27, 1864, Warren Goodale Letters, MHS; Bailey, *A Private Chapter of the War,* 33, 79; Samuel Storrow to parents, February 5, 1863, Samuel Storrow Papers, CW Correspondence, reel 9, MHS.

54. Adoniram Judson Withrow to wife [Libertatia], December 8, 1862, Adoniram Judson Withrow Letters (typescript), SHSIa-IC.

55. Humphrey Hughes Hood to wife, February 7, 1863, Humphrey Hughes Hood Correspondence, IllSHL.

56. Lyman W. Ayer to unknown, April 23, 1863, Lyman W. Ayer Letter, Federal Collection, TSLA.

57. William J. Gibson to children, March 25, 1862, William J. Gibson Journal (typescript), HCWRTC, USAMHI.

58. Robert Hubbard to wife Nellie, July 20, 1863, Robert Hubbard Papers (typescript), Civil War Manuscripts Collection, YUL.

59. Humphrey Hughes Hood to wife, February 18, 1863, Humphrey Hughes Hood Correspondence, IllSHL.

60. F. W. Gates to Richard Yates, February 23, 1863, Yates Family Papers, IllSHL.

61. Allan Nevins, *The War for the Union*, vol. 4, *The Organized War to Victory, 1864–1865* (New York: Charles Scribner's Sons, 1971), 93.

62. Daniel Wallace Adams, "Illinois Soldiers and the Emancipation Proclamation," *Journal of the Illinois State Historical Society* 67 (September 1967): 408–10; Glatthaar, *Forged in Battle,* 9; McPherson, *Battle Cry of Freedom,* 557–63.

63. Thomas Tharp to Sarah M. Resley, April 3, 1863, John Resley Collection, SHSIa-IC.

64. Joshua W. Haas to Frederick Haas, January 3, 1863, Joshua W. Haas Reprint of letter, CWMC, USAMHI.

65. Jasper Barney to [J. Dinsmore], October 24, 1862, J. Dinsmore Collection, IllSHL; also see John Fuson to parents, July 2, 1863, Dieck Collection, TSLA; P. Gamble to Lucian B. Case, April 2, 1863, Lucian B. Case Papers, CHS; *Free South,* January 27, 1863; David Logan Houser to Malvina, November 20, 1863, David Logan Houser Letters, SHSIa-IC.

66. "Publico," E. B. Quiner Papers: Correspondence of the Wisconsin Volunteers (microfilm), reel 3, vol. 8, p. 193, SHSW.

67. L. S. Livermore, E. B. Quiner Papers: Correspondence of the Wisconsin Volunteers (microfilm), reel 3, vol. 9, p. 220, SHSW.

68. Myron Underwood to wife, March 20, 1864, Myron Underwood Letters, UIaL.

69. Resolutions on the Conduct of the War Adopted by the Officers and Enlisted Men from Illinois Stationed at Bolivar, Tennessee, February 13, 1863, Yates Family Papers, IllSHL.

70. William R. Rapson to brother, March 21, 1863, William R. Rapson Collection, WRHS.

71. J. Newman Kirkpatrick to sister and brother, May 20, 1863, Kirkpatrick Family Papers, WHMC.

72. Robert Hubbard to wife Nellie, April 16, 1863, Robert Hubbard Papers (typescript), Civil War Manuscripts Collection, YUL.

73. *Free South,* January 17, 1863.

74. George Fowle, *Letters to Eliza,* ed. Margery Greenleaf (Chicago: Follett Publishing Co., 1970), 19.

75. Robert Gooding to brother, May 4, 1963, Robert Gooding Collection, WHMC.

76. John Hiller, draft of a letter to the editor [late 1863 or early 1864] submitted to John Culver, Hiller Family Papers, WHMC.

77. Abbott, *Fallen Leaves,* 161–62.

78. "A Private," Company E, 130th Illinois Infantry, to Richard Yates, January 4, 1863, Yates Family Papers, IllSHL; Benjamin F. Ashenfelter to father Churchman, March 1, 1863, Benjamin F. Ashenfelter Letters (photocopies), HCWRTC, USAMHI; David P. Craig to wife, January 25, 1863, David P. Craig Letters, IndSHL; Voleny G. Barbour to Lucian B. Case, August 14, 1863, Lucian B. Case Papers, CHS; John C. Dinsmore to wife, September 26, 1863, John C. Dinsmore Letters, IllSHL; John C. Ellis to nephew, February [1863], Ellis-Marshall Family Papers, HCWRTC, USAMHI; Humphrey Hughes Hood to wife, February 15, 1863, Humphrey Hughes Hood Correspondence, IllSHL.

79. Current, *The History of Wisconsin,* 2:299.

80. Levi A. Ross Diary, February 3, 1863, Levi A. Ross Diary (typescript) and Letters, IllSHL.

81. Peter Eltinge to father, January 6, 1864, Eltinge-Lord Family Papers, DUL.

82. *Jonesboro (Illinois) Gazette,* February 7, 1863.

83. D. A. Kreiling to friend Charles, August 22, 1863, Isaac Farver Collection, IndSHL.

84. Richard R. Puffer to sister, October 17, 1862 and February 12, 1863, Richard R. Puffer Letters, CHS.

85. Arthur B. Carpenter to parents, May 13, 1863, Arthur B. Carpenter Papers, Civil War Manuscripts Collection, YUL; also see "A Private," Company E, 130th Illinois Infantry, to Richard Yates, January 4, 1863, Yates Family Papers, IllSHL; George Avery to Lizzie, February 23, 1862, George Smith Avery Letters, CHS.

86. Thomas J. Green et al., Petition to Zebulon Baird Vance, March 30, 1864, Thomas Jefferson Green Papers, SHC, UNC.

87. Arthur W. Bergeron Jr., "Free Men of Color in Grey," *CWH* 32 (September 1986): 248; Ira Berlin, ed. *Freedom: A Documentary History of Emancipation, 1861–1867.* Series 2, *The Black Military Experience* (New York: Cambridge University Press, 1982), 279; Charles H. Wesley, "Employ of Negroes in the Confederate Army," *Journal of Negro History* 4 (July 1919): 243.

88. Berlin, *Freedom,* 279.

89. Ibid., 281.

90. McPherson, *Battle Cry of Freedom,* 831.

91. Beringer et al., *Why the South Lost the Civil War,* 377, 379.

92. Robert F. Durden, *The Gray and the Black: The Confederate Debate on Emancipation* (Baton Rouge: Louisiana State University Press, 1972), 31, 65; Wesley, "Employ of Negroes in the Confederate Army," 243.

93. McPherson, *Battle Cry of Freedom,* 833; Emory M. Thomas, *The Confederate Nation, 1861–1865* (New York: Harper and Row, 1979), 263.

94. McPherson, *Battle Cry of Freedom,* 833–34.

95. Nathaniel W. Stephenson, "The Question of Arming the Slaves," *AHR* 18 (January 1918): 300; also see Wesley, "Employ of Negroes in the Confederate Army," 251.

96. Stephenson, "The Question of Arming the Slaves," 306.

97. Durden, *The Gray and the Black,* 235.

98. Ervin L. Jordan Jr. *Black Confederates and Afro-Yankees in Civil War Virginia* (Charlottesville: University of Virginia Press, 1995), 246, 250–51; Stephenson, "The Question of Arming the Slaves," 300; Wesley, "Employ of Negroes in the Confederate Army," 251.

99. Richard Rollins, "Black Southerners in Gray," in *Black Southerners,* ed. Richard Rollins (Murfreesboro, Tenn.: Southern Heritage Press, 1994), 27.

100. Theodore Gillard Trimmier to wife Mary, August 7, 1863, Theodore Gillard Trimmier Papers, TSLA.

101. Durden, *The Gray and the Black,* 217–18; Berlin, *Freedom,* 297.

102. Durden, *The Gray and the Black,* 219–23.

103. Berlin, *Freedom,* 298–99.

104. Charles L. Anthony to father, January 17, 1865, Anthony Family Papers, VSLA.

105. Lundsford Yandell to Lundsford Yandell Jr., February 26, 1865, Yandell Family Papers, TFC.

106. Joseph Branch O'Bryan to sister, January 20, 1865, Joseph Branch O'Bryan Papers, TSLA.

107. Samuel H. Sublet to mother, March 24, 1865, Thomas Kelley Papers, DUL.

108. Edwin Hedge Fay to wife, January 14, 1863, in *"This Infernal War";* also see Lundsford Yandell to Lundsford Yandell Jr., January 29, 1865, Yandell Family Papers, TFC.

109. George R. Elliott Diary, February 19, 1863, Collins D. Elliott Papers, TSLA; also see A. T. Fielder Diary, January 23, 1865, TSLA; Thomas C. Jackson to [wife] Jose, February 8, 1865, William P. Palmer Collection, WRHC.

110. "J.D." Petition to Jefferson Davis from soldier[s] in the II Corps, February 5, 1865 (typescript), Alder Bell Collection, VSLA.

111. Lewis Henry Webb Diary, January 25 and February 6, 1865, Webb Family Papers, SHC, UNC.

112. John Hendricks Kinyoun to wife, March 28, 1865, John Hendricks Kinyoun Papers, DUL; also see Eppa Hunton to wife, February 10, 1865, Hunton Family Papers, VHS.

113. Theodore Gillard Trimmier to Mary, February 2, 1865, Theodore Gillard Trimmier Papers, TSLA.

114. Eppa Hunton to wife, February 27, 1865, Hunton Family Papers, VHS.

115. James B. Walton to Mrs. M. A. Walton, February 6, 1865, Walton-Glenny Family Papers, 1855–1967, Williams Research Center, HNOC.

116. Robert Franklin Bunting to the *Telegraph,* February 17, 1865, Robert Franklin Bunting Letters (transcript), TSLA; also see Alexander H. Bolton to sister, January 26, 1865, Bolton Family Papers, VHS; Thomas W. Hardin to wife [Kate], February 4, 1863, Hardin Family Letters, AHC.

117. The number of respondents was too small for a reliable statistical measurement.

118. Daniel Abernathy to wife, February 4, 16, 25, 1865, Daniel Abernathy Papers, DUL.

119. R. M. Lyons to S. B. Shotwell, March 22, 1863, Shotwell Family Papers, OHS.

120. Fred M. Clarke to father, December 15, 1862, William Penn Clarke Collection, SHSIa-DM.

121. B. F. Moulton to father, April 29, 1865, William P. Palmer Collection, WRHS; also see Henry C. McArthur Diary, April 19, 1865, SHSIa-DM.

122. Abial Hall Edwards, April 26, 1865, in *"Dear Friend Anna,"* ed. Beverly Hayes Kallgren and James L. Crouthamel (Orono: University of Maine Press, 1992), 126.

123. Robert Baird to brother, January 10, 1864, Robert Baird Papers, OHS.

124. David S. Seibert to father, December 29, [1864], Seibert Family Papers, HCWRTC, USAMHI.

125. Zerah Coston Monks to Misses A[nnie] and E. E. Rohrer, March 2, 1864, Monks Family Papers, WRHS.

126. Henry Clinton Forbes to sister Flavilla, May 8, 1865, Henry Clinton Forbes Letters, OHS; also see Lt. E. E. Bryant to editor, E. B. Quiner Papers: Correspondence of the Wisconsin Volunteers (microfilm), reel 3, vol. 8, pp. 163, 168, SHSW.

127. William J. Gibson to children, March 25, 1862, William J. Gibson Journal (typescript), HCWRTC, USAMHI.

128. Edward Prince to Richard Yates, July 15, 1864, Yates Family Papers, IllSHL.

129. William Whatley Pierson Jr., "The Committee on the Conduct of the War," *AHR* 23 (April 1918): 572; Nevins, *The War for the Union*, 4:84–85.

130. John William Green Diary (transcript), May 4, 1865, TFC.

131. John Joyes Jr. Diary, February 10, 1865, TFC.

132. Bragg, *Letters of a Confederate Surgeon*, 271–72.

133. Elbridge Gerry Littlejohn to [wife], May 4, 1865, in "Civil War Letters, Part II," ed. Vicki Betts, *Chronicles of Smith County* 18 (Summer 1979): 37.

134. George Washington Dillon Diary, April 9, 1865, TSLA.

135. Francis Warrington Dawson to father, June 13, 1865, Francis Warrington Dawson Letters, DUL.

136. T[itus] P[omponius] Atticus Bibb to friend Brown, May 30, 1865, Orlando Brown Papers, TFC.

137. T[itus] P[omponius] Atticus Bibb to friend Brown, May 30, 1865, Orlando Brown Papers, TFC.

138. Almond and Verba, *The Civic Culture*.

139. Robert David Jamison, *Letters and Recollections of a Confederate Soldier, 1860–1865*, comp. Henry Downs Jamison Jr. (Nashville, Tenn.: privately published, 1964), 80.

140. Obed William Carr Diary (transcript), April 17, 1865, DUL; also see John Francis Shaffner to unknown, January 1, 1865, John Francis Shaffner Papers, NCSA.

141. Jamison, *Letters and Recollections of a Confederate Soldier*, 79.

142. Samuel B. Johnson to sister, April 14, 1865, Johnson Family Papers, VSLA.

143. Poché, September 19, 1864, in *A Louisiana Confederate*.

144. Francis Atherton Boyle Diary (typescript), April 30, 1865, SHC, UNC; also see John A. Gibson Diary, April 27, 1865, Gibson Family Papers, VHS.

145. John Hampden Chamberlayne to mother, February 13, 1865, John Hampden

Chamberlayne Papers, VHS; also see William Marrin to Pierre Gustave Toutant Beaure-gard, June 19, 1865, Pierre Gustave Toutant Beauregard Letters, Williams Research Center, HNOC.

146. James B. Walton to [Mrs. James B. Walton], [ca. 1865], Walton-Glenny Family Papers, 1855–1967, Williams Research Center, HNOC.

147. Corrected chi square $= 1.78$, df $= 1$, probability of chance .18.

148. Joseph Branch O'Bryan to sister, February 24, 1865, Joseph Branch O'Bryan Papers, TSLA.

149. R. H. Bacot to sister, January 18, 1865, R. H. Bacot Letters, NCSA.

150. Elijah P. Petty to brother Thomas, February 16, 1864, in *Journey to Pleasant Hill*, 325; also see Edwin H. Fay to wife, February 19, 1863, in *"This Infernal War."*

151. Beringer et al., *Why the South Lost the Civil War*, 310, 339, 436–38.

152. Ibid., 368–69.

153. Ibid., 436.

154. Alfred Patton to brother, June 9, 1865, Patton-Scott Family Papers, WHMC.

CHAPTER 5: **Leaders and Politics**

1. R. H. Bacot to sister, April 24, 1864, R. H. Bacot Letters, NCSA; Samuel Thompson Foster, July 19, 1864, in *One of Cleburne's Command*, ed. Norman D. Brown (Austin: University of Texas Press, 1980); Macon Bonner to wife, June 5, 1864, Macon Bonner Papers, SHC, UNC.

2. Laurence Massillon Keitt to wife, January 13 and 22 and February 11, 1864, Laurence Massillon Keitt Letters, SHC, UNC.

3. Edwin H. Fay to wife, January 13, 1864, in *"This Infernal War."*

4. Jacques Alfred Charbonnet Diary (original in French), August 22, 1863, TUL.

5. Laurence Massillon Keitt to wife, January 17, 1864, Laurence Massillon Keitt Letters, SHC, UNC.

6. William Johnson Pegram to sister, January 16, 1863, Pegram-Johnson-McIntosh Family Papers, VHS; also see McPherson, *Battle Cry of Freedom*, 79.

7. Laurence Massillon Keitt to wife, January 27, 1864, Laurence Massillon Keitt Letters, SHC, UNC.

8. Charles E. Denoon to brother, November 22, 1863, Denoon Family Papers, VSLA.

9. Felix G. Buchanan to father, March 13, 1865, Buchanan-McClellan Collection, SHC, UNC.

10. Henry St. Paul, "Our Home and Foreign Policy," *Mobile Register*, November 1863.

11. Samuel Thompson Foster, July 19, 1864, in *One of Cleburne's Command*.

12. William Johnson Pegram to wife, July 21, 1864, Pegram-Johnson-McIntosh Family Papers, VHS.

13. Edwin H. Fay to wife, July 10, 1863, in *"This Infernal War."*

14. Laurence Massillon Keitt to wife, January 22 and 27, 1864, Laurence Massillon Keitt Letters, SHC, UNC.

15. James C. Zimmerman to wife Adeline, August 16, 1863, James C. Zimmerman Papers, DUL.

16. Edwin H. Fay to wife, January 9, 1864, in *"This Infernal War"*; Laurence Massillon Keitt to wife, January 22, 1864, Laurence Massillon Keitt Letters, SHC, UNC.

17. James C. Zimmerman to wife Adeline, August 5, 1863, James C. Zimmerman Papers, DUL.

18. Jacques Alfred Charbonnet Diary (original in French), August 6, 1863, TUL: "Dans les révolutions l'écume monte à la surface—l'honnête homme seul souffre et ne parvient pas—c'est pourquoi Dieu bénit rarement les révolutions."

19. Francis Warrington Dawson to father, January 13, 1865, Francis Warrington Dawson Letters, DUL.

20. Jonathan Thomas Knight to wife Susan, [August] 1863, Jonathan Thomas Knight Letters (typescript) Confederate Collection, TSLA.

21. Jonathan Thomas Knight to wife Susan, August 15, 1863, Jonathan Thomas Knight Letters (typescript), Confederate Collection, TSLA.

22. Theophilus Perry to wife, July 16, 1863, Persley Person Papers, DUL.

23. J. J. Wilson to father, January 6, 1864, J. J. Wilson Papers, MDAH; Edwin W. Bearse to mother, September 23, 1864, Edwin W. Bearse Correspondence, CW Correspondence, MHS; Charles Beath to Isaac Funk, February 19, 1864, Isaac Funk Collection, IllSHL; James Madden to Cornelius Madden, June 25, 1863, Cornelius Madden Papers, OHS; Luther Furney to Lucian B. Case, November 13, 1863, Lucian B. Case Papers, CHS; Peter Eltinge to father, February 9, 1864, Eltinge-Lord Family Papers, DUL; Dayton E. Flint to father, September 11, 1864, Dayton E. Flint Letters (typescript), CWMC, USAMHI; Amos C. Weaver to mother, July 11, 1864, Amos C. Weaver Letters, IndHS; Nevins, *The War for the Union,* 2:193.

24. John Walter Lee to father, March 5, 1865, John Walter Lee Letters, SHSIa-IC.

25. Edward Griswold to sister, October 12, 1864, Griswold Papers, DUL.

26. Humphrey Hughes Hood to wife, September 13, 1864, Humphrey Hughes Hood Correspondence, IllSHL.

27. Harold M. Hyman, "Elections of 1864," in *History of Presidential Elections,* vol. 3, *1848–1868,* ed. Arthur M. Schlesinger Jr. (New York: Chelsea House Publishers, 1985), 1155.

28. Ibid., 1165–66.

29. Ibid., 1167.

30. William Frank Zornow, *Lincoln and the Party Divided* (1954; reprint, Westport, Conn.: Greenwood Press, 1972), 10–11.

31. Ibid., 28, 52, 73, 87–88; T. Harry Williams, *Lincoln and the Radicals* (1941; reprint, Madison: University of Wisconsin Press, 1965), 312; Hyman, "Elections of 1864," 1166.

32. Hyman, "Elections of 1864," 1167–69; Zornow, *Lincoln and the Party Divided,* 16, 111; Howard C. Westwood, "The Joint Committee on the Conduct of the War—A Look at the Record," *Lincoln Herald* 80 (Spring 1978): 3–5; Brian Holden Reid, "Historians and the Joint Committee on the Conduct of the War, 1861–1865," *CWH* 38 (December 1992): 320–29.

33. William C. Harris, "Conservative Unionists and the Presidential Election of 1864," *CWH* 38 (December 1992): 301; Dell, *Lincoln and the War Democrats* 294–95.

34. Hyman, "Elections of 1864," 1171; Zornow, *Lincoln and the Party Divided*, 132–33, 149–53; John A. Rawley, *The Politics of Union: Northern Politics during the Civil War* (Hinsdale, Ill.: Dryden Press, 1974), 154–55.

35. Abial Hall Edwards to Anna, April 26, 1865, in *"Dear Friend Anna"*; Humphrey Hughes Hood to wife, February 18 and June 22, 1863, Humphrey Hughes Hood Correspondence, IllSHL; Andrew R. Linscott to parents, October 3, 1863, Andrew R. Linscott Correspondence, MHS.

36. John L. Mcnaugh to James Addison Cravens, February 22, 1863 (draft), James Addison Cravens Papers, Lilly Library, Indiana University.

37. Henry Livermore Abbott to father, May [7], 1863, in *Fallen Leaves*.

38. George M. Barnard Jr. to father, January 6, 1863, George M. Barnard Papers, CW Correspondence, reel 17, MHS.

39. Robert Hubbard to wife, August 7, 1863, Robert Hubbard Papers (typescript), Civil War Manuscripts Collection, YUL.

40. Henry Livermore Abbott to mother, September 18, 1863, and February 8, 1864, in *Fallen Leaves*.

41. Dayton E. Flint to father, January 27, 1863, Dayton E. Flint Letters (typescript), CWMC, USAMHI; also see Clement Hoffman to mother, June 23, 1863, Clement Hoffman Letters (photocopies), HCWRTC, USAMHI.

42. Benton, *Voting in the Field*, 125.

43. W. H. Sanders to father, September 5, 1863, William P. Palmer Collection, WRHS.

44. Petition of May 7, 1864, by Drury Township Voters, Yates Family Papers, IllSHL.

45. William H. Pittenger Diary, November 8, 1864, OHS.

46. Order by Colonel W. A. Owen, August 12, 1864, Bryan Grimes Papers, NCSA.

47. Paul D. Escott, *Many Excellent People: Power and Privilege in North Carolina, 1850–1900* (Chapel Hill: University of North Carolina Press, 1985), 3–16, 22–24.

48. Thomas Perkins Abernethy, *From Frontier to Plantation in Tennessee: A Study in Frontier Democracy* (1932; reprint, University: University of Alabama Press, 1976), 309, 314, 322; also see Escott, *Many Excellent People*, 23.

49. William Inwood to Oliver Morton, July 29, 1864, Governor Oliver P. Morton Papers, IndSA.

50. Cremin, ed., *The Republic and the School*, 93–94; also see Hess, *Liberty, Virtue, and Progress*, 59.

51. John D. Inskeep Diary, October 11, 1864, OHS; also see Alexander G. Downing Diary, November 7, 1864, in *Downing's Civil War Diary*, ed. Olynthus B. Clark (Des Moines: Historical Department of Iowa, 1916); Francis R. Baker Diary (transcript), October 20, 1864, IllSHL.

52. Henry H. Stone Diary (typescript), November 8, 1864, HCWRTC, USAMHI.

53. George Marion Shearer Diary, November 8 and 11, 1864, SHSIa-IC; also see John W. Northrop Diary of Prison Life (transcript), November 8, 1864, WRHS.

54. John W. Northrop Diary of Prison Life (transcript), [November] 16, 1864, WRHS.

55. Tilmon D. Kyger to sister Sarah, October 8, 1864, Tilmon D. Kyger Letters, IllSHL; James Austin Connolly Journal (typescript), November 8, 1864, James Austin Connolly Papers, IllSHL; Nelson Purdum Diary, November 8, 1864, OHS; Ephraim Franklin Brower Diary (typescript), November 9, 1864, CWMC, USAMHI.

56. Benton, *Voting in the Field*, 4; McPherson, *Battle Cry of Freedom*, 804.

57. Nevins, *The War for the Union*, 4:135–36; Benton, *Voting in the Field*, 9.

58. Benton, *Voting in the Field*, 15, 122–23.

59. Edward Maxwell Benton, "Soldier Voting in Iowa," *Iowa Journal of History and Politics* 39 (January 1931): 31; Benton, *Voting in the Field*, 49–50.

60. Benton, *Voting in the Field*, 17, 180.

61. Benton, "Soldier Voting in Iowa," 32–36, 36–37.

62. Simon Bennage Diary (photocopy), November 8, 1864, CWMC, USAMHI.

63. Benton, "Soldier Voting in Iowa," 28.

64. Benton, *Voting in the Field*, 221.

65. P. G. Hubbard, "The Lincoln-McClellan Presidential Election in Illinois" (Ph.D. diss., University of Illinois, 1949), 183.

66. Stedman Hatch to Ozias Hatch, August 16, 1864, Ozias M. Hatch Papers, IllSHL.

67. Hubbard, "The Lincoln-McClellan Presidential Election in Illinois," 179–81,184.

68. Ibid., 177–78, 184–5; Harris, "Conservative Unionists and the Presidential Election of 1864," 316; McPherson, *Battle Cry of Freedom*, 804.

69. Nevins, *The War for the Union*, 4:138.

70. Joel Griswold to sister, September 20, 1863, Griswold Papers, DUL.

71. John Walter Lee to father, September 6, 1864, John Walter Lee Letters, SHSIa-IC.

72. William Foster to Kate, November 9, 1864, William Foster Papers, WRHS.

73. Edward Griswold to sister, October 12, 1864, Griswold Papers, DUL.

74. Carlos Parsons Lyman Diary, November 8, 1864, Carlos Parsons Lyman Diaries and Letters, WRHS; also see *OR*, (Washington, D.C.: Government Printing Office, 1891–99), ser. 1, vol. 42, pt. 3, pp. 565–70, 579, 650–61; McPherson, *Battle Cry of Freedom*, 804; Joseph T. Glatthaar, *The March to the Sea and Beyond* (New York: New York University Press, 1986), 47.

75. Harris, "Conservative Unionists and the Presidential Election of 1864," 318; see also McPherson, *Battle Cry of Freedom*, 805, which contends that only the New York and Connecticut elections may have been decided by the soldier vote. Zornow, *Lincoln and the Party Divided*, 202, concurs with McPherson.

76. Benton, "Soldier Voting in Iowa," 38–39.

77. Samuel Augustus Wildman to father, September 15, 1864, Wildman Family Papers, OHS.

78. David Logan Houser to Malvina, September 23, 1864, David Logan Houser Letters, SHSIa-IC.

79. E. B. Dowd to B. F. Moulton, November 10, 1864, William P. Palmer Collection, WRHS.

80. Luther Short to father, June 22 and September 8, 1864, Luther Short Letters, IndSHL.

81. Zerah Coston Monks to Hattie, August 15, 1864, Monks Family Papers, WRHS.

82. George Shuman to Fannie, November 4, 1864, George Shuman Letters (photocopies), HCWRTC, USAMHI; also see Edwin Bearse to mother, October 4, 1864, Edwin W. Bearse Correspondence, CW Correspondence, MHS; William Church to Ella, September 3, 1864, William H. Church Papers, SHSW; Richard Lew Dawson to father and mother, September 24, 1864, Richard Lew Dawson Letters, IndHSL; William B. Britton to editors of the *Gazette,* October 27, 1863, William B. Britton Papers, WRHS; James Easton to brother, August 24, 1864, Joseph Easton Collection, OHS; Humphrey Hughes Hood to wife, October 10, 1864, Humphrey Hughes Hood Correspondence, IllSHL; Andrew R. Linscott to parents, October 6, 1864, Andrew R. Linscott Correspondence, MHS.

83. Samuel Storrow to mother, November 3, 1864, Samuel Storrow Papers, CW Correspondence, reel 9, MHS.

84. Harris, "Conservative Unionists and the Presidential Election of 1864," 302–14.

85. Benton, *Voting in the Field,* 4; Nevins, *The War for the Union,* 1:104.

86. McPherson, *Battle Cry of Freedom,* 403; Tallies of Votes Cast by Soldiers and Regimental Elections, 1862–1864, Confederate States of America Archives, State Governments, Georgia, DUL; Roster of Voters of the 29th Georgia Cavalry Battalion, January 4, 1865, R. W. Wade Papers, LLC, USAMHI; Douglas, *Douglas's Texas Battery, CSA,* 124; Tennessee Secretary of State, Tennessee Election Returns, State Wide General Election for Governor, C.S.A. Congress, State Legislature, August 6, 1863.

87. Marc W. Kruman, *Parties and Politics in North Carolina, 1836–1865* (Baton Rouge: Louisiana State University Press, 1983), 244–48.

88. William R. Trotter, *Silk Flags and Cold Steel: The Civil War in North Carolina: The Piedmont* (Winston Salem, N.C.: John Blair, 1988), 198.

89. Ibid., 204–5.

90. Elizabeth Reid Murray, *Wake Capital and County of North Carolina,* (Raleigh: Capital County Publishing, 1983), 1:485–86.

91. John G. Barrett, *The Civil War in North Carolina* (Chapel Hill: University of North Carolina Press, 1963), 198; also see Phillip Shaw Paludan, *Victims: A True Story of the Civil War* (Knoxville: University of Tennessee Press, 1981), 56–83.

92. Seaton Gales to wife, August 14, 1863, Seaton Gales Papers, NCSA; Martin Malone Gash to sister, June 18, 1864, Martin Malone Gash Papers, NCSA; James E. Green Diary, July 12, 1863, James E. Green Papers (typescript), SHC, UNC; John Francis Shaffner to Carrie, March 27, 1864, John Francis Shaffner Papers, NCSA.

93. James W. Biddle to Rosa, December 7, 1863, Samuel Simpson Biddle Papers, DUL.

94. Peter Newport Bragg to Josephine, September 18, 1864, in Bragg, *Letters of a Confederate Surgeon;* also see James Postell Douglas to [wife] Sallie, September 14, 1864, in *Douglas's Texas Battery, CSA;* and Carl H. Moneyhon, *The Impact of the Civil War and Reconstruction on Arkansas: Persistence in the Midst of Ruin* (Baton Rouge: Louisiana State University Press, 1994), 156–58.

95. Donald Bradford Dodd, "Unionism in Northwest Alabama through 1865" (master's thesis, Auburn University, 1966), 45–48, 50–51.

96. Charles Faulker Bryan Jr., "The Civil War in East Tennessee: A Social, Political, and Economic Study" (Ph.D. diss., University of Tennessee, 1978), 88, 92, 95, 98–101.

97. Bailey, *A Private Chapter of the War,* 144.

98. Lewis B. Blackford, December 12, 1863, Blackford Family Papers, SHC, UNC.

99. Corrected chi square $= 20.93$, df $= 1$, probability of chance $= 0$; phi was a weak .14; also see Jimmerson, *The Private Civil War,* 222.

100. William Birkley to Richard Yates, May 23, 1863, Yates Family Papers, IllSHL.

101. Corrected chi square $= 2.01$, df $= 1$, probability of chance $= .16$, Phi a weak .06.

102. James R. Slack to wife Ann, October 31, 1863, James R. Slack Papers, IndSHL. Army resolutions thundered the army's anger toward traitors at home (Resolutions of Officers of the 82d [Illinois] Regiment, February 14, 1863, Yates Family Papers, IllSHL).

103. Matthew R. Perry to brother, September 5, 1864, Matthew R. Perry Letters (copies), SHSW.

104. James F. Dunn to Jacob Ammen, April 25, 1863, Jacob Ammen Papers, IllSHL.

105. John Francis Shaffner to unknown, February 4, 1863, John Francis Shaffner Papers, NCSA; also see Caleb Hadley Beale to [parents], July 16, 1863, Caleb Hadley Beale Correspondence, CW Correspondence, MHS.

106. Charles Beath to Isaac Funk, February 19, 1863, Isaac Funk Collection, IllSHL.

107. Andrew Bush to [wife] Mary, March 26, 1863, Andrew Bush Letters (transcript), IndSHL.

108. Cyrus F. Boyd, January 1863, in *The Civil War Diary of Cyrus F. Boyd; Chicago Tribune,* January 26, 1863; William H. Church to Ella, September 3, 1864, William H. Church Papers, SHSW; Andrew Bush to [wife] Mary, March 26, 1863, Andrew Bush Letters (transcript), IndSHL.

109. Macon Bonner to [wife], April 13, 1864, Macon Bonner Papers, SHC, UNC.

110. Elias Davis to wife, August 14, 1863, Elias Davis Papers, SHC, UNC.

111. George W. Guess to Sarah Cockrell, April 8, 1863, Sarah Cockrell Papers, DUL.

112. Issashar Davis to friend William, January 14, 1863, Oscar Faulkner and Holt Family Papers, SHSIa-DM.

113. *Jonesboro (Illinois) Gazette,* January 7 and 24 and February 7, 1863; *Chicago Tribune,* January 26, 1863.

114. Humphrey Hughes Hood to wife, May 6, 1863, Humphrey Hughes Hood Correspondence, IllSHL.

115. E. B. Quiner Papers: Correspondence of the Wisconsin Volunteers (microfilm), reel 3, vol. 9, pp.104–5, SHSW.

116. Levi A. Ross Diary (transcript), October 31, 1864, IllSHL.

117. Frank Shearer to sister Mollie, March 26, 1863, George Marion Shearer Diary, SHSIa-IC; also see Oscar Adams to Minnie, February 26, 1863, Oscar Adams Letter, CWMC, USAMHI; James F. Drish to wife, August 3 and 9, 1863, James F. Drish Letters, IllSHL.

118. S. C. Bishop to mother, February 1, 1863, in "Indiana Troops at Helena: Part V," *Phillips County Historical Quarterly* 18 (June-September 1980): 2.

119. Samuel Storrow to parents, January 22, 1863, Samuel Storrow Papers, CW Correspondence, reel 9, MHS.

120. Enoch Whitley to Stephen Emert, June 18, 1863, Stephen Emert Collection, IndHS.

121. John Francis Shaffner to unknown, February 4, 1863, John Francis Shaffner Papers, NCSA; also see Benjamin F. Ashenfelter to father, August 23, 1863, Benjamin F. Ashenfelter Letters (photocopies), HCWRTC, USAMHI; David P. Craig to wife, January 25, 1863, David P. Craig Letters, IndSHL; Issashar Davis to friend William, May 22, 1863, Oscar Faulkner and Holt Family Papers, SHSIa-DM; Luther Furney to Lucian B. Case, August 23, 1863, Lucian B. Case Papers, CHS.

122. Cyrus F. Boyd, February 24, 1863, in *The Civil War Diary of Cyrus F. Boyd*.

123. Elijah P. Petty to wife, January 29, 1863, in *Journey to Pleasant Hill*.

124. William H. Philips, October 14, 1863, Philips Collection, OHS.

125. James W. Ames to mother, June 15, 1863, John W. Ames Letters (typescript), LLC, USAMHI.

126. Oscar Cram to Ellen, July 14, 1864, Oscar Cram Letters, CWMC, USAMHI.

127. Carlos Parsons Lyman to "Dear Ones at Home," July 29, 1863, Carlos Parsons Lyman Diaries and Letters, WRHS.

128. John W. Baldwin to [wife] Gussie, June 16, 1863, James W. Baldwin Correspondence, OHS.

129. Levi A. Ross to father, June 26, 1863, Levi A. Ross Diary (typescript) and Letters, IllSHL.

130. Bergun H. Brown to mother, June 21, 1863, Bergun H. Brown Collection (typescript), WHMC; also see John W. Baldwin to [wife] Gussie, September 1, 1863, James W. Baldwin Correspondence, OHS; Macon Bonner to wife, April 12, 1863, Macon Bonner Papers, SHC, UNC.

131. John W. Baldwin to [wife] Gussie, June 14, 1863, James W. Baldwin Correspondence, OHS.

132. William Foster to Kate, January 24, 1863, William Foster Papers, WRHS.

133. Macon Bonner to wife, January 6, 1864, Macon Bonner Papers, SHC, UNC.

134. John F. Sale to uncle, February 13, 1864, John F. Sale Correspondence, VSLA.

135. John H. Burrill to parents, August 1, 1863, John H. Burrill Letters (typescript), CWTIC, USAMHI.

136. Issashar Davis to friend William, January 4, 1863, Oscar Faulkner and Holt Family Papers, SHSIa-DM; also see David Seibert to father, April 4, 1865, Seibert Family Papers, HCWRTC, USAMHI; Ephraim S. Holloway to son, April 6, 1863, Ephraim S. Holloway Letters (typescript), OHS; Daniel Faust to sister, November 24, 1864, Daniel Faust Letters (photocopies), HCWRTC, USAMHI; William Pedrick to brother, March 11, 1863, Benjamin Pedrick Papers, DUL.

137. David Goodrich James to parents, March 23, 1863, David Goodrich James Collection, SHSW.

138. Mason Brayman to Richard Yates, February 16, 1863, Yates Family Papers, IllSHL;

also see William B. Britton to editors of the *Gazette*, July 21, 1863, William B. Britton Papers, WRHS.

139. Lona Burt to husband Richard, October 25, 1864, Richard W. Burt Papers, WHMC.

140. James F. Drish to wife, July 18, 1863, James F. Drish Letters, IllSHL.

141. John McAuley Palmer to Richard Yates, January 18, 1863, Yates Family Papers, IllSHL.

142. James S. Thomas to sister [Laura], February 9, 1863, James S. Thomas Letters, IndHS.

143. David A. Whitehorn to father and mother, February 17, 1864, David A. Whitehorn Letters, IndHS.

144. George S. Richardson to mother and father, April 2, 1863, George S. and William A. Richardson Letters (typescript), SHSIa-IC.

145. Benjamin F. Ashenfelter to father Churchman, August 23, 1863, Benjamin F. Ashenfelter Letters (photocopies), HCWRTC, USAMHI; James Postell Douglas to [wife] Sallie, September 14, 1863, in *Douglas's Texas Battery, CSA;* Day Elmore to parents, November 8, 1864, Lucian B. Case Papers, CHS.

146. Peter Guerrant Jr. to Uncle William, October 9, 1864, Guerrant Family Papers, VHS.

147. George W. Grubbs to sisters, July 7, 1865, George W. Grubbs Letters, IndSHL.

148. Edward J. Bartlett to Martha, November 4, 1863, Edward J. Bartlett Papers, CW Correspondence, reel 1, MHS.

149. Corrected chi square = 51.923, df = 1, probability of chance = 0, phi a weak .23.

150. Fred M. Clarke to father, December 3, 1862, William Penn Clarke Collection, SHSIa-DM; also see John W. Northrop Diary of Prison Life (transcript), May 6, 1864, WRHS.

151. Paul Grima to father, November 11, 1864, (author's translation from the French), Grima Family Papers, 1856–1921, Williams Research Center, HNOC.

152. Arthur B. Carpenter to parents, August 14, 1864, Arthur B. Carpenter Papers, Civil War Manuscripts Collection, YUL; also see Andrew McNeil to friend Porter, August 16, 1863, Frederick Chesson Papers, CWTIC, USAMHI.

153. John Francis Shaffner to unknown, May 8, 1863, John Francis Shaffner Papers, NCSA; also see Junius Newport Bragg to Josephine, February 1, 1864, in *Letters of a Confederate Surgeon.*

154. Zornow, *Lincoln and the Party Divided,* 106, 108–9.

155. William Peel Diary, August 19, 1864, MDAH.

156. Edwin H. Fay to Sarah, October 23, 1863, in *"This Infernal War";* also see Laurence Massillon Keitt to wife, February 26, 1864, Laurence Massillon Keitt Letters, SHC, UNC.

157. J. D. Sprake Diary (typescript), August 20, 1864, TFC.

158. James B. Walton to Mrs. James B. Walton, August 31, 1864, Walton-Glenny Family Papers, 1855–1967, Williams Research Center, HNOC.

159. Macon Bonner to wife, September 23, 1864, Macon Bonner Papers, SHC, UNC.

160. Edwin H. Fay to wife Sarah, April 25, 1864, in *"This Infernal War."*

161. Thomas T. Colman to parents, August 31, 1864, Colman-Hayter Family Papers, WHMC.

162. James Postell Douglas to wife, May 20, 1864, in *Douglas's Texas Battery, CSA.*

163. William C. McClellan to sister, September 25, 1864, Buchanan-McClellan Collection, SHC, UNC; James N. Orr to mother, July 18, 1864, in A. L. Orr, Henry Goodloe Orr, and James N. Orr, *Campaigning with Parson's Texas Brigade, CSA,* ed. John Q. Anderson (Hillsboro, Tex.: Hill Junior College Press, 1967).

164. William Johnson Pegram to sister, September 1, 1864, Pegram-Johnson-McIntosh Family Papers, VHS.

165. J. D. Sprake Diary (typescript), October 19, 1864, TFC.

166. William Biggs to sister, November 12, 1864, Asa Biggs Papers, DUL; also see Joseph C. Sharp to wife, September 14, 1864, Joseph C. Sharp Letters, AHC.

167. Junius Newport Bragg to Josephine, March 12, 1863, in *Letters of a Confederate Surgeon.*

168. Junius Newport Bragg to wife, November 24, 1864, in ibid.

169. Peter Cross to wife, November 4, 1864, John M. Wright Family Papers, NCSA.

170. John Francis Shaffner to unknown, December 3, 1864, John Francis Shaffner Papers, NCSA.

171. Poché, January 22, 1865, in *A Louisiana Confederate.*

172. John W. Ames to mother, July 26, 1863, John W. Ames Letters (typescript), LLC, USAMHI.

173. George Smith Avery to Lizzie Little, June 22, 1864, George Smith Avery Letters, CHS.

174. Robert Hubbard to Nellie, April 4, October 11, and November 15, 1863, Robert Hubbard Papers (typescript), YUL; Edward J. Bartlett to Martha, November 19, 1863, Edward J. Bartlett Papers, CW Correspondence, reel 1, MHS.

175. James L. Burhalter Diary, May 7, 1864, IllSHL.

176. William Samuel Woods to sister, February 8, 1863, MC.

177. John Francis Shaffner to friend, February 1, 1863, John Francis Shaffner Papers, NCSA.

178. Robert Franklin Bunting to the *Telegram,* March 3, 1863, Robert Franklin Bunting Letters (transcript), TSLA; also see Elias Davis to wife, February 3, 1863, Elias Davis Papers, SHC, UNC; Edwin H. Fay to wife, February 22, 1863, in *"This Infernal War."*

179. Felix Buchanan to sister, January 31, [1863], Buchanan-McClellan Collection, SHC, UNC; also see William Bailey Clement to Mattie, May 3, 1863, William Bailey Clement Papers, NCSA.

180. John Hampden Chamberlayne to [doctor], June 4, 1863, John Hampden Chamberlayne Papers, VHS.

181. Edwin H. Fay to wife Sarah, July 23, 1863, in *"This Infernal War."*

182. Clifton V. Higganbotham to uncle, July 11, 1864, Clifton V. Higganbotham Letter, VHS.

183. Charles Jackson Paine to brother, January 28, 1863, Charles Jackson Paine Letters, MHS.

184. Charles E. Denoon to brother, November 22, 1863, Denoon Family Papers, VSLA.

185. Dan Scully Diary, May 26, 1864, LHA Coll., TUL.

186. Daniel Gookin to wife, April 4, 1865, Daniel Gookin Letters, LLC, USAMHI.

187. Eugene Marshall Diary (typescript), March 30, 1863, DUL; McPherson, *Battle Cry of Freedom*, 440.

188. Patrick, *Reluctant Rebel,* 89–90; John Francis Shaffner to friend, February 1 and September 29, 1863, John Francis Shaffner Papers, NCSA; Edwin H. Fay to wife Sarah, April 28, 1863, in *"This Infernal War";* James Postell Douglas to wife Sallie, July 4, 1863, in *Douglas's Texas Battery, CSA;* William Peel Diary, July 3, 1864, MDAH; J. G. Harvey to the *Beacon* (Greenville, Alabama), March 21, 1864, Miscellaneous Civil War Letters, AlaDAH.

189. James W. Albright Diary (typescript), July 5, 1864, SHC, UNC.

190. William Peel Diary, November 10, 1864, William Peel Diary, MDAH.

191. Daniel P. Wade to wife, March 1, 1863, Daniel P. Wade Letters (transcript), TUL.

192. Jacques Alfred Charbonnet Diary (original in French), October 5, 1863, TUL; Elias Davis to wife, November 4, 1863, Elias Davis Papers, SHC, UNC; John Francis Shaffner to unknown, March 6, 1863, John Francis Shaffner Papers, NCSA.

193. John Francis Shaffner to friend, January 22, 1863, John Francis Shaffner Papers, NCSA.

194. Junius Newport Bragg to Josephine, February 14, 1864, in *Letters of a Confederate Surgeon.*

195. James E. Green Diary, July 19, 1863, James E. Green Papers (typescript), SHC, UNC.

196. William R. Rapson to brother, March 21, 1863, William R. Rapson Collection, WRHS.

197. Corrected chi square $= 5.96$, df $= 1$, probability of chance $= .01$, phi only .08.

198. William H. Bradbury to wife, January 23, 1863, William H. Bradbury Correspondence, LC.

199. William Bailey Clement to [wife] Mattie, January 2, 1863, William Bailey Clement Papers, NCSA; Patrick, *Reluctant Rebel,* 253.

200. W. D. Wildman to [Miss Greggs], February 8, 1863, Wildman Family Papers, OHS.

201. Humphrey Hughes Hood to wife, August 2, 1863, Humphrey Hughes Hood Correspondence, IllSHL.

202. D.P. Crook, *Diplomacy during the American Civil War* (New York: John Wiley and Sons, 1975), 155, 159–61.

203. Henry Mortimer Favrot Diary (French transcript), May 22, 1863, TUL.

204. Isaac Newton Brownlow to Mrs. E. F. Brownlow, May 26, 1863, Isaac Newton Brownlow Letters, AHC.

205. Crook, *Diplomacy during the American Civil War,* 161–62.

206. Patrick, *Reluctant Rebel*, 101–2.

207. Edwin H. Fay to wife Sarah, July 23, 1864, in *"This Infernal War."*

208. Jacques Alfred Charbonnet Diary (original in French), August 21, 1863, TUL.

209. Elias Davis to wife, December 17, 1863, Elias Davis Papers, SHC, UNC; also see Francis Warrington Dawson to mother, June 26, 1864, Francis Warrington Dawson Letters, DUL.

210. Peter M. Wright to sister, November 17, 1863, Wright Family Correspondence, VSLA.

211. Humphrey Hughes Hood to Chase, March 14, 1863, Humphrey Hughes Hood Correspondence, IllSHL.

212. C. Fackler to sister, March 26, 1863, C. Fackler Letters (typescript), DUL.

213. Henry Lea Graves to Cora, January 22, 1863, Mebane and Graves Papers, SHC, UNC.

214. Frank M. Parker to wife, March 17, 1864, Frank M. Parker Papers, NCSA.

215. William Johnson Pegram to [sister] Jennie, January 8, 1863, Pegram-Johnson-McIntosh Family Papers, VHS.

216. Charles Woodward Hutson to mother, February 2, 1863, Hutson Family Papers, TUL.

217. Arthur B. Carpenter to parents, September 2, 1863, Arthur B. Carpenter Papers, Civil War Manuscripts Collection, YUL.

218. Eugene Marshall Diary (typescript), July 31, 1863, DUL.

219. James F. Drish to wife, August 3, 1863, James F. Drish Letters, IllSHL.

220. Rawleigh William Downman to [wife] Mary Alice, April 23, 1865, Downman Family Papers, VHS.

221. Francis Atherton Boyle Diary (transcript), April 16, 1865, SHC, UNC.

222. John Joyes Jr. Diary, April 15, 1865, TFC.

223. Joseph Weddell Diary, April 20, 1865, William P. Palmer Collection, WRHS.

224. John Walter Lee to father, April 19, 1865, John Walter Lee Papers, SHSIa-IC.

225. Joseph F. Ward to father and mother, April 16, 1865, Joseph F. Ward Letters, CHS.

226. Sondus W. Haskell to mother, April 28, 1865, Sondus W. Haskell Letters (photocopies), LLC, USAMHI.

227. Wilson S. Miller to father, April 18, 1865, Wilson S. Miller Letters, Federal Collection, TSLA.

228. Emerson Opdycke to wife, April 19, 1865, Emerson Opdycke Papers, OHS.

229. A. A. Rigby Journal, April 18, 1865, SHSIa-DM; Benjamin R. Hieronymous Diary (typescript), April 30, 1865, IllSHL; S. B. Herrington to wife, April 22, 1865, S. B. Herrington Papers, OHS.

230. Abial Hall Edwards to Anna, April 16, 1865, in *"Dear Friend Anna."*

231. B. F. Moulton to father, April 23, 1865, William P. Palmer Collection, WRHS.

232. Hattie Rohrer to Zerah Coston Monks, April 20, 1865, Monks Family Papers, WRHS.

233. Alfred Patton to brother, June 9, 1865, Patton-Scott Family Papers, WHMC.

234. Thomas C. Honnell to brother Eli, April 18, 1865, Thomas C. Honnell Papers, OHS.

235. L. C. Ludlow to cousin Warren, May 4, 1865, Warren D. Stafford Papers, SHSIa-IC; also see Emerson Opdycke to wife, April 29, 1865, Emerson Opdycke Papers, OHS; Benjamin R. Hieronymous Diary (typescript), April 30, 1865, IllSHL.

236. John D. Inskeep Diary, April 18, 1865, John D. Inskeep Papers, OHS.

237. Thomas C. Honnell to Benjamin Epler, April 21, 1865, Thomas C. Honnell Papers, OHS; also see John O. Gay to sister, April 1865, John O. Gay Letters, Civil War Manuscripts Collection, YUL.

CHAPTER 6: The Caesarist Impulse

1. Richard Gabriel and Paul L. Savage, *Crisis in Command* (New York: Hill and Wang, 1978), 54; William Darryl Henderson, *Cohesion: The Human Element in Combat* (Washington, D.C.: National Defense University Press, 1985), 109; Robert L. Egbert et al. *The Characteristics of Fighters and Non-Fighters* (Fort Ord, Calif.: Human Research Unit no. 2, 1954), 3; John Keegan, *The Mask of Command* (New York: Penguin, 1988).

2. Faivre, *Les Nations armées,* 10.

3. James Austin Connolly Diary, October 11, 1864, James Austin Connolly Papers, IllSHL.

4. William Hamilton to mother, September 4, 1863, William Hamilton Letters, LC.

5. Ellis, *Armies in Revolution,* 63–64.

6. Cohen, *Citizens and Soldiers,* 34.

7. Lee Kennett, *G.I.: The American Soldier in World War II* (New York: Warner Books, 1989), 83, 88.

8. Ellis, *Armies in Revolution,* 16, 34, 242.

9. *Mobile Advertiser and Register,* October 26, 1861.

10. Richard Cobb, *The People's Armies* (New Haven: Yale University Press, 1987), 134.

11. Bertaud, *The Army of the French Revolution,* 39.

12. These ideas are discussed regarding the modern American professional army in Peter Maslowski, "Army Values and American Values," *Military Review* 70 (April 1990): 19.

13. Humphrey Hughes Hood to wife, January 29, 1863, Humphrey Hughes Hood Correspondence, IllSHL.

14. John W. Ames to mother, February 15, 1863, John W. Ames Letters (typescript), LLC, USAMHI; see also Williams, "Voters in Blue," 203.

15. [H. J.] Hamilton to Elihu B. Washburne, January 18, 1863, Elihu B. Washburne Papers, LC.

16. J. F. Ankeny to Elihu B. Washburne, February 3, 1863, Elihu B. Washburne Papers, LC.

17. Richard R. Puffer to sister, February 12, 1863, Richard R. Puffer Papers, CHS; also see Zerah Coston Monks to Hattie, February 23, 1863, Monks Family Papers, WRHS;

Emerson Opdycke to wife, May 24, 1863, Emerson Opdycke Papers, OHS; Henry Livermore Abbott to father, July 27, 1863, in *Fallen Leaves*.

18. Macon Bonner to wife, December 28, 1863, Macon Bonner Papers, SHC, UNC.

19. Brigadier Truman Seymour, "Military Education: A Vindication of West Point and the Regular Army," *Army and Navy Journal,* September 24, 1864, (copy in Massachusetts Governor, Executive Letterbooks, ser. 567X, MSA).

20. Maslowski, "Army Values and American Values," 20.

21. Corrected chi square $= 3.18$, $df = 1$, probability of chance .07, and phi only $= .12$.

22. Emerson Opdycke to wife, May 24, 1863, Emerson Opdycke Papers, OHS.

23. Henry Livermore Abbott to father, July 23, 1863, in *Fallen Leaves*.

24. Williams, "Voters in Blue," 200.

25. These results come with the caveat that the corrected chi square only yielded .83, $df = 1$, and there were a high probability of error of .36 and a phi of .09.

26. Henry Bruce Scott to Lizzie, June 3, 1863, Henry Bruce Scott Papers (typescript), MHS; also see George M. Barnard Jr. to father, July 17, 1863, George M. Barnard Papers, CW Correspondence, reel 17, MHS.

27. Samuel Storrow to parents, May 17, 1863, Samuel Storrow Papers, CW Correspondence, reel 9, MHS.

28. William Hamilton to mother, January 6, 1863, William Hamilton Letters, LC.

29. Moore, *Conscription and Conflict in the Confederacy,* 343–44.

30. *OR,* ser. 1, vol. 52, pt. 2, pp. 586–92. Other signatories were: Brigadier General D. C. Govan; Colonel John E. Murray, 5th Arkansas Infantry; Colonel G. F. Baucum, 8th Arkansas Infantry; Lieutenant Colonel Peter Snyder, 6th and 7th Arkansas Infantry; Lieutenant Colonel E. Warfield, 2d Arkansas Infantry; Brigadier General M. P. Lowrey; Colonel A. B. Hardcastle, 32d and 45th Mississippi Infantry; Major F. A. Ashford, 16th Alabama Infantry; Colonel John W. Colquitt, 1st Arkansas Infantry; Major Rich J. Person, 3d and 5th Confederate Infantry; Major G. S. Deakins, 8th and 35th Tennessee Infantry; Captain J. H. Collett, 7th Texas Infantry; Brigadier General J. H. Kelly, Cavalry Division.

31. Ibid., ser. 1, vol. 52, pt. 2, pp. 586–92.

32. General Joseph E. Johnston, General William Joseph Hardee, Major General William H. T. Walker, Major General Alexander P. Stewart, and Brigadier General Thomas C. Hindman.

33. Moore, *Conscription and Conflict in the Confederacy,* 344.

34. Brigadier General James Patton Anderson to Lieutenant General Leonidas Polk, January 14, 1864, *OR,* ser. 1, vol. 52, pt. 2, II, pp. 599, 608.

35. Stephenson, "The Question of Arming the Slaves," 300; Wesley, "Employ of Negroes in the Confederate Army," 251; Jordan, *Black Confederates and Afro-Yankees in Civil War Virginia,* 242.

36. Nevins, *The War for the Union,* 2:325, 329.

37. Day Elmore to parents, November 8, 1864, Lucian B. Case Papers, CHS.

38. Robert Steele to father and mother, January 5, 1863, Robert Steele Letters, SHSW.

39. Unknown to Lieutenant Colonel E. C. Yellowley, April 15, 1864, SHC, UNC.

40. Dell, *Lincoln and the War Democrats,* 10.

41. Alexander Downing Diary, October 13, 1863, in *Downing's Civil War Diary.*

42. Current, *The History of Wisconsin,* 2:409.

43. Nevins, *The War for the Union,* 4:141.

44. Dell, *Lincoln and the War Democrats,* 11.

45. Hubbard, "The Lincoln-McClellan Presidential Election in Illinois," 176.

46. U.S. Senate, *Report of the Joint Committee on the Conduct of the War,* 38th Cong., 2d sess., 1865, 15.

47. Peter Newport Bragg to Josephine, July 30, 1863, in Bragg, *Letters of a Confederate Surgeon.*

48. Zebulon Baird Vance to wife, May 31, 1861, Zebulon Baird Vance and Harriet Espy Letters, NCSA. E. W. Gantt, commander of the 12th Arkansas Infantry, changed sides to fight against his state; see Michael B. Dougan, *Confederate Arkansas: The People and Policies of a Frontier State in Wartime* (University: University of Alabama Press, 1976), 110–11.

49. Luther Furney to Lucian B. Case, October 17, 1863, Lucian B. Case Papers, CHS.

50. Theodore Lyman III to wife, October 19, 1864, Lyman Family Papers, MHS.

51. Mrs. Blenderhill to Benjamin F. Wade, February 25, 1863, E. B. Ward to Benjamin F. Wade, February 7, 1863, Benjamin F. Wade Papers, LC; Petition from the 45th Illinois Infantry to Elihu B. Washburne, April 2, 1863, Elihu B. Washburne Papers, LC.

52. A. S. Webb to sister, August 10, 1863, Webb Collection, NCSA.

53. Fisher Alison to Elihu B. Washburne, January 29, 1863, Elihu B. Washburne Papers, LC.

54. George Hay to Elihu B. Washburne, February 12, 1863, Elihu B. Washburne Papers, LC.

55. Williams, "Voters in Blue," 190.

56. Ibid., 189, 190–92.

57. [W. McConnelly] to Benjamin F. Wade, February 6, 1863, Benjamin F. Wade Papers, LC; Williams, "Voters in Blue," 193.

58. J. Maple to Lyman Trumbull, December 28, 1862, Lyman Trumbull Papers, LC.

59. J. Noble to Elihu B. Washburne, January 24, 1863, Elihu B. Washburne Papers, LC.

60. Montgomery C. Meigs to Henry C. Wilson, January 16, 1863, John Sherman Papers, LC.

61. Samuel R. Curtis to Elihu B. Washburne, January 30, 1863, Elihu B. Washburne Papers, LC.

62. Nevins, *The War for the Union,* 3:134–35.

63. Benjamin F. Butler to Henry Wilson, February 22, 1863, Henry Wilson Papers, LC.

64. Resolution of the Military Committee of Knox County, July 1863, Ohio Governor and Adjutant General, Correspondence, OHS; D. D. Benedict, president of Union League at Greenfield, Ohio, to David Tod, June 29, 1863, Ohio Governor and Adjutant General, Correspondence, OHS.

65. Nevins, *The War for the Union,* 2:314.

66. "Voters, Read!" handbill, ca. September 1863, William McCoy Papers, WRHS.

67. For example, John G. Stephenson to Oliver H. Morton, May 8, 1863, 19th Indiana Regimental File, Correspondence, IndSA.

68. A. Jackson to Oliver H. Morton, January 18, 1864, Ind. Adj. Gen. Rec., IndSA.

69. A. Jackson to Oliver H. Morton, January 18, 1864, Ind. Adj. Gen. Rec., IndSA.

70. Resolution of the citizens of Stoneport, Saline County, Illinois, to Richard Yates, February 15, 1862, Yates Family Papers, IllSHL; also see John Petit to Oliver H. Morton, January 18, 1864, Ind. Adj. Gen. Rec., IndSA; George A. Thornton and other citizens of Bedford, Indiana, to Oliver H. Morton, February 25, 1863, Ind. Adj. Gen. Rec., IndSA; Isaac Van Devanter to Oliver H. Morton, February 13, 1863, Ind. Adj. Gen. Rec., IndSA; Petition of citizens of Lawrenceburgh, Indiana, March 10, 1865, Ind. Adj. Gen. Rec., IndSA; George W. Roby to Benjamin F. Wade, January 28, 1863, Benjamin F. Wade Papers, LC; George N. Geddel to Abraham Lincoln, March 10, 1863, John Sherman Papers, LC; Moses Pratt to Richard Yates, February 6, 1863, Yates Family Papers, IllSHL; Petition of citizens of Onarga, Iroquois County, Illinois, to Richard Yates, received April 22, 1863, Yates Family Papers, IllSHL; O. B. Maples to Richard Yates, February 17, 1863, Yates Family Papers, IllSHL; Merredith H. Kidd to Lazarus Noble, April 20, 1864, Ind. Adj. Gen. Corres., IndSA; D. H. Gilmer to Richard Yates, February 28, 1863, Yates Family Papers, IllSHL; J. B. Cummings et al. at the County Court House of McDonough County, petition to Richard Yates, February 16, 1863, Yates Family Papers, IllSHL; McThomas Slaughter to Oliver Morton, October 13, 1863, and March 28, 1864, Ind. Adj. Gen. Rec., IndSA; James Brooks to Oliver Morton, October 9, 1863, Ind. Adj. Gen. Rec., IndSA.

71. Nathan Hayward to father, March 1, 1863, William P. Palmer Collection, WRHS.

72. John W. Ames to mother, May 31, 1863, John W. Ames Letters (typescript), LLC, USAMHI; T. S. Bunker to Benjamin F. Wade, February 24, 1863, Benjamin F. Wade Papers, LC; Charles M. Burrows to Richard Yates, March 24, 1864, Yates Family Papers, IllSHL; Captain A. Rounds to Zachariah Chandler, January 31, 1863, Zachariah Chandler Papers, LC; R. B. Avery to Richard Yates, February 27, 1863, Illinois Governors' Correspondence, IllSA; E. R. Williams to Richard Yates, February 9, 1863, Yates Family Papers, IllSHL; Strawn to Richard Yates, May 19, 1863, Yates Family Papers, IllSHL; Andrew Miller to Richard Yates, March 12, 1863, Yates Family Papers, IllSHL; E. Higgins to Charles W. Hill, July 22, 1863, Ohio Governor and Adjutant General, Correspondence, OHS.

73. The case of David Franklin Caldwell of North Carolina reflected the importance of political reliability to a military career during the Civil War; see William S. Powell, ed., *Dictionary of North Carolina Biography* (Chapel Hill: University of North Carolina Press, 1979), 1:303.

74. Walter DuBose to John, June 7, 1863, Walter DuBose Letters, CWLC, AlaDAH.

75. Augustus Summerfield Merrimon to Zebulon Baird Vance, October 22, 1864, Zebulon Baird Vance Collection (microform), NCSA.

76. D. Pinckney Johnstone, Postmaster [Dunn's Rock], to Zebulon Baird Vance, September 11, 1863, Zebulon Baird Vance Collection (microform), NCSA.

77. W. H. T. Walker to Braxton Bragg, March 8, 1864, William P. Palmer Collection, WRHS.

78. James L. Selfridge to Andrew Curtin, April 15, 1863, Andrew G. Curtin Letters, HCWRTC, USAMHI; *Free South,* January 27, 1863.

79. [Brigadier General John Hawkins] to Elihu G. Washburne, [February 1863], Elihu B. Washburne Papers, LC; also see C. [Gatch], secretary of the Military Committee of Kenton, Ohio, to Charles Hill, July 27, 1863, Ohio Governor and Adjutant General, Correspondence, OHS.

80. S. Noble to Lyman Trumbull, February 24, 1863, Lyman Trumbull Papers, LC.

81. [W. McConnelley] to Benjamin F. Wade, February 8, 1863, Benjamin F. Wade Papers, LC.

82. Anonymous to John Albion Andrew, April 17, 1861, Massachusetts Governor, Executive Letterbooks, ser. 567X, MSA.

83. "A Friend" to John Albion Andrew, September 3, 1861, Massachusetts Governor, Executive Letterbooks, ser. 567X, MSA.

84. W. O. Jones to Richard Yates, February 4, 1863, Yates Family Papers, IllSHL.

85. George Y. Atkinson to Oliver P. Morton, July 11, 1863, Governor Oliver P. Morton Papers, IndSA; also see Thomas W. Bennett to Oliver Morton, October 20, 1863, Governor Oliver P. Morton Papers, IndSA; also see "Scribus" in *State Journal,* E. B. Quiner Papers: Correspondence of the Wisconsin Volunteers (microfilm), reel 3, vol. 10, pp. 405–6, SHSW; "A.E." in the *Patriot,* E. B. Quiner Papers: Correspondence of the Wisconsin Volunteers (microfilm), reel 3, vol. 9, pp. 129, 134, SHSW; "Thomper" in the *Sentinel,* E. B. Quiner Papers: Correspondence of the Wisconsin Volunteers (microfilm), reel 3, vol. 9, p. 19, SHSW; Edwin H. Fay to wife Sarah, July 23, 1863, in *"This Infernal War";* Miles McCabe to Richard Yates, February 25, 1863, Yates Family Papers, IllSHL; Frederick Lloyd to William Penn Clarke, November 15, 1862, William Penn Clarke Collection, SHSIa-DM; David Logan Houser to Malvina, May 11, 1864, David Logan Houser Letters, SHSIa-IC.

86. J. George Hubbard to John A. Andrew, January 19, 1863, Massachusetts Governor, Executive Letterbooks, ser. 567X, MSA.

87. John A. Hawke to Edwin H. Stanton, September 17, 1863, Edwin H. Stanton Papers, LC.

88. John A. Dix to Edwin H. Stanton, August 16, 1863, Edwin H. Stanton Papers, LC.

89. Major General Keyes to Edwin H. Stanton, May 12, 1863, Edwin H. Stanton Papers, LC.

90. Emile Bourlier to members of Union League in Philadelphia, September 1864, to William P. Palmer Collection, WRHS.

91. [T. L. Leybold] to Owen Lovejoy, February 25, 1863, Benjamin F. Wade Papers, LC.

92. Henry Livermore Abbott to father, May [7], 1863, in *Fallen Leaves.*

93. John G. Barnard to Edwin H. Stanton, January 22, 1863, January 24, 1863, Edwin H. Stanton Papers, LC; Edwin H. Stanton to General John G. Barnard, January 22, 1863, Edwin H. Stanton Papers, LC; also see Emerson Opdycke to wife, June 14, 1863 (copy),

Emerson Opdycke Papers, OHS; Alfred B. Cree to wife Mattie, June 30, 1864, Alfred B. Cree Correspondence, UIaL.

94. Jno. R. Brown to Richard Yates, August 31, 1864, Yates Family Papers, IllSHL.

95. Pierson, "The Committee on the Conduct of the War," 555–57.

96. Westwood, "The Joint Committee on the Conduct of the War—A Look at the Record," 5, 8.

97. U.S. Senate, *Report of the Joint Committee on the Conduct of the War*, xv.

98. Westwood, "The Joint Committee on the Conduct of the War—A Look at the Record," 7.

99. Examination of Mary Ann Pitman by Colonel J. P. Sanderson, Provost Marshal General of Missouri, June 20, 1864, in St. Louis, *OR*, ser. 2, vol. 7, p. 349.

100. J. B. Devoe to J. P. Sanderson, Provost Marshal General, Department of Missouri, June 17, 1864, ibid., ser. 2, vol. 7, pp. 354–56.

101. U.S. Senate, *Report of the Joint Committee on the Conduct of the War*, xxxii.

102. John J. Hight, *History of the Fifty-Eighth Regiment of Indiana Volunteer Infantry* (Princeton, N.J.: Press of the Clarion, 1895), 426–27.

103. James Austin Connolly Diary, December 4, 8, 9, 13, 18, 1864, James Austin Connolly Papers, IllSHL.

104. John A. Marshall, *American Bastille: A History of the Illegal Arrests and Imprisonment of American Citizens during the Late Civil War* (1869; reprint, New York: Da Capo Press, 1970), 245.

105. DOC GO, 1863–64, no. 253, October 23, 1863; also see DOC GO, 1863–64, no. 30, February 24, 1863; GCMO, 1863–65, no. 29, February 4, 1863.

106. GCMO, 1863–65, no. 267, August 30, 1864.

107. GCMO, 1863–65, no. 171, April 21, 1864.

108. DOC GO, 1863 64, no. 131, June 6, 1863.

109. WDGO, 1863–65, no. 318, February 19, 1863.

110. WDGO, 1863–65, no. 242, July 28, 1863.

111. DOC GO, 1863–64, no. 142, October 4, 1864; DOC GO, 1863–64, no. 42, March 7, 1863; AOP G&CMO, 1863–65, no. 69, September 14, 1863; WDGO, 1863–65, no. 377, November 21, 1863; John B. B. Trussel, Commanders of Pennsylvania Civil War Regiments, vi, HCWRTC, USAMHI.

112. DOC GO, 1863–64, no. 85, April 19, 1863.

113. DOC GO, 1863–64, no. 134, June 6, 1863; also see WDGO, 1863–65, no. 117, March 24, 1864.

114. WDGO, 1863–65, no. 89, April 6, 1863.

115. George Shuman to Fannie, June 7, 1863, George Shuman Letters (photocopies), HCWRTC, USAMHI.

116. John Vestal Hadley to Mary [Hill], August 5, 1863, John Vestal Hadley to Mary [Hill] Letters, Lilly Library, Indiana University.

117. Marshall, *American Bastille*, 559–61, 569.

118. Hubbard, "The Lincoln-McClellan Presidential Election in Illinois," 186.

119. Van S. Bennett Diary, March 25, 1863, SHSW.

120. A. S. Webb to sister, August 10, 1863, Webb Collection, NCSA; also see H. A. Yellowley to brother, August 4, 1864, Edward Clements Yellowley Papers, SHC, UNC.

121. Fred M. Clarke to father, October 6, 1862, William Penn Clarke Collection, SHSIa-DM.

122. James L. Selfridge to Andrew G. Curtin, April 15, 1863, Andrew G. Curtin Letters, HCWRTC, USAMHI.

123. Lansden J. Cox to wife, July 12, 1863, Lansden J. Cox Letters, IllSHL.

124. "Quidam" in the *Spectator,* E. B. Quiner Papers: Correspondence of the Wisconsin Volunteers (microfilm), reel 3, vol. 10, pp. 411–12, SHSW; Henry F. Young, E. B. Quiner Papers: Correspondence of the Wisconsin Volunteers (microfilm), reel 3, vol. 8, pp. 397–98, SHSW.

125. AOP G&CMO, Special Order no. 30, February 1, 1863.

126. WDGO, 1863–65, no. 156, April 23, 1863.

127. Mark E. Neely Jr. *The Fate of Liberty: Abraham Lincoln and Civil Liberties* (New York: Oxford University Press, 1991), 115, 162–74.

128. Unknown to Hartsfield, July 24, 1864, Miscellaneous Letters, CWLC, AlaDAH.

129. "Two Madison Boys," E. B. Quiner Papers: Correspondence of the Wisconsin Volunteers (microfilm), reel 3, vol. 9, pp. 312–13.

130. Erastus Fairbanks to Justin Smith Morrill, February 16, 1863, Justin Smith Morrill Papers, LC.

131. William Tecumseh Sherman to Lazarus Noble, May 20, 1864, Ind. Adj. Gen. Corres., IndSA.

132. Zornow, *Lincoln and the Party Divided,* 200; Samuel G. Swain to brother, January 2, 1863, Samuel Swain Papers, SHSW; William H. Warren to wife [Rosina], December 29, 1862, Yates Family Papers, IllSHL.

133. Humphrey Hughes Hood to wife, February 21, 1863, Humphrey Hughes Hood Correspondence, IllSHL.

134. Francis H. Bruce to mother, April 21, 1863, Francis Bruce Letters, IllSHL; Humphrey Hughes Hood to wife, April 13, 1863, Humphrey Hughes Hood Correspondence, IllSHL; N. R. Gill to Richard Yates, Yates Family Papers, March 24, 1863, IllSHL.

135. William H. Bradbury to wife, February 17, and April 14, 1864, William H. Bradbury Correspondence, LC.

136. Samuel Storrow to parents, March 3, 1863, Samuel Storrow Papers, CW Correspondence, reel 9, MHS; J. W. Hughes to Elihu B. Washburne, February 20, 1863, Elihu B. Washburne Papers, LC; F. W. Gates to Richard Yates, January 23, 1863, Yates Family Papers, IllSHL.

137. Cyrus F. Boyd, March 1863, in *The Civil War Diary of Cyrus F. Boyd.*

138. A cascade of resolutions supporting emancipation reached the state government from the 15th, 43d, 46th, 61st, 76th, 117th, and 124th Illinois Infantries (*Chicago Tribune,* February 26, 1863).

139. Humphrey Hughes Hood to wife, February 12, 1863, Humphrey Hughes Hood Correspondence, IllSHL.

140. Robert Hubbard to wife, March 18, 1863, Robert Hubbard Papers (typescript), Civil War Manuscripts Collection, YUL.

141. James P. Banta Diary, January 2, 1863, IndHS.

142. Francis F. Audsley to wife, September 8, 1864, Francis F. Audsley Letters, WHMC.

143. Zornow, *Lincoln and the Party Divided*, 200.

144. Nevins, *The War for the Union*, 3:166.

145. John L. Mathews to "Madam," November 30, 1864, John L. Mathews Letters (typescript), SHSIa-IC; Daniel Faust to mother, January 5, 1863, Daniel Faust Letters (photocopies), HCWRTC, USAMHI; *Free South*, January 10, 1863.

146. Benton, *Voting in the Field*, 122–23.

147. Oscar Osburn Winther, "The Soldier Vote in the Election of 1864," *New York History* 25 (1944): 441–42; Nathaniel Parmeter Diary (typescript), October 11, 1864, OHS.

148. William J. Abernathy Diary, November 9, 1864, Daniel Abernathy Papers, DUL.

149. Winther, "The Soldier Vote in the Election of 1864," 453.

150. Hubbard, "The Lincoln-McClellan Presidential Election in Illinois," 187; Nathaniel Parmeter Diary (typescript), October 11, 1864, OHS; "A Soldier," E. B. Quiner Papers: Correspondence of the Wisconsin Volunteers (microfilm), reel 3, vol. 9, p. 124, SHSW.

151. Benton, "Soldier Voting in Iowa," 36.

152. F. F. Coleman in the *Patriot*, E. B. Quiner Papers: Correspondence of the Wisconsin Volunteers (microfilm), reel 3, vol. 9, p. 95.

CHAPTER 7: The "Hard War"

1. Leo Tolstoy, *War and Peace* (1869; reprint, New York: Simon and Schuster, 1942), bk. 10, ch. 25, pp. 864–65.

2. Hoffman Nickerson, *The Armed Horde, 1793–1939: A Study of the Rise, Survival, and Decline of the Mass Army* (New York: G. P. Putnam's Sons, 1940), 14.

3. Ibid., ix; Reuven Gal, "Limits of Military Legitimacy and Its Relation to Military Commitment," in *Legitimacy and Commitment in the Military,* ed. Thomas C. Wyatt and Reuven Gal (Westport, Conn.: Greenwood Press, 1990), 6.

4. Nickerson, *The Armed Horde,* 40–42, 59, 61, 63, 73–74.

5. Allan R. Millett, Murray Williamson, and Kenneth Watman, "The Effectiveness of Military Organizations," in *Military Effectiveness,* ed. Allan R. Millett and Murray Williamson (Boston: Allen and Unwin, 1988), 1:8.

6. Clausewitz, *War, Politics, and Power,* 65.

7. Nickerson, *The Armed Horde,* 65.

8. Paddy Griffith, *Battle Tactics of the Civil War* (New Haven: Yale University Press, 1989), 10.

9. Nickerson, *The Armed Horde,* 167.

10. Corrected chi square = 82.602, df = 1, probability of error = 0, but phi only .29.

11. Andrew R. Linscott to parents, October 7, 1864, Andrew R. Linscott Correspondence, CW Correspondence, MHS.

12. Francis F. Audsley to Harriet, November 3, 1863, Francis F. Audsley Letters, WHMC.

13. Mark Grimsley, *The Hard Hand of War: Union Policy toward Southern Civilians, 1861–1865* (New York: Cambridge University Press, 1995), 2–4, 174–75.

14. Ibid., 39–46.

15. Stephen V. Ash, *When the Yankees Came: Conflict and Chaos in the Occupied South, 1861–1865* (Chapel Hill: University of North Carolina Press, 1995), 56–58, 69.

16. Charles Royster, *The Destructive War: William Tecumseh Sherman, Stonewall Jackson, and the Americans* (New York: Alfred A. Knopf, 1991), 267.

17. Grimsley, *The Hard Hand of War,* 222–23.

18. Peter Newport Bragg to Josephine, January 1, 1863, in Bragg, *Letters of a Confederate Surgeon.*

19. "Resolution of Officers of the Iowa Regiments at Corinth," February 23, 1863, Company F, 2d Iowa, 7th Corporal to Captain, Voltaire P. Twombly Correspondence, SHSIa-DM.

20. George S. Richardson to mother, June 4, 1863, George S. and William A. Richardson Letters (typescript), SHSIa-IC.

21. Brian Holden Reid, "Historians and the Joint Committee on the Conduct of the War," 329.

22. Cyrus F. Boyd, February 15, 1863, in *The Civil War Diary of Cyrus F. Boyd;* also see Humphrey Hughes Hood to wife, July 21, 1863, Humphrey Hughes Hood Correspondence, IllSHL; James J. Nelson to Oliver Morton, July 14, 1864, Governor Oliver P. Morton Papers, IndSA.

23. Mark E. Neely Jr. "Was the Civil War a Total War?" *CWH* 37 (March 1991): 11, 15, 18–19, 21, 23.

24. Ibid., 23.

25. Ibid.

26. Robert Mitchell Jr. to friend Mumm, August 11, 1864, Robert Mitchell Jr. Letters and Diaries, Briggs-Mitchell Family Papers, CHS; also see George Shuman to Fannie, January 8, 1865, George Shuman Letters (photocopies), HCWRTC, USAMHI.

27. Glatthaar, *The March to the Sea and Beyond,* 122.

28. DeWitt Clinton Loudon to Hannah, January 1, 1863, Dewitt Clinton Loudon Papers, OHS.

29. Harvey Graham to wife, April 16, 1863, Dr. Graeme O'Geran Collection, SHSIa-DM.

30. McPherson, *Battle Cry of Freedom,* 500.

31. Joseph Kohout to family, August 12, 1864, Joseph Kohout Letters, UIaL; also see Carlos Parsons Lyman, March 2, 1863, Carlos Parsons Lyman Diaries and Letters, WRHS.

32. John W. Baldwin to Gussie, April 20, 1863, James W. Baldwin Correspondence, OHS.

33. Edward S. Solomon, Resolution of the Officers of the 82d Illinois, February 14, 1863, Yates Family Papers, IllSHL.

34. Nickerson, *The Armed Horde,* 170.

35. Edward Hagerman, *The American Civil War and the Origins of Modern Warfare: Ideas, Organization, and Field Command* (Bloomington: Indiana University Press, 1988), 47.

36. Nevins, *The War for the Union,* 2:466.

37. Glatthaar, *The March to the Sea and Beyond,* xii.

38. Faivre, *Les Nations armées,* 25; Bertaud, *The Army of the French Revolution,* 76, 236.

39. [W. McConnelley] to Benjamin F. Wade, February 8, 1863, Benjamin F. Wade Papers, LC.

40. Griffith, *Battle Tactics of the Civil War,* 140, 163; Hagerman, *The American Civil War and the Origins of Modern Warfare,* 3–4.

41. Griffith, *Battle Tactics of the Civil War,* 61.

42. Ibid., 66, 140, 163.

43. Frank and Reaves, *"Seeing the Elephant,"* 88–91.

44. Henry Jerry Osterhoudt, "The Evolution of the U.S. Army Assault Tactics, 1778–1919: The Search for a Sound Doctrine" (Ph.D. diss., Duke University, 1986), 87.

45. Nevins, *The War for the Union,* 3:209.

46. Glatthaar, *The March to the Sea and Beyond,* 38.

47. Hagerman, *The American Civil War and the Origins of Modern Warfare,* 172.

48. Glatthaar, *The March to the Sea and Beyond,* 121–22; Hagerman, *The American Civil War and the Origins of Modern Warfare,* 14, 34.

49. Hagerman, *The American Civil War and the Origins of Modern Warfare,* 119, 170, 204–5, 208.

50. John Wesley Marshall Journal (typescript), September 26, 1863, OHS.

51. Bertaud, *The Army of the French Revolution,* 155, 232–33.

52. Humphrey Hughes Hood to wife, September 10, 1863, Humphrey Hughes Hood Correspondence, IllSHL.

53. Nickerson, *The Armed Horde,* 22; Thucydides, *History of the Peloponnesian War,* trans. Rex Warner (New York: Penguin Books), 5:85–113.

54. John Blair Diary, June 10, 1864, Confederate Collection, TSLA; AOP G&CMO, 1863–65, nos. 21 and 194, July 7, 1863, and July 8, 1864.

55. Clausewitz, *War, Politics, and Power,* 63, 99.

56. Elliott P. Chodoff, "Ideology and Primary Groups," *AFS* 9 (Summer 1983): 575.

57. Griffith, *Battle Tactics of the Civil War,* 51, 98; Jock Haswell, *Citizen Armies* (London: P. Davies, 1973), 112; Hess, *Liberty, Virtue, and Progress,* 63.

58. Chodoff, "Ideology and Primary Groups," 572–73; *Battles and Leaders of the Civil War* (New York: Yoseloff, 1956), 1:539, 4:289.

59. Haswell, *Citizen Armies,* 112.

60. George L. Mosse, *Fallen Soldiers: Reshaping the Memory of the World Wars* (New York: Oxford University Press, 1990), 31; Royster, *The Destructive War,* 34–39, 256–57.

61. Regarding the First World War's British volunteers, see Reader, *At Duty's Call*.

62. Griffith, *Battle Tactics of the Civil War*, 80–81.

63. Hagerman, *The American Civil War and the Origins of Modern Warfare*, 22.

64. Nickerson, *The Armed Horde*, 16–17.

65. Ibid., 30; also see Clausewitz, *War, Politics, and Power*, 78.

66. Clausewitz, *War, Politics, and Power*, 84.

67. Edwin H. Fay to wife Sarah, July 10, 1863, in *"This Infernal War"*; John Hampden Chamberlayne to mother, May 9, 1863, John Hampden Chamberlayne Papers, VHS; George W. Guess to Sarah Cockrell, January 17, 1863, Sarah Cockrell Papers, DUL.

68. Humphrey Hughes Hood to wife, September 20, 1864, Humphrey Hughes Hood Correspondence, IllSHL.

69. Foner, *Politics and Ideology in the Age of the Civil War*, 24; Daniel Faust to brother, May 7, 1863, Daniel Faust Letters (photocopies), HCWRTC, USAMHI.

70. William J. Gibson to children, March 25, 1862, Gibson Family Papers, VHS.

71. Cyrus F. Boyd Diary, February 15, 1863, in *The Civil War Diary of Cyrus F. Boyd; Jonesboro (Illinois) Gazette*, February 14, 1863.

72. There were fifty-six Union soldiers who were highly politically sophisticated and who discussed emancipation in their letters and diaries. Corrected chi square = 17.534, df = 1, probability of error = 0. However, when all Union soldiers who discussed slavery (N = 613) were included, only 27 percent supported emancipation. Corrected chi square in this case was 62.005, df = 1, probability of error = 0.

73. Levi A. Ross to father and mother, December 16, 1864, Levi A. Ross Diary and Letters, IllSHL.

74. Lucius V. Wood to parent, January 31, 1863, Julius V. Wood Correspondence, WRHS.

75. Joseph C. Sharp to wife, September 8, 1864, Joseph C. Sharp Letters, AHC.

76. Unknown soldier of the 4th Wisconsin Infantry, E. B. Quiner Papers: Correspondence of the Wisconsin Volunteers (microfilm) reel 3, vol. 8, p. 216.

77. Myron Underwood to wife, March 20, 1864, Myron Underwood Letters, UIaL.

78. Isaac Babel, *Collected Short Stories* (New York: New American Library, 1974), 30–31.

79. *Free South* (Beaufort, South Carolina), January 17, 1863.

80. Ira Miltmore to wife, July 4, 1863, Clarion I. Miltmore Papers, CHS.

81. Voleny G. Barbour to Lucian B. Case, August 14, 1863, Lucian B. Case Papers, CHS; also see Junius Newport Bragg to Josephine, January 1, 1863, in *Letters of a Confederate Surgeon*, 107.

82. Robert Franklin Bunting to editor of the *Tri Weekly Telegraph*, January 6, 1863, Robert Franklin Bunting Letters (transcript), TSLA.

83. "Buck" [William S.] Long to A. S. Webb's sister, August 10, 1863, Webb Family Papers, SHC, UNC.

84. Joseph Branch O'Bryan to sister, July 30, 1864, Joseph Branch O'Bryan Papers, TSLA.

85. Patrick, *Reluctant Rebel*, 201–2.

86. Henry Goodloe Orr to sister, July 2, 1863, in *Campaigning with Parson's Texas Brigade, CSA*.

87. Alva C. Griest Journal (typescript), January 21, 1863, HCWRTC, USAMHI.

88. James C. Parrott to wife, January 27, 1865, James C. Parrott Letters, SHSIa-IC.

89. De Have Norton to father, May 3, 1862, De Have Norton Papers, SHSW.

90. John Wesley Marshal Journal (typescript), July 13, 1863, OHS.

91. John Lane Stuart to brother Charles, July 22, 1863, John Lane Stuart Letters, DUL; "W.P.M.," E. B. Quiner Papers: Correspondence of the Wisconsin Volunteers (microfilm), reel 3, vol. 8, pp. 229–30, SHSW.

92. George C. Brown Reminiscences, Brown-Ewell Papers, TSLA.

93. Myron Underwood to wife, March 20, 1864, Myron Underwood Letters, UIaL.

94. Frank M. Myers to home folks, May 16, 1864, Frank M. Myers Letters (typescript), CWTIC, USAMHI.

95. William Foster to Kate, September 5, 1864, William Foster Papers, WRHC.

96. Michael Fellman, *Inside War* (New York: Oxford University Press, 1989), 110–11.

97. Harriet Audsley to husband [Francis], January 30, 1864, Francis F. Audsley Letters, WHMC; Henry Goodloe Orr to sister, February 8, 1864, in *Campaigning with Parson's Texas Brigade, CSA; OR*, ser. 2, vol. 7, pp. 1060–62.

98. Major General W. T. Sherman to General Burnside, June 21, 1863, U.S. Adjutant General, Partial Compilation of Documents Relating to Extreme Repressive Measures in the Conduct of the Civil War, RG 94, NA; also see Arthur B. Carpenter to parents, September 22, 1864, Arthur B. Carpenter Papers, Civil War Manuscripts Collection, YUL; Jimmerson, *The Private Civil War*, 138.

99. John Francis Shaffner to Carrie, October 8, 1864, John Francis Shaffner Papers, NCSA; George Shuman to Fannie, June 7, 1863, George Shuman Letters (photocopies), HRCWRT, USAMHI; *OR*, ser. 2, vol. 7, p. 50.

100. Alexander G. Downing, March 2, 1865, in *Downing's Civil War Diary*.

101. Macon Bonner to wife, May 15, 1864, Macon Bonner Papers, SHC, UNC.

102. Bailey, *A Private Chapter of the War*, 7–9, 25–26.

103. James W. Chapin, March 7, 1865, in "A Yank in the Carolinas Campaign," ed. Donald E. Reynolds and Max H. Kele, *North Carolina Historical Review* 46 (1969).

104. Humphrey Hughes Hood to wife, September 30, 1864, Humphrey Hughes Hood Correspondence, IllSHL.

105. *OR*, ser. 2, vol. 6, p. 1029.

106. Luther L. Swank to Katie, August 25, 1864, Luther L. Swank Letters (typescript), VHS.

107. Uriah N. Parmelee to brother Sam, April 7, 1864, Samuel Spencer and Uriah N. Parmelee Papers, DUL; John H. Burrill to parents, March 21, 1864, John H. Burrill Letters (typescript), CWTIC, USAMHI; Major General W. T. Sherman to Major General J. B. Steadman, June 23, 1864, U.S. Adjutant General, Partial Compilation of Documents Relating to Extreme Repressive Measures in the Conduct of the Civil War, RG 94, NA;

Downing, December 10, 1864, in *Downing's Civil War Diary;* Hight, *History of the Fifty-Eighth Regiment of Indiana Volunteer Infantry,* 468.

108. William Peel Diary, April 16, 1864, MDAH; Luther L. Swank to Katie, August 25, 1864, Luther L. Swank Letters (typescript), VHS; Richard P. White to cousin, April 23, 1864, Ross Family Correspondence, VSLA.

109. James S. Thomas to sister, May 23, 1863, James S. Thomas Correspondence, IndHS.

110. Leonard F. Parker Diary, June 18, 1864, SHSIa-IC.

111. William T. Sherman to Edwin H. Stanton, April 23, 1864, Edwin H. Stanton Papers, LC.

112. Glatthaar, *Forged in Battle,* 133.

113. Gregory J. W. Urwin, "'We Cannot Treat Negroes . . . as Prisoners of War': Racial Atrocities and Reprisals in Civil War Arkansas," *CWH* 42 (September 1996): 196–98.

114. Glatthaar, *Forged in Battle,* 156; also see William D. Matter, *If It Takes All Summer* (Chapel Hill: University of North Carolina Press, 1988), 80, regarding another Virginia incident.

115. Edwin H. Fay to wife Sarah, April 25, 1864, in *"This Infernal War."*

116. *OR,* ser. 2, vol. 7, pp. 459–60.

117. Glatthaar, *Forged in Battle,* 155.

118. *OR,* ser. 2, vol. 7, pp. 967–69, 987–88.

119. William Johnson Pegram to Jenny, August 1, 1864, Pegram-Johnson-McIntosh Family Papers, VHS.

120. Lance Janda, "Shutting the Gates of Mercy: The American Origins of Total War, 1860–1880," *American Journal of Military History* 59 (January 1995): 12–20; Jimmerson, *The Private Civil War,* 130.

121. G. H. Munn to Robert Mitchell, August 11, 1862, Robert Mitchell Jr. Letters and Diaries, Briggs-Mitchell Family Papers, CHS; also see Lieutenant General U. S. Grant to Major General Sheridan, August 26, 1864, U.S. Adjutant General, Partial Compilation of Documents Relating to Extreme Repressive Measures in the Conduct of the Civil War, RG 94, NA.

122. Nevins, *The War for the Union,* 2:293, 296.

123. Major General P. H. Sheridan to Lieutenant General U. S. Grant, October 7, 1864, U.S. Adjutant General, Partial Compilation of Documents Relating to Extreme Repressive Measures in the Conduct of the Civil War, RG 94, NA.

124. [P. G. Bier] Assistant Adjutant General, to Major T. Quinn, Commanding 1st New York Cavalry, May 30, 1864, and Lieutenant General U. S. Grant to Major General Sheridan, August 26, 1864, both in U.S. Adjutant General, Partial Compilation of Documents Relating to Extreme Repressive Measures in the Conduct of the Civil War, RG 94; also see Edward G. Longacre, "Judson Kilpatrick," *Civil War Times Illustrated* 10 (January 1971): 32–33.

125. Nevins, *The War for the Union,* 3:29, 379, 430; James Austin Connolly Journal, November 23, 1864, James Austin Connolly Papers, IllSHL; Andrew Bush to wife, No-

vember 9, 1864, Andrew Bush Letters (typescript), IndSHL; Greenville [South Caro-lina] Ladies Association Minutes, DUL; J. G. Harvey, letter to the *Beacon* (Greenville, Ala-bama) April 25, 1863; Thomas Hopkins Deavenport Diary, September 23, 1864, TSLA. Yankee raiding parties were making "beggars of the richest," lamented a Confederate (Francis Warrington Dawson to mother, December 25, 1864, Francis Warrington Daw-son Letters, DUL); also see Thomas Hopkins Deavenport Diary, April 28, 1864, TSLA.

126. Report by William S. Kochersperger, sergeant, Company L, 20th Pennsylvania Cavalry, to Major John S. Schultze, Assistant Adjutant General, Harrisburg, August 9, 1864, U.S. Adjutant General, Partial Compilation of Documents Relating to Extreme Repressive Measures in the Conduct of the Civil War, RG 94, NA; also see Lieutenant General Jubal A. Early's order to General McCausland, July 28, 1864, U.S. Adjutant General, Partial Compilation of Documents Relating to Extreme Repressive Measures in the Conduct of the Civil War, RG 94, NA; Thomas Colman to parents, April 29, 1863, Colman-Hayter Family Papers, WHMC. The Confederate cavalry stole supplies and seized women when the Southern quartermaster corps could not furnish the former and money could not buy the latter (Patrick, *Reluctant Rebel*, 200).

127. Dougan, *Confederate Arkansas,* 103.

128. Nevins, *The War for the Union,* 2:403.

129. Martin V. Ewing Civil War Diary (typescript), June 23, 1863, Wilbur H. Tracy Pa-pers, WHMC.

130. Nevins, *The War for the Union,* 2:288.

131. Humphrey Hughes Hood to wife, January 23 and June 26, 1863, Humphrey Hughes Hood Correspondence, IllSHL; John William Murray to wife, May 23, 1863, John William Murray Letters (photocopies), VSLA; Theodore Gillard Trimmier to Mary, June 7, 1863, Theodore Gillard Trimmier Papers, TSLA.

132. Sam Keen, *Faces of the Enemy: Reflections of the Hostile Imagination* (San Fran-cisco: Harper and Row, 1986).

133. Westwood, "The Joint Committee on the Conduct of the War—A Look at the Record," 9.

134. William Johnson Pegram to sister, October 24, 1864, Pegram-Johnson-McIntosh Family Papers, VHS; Charles Hart Olmstead to wife, September 12, 1864, Charles Hart Olmstead Papers, SHC, UNC.

135. Macon Bonner to wife, July 6, 1864, and November 1, [1864], Macon Bonner Pa-pers, SHC, UNC.

136. John Marshall Martin to Sallie, October 8, 1864, John Marshall Martin Let-ters, VHS.

137. Day Elmore to parents, November 8, 1864, Lucian B. Case Papers, CHS.

138. John Francis Shaffner to Carrie, April 24, 1864, John Francis Shaffner Papers, NCSA; also see Alcinus Ward Fenton to brother Shrub, January 16, 1864, Alcinus Ward Fenton Papers, WRHS.

139. Elias Davis to wife, March 27, 1864, Elias Davis Papers, SHC, UNC.

140. Day Elmore to parents, November 8, 1864, Lucian B. Case Papers, CHS.

141. Joseph C. Sharp to wife, October 14, 1864, Joseph C. Sharp Letters, AHC. Generals including Lee, Hood, and Johnston realized that they were political allies of McClellan (McPherson, *Battle Cry of Freedom*, 650).

142. Neely, "Was the Civil War a Total War?" 27; Janda, "Shutting the Gates of Mercy," 8.

143. Nevins, *The War for the Union*, 2:154–56.

144. Robert Gooding to brother, May 5 and 19, 1863, Robert Gooding Collection, WHMC.

145. McPherson, *Battle Cry of Freedom*, 335.

146. Neely, "Was the Civil War a Total War?" 24.

147. Major General David Hunter to Edwin H. Stanton, April 30, 1863, Edwin H. Stanton Papers, LC.

148. Bailey, *A Private Chapter of the War*, 76; also see Thomas Wentworth Higginson, *Army Life in a Black Regiment* (1900; reprint, Boston: Beacon Press, 1962), 146, regarding "pirating" operations along the Carolina-Florida coast.

149. Kenneth M. Stampp, *The Era of Reconstruction, 1865–1877* (New York: Alfred A. Knopf, 1966), 125.

150. William Biggs to father, June 27, 1864, Asa Biggs Papers, DUL.

151. James Peter Williams to sister, June 4, 1863, James Peter Williams Letter (typescript), VSLA.

CHAPTER 8: The War against Dissidents

1. Frank and Reaves, "*Seeing the Elephant*," 54–61, 137; Reid Mitchell, *The Vacant Chair* (New York: Oxford University Press, 1993), 26, 32.

2. Firth, *Cromwell's Army*, 346–47.

3. Ibid., 351.

4. Arthur Marwick, "Problems and Consequences of Organizing Society for Total War," in *Mobilization for Total War: The Canadian, American, and British Experience, 1914–1918, 1939–1945*, ed. N. F. Dreiziger (Montreal: Wilfrid Laurier Press, 1981), 4, explains that no two societies respond to war in the same way. Each society has its own mix of traits that determine the nature of its response. Hence, no universal predictive model can explain outcomes. Also, responses vary according to the extent of involvement in the war.

5. Bertaud, *The Army of the French Revolution*, 28.

6. Ibid., 204.

7. *Howard (Indiana) Tribune*, November 5, 1861; *Steubenville (Ohio) Herald*, November 26, 1861, January 26, 1862.

8. G. W. Hodges to [wife] Marana, April 25, 1863, G. W. Hodges Collection, WRHS.

9. *Natchez (Mississippi) Daily Courier*, October 23, 1861.

10. George M. Barnard Jr. to father, July 4, 1863, George M. Barnard Papers, CW Correspondence, reel 17, MHS.

11. Elijah J. Petty to wife, April 16, 1863, in *Journey to Pleasant Hill*.

12. William McCutcheon to J. M. Cole, March 9, 1862, James M. Cole Papers, IllSHL.

13. Ellis, *Armies in Revolution*, 64; also see Martin L. Van Creveld, *Fighting Power: German and U.S. Army Performance, 1939–1949* (Westport, Conn.: Greenwood Press, 1982), 20–21; Henderson, *Cohesion*, 42. Alexander Hamilton fought an uphill fight to convince his fellow citizens of the need to have any national army. His *Federalist* 22 calling for a national army and criticizing the state militia system elicited a storm of criticism.

14. *Van Buren (Arkansas) Press*, September 25, 1861.

15. Leander Stillwell, *The Story of A Common Soldier of Army Life in the Civil War, 1861–1865* (n.p.: Franklin Hudson, 1920), 11.

16. "Journal of the Orleans Guard," Walton-Glenny Family Papers, 1855–1967, Williams Research Center, HNOC.

17. *New Orleans Daily Crescent*, January 11, 1862.

18. See Van Creveld, *Fighting Power*, 43, 45, 74.

19. The same ties between the home front and the fighting forces existed in World War I, but in World War II territorial recruitment played a lesser role in army organizations. Nevertheless, some of the best units in the Second World War were territorially recruited: the 45th National Guard division exemplified this tradition. But modern personnel policy was premised on spreading losses nationally. If a territorially recruited outfit sustained heavy casualties, there would be high political costs and a tremendous negative impact on the morale of a community. However, the actual loss to army cohesion could be worse if heterogenous units composed of alienated replacements were thrown into combat, as was confirmed by the German experience in World War II. Such units lacked resilience during the early stages of the war. They needed the bonding effect of territorial recruitment during the interval before the unit developed an esprit de corps. Gabriel and Savage, *Crisis in Command*, 41, argue that by the Vietnam War, home front ties to specific units had limited effect on troop morale.

20. For a study of civilian relief efforts, see Robert H. Bremner, *The Public Good: Philanthropy and Welfare in the Civil War Era* (New York: Alfred A. Knopf, 1980), 35–91.

21. Junius Newport Bragg to Josephine, February 20, 1863, in *Letters of a Confederate Surgeon*.

22. Dougan, *Confederate Arkansas*, 97.

23. *Aurora (Illinois) Beacon*, May 15, 1862.

24. Michael Barton, *Goodmen: The Character of the Civil War Soldier* (University Park: Pennsylvania State University Press, 1981); also see Moran, *The Anatomy of Courage*.

25. John W. Baldwin to [wife] Gussie, December 13, 1863, James W. Baldwin Correspondence, OHS.

26. Henderson, *Cohesion*, 10.

27. See Marwick, "Problems and Consequences of Organizing Society for Total War," 16–17; and Modris Eksteins, *Rites of Spring: The Great War and the Birth of the Modern Age* (New York: Anchor Books, 1990), 181. Both books describe the role of propaganda in motivating troops in democratic and totalitarian societies.

28. Firth, *Cromwell's Army*, 20–21, 312.

29. This paralleled the ten thousand personal stereos and twenty-two thousand copies of *Stars and Stripes* that the government parceled out to the troops in the Gulf War (*New York Times,* September 6 and 15, 1990).

30. Laurence Massillon Keitt to A. Dudley Mann, [April 1864], Laurence Massillon Keitt Letters, SHC, UNC.

31. John A. Hooper to wife, August 12, 1864, John A. Hooper Letters (typescript), SHC, UNC.

32. Henderson, *Cohesion,* 11, 24.

33. Ibid., 44, 62.

34. John Kennedy Coleman Diary (printed version of original), March 14, 1865, CWTIC, USAMHI; regarding other wars, see Eksteins, *Rites of Spring,* 229, and Paul Fussell, *Wartime: Understanding and Behavior in the Second World War* (New York: Oxford University Press, 1989), 145.

35. Dewitt Clinton Loudon to Hannah, January 23, 1863, Dewitt Clinton Loudon Papers, OHS.

36. "WQ" to Captain Charles B. Johnson, February 27, 1865, Charles B. Johnson Papers, AHC.

37. W. B. Britton to the *Gazette,* August 31, 1863, E. B. Quiner Papers: Correspondence of the Wisconsin Volunteers (microfilm), reel 3, vol. 9, p. 10.

38. Franklin Gaillard to Maria, September 6, 1863, Franklin Gaillard Letters (typescript), SHC, UNC.

39. George R. Elliott Diary, September 7, 1863, Collins D. Elliott Papers, TSLA.

40. Robert Hubbard to wife Nellie, July 17, 1863, Robert Hubbard Papers (typescript), Civil War Manuscripts Collection, YUL.

41. Franklin Gaillard to Maria, September 6, 1863, Franklin Gaillard Letters (typescript), SHC, UNC.

42. John H. Burrill to parents, September 13, 1863, John H. Burrill Letters (typescript), CWTIC, USAMHI; also see David Goodrich James to parents, March 23, 1863, David Goodrich James Collection, SHSW; and George Edward Fowle to Eliza [Caldwell], July 18, 1863, in *Letters to Eliza.*

43. John Lewis to wife, March 14, 1863, John Lewis Letter (typescript), LLC, USAMHI.

44. Edwin H. Fay to wife, February 12, 1863, in *"This Infernal War";* also see Petty, *Journey to Pleasant Hill,* 126; Jonas H. Brown Diary, [May 30, 1864], Wendell W. Lang Jr. Collection, USAMHI; William Biggs to sister, October 29, 1864, Asa Biggs Papers, DUL; Peter Newport Bragg to Josephine, January 1, 1863, in Bragg, *Letters of a Confederate Surgeon;* Captain P. H. Colburn to Selectmen of the Town of Middleton, Massachusetts, December 19, 1863, Oscar Cram Letters, CWMC, USAMHI.

45. Petition by Officers of North Carolina Troops in the Army of Northern Virginia to Senator William Alexander Graham, February 27, 1865, William Alexander Graham Papers, SHC, UNC.

46. George Shuman to [wife] Fannie, June 21, 1863, George Shuman Letters (photocopies), HCWRTC, USAMHI.

47. Luther B. Furney to Lucian B. Case, August 23, 1863, Lucian B. Case Papers, CHS.

48. John F. Sale to aunt, January 23, 1864, John F. Sale Correspondence, VSLA.

49. George Shuman to [wife] Fannie, June 21, 1863, George Shuman Letters (photocopies), HCWRTC, USAMHI.

50. David Goodrich James to parents, March 23, 1863, David Goodrich James Collection, SHSW.

51. Luther B. Furney to Lucian B. Case, November 14, 1864, Lucian B. Case Papers, CHS.

52. Clement Laird Vallandigham to Horatio Seymour, May 21, 1863, Clement Laird Vallandigham Letter, OHS.

53. John H. Stibbs to father, February 23, 1863, Stibbs Family Papers, TUL; also see Amanda Chittenden to husband [George], June 14, 1863, George F. Chittenden Letters, IndSHL; David Logan Houser to Malvina, August 14, 1863, David Logan Houser Letters, SHSIa-IC; James F. Drish to wife, August 8, 1863, James F. Drish Letters, IllSHL; Humphrey Hughes Hood to wife, July 24, 1864, Humphrey Hughes Hood Correspondence, IllSHL; "R," E. B. Quiner Papers: Correspondence of the Wisconsin Volunteers (microfilm), reel 3, vol. 9, p. 154.

54. [W. McConnelley] to Benjamin F. Wade, February 8, 1863, Benjamin F. Wade Papers, LC; R. R. Crosby to Elihu B. Washburne, February 2, 1863, Elihu B. Washburne Papers; Sprague, *Freedom under Lincoln*, 174.

55. Dr. John Culver to John Hiller, November 30, 1863, Hiller Family Papers, WHMC.

56. Resolution of Officers of the Iowa Regiments at Corinth, February 23, 1863, Company F, 2d Iowa Infantry, 7th Corporal to Captain, Voltaire P. Twombly Correspondence, SHSIa-DM; also see Daniel Curry to Robert Conley, December 7, 1863, Robert G. Conley Letters, IndHS.

57. George S. Richardson to father and mother, August 9, 1863, George S. and William A. Richardson Letters (typescript), SHSIa-IC.

58. David Goodrich James to parents, March 23, 1863, David Goodrich James Collection, SHSW; also see Charles Beath to Isaac Funk, February 19, 1864, Isaac Funk Collection, IllSHL; F. M. Sparks to Richard Yates, April 21, 1863, Yates Family Papers, IllSHL.

59. Myron Underwood to wife, April 8, 1863, Myron Underwood Letters, UIaL.

60. Alonzo Van Vlack to family, August 11, 1864, Alonzo Van Vlack Papers, CWLC, AlaDAH.

61. Paul McNeil to Colonels Jones and Swan, January 2, 1863, Governor John Letcher Executive Papers, VSLA; Paul Garvey to John Letcher, January 10, 1863, Governor John Letcher Executive Papers, VSLA.

62. D. B. Worth to Zebulon Baird Vance, August 20, 1863, April 25 and August 20, 1864, Zebulon Baird Vance Collection (microform), NCSA.

63. W. L. Bryan to [Zebulon Baird Vance], April 20, 1863, Zebulon Baird Vance Collection (microform), NCSA.

64. Lieutenant Colonel W. J. Martin to Zebulon Baird Vance, August 24, 1863, Zebulon Baird Vance Collection (microform), NCSA.

65. John P. Nissen to Zebulon Baird Vance, August 29, 1862, Zebulon Baird Vance Collection (microform), NCSA.

66. R. Emerson Jr. to Elihu B. Washburne, January 26, 1863, Elihu B. Washburne Papers, LC.

67. T. Barnes to General Jacob Ammen, General Memoranda ca. May 1863, Jacob Ammen Papers, IllSHL; N. R. Gill to Richard Yates, March 24, 1863, Yates Family Papers, IllSHL; L. Thomas, adjutant general, to commanding officer, Fort Leavenworth, Kansas, March 11, 1863, U.S. Adjutant General, Letters Sent, 1863, RG 94, NA; Benjamin F. Johnson to Oliver P. Morton, August 28, 1864, Governor Oliver P. Morton Papers, IndSA; "A Friend" to Oliver P. Morton, July 3, 1863 (photocopy), Governor Oliver P. Morton Papers, IndSA; Thomas Wildman to Richard Yates, February 9, 1863, Yates Family Papers, IllSHL; W. R. Smith to David Tod, July 14, 1863, Ohio Governor and Adjutant General, Correspondence, OHS; John Kissell to Charles W. Hill, July 24, 1863, Ohio Governor and Adjutant General, Correspondence, OHS.

68. J. George Hubbard to John Albion Andrew, January 19, 1863, Massachusetts Governor Executive Letterbooks, ser. 567X, MSA.

69. "A Citizen" to John Albion Andrew, n.d., Massachusetts Governor Executive Letterbooks, ser. 567X, MSA.

70. "Not a Nager" to John Albion Andrew, August 2, 1864, Massachusetts Governor Executive Letterbooks, ser. 567X, MSA.

71. William Peel Diary, February 29, 1864, MDAH.

72. George H. Harlow to Richard Yates, June 30, 1863, Yates Family Papers, IllSHL.

73. Wood Gray, *The Hidden Civil War: The Story of the Copperheads* (1942; reprint, New York: Viking Press, 1964), 194.

74. George W. Worthman to Zebulon Baird Vance, May 10, 1863, Thomas Merritt Pittman Papers, NCSA.

75. Petition from Citizens of Marion District, May 2, 1862, James Chestnut Jr. Papers, DUL.

76. Brigadier General John H. Winder to John Letcher, March 4, 1863, Governor John Letcher Executive Papers, VSLA; Crawford, "Confederate Volunteering and Enlistment in Ashe County, North Carolina," 33.

77. Paludan, *Victims,* 60–61.

78. F. Roy Johnson, "The Roanoke-Chowan Story," 100, F. Roy Johnson Papers, NCSA.

79. The term originated with the Buffalo Know-Nothings of the 1850s.

80. Johnson, "The Roanoke-Chowan Story," 96–105, F. Roy Johnson Papers, NCSA.

Opposition to the war among the poorer classes in North Carolina had its origins in the Locofoco movement of the 1850s. Locofocoism stemmed from a working men's organization that arose when railroads and manufacturing came to the South. This left-wing Democrat movement supported Holden's peace policy and opposed what its members believed was a rich man's war and a poor man's fight. See William T. Auman and David D. Scarboro, "The Heroes of America in the Civil War in North Carolina," *North Carolina Historical Review* 58 (October 1981): 350.

81. McPherson, *Battle Cry of Freedom*, 613.

82. Moore, *Conscription and Conflict in the Confederacy*, 152–53; Paludan, *Victims*, 62–64, 70.

83. Dial, Wilse, and Brothers to Captain Quill Hunter, July 29, 1863, Wilse Dial and Brothers Letter, SHC, UNC.

84. Barrett, *The Civil War in North Carolina*, 196.

85. "Bella" to [brother] Ike, June 21, 1863, OHS.

86. Gray, *The Hidden Civil War*, 111.

87. Current, *The History of Wisconsin*, 2:315–16.

88. I. Gillespie to John McAuley Palmer, December 28, 1863, Yates Family Papers, IllSHL.

89. Wife to John McAuley Palmer, November 22, 1863, Yates Family Papers, IllSHL.

90. Jacob Ammen to Richard Yates, August 12, 1863, Yates Family Papers, IllSHL.

91. Richard Yates to Edwin H. Stanton, February 2, 1863, Edwin H. Stanton Papers, LC.

92. Richard Yates et al. to Abraham Lincoln, March 1, 1863 (copy), Yates Family Papers, IllSHL; Andrew Millen to Richard Yates, January 21, 1863, Yates Family Papers, IllSHL.

93. Margaret Hiller to brother, May 10, 1863, Hiller Family Papers, WHMC.

94. Gray, *The Hidden Civil War*, 113.

95. Humphrey Hughes Hood to wife, February 4, 1863, Humphrey Hughes Hood Correspondence, IllSHL.

96. [Illegible] to Elihu B. Washburne, January 26, 1863, Elihu B. Washburne Papers, LC.

97. [Steven V. Campbell] to Benjamin F. Wade, February 7, 1863, Benjamin F. Wade Papers, LC.

98. Sprague, *Freedom under Lincoln*, 155–56.

99. S. H. Melvin et al. to Lyman Trumbull, January 27, 1863, Lyman Trumbull Papers, LC; John Corstack et al. to Lyman Trumbull, March 10, 1863, Lyman Trumbull Papers, LC; wife to John McAuley Palmer, January 7, 1863, Yates Family Papers, IllSHL.

100. James W. Ames to mother, July 19, 1863, John W. Ames Letters (typescript), LLC, USAMHI.

101. [W. McConnelley] to Benjamin F. Wade, February 8, 1863, Benjamin F. Wade Papers, LC.

102. George Wise to son, April 29, 1864, Wise Family Papers, VSLA.

103. *OR*, ser. 2, vol. 6, pp. 54–55.

104. Paludan, *Victims*, 56–57.

105. Murray, *Wake Capital and County of North Carolina*, 1:485–86.

106. *OR*, ser. 2, vol. 6, pp. 18–19; McPherson, *Battle Cry of Freedom*, 697.

107. Charges against Union sympathizers brought to 45th Virginia Regiment, Con-

federate States of America, Executive Departments, Justice Department Papers, SHC, UNC.

108. Opinion of Attorney General [John Randolph Tucker], December 30, 1862, January 3, 1863, Governor John Letcher Executive Papers, VSLA; Samuel W. Camahan, mayor of Abingdon, to John Letcher, December 31, 1862, Governor John Letcher Executive Papers, VSLA.

109. Dougan, *Confederate Arkansas,* 5, 90–91.

110. Oliver P. Morton to Edwin H. Stanton, February 9, 1863, Edwin H. Stanton Papers, LC. Lincoln suspended habeas corpus, and local authorities began making arrests (*OR,* ser. 2, vol. 6, pp. 4–10; Sprague, *Freedom under Lincoln,* 116–17; Current, *The History of Wisconsin,* 2:319; McPherson, *Battle Cry of Freedom,* 493; Nevins, *The War for the Union,* 4:127).

111. McPherson, *Battle Cry of Freedom,* 434.

112. George Davis to E. J. Hale, January 16, 1863, Edward Jones Hale Papers, NCSA.

113. Frederick Fitzgerald to E. J. Hale, July 24, 1863, Edward Jones Hale Papers, NCSA; Murray, *Wake Capital and County of North Carolina,* 1:494; McPherson, *Battle Cry of Freedom,* 696.

114. Humphrey Hughes Hood to wife, September 21, 1864, Humphrey Hughes Hood Correspondence, IllSHL.

115. Gray, *The Hidden Civil War,* 165.

116. James H. Leonard to Mary [Sheldon], October 8, 1863, James H. Leonard Letters, SHSW.

117. Dell, *Lincoln and the War Democrats,* 207; Nevins, *The War for the Union,* 2:388.

118. Gray, *The Hidden Civil War,* 141–42, 165.

119. Frank L. Klement, *The Limits of Dissent* (Lexington: University Press of Kentucky, 1970), 183.

120. Resolution of Officers of the Iowa Regiments at Corinth, February 23, 1863, Company F, 2d Iowa Infantry, 7th Corporal to Captain, Voltaire P. Twombly Correspondence, SHSIa-DM; Daniel Curry to Robert Conley, December 7, 1863, Robert G. Conley Letters, IndHS.

121. Nevins, *The War for the Union,* 4:128.

122. Sprague, *Freedom Under Lincoln,* 143–46.

123. A. S. Young, secretary of the Military Committee of Montgomery County, to Adjutant General Charles W. Hill, July 11, 1863, Ohio Governor and Adjutant General Correspondence, OHS.

124. Neely, *The Fate of Liberty,* 69.

125. *OR,* ser. 2, vol. 7, p. 356.

126. Dougan, *Confederate Arkansas,* 90–91.

127. *OR,* ser. 2, vol. 5, p. 838; Gray, *The Hidden Civil War,* 137, 154–55.

128. *OR,* ser. 2, vol. 6, p. 432.

129. Dell, *Lincoln and the War Democrats,* 240.

130. Zornow, *Lincoln and the Party Divided,* 202.

131. McPherson, *Battle Cry of Freedom,* 618.

132. Nevins, *The War for the Union*, 4:128.

133. Dell, *Lincoln and the War Democrats*, 215; Gray, *The Hidden Civil War*, 145.

134. General Order no. 10, Headquarters, District of the Border (Kansas City), August 18, 1863, Major and Chief of Staff P. B. Plumb, U.S. Adjutant General, Partial Compilation of Documents Relating to Extreme Repressive Measures in the Conduct of the Civil War, RG 94, NA.

135. General Orders no. 11, Headquarters, District of the Border (Kansas City), August 25, 1863, Acting Assistant Adjutant General, U.S. Adjutant General, Partial Compilation of Documents Relating to Extreme Repressive Measures in the Conduct of the Civil War, RG 94, NA.

136. *OR,* ser. 2, vol. 5, p. 693.

137. Nevins, *The War for the Union*, 2:397.

138. Neely, *The Fate of Liberty*, 167–68.

139. Nevins, *The War for the Union*, 4:128.

140. DOC GO, 1865, General Order no. 30, May 6, 1865.

141. *OR,* ser. 2, vol. 6, p. 23.

142. Brigadier General John Henry Winder to John Letcher, April 6, 1863, Governor John Letcher Executive Papers, VSLA.

143. Neely, *The Fate of Liberty*, 168–69, 172, 173.

144. James S. Thomas to sister, March 11, 1863, James S. Thomas Letters, IndHS.

145. John McAuley Palmer to wife, June 12, 1863, Yates Family Papers, IllSHL.

146. Poché, November 11, 1864, in *A Louisiana Confederate.*

147. Thomas Settle Jr. to Zebulon Baird Vance, October 4, 1864, Zebulon Baird Vance Collection (microform), NCSA.

148. Paludan, *Victims,* 71–72.

149. Neely, *The Fate of Liberty*, 110–11.

150. Bailey, *A Private Chapter of the War,* 92; Dougan, *Confederate Arkansas,* 115; A. Coleman Bowman to John Letcher, February 10, 1863, Governor John Letcher Executive Papers, VSLA.

151. Confed. GO, 1863–65, General Order no. 47 restated the act of April 21, 1862, NA.

152. William Bailey Clement to wife, [August] 21, 1864, William Bailey Clement Papers, NCSA; Moore, *Conscription and Conflict in the Confederacy,* 121.

153. Alfred Pirtle to Jane, August 13, 1863, Alfred Pirtle Civil War Letters, TFC.

154. John W. Harris to mother, March 27, 1863, John W. Harris Letters, Confederate Collection, TSLA.

155. William Clarke Quantrill to Sterling Price, December 23, 1864, Charles Colcock Jones Jr. Collection, DUL. Arkansas and other states enrolled every able-bodied man into military service. Arkansas often assigned them to home-guard outfits to carry out raids against Union sympathizers in the northern part of the state. See Samuel M. Scott to Harris Flanagin, April 27, 1863, Kie Oldham Papers, AHC.

156. Humphrey Hughes Hood to wife, January 29, 1863, Humphrey Hughes Hood Correspondence, IllSHL.

157. William P. Cook to Richard Yates, June 23, 1863, Yates Family Papers, IllSHL.

158. Dell, *Lincoln and the War Democrats*, 206.

159. D. D. Benedict, president of the Union League of Greenfield, Ohio, to David Tod, June 29, 1863, Ohio Governor and Adjutant General Correspondence, OHS.

160. Confederate League Subscription Book, DUL.

161. Nevins, *The War for the Union*, 3:162.

162. Zornow, *Lincoln and the Party Divided*, 32, 179; also see Robert Hubbard to wife Nellie, April 16, May 18, 1863, Robert Hubbard Papers (typescript), Civil War Manuscripts Collection, YUL.

163. E. A. Small to Elihu B. Washburne, January 17, 1863, Elihu B. Washburne Papers, LC; Clement M. Silvestro, *Rally round the Flag: The Union Leagues in the Civil War* (Ann Arbor: University of Michigan Press, 1966), 3–4; Gray, *The Hidden Civil War*, 143–44; Nevins, *The War for the Union*, 3:162–65.

164. Rose, *Victorian America and the Civil War*, 137.

165. Amos F. Way to Richard Yates, June 23, 1863, Yates Family Papers, IllSHL; Silvestro, *Rally round the Flag*, 9.

166. Silvestro, *Rally round the Flag*, 9; Jimmerson, *The Private Civil War*, 221; Nevins, *The War for the Union*, 3:165.

167. Silvestro, *Rally round the Flag*, 3, 9.

168. *Goshen (Indiana) Democrat*, June 25, 1863, copy in Ind. Adj. Gen. Corres., IndSA.

169. Silvestro, *Rally round the Flag*, 9.

170. Charles Beath to Isaac Funk, February 19, 1863, Isaac Funk Collection, IllSHL.

171. Francis S. Minger to P. P. Enos, September 25, 1863, Ozias M. Hatch Papers, IllSHL; also see Frank L. Klement, *Dark Lanterns: Secret Political Societies, Conspiracies, and Treason Trials in the Civil War* (Baton Rouge: Louisiana State University Press, 1984), 55.

172. Harriet (Hiller) Spruance to brother Royal, March 22, 1863, Hiller Family Papers, WHMC.

173. Milton Hathaway to Richard Yates, February 17, 1863, Yates Family Papers, IllSHL.

174. Jonathan Richmond to Richard Yates, February 9, 1863, Yates Family Papers, IllSHL. Similar organizations took to the saddle in Indiana and Ohio (A. C. Harris to Oliver P. Morton, Governor Oliver P. Morton Papers, IndSA; S. S. Fisher to Charles W. Hill, July 18, 1863, Ohio Governor and Adjutant General Correspondence, OHS.

175. Klement, *The Limits of Dissent*, 320–22.

Bibliography

BOOKS, ARTICLES, AND DISSERTATIONS

Abbott, Henry Livermore. *Fallen Leaves.* Edited by Robert Garth Scott. Kent, Ohio: Kent State University Press, 1991.

Abernethy, Thomas Perkins. *From Frontier to Plantation in Tennessee: A Study in Frontier Democracy.* 1932. Reprint, University: University of Alabama Press, 1976.

Abramson, Paul R., and Ada W. Finifter. "On the Meaning of Political Trust: New Evidence from Items Introduced in 1978." *American Journal of Political Science* 25 (May 1981): 297–307.

Adams, Daniel Wallace. "Illinois Soldiers and the Emancipation Proclamation." *Journal of the Illinois State Historical Society* 67 (September 1967): 408–10.

Adams, Michael C. C. "White Volunteer Soldiers in the American Civil War." *Reviews in American History* 16 (June 1988): 222–26.

Adelman, Jonathan R. *Revolutionary Armies.* Westport, Conn.: Greenwood Press, 1980.

Adorno, Theodor W., et al. *The Authoritarian Personality.* New York: Harper and Row, 1950.

Almond, Gabriel A., and Sidney Verba. *The Civic Culture: Political Attitudes and Democracy in Five Nations.* Boston: Little, Brown and Co., 1965.

Ambrose, Stephen E. *Upton and the Army.* Baton Rouge: Louisiana State University Press, 1964.

Aristotle. *Nicomachean Ethics.* Chicago: Encyclopaedia Britannica–Great Books, 1952.

Ash, Stephen V. *When the Yankees Came: Conflict and Chaos in the Occupied South, 1861–1865.* Chapel Hill: University of North Carolina Press, 1995.

Auman, William T., and David D. Scarboro. "The Heroes of America in the Civil War in North Carolina." *North Carolina Historical Review* 58 (October 1981): 327–63.

Babel, Isaac. *Collected Short Stories.* New York: New American Library, 1974.

Bailey, Fred Arthur. *Class and Tennessee's Confederate Generation.* Chapel Hill: University of North Carolina Press, 1987.

Bailey, George W. *A Private Chapter of the War (1861–1865).* St. Louis: G. I. Jones and Co., 1880.

Baker, Jean H. *Affairs of Party: The Political Culture of Northern Democrats in the Mid-Nineteenth Century* (Ithaca: Cornell University Press, 1983.

Barrett, John G. *The Civil War in North Carolina*. Chapel Hill: University of North Carolina Press, 1963.

Barton, Michael. *Goodmen: The Character of the Civil War Soldier*. University Park: Pennsylvania State University Press, 1981.

——. Review of *We Need Men: The Union Draft in the Civil War,* by James W. Geary. *American Historical Review* 97 (December 1992): 1598–99.

Bartov, Omer. *Hitler's Army*. New York: Oxford University Press, 1991.

Battles and Leaders of the Civil War. 4 vols. New York: Yoseloff, 1956.

Baynes, John. *Morale: A Study of Men and Courage*. London: Cassell, 1967.

Beatty, Bess, and Judy Caprio, eds. "How Long Will this Misery Continue." *Civil War Times Illustrated* (February 1981): 20–23.

Behan, Charles I. "A Louisiana Soldier's Comments on Unionist Sentiment in Eastern Tennessee." *Louisiana History* 21 (Winter 1980): 92–93.

Benton, Edward Maxwell. "Soldier Voting in Iowa." *Iowa Journal of History and Politics* 39 (January 1931): 27–41.

Benton, Josiah. *Voting in the Field*. Boston: privately published, 1915.

Bergeron, Arthur W., Jr. "Free Men of Color in Grey." *Civil War History* 32 (September 1986): 247–55.

Beringer, Richard E., Herman Hattaway, Archer Jones, and William N. Still Jr. *Why the South Lost the Civil War*. Athens: University of Georgia Press, 1986.

Berlin, Ira, ed. *Freedom: A Documentary History of Emancipation, 1861–1867*. Series II. *The Black Military Experience*. New York: Cambridge University Press, 1982.

Bertaud, Jean-Paul. *The Army of the French Revolution*. Princeton: Princeton University Press, 1988.

Best, Geoffrey. *War and Society in Revolutionary Europe, 1770–1870*. New York: Oxford University Press, 1986.

Bishop, S. C. "Indiana Troops at Helena: Part V." *Phillips County Historical Quarterly* 18 (June 1980): 1–8.

Blaine, Norfleet E. "Dear Mother . . . Letters of Major and Lt. Col. Pillow." *Phillips County Historical Quarterly* 17 (December 1978): 18–24.

Boyd, Cyrus F. *The Civil War Diary of Cyrus F. Boyd: Fifteenth Iowa Infantry, 1861–1863*. Edited by Mildred Throne. Iowa City: State Historical Society of Iowa, 1953.

Bragg, Junius Newport. *Letters of a Confederate Surgeon, 1861–1865*. Edited by T. J. Gaughan. Camden, Ark.: Gaughan, 1960.

Bremner, Robert H. *The Public Good: Philanthropy and Welfare in the Civil War Era*. New York: Alfred A. Knopf, 1980.

Brinton, Crane. *The Anatomy of Revolution*. New York: Vintage, 1956.

Bryan, Charles Faulker, Jr. "The Civil War in East Tennessee: A Social, Political, and Economic Study." Ph.D. diss., University of Tennessee, 1978.

Cain, Marvin R. "A Face of Battle Needed: An Assessment of Motives and Men in Civil War Historiography." *Civil War History* 28 (1982): 5–27.

Campbell, Andrew Jackson. *Civil War Diary.* Edited by Jill Knight Garrett. Columbia, Tenn.: privately published, 1965.

Chamberlain, Robert S. "The Northern State Militia." *Civil War History* 4 (June 1958): 105–18.

Chambers, Henry A. *Diary.* Edited by T. H. Piearce. Wendell, N.C.: Broadfoot's Bookmark, 1983.

Chapin, James W. "A Yank in the Carolinas Campaign." Edited by Donald E. Reynolds and Max H. Kele. *North Carolina Historical Review* 46 (1969): 42–57.

Chazel, François. "Les ruptures révolutionnaires." In *Traité de Science Politique,* edited by Madeleine Gravitz and Jean Leca. Paris: Presses Universitaires de France, 1985.

Child, Lydia Maria Francis. *The Mother's Book.* 1831. Reprint, Old Saybrook, Conn.: Applewood Books, 1992.

Chodoff, Elliott P. "Ideology and Primary Groups." *Armed Forces and Society* 9 (Summer 1983): 569–93.

Chong, Dennis, Herbert McClosky, and John Zaller. "Patterns of Support of Democratic Capitalist Values in the United States." *British Journal of Politics* 13 (October 1983): 401–40.

Chorley, Katherine. *Armies and the Art of Revolution.* London: Faber and Faber, 1943.

Claude, Inis L., Jr. "Just Wars: Doctrines and Institutions." *Political Science Quarterly* 95 (Spring 1980): 83–96.

Clausewitz, Karl von. *War, Politics, and Power: Selections from "On War" and "I Believe and Profess."* Edited and translated by Edward M. Collins. 1833. Reprint, Chicago: Gateway, 1962.

Cobb, Richard. *The People's Armies.* New Haven: Yale University Press, 1987.

Cohen, Eliot. *Citizens and Soldiers.* Ithaca: Cornell University Press, 1985.

Cook, Timothy E. "The Bear Market in Political Socialization and the Costs of Misunderstood Psychological Theories." *American Political Science Review* 79 (December 1985): 1079–93.

Cotton, Charles A. "Commitment in Military Systems." In *Legitimacy and Commitment in the Military,* edited by Thomas C. Wyatt and Reuven Gal. Westport, Conn.: Greenwood Press, 1990.

Crawford, Martin. "Confederate Volunteering and Enlistment in Ashe County, North Carolina." *Civil War History* 37 (March 1991): 29–50.

Cremin, Lawrence A., ed. *The Republic and the School: Horace Mann on the Education of the Free Men.* New York: Teachers College, Columbia University, 1957.

Crook, D. P. *Diplomacy during the American Civil War.* New York: John Wiley and Sons, 1975.

Current, Richard N. *The History of Wisconsin.* Vol. 2, *The Civil War Era, 1848–1873.* Madison: State Historical Society of Wisconsin, 1976.

Dahl, Robert A. *Modern Political Analysis.* 4th ed. Englewood Cliffs, N.J.: Prentice-Hall, 1984.

Davis, David Brion, ed. *Antebellum American Culture.* Boston: D. C. Heath, 1979.

Daniel, Larry J. *Soldiering in the Army of the Tennessee.* Chapel Hill: University of North Carolina Press, 1991.

DeBerru, John H. "Confederate Tennessee." Ph.D. diss., University of Kentucky, 1967.

Dell, Christopher. *Lincoln and the War Democrats.* Rutherford, N.J.: Fairleigh Dickinson University Press, 1975.

Demosthenes. *Harangues.* Book 2. Paris: Société d'Edition "Les Belles Lettres," 1955.

Denoon, Charles E. *Charlie's Letters.* Edited by Richard T. Couture. Farmville, Va.: Couture, 1989.

Dickerson, Mark O., and Thomas Flanagan. *An Introduction to Government and Politics: A Conceptual Approach.* Toronto: Methuen, 1982.

Dodd, Donald Bradford. "Unionism in Northwest Alabama through 1865." Master's thesis, Auburn University, 1966.

Dougan, Michael B. *Confederate Arkansas: The People and Policies of a Frontier State in Wartime.* University: University of Alabama Press, 1976.

Douglas, James Postell. *Douglas's Texas Battery, CSA.* Edited and compiled by Lucia Rutherford. Tyler, Tex.: Smith County Historical Society, 1966.

Dower, John W. *War without Mercy.* New York: Pantheon Books, 1986.

Downing, Alexander G. *Downing's Civil War Diary.* Edited by Olynthus B. Clark. Des Moines: Historical Department of Iowa, 1916.

Drescher, Seymour, David Sabean, and Allan Sharlin, eds. *Political Symbolism in Modern Europe: Essays in Honor of George L. Mosse.* New Brunswick, N.J.: Transaction Books, 1982.

Dupuy, Trevor. "Analyzing Trends in Ground Combat." *History, Numbers and War* 1 (Summer 1977): 77–83.

Durden, Robert F. *The Gray and the Black: The Confederate Debate of Emancipation.* Baton Rouge: Louisiana State University Press, 1972.

Earnhart, Hugh C. "Commutation: Democratic or Undemocratic?" *Civil War History* 12 (June 1966): 132–42.

Edwards, Abial Hall. *"Dear Friend Anna."* Edited by Beverly Hayes Kallgren and James L. Crouthamel. Orono: University of Maine Press, 1992.

Edwards, Joseph R., comp. "Civil War and Reconstruction." *Phillips County Historical Quarterly* 16 (June 1979): 1–23.

Egbert, Robert L., et al. *The Characteristics of Fighters and Non-Fighters.* Fort Ord, Calif.: Human Research Unit no. 2, 1954.

Eksteins, Modris. *Rites of Spring: The Great War and the Birth of the Modern Age.* New York: Anchor Books, 1990.

Ellis, John. *Armies in Revolution.* New York: Oxford University Press, 1974.

———. *The Sharp End of War.* North Pomfret, Vt.: David and Charles, 1980.

Escott, Paul D. *Many Excellent People: Power and Privilege in North Carolina, 1850–1900.* Chapel Hill: University of North Carolina Press, 1985.

Eskridge, M. B. "Who Must Not Feel Its Anxiety and Gloom?" *Pulaski County Historical Society Bulletin* 1 (November 1955): 34.

Eysenck, Hans J. *The Psychology of Politics.* London: Routledge and K. Paul, 1954.

Faivre, Maurice. *Les Nations armées*. Paris: Economica, 1988.

Fay, Edwin H. *"This Infernal War": The Confederate Letters of Sgt. Edwin H. Fay*. Edited by Bell I. Wiley. Austin: University of Texas Press, 1958.

Fellman, Michael. *Inside War*. New York: Oxford University Press, 1989.

Finley, M. I. *Politics in the Ancient World*. 1983. Reprint, New York: Cambridge University Press, 1984.

Firth, Charles H. *Cromwell's Army*. London: Methuen, 1962.

Foner, Eric. *Politics and Ideology in the Age of the Civil War*. New York: Oxford University Press, 1980.

Foster, Samuel Thompson. *One of Cleburne's Command*. Edited by Norman D. Brown. Austin: University of Texas Press, 1980.

Fowle, George. *Letters to Eliza*. Edited by Margery Greenleaf. Chicago: Follett Publishing Co., 1970.

Frank, Joseph Allan, and George Reaves. *"Seeing the Elephant": Raw Recruits at the Battle of Shiloh*. Westport, Conn.: Greenwood Press, 1989.

Fussell, Paul. *The Great War and Modern Memory*. London: Oxford University Press, 1975.

———. *Wartime: Understanding and Behavior in the Second World War*. New York: Oxford University Press, 1989.

Gabriel, Richard, and Paul L. Savage. *Crisis in Command*. New York: Hill and Wang, 1978.

Gal, Reuven. "Limits of Military Legitimacy and Its Relation to Military Commitment." In *Legitimacy and Commitment in the Military*, edited by Thomas C. Wyatt and Reuven Gal. Westport, Conn.: Greenwood Press, 1990.

Gallagher, Gary W. "Lee's Army Has Not Lost Any of Its Prestige." In *The Third Day at Gettysburg and Beyond*, edited by Gary W. Gallagher. Chapel Hill: University of North Carolina Press, 1994.

Galvin, John R. *The Minute Men*. New York: Pergamon-Brassey's, 1989.

Ganoe, William A. *The History of the United States Army*. New York: D. Appleton, 1942.

Geary, James W. "Civil War Conscription in the North: A Historiographical Overview." *Civil War History* 32 (September 1986): 208–28.

———. *We Need Men: The Union Draft in the Civil War*. DeKalb: Northern Illinois University Press, 1991.

George, Alexander L. "Primary Groups, Organization, and Military Performance." In *Handbook of Military Institutions*, edited by Roger W. Little. Beverly Hills, Calif.: Sage Publications, 1971.

Gibbon, Edward. *The Decline and Fall of the Roman Empire*. 3 vols. New York: Modern Library, n.d.

Glatthaar, Joseph T. *Forged in Battle*. New York: Meridian Books, 1991.

———. *The March to the Sea and Beyond*. New York: New York University Press, 1986.

Gray, Wood. *The Hidden Civil War: The Story of the Copperheads*. 1942. Reprint, New York: Viking Press, 1964.

Griffith, Paddy. *Battle Tactics of the Civil War*. New Haven: Yale University Press, 1989.

Grimsley, Mark. *The Hard Hand of War: Union Policy toward Southern Civilians, 1861–1865.* New York: Cambridge University Press, 1995.

Hagerman, Edward. *The American Civil War and the Origins of Modern Warfare: Ideas, Organization, and Field Command.* Bloomington: Indiana University Press, 1988.

Hallock, Judith Lee. *Braxton Bragg and Confederate Defeat.* Vol. 2. Tuscaloosa: University of Alabama Press, 1991.

Hansen, J. T., A. Susan Owen, and Michael Patrick Madden. *Parallels: The Soldiers' Knowledge and the Oral History of Contemporary Warfare.* New York: Aldine de Gruyter, 1992.

Harris, Emily J. "Sons and Soldiers: Deerfield, Massachusetts, and the Civil War." *Civil War History* 30 (June 1984): 157–71.

Harris, William C. "Conservative Unionists and the Presidential Election of 1864." *Civil War History* 38 (December 1992): 298–318.

Haswell, Jock. *Citizen Armies.* London: P. Davies, 1973.

Henderson, William Darryl. *Cohesion: The Human Element in Combat.* Washington, D.C.: National Defense University Press, 1985.

Herodotus. *The History.* Chicago: Encyclopaedia Britannica–Great Books, 1952.

Hess, Earl J. *Liberty, Virtue, and Progress: Northerners and Their War for the Union.* New York: New York University Press, 1988.

Higginson, Thomas Wentworth. *Army Life in a Black Regiment.* 1900. Reprint, Boston: Beacon Press, 1962.

Hight, John J. *History of the Fifty-Eighth Regiment of Indiana Volunteer Infantry.* Princeton, N.J.: Press of the Clarion, 1895.

Holmes, Richard. *Firing Line.* Harmondsworth, England: Penguin Books, 1986.

Hopkins, Anne H., and William Lyons. *Studies in Tennessee Politics: Tennessee Votes, 1799–1976.* Knoxville: University of Tennessee Bureau of Public Administration, 1978.

Horrocks, James. *My Dear Parents: The Civil War Seen by an English Union Soldier.* Edited by A. S. Lewis. New York: Harcourt Brace Jovanovich, 1982.

Hubbard, P. G. "The Lincoln-McClellan Presidential Election in Illinois." Ph.D. diss., University of Illinois, 1949.

Huntington, Samuel. *Political Order in Changing Societies.* New Haven: Yale University Press, 1969.

Hyman, Harold M. "Elections of 1864." in *History of Presidential Elections,* vol. 3, *1848–1868,* edited by Arthur M. Schlesinger Jr. New York: Chelsea House Publishers, 1985.

Jamison, Robert David. *Letters and Recollections of a Confederate Soldier, 1860–1865.* Compiled by Henry Downs Jamison Jr. Nashville, Tenn.: privately published, 1964.

Janda, Lance. "Shutting the Gates of Mercy: The American Origins of Total War, 1860–1880." *American Journal of Military History* 59 (January 1995): 7–26.

Janowitz, Morris. *Sociology and the Military Establishment.* New York: Sage Foundation, 1959.

Jimmerson, Randall C. *The Private Civil War.* Baton Rouge: Louisiana State University Press, 1988.

Jones, James. *The Thin Red Line.* 1962. Reprint, New York: Avon Books, 1975.

Jordan, Amos A., Jr. "Troop Information and Indoctrination." In *Handbook of Military Institution,* edited by Roger W. Little. Beverly Hills, Calif.: Sage Publications, 1971.

Jordan, Ervin L., Jr. *Black Confederates and Afro-Yankees in Civil War Virginia.* Charlottesville: University of Virginia Press, 1995.

Jouvenel, Bertrand de. *The Pure Theory of Politics.* New Haven: Yale University Press, 1963.

Kammen, Michael. *A Machine That Would Go of Itself: The Constitution in American Culture.* New York: Alfred A. Knopf, 1987.

Kaser, David. *Books and Libraries in Camp and Battle.* Westport, Conn.: Greenwood Press, 1984.

Keegan, John. *The Mask of Command.* New York: Penguin, 1988.

Keen, Sam. *Faces of the Enemy: Reflections of the Hostile Imagination.* San Francisco: Harper and Row, 1986.

Kellett, Anthony. *Combat Motivation.* Boston: Kluwer Nijhoff, 1982.

Kemp, Thomas R. "Community and War: The Civil War Experience of Two New Hampshire Towns." In *Toward a Social History of the American Civil War: Exploratory Essays,* edited by Maris A. Vinovskis. New York: Cambridge University Press, 1990.

Kennett, Lee. *G.I.: The American Soldier in World War II.* New York: Warner Books, 1989.

Klement, Frank L. *Dark Lanterns: Secret Political Societies, Conspiracies, and Treason Trials in the Civil War.* Baton Rouge: Louisiana State University Press, 1984.

———. *The Limits of Dissent.* Lexington: University Press of Kentucky, 1970.

Kruman, Marc W. *Parties and Politics in North Carolina, 1836–1865.* Baton Rouge: Louisiana State University Press, 1983.

Lang, Donald L. "Values: The Ultimate Determinants of Commitment and Legitimacy." In *Legitimacy and Commitment in the Military,* edited by Thomas C. Wyatt and Reuven Gal. Westport, Conn.: Greenwood Press, 1990.

Lasswell, Harold D., and Abraham Kaplan. *Power and Society: A Framework for Political Inquiry.* New Haven: Yale University Press, 1950.

Lee, James Melvin. *History of American Journalism.* Boston: Houghton Mifflin, 1917.

Leverrier, J. *Naissance de l'armée nationale.* Paris: Editions sociales, 1939.

Linderman, Gerald F. *Embattled Courage.* New York: Free Press, 1987.

Littlejohn, Elbridge Gerry. "Civil War Letters, Part II." Edited by Vicki Betts. *Chronicles of Smith County* 18 (Summer 1979): 11–50.

Longacre, Edward G. "Judson Kilpatrick." *Civil War Times Illustrated* 10 (January 1971): 24–30.

Luskin, Robert C. "Measuring Political Sophistication." *American Journal of Political Science* 31 (November 1987): 856–99.

Lynn, John A. *Bayonets of the Republic: Motivation and Tactics in the Army of Revolutionary France.* Chicago: University of Illinois Press, 1984.

Machiavelli, Niccolo. *Discourses.* New York: Penguin, 1987.

Madsen, Douglas. "Political Self-Efficacy Tested." *American Political Science Review* 81 (June 1987): 571–81.

Mahon, John K. "Civil War Infantry Assault Tactics." In *Military Analysis of the Civil War,* edited by T. Harry Williams. Millwood, N.J.: KTO Press, 1977.

Manning, Frederick J., and David H. Marlowe. "The Legitimation of Combat for the Soldier." In *Legitimacy and Commitment in the Military,* edited by Thomas Wyatt and Reuven Gal. Westport, Conn.: Greenwood Press, 1990.

Marshall, John A. *American Bastille: A History of the Illegal Arrests and Imprisonment of American Citizens during the Late Civil War.* 1869. Reprint, New York: Da Capo Press, 1970.

Marwick, Arthur. "Problems and Consequences of Organizing Society for Total War." In *Mobilization for Total War: The Canadian, American, and British Experience, 1914–1918, 1939–1945,* edited by N. F. Dreiziger. Montreal: Wilfrid Laurier Press, 1981.

Maslowski, Peter. "Army Values and American Values." *Military Review* 70 (April 1990): 10–23.

Matter, William D. *If It Takes All Summer.* Chapel Hill: University of North Carolina Press, 1988.

McConnell, Stuart. *Glorious Contentment: The Grand Army of the Republic, 1865–1900.* Chapel Hill: University of North Carolina Press, 1992.

McCrary, Peyton. "The Party of Revolution: Republican Ideas about Politics and Social Change, 1862–1867." *Civil War History* 30 (December 1984): 330–50.

McPherson, James M. "Abraham Lincoln and the Second American Revolution." In *Abraham Lincoln and the American Political Tradition,* edited by John L. Thomas. Amherst: University of Massachusetts Press, 1986.

———. *Battle Cry of Freedom.* New York: Oxford University Press, 1988.

———. *For Cause and Comrades: Why Men Fought in the Civil War.* New York: Oxford University Press, 1997.

———. *What They Fought For, 1861–1865.* Baton Rouge: Louisiana State University Press, 1994.

Meneely, Alexander Howard. *The War Department, 1861.* New York: AMS Press, 1970.

Michie, Peter S. *The Life and Letters of Emory Upton.* 1885. Reprint, New York: Arno Press, 1979.

Milgram, James W. "A Turncoat's Correspondence." *Confederate Philatelist* 12 (January 1967): 1–21.

Millett, Allan R., Murray Williamson, and Kenneth Watman. "The Effectiveness of Military Organizations." In *Military Effectiveness.* vol. 1, *The First World War,* edited by Allan R. Millett and Murray Williamson. Boston: Allen and Unwin, 1988.

Mitchell, Reid. *Civil War Soldiers.* New York: Viking Penguin, 1988.

———. "The Northern Soldier and His Community." In *Toward a Social History of the*

American Civil War: Exploratory Essays, edited by Maris A. Vinovskis. New York: Cambridge University Press, 1990.

———. *The Vacant Chair*. New York: Oxford University Press, 1993.

Moneyhon, Carl H. *The Impact of the Civil War and Reconstruction on Arkansas: Persistence in the Midst of Ruin*. Baton Rouge: Louisiana State University Press, 1994.

Moore, Albert Burton. *Conscription and Conflict in the Confederacy*. New York: Hillary Publishers, 1963.

Moran, Lord Charles. *The Anatomy of Courage*. 1945. Reprint, London: Constable, 1966.

Moskos, Charles C. *The American Enlisted Man*. New York: Sage, 1970.

Mosse, George L. *Fallen Soldiers: Reshaping the Memory of the World Wars*. New York: Oxford University Press, 1990.

Murdock, Eugene C. *One Million Men: The Civil War Draft in the North*. Madison: State Historical Society of Wisconsin, 1971.

———. "Was It a 'Poor Man's Fight?'" *Civil War History* 10 (September 1964): 241–45.

Murray, Elizabeth Reid. *Wake Capital and County of North Carolina*. Raleigh: Capital County Publishing, 1983.

Neely, Mark E., Jr. *The Fate of Liberty: Abraham Lincoln and Civil Liberties*. New York: Oxford University Press, 1991.

———. "Was the Civil War a Total War?" *Civil War History* 37 (March 1991): 5–28.

Nevins, Allan. *The War for the Union*. Vol. 1, *The Improvised War, 1861–1862*. New York: Charles Scribner's Sons, 1959.

———. *The War for the Union*. Vol. 2, *The War Becomes Revolution, 1862–1863*. New York: Charles Scribner's Sons, 1960.

———. *The War for the Union*. Vol. 3, *The Organized War, 1863–1864*. New York: Charles Scribner's Sons, 1971.

———. *The War for the Union*. Vol. 4, *The Organized War to Victory, 1864–1865*. New York: Charles Scribner's Sons, 1971.

Nickerson, Hoffman. *The Armed Horde, 1793–1939: A Study of the Rise, Survival, and Decline of the Mass Army*. New York: G. P. Putnam's Sons, 1940.

Orr, A. L., Henry Goodloe Orr, and James N. Orr. *Campaigning with Parson's Texas Brigade, CSA*. Edited By John Q. Anderson. Hillsboro, Tex.: Hill Junior College Press, 1967.

Osterhoudt, Henry Jerry. "The Evolution of the U.S. Army Assault Tactics, 1778–1919: The Search for a Sound Doctrine." Ph.D. diss., Duke University, 1986.

Paludan, Phillip Shaw. *"The People's Contest": The Union and Civil War, 1861–1865*. New York: Harper and Row, 1988.

———. *Victims: A True Story of the Civil War*. Knoxville: University of Tennessee Press, 1981.

Parker, H. A. "Reaping the Whirlwind." Edited by Edward Longacre. *Manuscripts* 32 (Winter 1980): 54–57.

Patrick, Robert. *Reluctant Rebel*. Edited by F. Jay Taylor. Baton Rouge: Louisiana State University Press, 1959.

Petty, Elijah P. *Journey to Pleasant Hill: The Civil War Letters of Captain Elijah P. Petty,*

Walker's Texas Division CSA. Edited by Norman D. Brown. San Antonio: University of Texas Institute of Texan Culture, 1982.

Pierson, William Whatley, Jr. "The Committee on the Conduct of the War." *American Historical Review* 23 (April 1918): 550–76.

Plato. *Laws.* Chicago: Encyclopaedia Britannica–Great Books, 1952.

Poché, Felix Pierre. *A Louisiana Confederate: Diary of Felix Poché.* Edited by Edwin C. Bearss. Natchitoches: Louisiana Studies Institute, Northwestern State University, 1972.

Polybius. *Histories.* Translated by W. R. Paton. London: Cambridge University Press, 1954.

Poole, Miriam, and Robert Hoffsommer, eds. "No Rest for the Wicked." *Civil War Times Illustrated* 22 (September 1983): 16–31.

Powell, William S., ed. *Dictionary of North Carolina Biography.* Chapel Hill: University of North Carolina Press, 1979.

Rawley, John A. *The Politics of Union: Northern Politics during the Civil War.* Hinsdale, Ill.: Dryden Press, 1974.

Reader, W. J. *At Duty's Call.* Manchester, England: Manchester University Press, 1988.

Reid, Brian Holden. "Historians and the Joint Committee on the Conduct of the War, 1861–1865." *Civil War History* 38 (December 1992): 319–41.

Rollins, Richard. "Black Southerners in Gray." In *Black Southerners,* edited by Richard Rollins. Murfreesboro, Tenn.: Southern Heritage Press, 1994.

Rose, Anne C. *Victorian America and the Civil War.* New York: Cambridge University Press, 1992.

Rousseau, Jean-Jacques. *On the Origin of Inequality.* Chicago: Great Books–Encyclopaedia Britannica, 1952.

———. *On Political Economy.* Chicago: Encyclopaedia Britannica–Great Books, 1952.

Royster, Charles. *The Destructive War: William Tecumseh Sherman, Stonewall Jackson, and the Americans.* New York: Alfred A. Knopf, 1991.

Schama, Simon. *Citizen: A Chronicle of the French Revolution.* New York: Alfred A. Knopf, 1989.

Sears, David O. "Political Socialization." In *The Handbook of Political Science,* vol. 2, *Macropolitical Theory,* edited by Fred I. Greenstein and Nelson W. Polsby. Don Mills, Ont.: Addison-Wesley, 1975.

Shackelford, George Green. *George Wythe Randolph and the Confederate Elite.* Athens: University of Georgia Press, 1988.

Sheeran, Reverend James B. *Confederate Chaplain: A War Journal.* Edited by Rev. Joseph T. Durkin, S. J. Milwaukee: Bruce Publishing Co., 1960.

Silvestro, Clement M. *Ralley round the Flag: The Union Leagues in the Civil War.* Ann Arbor: University of Michigan Press, 1966.

Skocpol, Theda. *States and Social Revolutions.* New York: Cambridge University Press, 1979.

Smith, Eric R. A. N. "The Levels of Conceptualization: False Measures of Ideological Sophistication." *American Political Science Review* 74 (September 1980): 685–96.

Somerville, John. "Patriotism and War." *Ethics* 91 (July 1981): 568–78.

Sprague, Dean. *Freedom under Lincoln.* Boston: Houghton Mifflin, 1965.

Springhall, John. *Youth, Empire, and Society.* London: Croom Helm, 1977.

Stampp, Kenneth M. *The Era of Reconstruction, 1865–1877.* New York: Alfred A. Knopf, 1966.

Stephens, Lowdnes F. "Political Socialization of the American Soldier." *Armed Forces and Society* 31 (Summer 1993): 595–632.

Stephenson, Nathaniel W. "The Question of Arming the Slaves." *American Historical Review* 18 (January 1918): 295–308.

Stillwell, Leander. *The Story of a Common Soldier of Army Life in the Civil War, 1861–1865.* N.p.: Franklin Hudson, 1920.

Stouffer, Samuel A., et al. *The American Soldier.* Vol. 2, *Combat and Its Aftermath.* Princeton: Princeton University Press, 1949.

St. Paul, Henry. "Our Home and Foreign Policy." *Mobile Register,* November 1863. (Copy in Howard-Tilton Memorial Library, Tulane University, New Orleans.)

Sullivan, Dolores P. *William Holmes McGuffey: Schoolmaster of the Nation.* Rutherford, N.J.: Fairleigh Dickinson University Press, 1994.

Surles, R., ed. "I Fear . . . We Must Go Up." *Civil War Times Illustrated* 25 (February 1987): 30–39.

Tap, Bruce. "Race, Rhetoric, and Emancipation: The Election of 1862 in Illinois." *Civil War History* 39 (June 1993): 101–25.

Thomas, Emory M. *The Confederate Nation, 1861–1865.* New York: Harper and Row, 1979.

Thucydides. *History of the Peloponnesian War.* Translated by Rex Warner. New York: Penguin Books, 1972.

Tocqueville, Alexis de. *Democracy in America.* 2 vols. New York: Alfred A. Knopf, 1980.

Tolstoy, Leo. *War and Peace.* 1869. Reprint, New York: Simon and Schuster, 1952.

Trotter, William R. *Silk Flags and Cold Steel: The Civil War in North Carolina: The Piedmont.* Winston Salem, N.C.: John Blair, 1988.

Upton, Emory. *The Armies of Asia and Europe.* New York: Appleton and Co., 1878.

Urwin, Gregory J. W. "'We Cannot Treat Negroes . . . as Prisoners of War': Racial Atrocities and Reprisals in Civil War Arkansas." *Civil War History* 42 (September 1996): 193–210.

Van Creveld, Martin L. *Fighting Power: German and U.S. Army Performance, 1939–1949.* Westport, Conn.: Greenwood Press, 1982.

Van Doorn, Jacques. "Ideology and the Military." In *On Military Ideology,* edited by Jacques Van Doorn and Morris Janowitz. Rotterdam, Holland: Rotterdam University Press, 1971.

Walzer, Michael. *Just and Unjust Wars.* New York: Basic Books, 1977.

———. *Obligation: Essays on Disobedience, War, and Citizenship.* Cambridge: Harvard University Press, 1970.

Weber, Max. *The Theory of Political Organization.* 1947. Reprint, New York: Free Press, 1964.

Weissberg, Robert. *Political Learning, Political Choice, and Democratic Citizenship.*
    Englewood Cliffs, N.J.: Prentice-Hall, 1974.
Weller, J. G., and F. W. Foster. "Civil War Tactics." *Ordnance* 49 (November-December
    1964): 303-6.
Wesley, Charles H. "Employ of Negroes in the Confederate Army." *Journal of Negro
    History* 4 (July 1919): 239-53.
Westwood, Howard C. "The Joint Committee on the Conduct of the War—A Look at
    the Record." *Lincoln Herald* 80 (Spring 1978): 3-14.
Wilkinson, Rupert T. *The Broken Rebel.* New York: Harper and Row, 1972.
Williams, Robert W., and Ralph A. Wooster, eds. "With Wharton's Cavalry: The Civil
    War Letters of Private Isaac Dunbar Affleck." *Arkansas Historical Quarterly* 21
    (1962): 247-68.
Williams, T. Harry. *Lincoln and the Radicals.* 1941. Reprint, Madison: University of Wis-
    consin Press, 1965.
———. "The Return of Jomini—Some Thoughts on Recent Civil War Writings." *Mili-
    tary Affairs* 34 (1970): 127-31.
———. "Voters in Blue: The Citizen Soldiers of the Civil War." *Mississippi Valley His-
    torical Review* 31 (September 1944): 187-204.
Wilson, Richard W. "Political Socialization and Moral Development." *World Politics* 33
    (January 1981): 153-77.
Winther, Oscar Osburn. "The Soldier Vote in the Election of 1864." *New York History*
    25 (1944): 440-58.
Yager, Elizabeth F. "The Presidential Campaign of 1864 in Ohio." *Ohio Archaeological
    and Historical Quarterly* 34 (October 1925): 546-89.
Zimmerman, Marc A., and Julian Rappaport. "Citizen Participation, Perceived Control,
    and Psychological Empowerment." *American Journal of Community Psychology*
    16 (October 1988): 725-50.
Zornow, William Frank. *Lincoln and the Party Divided.* 1954. Reprint, Westport, Conn.:
    Greenwood Press, 1972.

NEWSPAPERS

Aurora (Illinois) Beacon
Chicago Tribune
Cripple (Headquarters, U.S. General Hospitals, Alexandria, Virginia)
Free South (Beaufort, South Carolina)
Goshen (Indiana) Democrat
Howard (Indiana) Tribune
Jonesboro (Illinois) Gazette
Memphis Daily Appeal (presently *Commercial Appeal,* Memphis, Tennessee)
Mobile (Alabama) Advertiser and Register
Natchez (Mississippi) Daily Courier

New Orleans Daily Crescent
New York Times
South Western Baptist (Tuskegee, Alabama)
Steubenville (Ohio) Herald
Van Buren (Arkansas) Press

GOVERNMENT DOCUMENTS

Army of the Potomac. General and General Court Martial Orders. Record Group no. 94. National Archives. Washington, D.C.

Confederate States of America. Adjutant and Inspector General's Office. General Orders. National Archives. Washington, D.C.

Confederate States of America. Executive Departments. Justice Department Papers. Southern Historical Collection, University of North Carolina. Chapel Hill.

Confederate States of America Archives. State Governments. Georgia. Tallies of Votes Cast by Soldiers and Regimental Elections, 1862–1864. Duke University Library. Durham, North Carolina.

51st Alabama Mounted Regiment. Papers. Alabama Department of Archives and History. Montgomery.

Illinois Adjutant General. Civil War Records. Regimental Papers. Commissions and Promotions File. Illinois State Archives. Springfield.

Illinois Adjutant General. Civil War Records. Regimental Papers. Miscellaneous Records. Illinois State Archives. Springfield.

Illinois Governors. Correspondence. Illinois State Archives. Springfield.

Indiana Adjutant General. Correspondence. Indiana State Archives, Indianapolis.

Indiana Adjutant General. Recommendations. Indiana State Archives. Indianapolis.

Leigh, Edwin. *Literacy in the United States.* Annual report of the Commissioner of Education, prepared for the Secretary of the Interior, U.S. Congress, 41st Cong., 3d sess., 1870, Executive Document 1, pt. 4 (Serial 1450) pp. 467–502.

Massachusetts Governor. Executive Letterbooks, Series 567X. Massachusetts State Archives. Boston.

Mississippi Secretary of State. Returns of Elections for Governor and State Officers. Also Town and County Officers and Members of the Legislature. Record Group 28, no. 35. Mississippi Department of Archives and History. Jackson.

19th Indiana Regimental File. Correspondence. Indiana State Archives. Indianapolis.

Ohio. *Annual Report of the Secretary of State to the Governor of the State of Ohio for the Year 1864.* Columbus: Richard Nevins, 1865.

Ohio. Governor and Adjutant General. Correspondence. Ohio Historical Society. Columbus.

Tennessee Secretary of State. Tennessee Election Returns. State Wide General Election for Governor, C.S.A. Congress, State Legislature, August 6, 1863. Tennessee State Library and Archives. Nashville.

20th Indiana Regiment File. Correspondence. Indiana State Archives. Indianapolis.

U.S. Adjutant General. Letters Sent, 1863. Record Group no. 94. National Archives. Washington, D.C.

U.S. Adjutant General. Partial Compilation of Documents Relating to Extreme Repressive Measures in the Conduct of the Civil War. Record Group no. 94. National Archives. Washington, D.C.

U.S. Senate. *Report of the Joint Committee on the Conduct of the War.* 38th Cong., 2d sess., 1865.

U.S. War Department. Department of the Cumberland. General Orders. Record Group no. 393. National Archives. Washington, D.C.

U.S. War Department. *General Court-Martial Orders, 1864.* Washington, D.C.: U.S. Government Printing Office, 1864.

U.S. War Department. *General Orders, 1863–65.* Washington, D.C.: U.S. Government Printing Office, 1863–65.

The War of the Rebellion: A Compilation of the Official Records of the Union and Confederate Armies. Washington, D.C.: U.S. Government Printing Office, 1891–99.

Wisconsin. *The Legislative Manual of the State of Wisconsin.* Madison: Atwood and Rublee State Printers, 1865.

MANUSCRIPT COLLECTIONS

Abernathy, Daniel. Papers. Duke University Library. Durham, North Carolina.

Abernathy, William Judson. Diaries. U.S. Army Military History Institute. Carlisle Barracks, Pennsylvania.

Abraham, James. Letters (typescript). Civil War Times Illustrated Collection. U.S. Army Military History Institute. Carlisle Barracks, Pennsylvania.

Adams, Oscar. Letters. February 24 and 26, 1863. Civil War Miscellaneous Collection. U.S. Army Military History Institute. Carlisle Barracks, Pennsylvania.

Adams, Tosh. Family Papers. Alabama Department of Archives and History. Montgomery.

Adams Brigade Papers. Howard-Tilton Memorial Library, Tulane University. New Orleans.

"Address to the Soldiers of Ohio" by the Ohio Democratic State Central Committee, September 15, 1863. Election pamphlet. Western Reserve Historical Society. Cleveland, Ohio.

Ainsworth, Jared L. Published manuscript by Richard J. De Vecchio (1971). Harrisburg Civil War Round Table Collection. U.S. Army Military History Institute. Carlisle Barracks, Pennsylvania.

Albright, James W. Diary (typescript). Southern Historical Collection. University of North Carolina. Chapel Hill.

Alexander, Alvin H. Letters. Civil War Miscellaneous Collection. U.S. Army Military History Institute. Carlisle Barracks, Pennsylvania.

Alexander, William D. Diary. Southern Historical Collection. University of North Carolina. Chapel Hill.

Ames, John W. Letters (typescript). Lewis Leigh Collection. U.S. Army Military History Institute. Carlisle Barracks, Pennsylvania.

Ammen, Jacob. Papers. Illinois State Historical Library. Springfield.

Andrew, John Albion. Papers. Massachusetts Historical Society. Boston.

Anonymous Commissary Sergeant Letter, April 4, 1864. Federal Collection. Tennessee State Library and Archives. Nashville.

Anthony Family Papers. Virginia State Library and Archives. Richmond.

Armfield, John G. Letters. North Carolina State Archives. Raleigh.

Army of the Tennessee. Miscellaneous Letters. Civil War Letters Collections. Alabama Department of Archives and History. Montgomery.

Arnold-McCollum Family Letters. Arkansas History Commission. Little Rock.

Ashenfelter, Benjamin F. Letters (photocopies). Harrisburg Civil War Round Table Collection. U.S. Army Military History Institute. Carlisle Barracks, Pennsylvania.

Ashley Family Papers. Civil War Miscellaneous Collection. U.S. Army Military History Institute. Carlisle Barracks, Pennsylvania.

Athey, W. C. Letters. Civil War Letters Collection. Alabama Department of Archives and History. Montgomery.

Atwood, Evans. Diary (typescript). Arkansas History Commission. Little Rock.

Audsley, Francis F. Letters. Western Historical Manuscript Collection. Columbia, Missouri.

Averett, Harrison H. Letters. Civil War Letters Collection. Alabama Department of Archives and History. Montgomery.

Avery, George Smith. Letters. Chicago Historical Society.

Ayer, Lyman W. Letter, April 23, 1863. Federal Collection. Tennessee State Library and Archives. Nashville.

Bacot, R. H. Letters. North Carolina State Archives. Raleigh.

Bagby, John Courts. Collection. Illinois State Historical Library. Springfield.

Bailey Diary. Louisiana Historical Collection. Howard-Tilton Memorial Library, Tulane University. New Orleans.

Baird, Robert. Papers. Ohio Historical Society. Columbus.

Baker, Francis R. Diary (transcript). Illinois State Historical Library. Springfield.

Baldwin, James W. Correspondence. Ohio Historical Society. Columbus.

Ballou, Schuyler S. Family Correspondence (typescript). Harrisburg Civil War Round Table Collection. U.S. Army Military History Institute. Carlisle Barracks, Pennsylvania.

Banks, Nathaniel P. Papers. Illinois State Historical Library. Springfield.

Banta, James P. Diary. Indiana Historical Society. Indianapolis.

Barnard, George M. Papers. Civil War Correspondence. Diaries and Journals on Microfilm, reel 17. Massachusetts Historical Society. Boston.

Barnes, William R. Letters. State Historical Society of Iowa. Des Moines.

Bartlett, Edward J. Papers. Civil War Correspondence. Diaries and Journals on Microfilm. Massachusetts Historical Society. Boston.

Bartlett, James W. Letter. Lewis Leigh Collection. U.S. Army Military History Institute. Carlisle Barracks, Pennsylvania.

Bates, Jesse P. Letters. Confederate Collection. Tennessee State Library and Archives. Nashville.

Baxter, Samuel Alexander. Papers. Ohio Historical Society. Columbus.

Baylor Family Papers. Virginia Historical Society (owner of the original documents). Richmond.

Beale, Caleb Hadley. Correspondence. Civil War Correspondence. Diaries and Journals on Microfilm. Massachusetts Historical Society. Boston.

Bean, William E. Letter. Western Historical Manuscript Collection. Columbia, Missouri.

Bearse, Edwin W. Correspondence. Civil War Correspondence. Diaries and Journals on Microfilm. Massachusetts Historical Society. Boston.

Beauregard, Pierre Gustave Toutant. Letters. Williams Research Center. Historic New Orleans Collection. New Orleans.

Bell, Alder. Collection. Virginia State Library and Archives. Richmond.

Bell, Charles J. Letter. Illinois State Historical Library. Springfield.

"Bella" to [brother] Ike, June 21, 1863. Anonymous correspondent's letter. Ohio Historical Society. Columbus.

Bellamy, William Jasper. Letters. Mississippi Department of Archives and History. Jackson.

Bennage, Simon. Diary (photocopy). Civil War Miscellaneous Collection. U.S. Army Military History Institute. Carlisle Barracks, Pennsylvania.

Bennett, Van S. Diary. State Historical Society of Wisconsin. Madison.

Bennette, J. Kelly. Diary (typescript). Southern Historical Collection. University of North Carolina. Chapel Hill.

Bennett-Stites-Fay Families Papers. Ohio Historical Society. Columbus.

Benson, Berry Greenwood. Papers. Southern Historical Collection. University of North Carolina. Chapel Hill.

Benson, Solon F. Papers. State Historical Society of Iowa. Des Moines.

Bent, Edward Dudley. Collection. Western Reserve Historical Society. Cleveland, Ohio.

Biddle, Samuel Simpson. Papers. Duke University Library. Durham, North Carolina.

Biggs, Asa. Papers. Duke University Library. Durham, North Carolina.

Billings, Sara. Letters. State Historical Society of Wisconsin. Madison.

Bishard, Daniel. Letters. State Historical Society of Iowa. Des Moines.

Blackford Family Papers. Southern Historical Collection. University of North Carolina. Chapel Hill.

Blair, John. Diary. Confederate Collection. Tennessee State Library and Archives. Nashville.

Blair, William L. Letters. State Historical Society of Iowa. Des Moines.

Blaisdell Family Correspondence. Howard-Tilton Memorial Library, Tulane University. New Orleans.

Bleckley, F. A. Papers. Duke University Library. Durham, North Carolina.

Bleckley, William L. Papers. Duke University Library. Durham, North Carolina.

Bolton Family Papers. Virginia Historical Society (owner of the original documents). Richmond.

Bond, R. T. Letters. Civil War Letters Collection. Alabama Department of Archives and History. Montgomery.

Bonner, Macon. Papers. Southern Historical Collection. University of North Carolina. Chapel Hill.

Boucher, John Vincent. Letter (typescript). Civil War Miscellaneous Collection. U.S. Army Military History Institute. Carlisle Barracks, Pennsylvania.

Bowen, Frederick F. Papers. Virginia Historical Society (owner of the original documents). Richmond.

Boyle, Francis Atherton. Diary (typescript). Southern Historical Collection. University of North Carolina. Chapel Hill.

Bradbury, William H. Correspondence. Library of Congress. Washington, D.C.

Brent, George W. Letters. Illinois State Historical Library. Springfield.

Brenton, R. A. Letters. Indiana Historical Society. Indianapolis.

Britton, William B. Papers. Western Reserve Historical Society. Cleveland, Ohio.

Brockway, George A. Diary. State Historical Society of Iowa. Des Moines.

Brower, Ephraim Franklin. Diary (transcript). Civil War Miscellaneous Collection. U.S. Army Military History Institute. Carlisle Barracks, Pennsylvania.

Brown, Bergun H. Collection (typescript). Western Historical Manuscript Collection. Columbia, Missouri.

Brown, Isaac. Collection. North Carolina State Archives. Raleigh.

Brown, J. R. Papers. Duke University Library. Durham, North Carolina.

Brown, Orlando. Papers. The Filson Club. Louisville, Kentucky.

Brown, R. E. Letter. Illinois State Historical Library. Springfield.

Brown-Ewell Papers. Tennessee State Library and Archives. Nashville.

Brownlow, Isaac Newton. Letters. Arkansas History Commission. Little Rock.

Bruce, Francis. Letters. Illinois State Historical Library. Springfield.

Brush Family Papers. Illinois State Historical Library. Springfield.

Buchanan, Daniel. Papers. Ohio Historical Society. Columbus.

Buchanan, Newell. Papers. Ohio Historical Society. Columbus.

Buchanan-McClellan Collection. Southern Historical Collection. University of North Carolina. Chapel Hill.

Buck, Samuel D. Papers. Duke University Library. Durham, North Carolina.

Buck, William F. Diary. Civil War Miscellaneous Collection. U.S. Military History Institute. Carlisle Barracks, Pennsylvania.

Buddemeyer Collection. Western Historical Manuscript Collection. Columbia, Missouri.

Bunting, Robert Franklin. Letters (transcript). Tennessee State Library and Archives. Nashville.

Burhalter, James L. Diary. Illinois State Historical Library. Springfield.

Burnett, John A. Papers. North Carolina State Archives. Raleigh.

Burns Family Papers. Mississippi Department of Archives and History. Jackson.

Burrill, John H. Letters (typescript). Civil War Times Illustrated Collection. U.S. Army Military History Institute. Carlisle Barracks, Pennsylvania.

Burt, Richard W. Papers. Western Historical Manuscript Collection. Columbia, Missouri.

Bush, Andrew. Letters (typescript). Indiana State Historical Library. Indianapolis.

Callaway, Jonathan W. Letters. Arkansas History Commission. Little Rock.

Calton, John Washington. Letters. North Carolina State Archives. Raleigh.

Campbell Family Papers. Southern Historical Collection. University of North Carolina. Chapel Hill.

Carpenter, Arthur B. Papers. Civil War Manuscripts Collection. Manuscripts and Archives. Sterling Memorial Library, Yale University. New Haven, Connecticut.

Carr, Obed William. Diary (transcript). Duke University Library. Durham, North Carolina.

Case, Lucian B. Papers. Chicago Historical Society.

Cauller, Samuel T. Letters (photocopies). Harrisburg Civil War Round Table Collection. U.S. Army Military History Institute. Carlisle Barracks, Pennsylvania.

Cavin, Milas A. Papers. North Carolina State Archives. Raleigh.

Chamberlayne, John Hampden. Papers. Virginia Historical Society (owner of the original documents). Richmond.

Chandler, Zachariah. Papers. Library of Congress. Washington, D.C.

Charbonnet, Jacques Alfred. Diary (original in French). Howard-Tilton Memorial Library, Tulane University. New Orleans.

Cherry, Lunceford R. Papers. Duke University Library. Durham, North Carolina.

Chesson, Frederick. Papers. Civil War Times Illustrated Collection. U.S. Army Military History Institute. Carlisle Barracks, Pennsylvania.

Chestnut, James, Jr. Papers. Duke University Library. Durham, North Carolina.

Chittenden, George F. Letters. Indiana State Historical Library. Indianapolis.

Christian Family Papers. Virginia Historical Society (owner of the original documents). Richmond.

Church, William H. Papers. State Historical Society of Wisconsin. Madison.

Clarke, William Penn. Collection. State Historical Society of Iowa. Des Moines.

Clement, William Bailey. Papers. North Carolina State Archives. Raleigh.

Cliburn, William. Papers. Mississippi Department of Archives and History. Jackson.

Click, Jacob B. Papers. Duke University Library. Durham, North Carolina.

Clift Family Papers. Tennessee State Library and Archives. Nashville.

Clover, N. I. Letters. Lewis Leigh Collection. U.S. Army Military History Institute. Carlisle Barracks, Pennsylvania.

Clover, William D. Letters. Lewis Leigh Collection. U.S. Army Military History Institute. Carlisle Barracks, Pennsylvania.

Cocke Family Papers. Virginia Historical Society (owner of the original documents). Richmond.

Cockrell, Sarah. Papers. Duke University Library. Durham, North Carolina.

Coggin, E. B. Letters. Civil War Letters Collection. Alabama Department of Archives and History. Montgomery.

Coghill, John Fuller. Papers. Southern Historical Collection. University of North Carolina. Chapel Hill.

Cohee, Benjamin. Letters. Harrisburg Civil War Round Table Collection. U.S. Army Military History Institute. Carlisle Barracks, Pennsylvania.

Coiner Family Letters (transcript). Virginia Historical Society (owner of the original documents). Richmond.

Cole, James M. Papers. Illinois State Historical Library. Springfield.

Coleman, D. Papers. Southern Historical Collection. University of North Carolina. Chapel Hill.

Coleman, John Kennedy. Diary (printed version of original). Civil War Times Illustrated Collection. U.S. Army Military History Institute. Carlisle Barracks, Pennsylvania.

Collier, Samuel P. Papers. North Carolina State Archives. Raleigh.

Collins, John Overton. Letters. Virginia Historical Society (owner of the original documents). Richmond.

Colman-Hayter Family Papers. Western Historical Manuscript Collection. Columbia, Missouri.

Company A, 18th Indiana. Protest Letter. Indiana State Historical Library. Indianapolis.

Confederate League. Subscription Book. Duke University Library. Durham, North Carolina.

Conley, R. T. Letters. Civil War Letters Collection. Alabama Department of Archives and History. Montgomery.

Conley, Robert G. Letters. Indiana Historical Society. Indianapolis.

Connelly, Jesse B. Diary. Indiana Historical Society. Indianapolis.

Connolly, James Austin. Papers. Illinois State Historical Library. Springfield.

Connor, Seldon. Letters (typescript). Civil War Times Illustrated Collection. U.S. Army Military History Institute. Carlisle Barracks, Pennsylvania.

Cooke, Flora Juliette. Collection. Chicago Historical Society.

Corpening Family Papers. Duke University Library. Durham, North Carolina.

Corson, William Clark. Letters. Virginia Historical Society (owner of the original documents). Richmond.

Cottle, John Clark. Letters. Illinois State Historical Library. Springfield.

Councill, Mary A. (Horton). Papers. Duke University Library. Durham, North Carolina.

Cowan, Nancy H. Papers. Duke University Library. Durham, North Carolina.

Cowand, Winifred A. Papers. Duke University Library. Durham, North Carolina.

Cox, Lansden J. Letters. Illinois State Historical Library. Springfield.

Craig, David P. Letters. Indiana State Historical Library. Indianapolis.

Craig, Mary E. Papers. Duke University Library. Durham, North Carolina.

Cram, Oscar. Letters. Civil War Miscellaneous Collection. U.S. Army Military History Institute. Carlisle Barracks, Pennsylvania.

Cravens, James Addison. Papers. Lilly Library, Indiana University. Bloomington.

Crawford, Abel H. Letters (transcript). Civil War Letters Collection. Alabama Department of Archives and History. Montgomery.

Crawford, Henry C. Collection. Western Historical Manuscript Collection. Columbia, Missouri.

Crawford, John Berryman. Papers. Mississippi Department of Archives and History. Jackson.

Crawford, William Ayers. Papers. Arkansas Historical Collection. Little Rock.

Cree, Alfred B. Correspondence. University of Iowa Library. Iowa City.

Crist Papers. Lilly Library, Indiana University. Bloomington.

Crosier, Adam. Collection. Indiana State Historical Library. Indianapolis.

Curry Family Papers. Alabama Department of Archives and History. Montgomery.

Curtin, Andrew G. Letters. Harrisburg Civil War Round Table Collection. U.S. Army Military History Institute. Carlisle Barracks, Pennsylvania.

Darling, Flora. Correspondence. Western Reserve Historical Society. Cleveland, Ohio.

Davis, Elias. Papers. Southern Historical Collection. University of North Carolina. Chapel Hill.

Davis, George T. Diaries. Tennessee State Library and Archives. Nashville.

Davison, Mary F. Papers. Duke University Library. Durham, North Carolina.

Dawson, Francis Warrington. Letters. Duke University Library. Durham, North Carolina.

Dawson, Nathaniel. Papers. Southern Historical Collection. University of North Carolina. Chapel Hill.

Dawson, Richard Lew. Letters. Indiana State Historical Library. Indianapolis.

Deane, Julia. Papers. Duke University Library. Durham, North Carolina.

Dearing Family Papers. Virginia Historical Society (owner of the original documents). Richmond.

Deavenport, Thomas Hopkins. Diary. Tennessee State Library and Archives. Nashville.

DeButts Family Papers. Virginia Historical Society (owner of the original documents). Richmond.

Denoon Family Papers. Virginia State Library and Archives. Richmond.

Dial, Wilse, and Brothers. Letter. Southern Historical Collection. University of North Carolina. Chapel Hill.

Dieck Collection. Tennessee State Library and Archives. Nashville.

Dillon, George Washington. Diary. Tennessee State Library and Archives. Nashville.

Dinsmore, John C. Letters. Illinois State Historical Library. Springfield.

Dodd, David Owen. Published Letters. Compiled by Dallas T. Herndon. Arkansas Historical Commission. Little Rock.

Doolan, John Calvin. Collection. The Filson Club. Louisville, Kentucky.

Dowd, John B. Papers. Harrisburg Civil War Round Table Collection. U.S. Army Military History Institute. Carlisle Barracks, Pennsylvania.

Downman Family Papers. Virginia Historical Society (owner of the original documents). Richmond.

Dragoo, John B. Correspondence. Indiana State Historical Library. Indianapolis.

Drenan, John Frank. Letters (photocopies). Lewis Leigh Collection. U.S. Army Military History Institute. Carlisle Barracks, Pennsylvania.

Drish, James F. Letters. Illinois State Historical Library. Springfield.

DuBose, Walter. Letters. Civil War Letters Collection. Alabama Department of Archives and History. Montgomery.

Dunn Family Papers. Virginia Historical Society (owner of the original documents). Richmond.

Dunn, Helim Hatch. Letters and Diaries. Indiana Historical Society. Indianapolis.

Durham, L. S. Letters. Virginia State Library and Archives. Richmond.

Easton, Joseph. Collection. Ohio Historical Society. Columbus.

Eberhart, Louicy Ann May. Reminiscences. Illinois State Historical Library. Springfield.

Edwards, Leroy Summerfield. Correspondence (typescript). Virginia Historical Society (owner of the original documents). Richmond.

Elliott, Collins D. Papers. Tennessee State Library and Archives. Nashville.

Elliott, George R. Diaries. Confederate Collection. Tennessee State Library and Archives. Nashville.

Ellis-Marshall Family Papers (photocopies). Harrisburg Civil War Round Table Collection. U.S. Army Military History Institute. Carlisle Barracks, Pennsylvania.

Eltinge-Lord Family Papers. Duke University Library. Durham, North Carolina.

Emert, Stephen. Collection. Indiana Historical Society. Indianapolis.

Emmons, Marius A. Letters (photocopies). Lewis Leigh Collection. U.S. Army Military History Institute. Carlisle Barracks, Pennsylvania.

Erwin, George Phifer. Papers. Southern Historical Collection. University of North Carolina. Chapel Hill.

Ewing, Martin V. Civil War Diary (typescript). Wilbur H. Tracy Papers. Western Historical Manuscript Collection. Columbia, Missouri.

Fackler, C. Letters (typescript). Duke University Library. Durham, North Carolina.

Fackler, James W. Letters (typescript). State Historical Society of Iowa. Des Moines.

Fair Family Papers (photocopies). Harrisburg Civil War Round Table Collection. U.S. Army Military History Institute. Carlisle Barracks, Pennsylvania.

Faller, John I. Correspondence (transcript). Harrisburg Civil War Round Table Collection. U.S. Army Military History Institute. Carlisle Barracks, Pennsylvania.

Farinholt, Benjamin Lyons. Letters. Virginia Historical Society (owner of the original documents). Richmond.

Farrar, Lee. Letter. Confederate Collection. Tennessee State Library and Archives. Nashville.

Farver, Isaac. Collection. Indiana State Historical Library. Indianapolis.

Faulkner, Oscar, and Holt Family Papers. State Historical Society of Iowa. Des Moines.

Faust, Daniel. Letters (photocopies). Harrisburg Civil War Round Table Collection. U.S. Army Military History Institute. Carlisle Barracks, Pennsylvania.

Favrot, Henry Mortimer. Diary (French transcript). Howard-Tilton Memorial Library, Tulane University. New Orleans.

Fee, James Frank. Letters (typescript). Indiana Historical Society. Indianapolis.

Fenton, Alcinus Ward. Papers. Western Reserve Historical Society. Cleveland, Ohio.

Fielder, A. T. Diary. Tennessee State Library and Archives. Nashville.

Fifer, Joseph Wilson. Letters. Illinois State Historical Library. Springfield.

Firebaugh, Samuel Angus. Diary (typescript). Southern Historical Collection. University of North Carolina. Chapel Hill.

Fisk, Wilbur. Letters. Civil War Times Illustrated Collection. U.S. Army Military History Institute. Carlisle Barracks, Pennsylvania.

Fleagle, Amos. Correspondence (photocopies). Harrisburg Civil War Round Table Collection. U.S. Army Military History Institute. Carlisle Barracks, Pennsylvania.

Fleck, Henry. Memoirs. Harrisburg Civil War Round Table Collection. U.S. Army Military History Institute. Carlisle Barracks, Pennsylvania.

Flint, Dayton E. Letters (typescript). Civil War Miscellaneous Collection. U.S. Army Military History Institute. Carlisle Barracks, Pennsylvania.

Foisie, John B. Letter. Civil War Miscellaneous Collection. U.S. Army Military History Institute. Carlisle Barracks, Pennsylvania.

Foote Family Papers. The Filson Club, Louisville, Kentucky.

Forbes, Henry Clinton. Letters. Ohio Historical Society. Columbus.

Forest, Robert J. Papers. Harrisburg Civil War Round Table Collection. U.S. Army Military History Institute. Carlisle Barracks, Pennsylvania.

Foskett, Liberty W. Letters. Civil War Times Illustrated Collection. U.S. Army Military History Institute. Carlisle Barracks, Pennsylvania.

Foster, William. Papers. Western Reserve Historical Society. Cleveland, Ohio.

Fowle, George Edward. Correspondence. Massachusetts Historical Society. Boston.

Francher, J. A. P. Diary. Confederate Collection. Tennessee State Library and Archives. Nashville.

Frank, Alexander. Papers. Duke University Library. Durham, North Carolina.

Fraser, Frederick. Papers. Duke University Library. Durham, North Carolina.

Frey, Augustus Beardslee. Letters. Illinois State Historical Library. Springfield.

Fuller, Joseph Pryor. Diary. Southern Historical Collection. University of North Carolina. Chapel Hill.

Funk, Isaac. Collection. Illinois State Historical Library. Springfield.

Furlow, Tim. Diary. Civil War Manuscripts Collection. Manuscripts and Archives. Sterling Memorial Library, Yale University. New Haven, Connecticut.

Furst, Luther C. Diary (typescript). Harrisburg Civil War Round Table Collection. U.S. Army Military History Institute. Carlisle Barracks, Pennsylvania.

Gaillard, Franklin. Letters (typescript). Southern Historical Collection. University of North Carolina. Chapel Hill.

Gales, Seaton. Papers. North Carolina State Archives. Raleigh.

Garnett, Thomas Stuart. Letters (typescript). Virginia State Library and Archives. Richmond.

Garrison, Josiah. Collection. Indiana State Historical Library. Indianapolis.

Gash, Martin Malone. Papers. North Carolina State Archives. Raleigh.

Gaston, Cyrus. Diaries. State Historical Society of Iowa. Des Moines.

Gay, Henry W. Letters. Civil War Miscellaneous Collection. U.S. Army Military History Institute. Carlisle Barracks, Pennsylvania.

Gay, John O. Papers. Civil War Manuscripts Collection. Manuscripts and Archives. Sterling Memorial Library, Yale University. New Haven, Connecticut.

Geer, Charles Franklin. Papers. Manuscripts and Archives. Sterling Memorial Library, Yale University Library. New Haven, Connecticut.

Gibbs, Benjamin Franklin. Letters. Federal Collection. Tennessee State Library and Archives. Nashville.

Gibson Family Papers. Virginia Historical Society (owner of the original documents). Richmond.

Gibson, William J. Journal (typescript). Harrisburg Civil War Round Table Collection. U.S. Army Military History Institute. Carlisle Barracks, Pennsylvania.

Gilbey, Eben. Letters (typescript). Civil War Times Illustrated Collection. U.S. Army Military History Institute. Carlisle Barracks, Pennsylvania.

Gill Family Papers. Civil War Manuscripts Collection. Manuscripts and Archives. Sterling Memorial Library, Yale University. New Haven, Connecticut.

Glazener, Abraham M. Letters (typescript). Civil War Times Illustrated Collection. U.S. Army Military History Institute. Carlisle Barracks, Pennsylvania.

Glines, Henry C. Diary and Letters. Civil War Manuscripts Collection. Manuscripts and Archives. Sterling Memorial Library, Yale University. New Haven, Connecticut.

Gooch, J. S. Letter. Southern Historical Collection. University of North Carolina. Chapel Hill.

Goodale, Warren. Letters. Massachusetts Historical Society. Boston.

Gooding, Robert. Collection. Western Historical Manuscript Collection. Columbia, Missouri.

Gookin, Daniel. Letters. Lewis Leigh Collection. U.S. Army Military History Institute. Carlisle Barracks, Pennsylvania.

Gordon, Thomas M. Letter. Lewis Leigh Collection. U.S. Army Military History Institute. Carlisle Barracks, Pennsylvania.

Graham, William Alexander. Papers. Southern Historical Collection. University of North Carolina. Chapel Hill.

Green, James E. Papers (typescript). Southern Historical Collection. University of North Carolina. Chapel Hill.

Green, John William. Diary (transcript). The Filson Club. Louisville, Kentucky.

Green, Thomas Jefferson. Papers. Southern Historical Collection. University of North Carolina. Chapel Hill.

Greenville [South Carolina] Ladies Association. Minutes. Duke University Library. Durham, North Carolina.

Greer, John C. Letters. Virginia State Library and Archives, Richmond.

Griest, Alva C. Journal (typescript). Harrisburg Civil War Round Table Collection. U.S. Army Military History Institute. Carlisle Barracks, Pennsylvania.

Griffith, John W. Diary. Ohio Historical Society. Columbus.

Grima Family Papers, 1856–1921. Williams Research Center. Historic New Orleans Collection. New Orleans.

Grimes, Bryan. Papers. North Carolina State Archives. Raleigh.

Grinnan Family Papers. Virginia Historical Society (owner of the original documents). Richmond.

Griswold Papers. Duke University Library. Durham, North Carolina.

Grubbs, George W. Letters. Indiana State Historical Library. Indianapolis.

Guerrant Family Papers. Virginia Historical Society (owner of the original documents). Richmond.

Guerrant-Green Letters. Haldeman Family Papers. The Filson Club. Louisville, Kentucky.

Guinan, Michael. Letters. Williams Research Center. Historic New Orleans Collection. New Orleans.

Haas, Joseph F. Reprint of letter. Civil War Miscellaneous Collection. U.S. Army Military History Institute. Carlisle Barracks, Pennsylvania.

Haas, Joshua W. Letters and Diary (typescript). Harrisburg Civil War Round Table Collection. U.S. Army Military History Institute. Carlisle Barracks, Pennsylvania.

Hadley, John Vestal, to Mary [Hill]. Letters. Lilly Library, Indiana University. Bloomington.

Hairston, Peter Wilson. Papers. Southern Historical Collection. University of North Carolina. Chapel Hill.

Hale, Edward Jones. Papers. North Carolina State Archives. Raleigh.

Hall, James Iredell. Papers. Southern Historical Collection. University of North Carolina. Chapel Hill.

Hamilton, William. Letters, Library of Congress. Washington, D.C.

Hanna, James R. Correspondence. Confederate Collection. Tennessee State Library and Archives. Nashville.

Hannaford, G. W. Letters. State Historical Society of Wisconsin. Madison.

Hard, Dudley J. Diary. Western Reserve Historical Society. Cleveland, Ohio.

Hardin Family Letters, Arkansas History Commission. Little Rock.

Hardman, C. T. Privately published letters. Civil War Letters Collection. Alabama Department of Archives and History. Montgomery.

Harlow Family Papers. Virginia Historical Society (owner of the original documents). Richmond.

Harper, George Washington. Papers. Southern Historical Collection. University of North Carolina. Chapel Hill.

Harris, John W. Letters. Confederate Collection. Tennessee State Library and Archives. Nashville.

Harrison Family Papers. Virginia Historical Society (owner of the original documents). Richmond.

Harrison, M. Ethridge. Collection. Virginia State Library and Archives. Richmond.

Harts, William Henry. Diary. Ohio Historical Society. Columbus.

Harvey, J. G. Letters to the *Beacon* (Greenville, Alabama). Miscellaneous Civil War Letters. Alabama Department of Archives and History. Montgomery.

Haskell, Oliver C. Diary. Indiana Historical Society. Indianapolis.

Haskell, Sondus W. Letters (photocopies). Lewis Leigh Collection. U.S. Army Military History Institute. Carlisle Barracks, Pennsylvania.

Hatch, Ozias M. Papers. Illinois State Historical Library. Springfield.

Haverly, Charles E. Letters. State Historical Society of Iowa. Des Moines.

Hayes, Charles C. Papers. Ohio Historical Society. Columbus.

Hayward, Nathan. Letters (transcript). Massachusetts Historical Society. Boston.

Healey, George W. Letters (typescript). State Historical Society of Iowa. Des Moines.

Heath, Jones Christian. Letter. Virginia State Library and Archives. Richmond.

Hedrick, Mrs. West. Papers. Indiana State Historical Library. Indianapolis.

Hefner, Marcus. Papers. North Carolina State Archives. Raleigh.

Hege, Constantine A. Letters. Lewis Leigh Collection, U.S. Army Military History Institute. Carlisle Barracks, Pennsylvania.

Henry, Jesse L. Letters. Duke University Library. Durham, North Carolina.

Henry, Robert W. Letters. State Historical Society of Iowa. Iowa City.

Herman, David. Diary (photocopy). Civil War Miscellaneous Collection. U.S. Army Military History Institute. Carlisle Barracks, Pennsylvania.

Herrington, S. B. Papers. Ohio Historical Society. Columbus.

Hieronymous, Benjamin R. Diary (typescript). Illinois State Historical Library. Springfield.

Higganbotham, Clifton V. Letter. Virginia Historical Society (owner of the original document). Richmond.

Hiller Family Papers. Western Historical Manuscript Collection. Columbia, Missouri.

Hills, James M. Letters. Chicago Historical Society.

Hincks Family Papers. Howard-Tilton Memorial Library, Tulane University. New Orleans.

Hinman, Wilbur F. Papers. Western Reserve Historical Society. Cleveland, Ohio.

Hinshaw, Thomas. Papers. Duke University Library. Durham, North Carolina.

Hodges, G. W. Collection. Western Reserve Historical Society. Cleveland, Ohio.

Hoffman, Clement. Letters (photocopies). Harrisburg Civil War Round Table Collection. U.S. Army Military History Institute. Carlisle Barracks, Pennsylvania.

Holloway, Ephraim S. Letters (typescript). Ohio Historical Society. Columbus.

Holloway, John William. Papers. Virginia Historical Society (owner of the original documents). Richmond.

Holmes, Conrad. Papers. Virginia Historical Society (owner of the original documents). Richmond.

Holmes, James Edward. Papers. Massachusetts Historical Society. Boston.

Holt, Theron P. Papers. State Historical Society of Wisconsin. Madison.

Homan, William Diary. Civil War Miscellaneous Collection. U.S. Army Military History Institute. Carlisle Barracks, Pennsylvania.

Honnell, Thomas C. Papers. Ohio Historical Society. Columbus.

Hood, Humphrey Hughes. Correspondence. Illinois State Historical Library. Springfield.

Hooper, John A. Letters (typescript). Southern Historical Collection. University of North Carolina. Chapel Hill.

Hoover Collection. Tennessee State Historical Library and Archives. Nashville.

Hopkins, Henry H. Letters. Duke University Library. Durham, North Carolina.

Horton, Charles M. Consolidated Crescent Regiment Letters. Louisiana Historical Association Collection. Howard-Tilton Memorial Library, Tulane University. New Orleans.

Horton, W. H. Letters. Southern Historical Collection. University of North Carolina. Chapel Hill.

Houser, David Logan. Letters. State Historical Society of Iowa. Iowa City.

Howard, Francis Marion. Letter. Lewis Leigh Collection. U.S. Army Military History Institute. Carlisle Barracks, Pennsylvania.

Howe, Hiram. Civil War Diaries. State Historical Society of Iowa. Iowa City.

Howe, James Henry. Letters. State Historical Society of Wisconsin. Madison.

Howland, Thomas. Correspondence. Civil War Correspondence. Diaries and Journals on Microfilm. Massachusetts Historical Society. Boston.

Hoyt, Henry. Letter. Civil War Miscellaneous Collection. U.S. Army Military History Institute. Carlisle Barracks, Pennsylvania.

Hubbard, Robert. Papers (typescript). Civil War Manuscripts Collection. Manuscripts and Archives. Sterling Memorial Library, Yale University. New Haven, Connecticut.

Hunton Family Papers. Virginia Historical Society (owner of the original documents). Richmond.

Hurter, Henry. Diary. Civil War Times Illustrated Collection. U.S. Army Military History Institute. Carlisle Barracks, Pennsylvania.

Hutson Family Papers. Howard-Tilton Memorial Library, Tulane University. New Orleans.

Hutspeth, R. H. Letters. North Carolina State Archives. Raleigh.

Hutt, Charles W. Personal Narrative. Alabama Department of Archives and History. Montgomery.

Hutton, Thomas Smith. Diary. Federal Collection. Tennessee State Library and Archives. Nashville.

Imboden, G. W. Letter. Lewis Leigh Collection. U.S. Army Military History Institute. Carlisle Barracks, Pennsylvania.

Ingalls, William Henry. Letters. Civil War Manuscripts Collection. Manuscripts and Archives. Sterling Memorial Library, Yale University. New Haven, Connecticut.

Inskeep, John D. Diary. Ohio Historical Society. Columbus.

Jackson, George. Papers. Ohio Historical Society. Columbus.

James, David Goodrich. Collection. State Historical Society of Wisconsin. Madison.

James Family Papers. Ohio Historical Society. Columbus.

James, William A. Papers. Duke University Library. Durham, North Carolina.

Janvrin, George. Letter. Howard-Tilton Memorial Library, Tulane University. New Orleans.

Jensen, Ellis E. Collection. State Historical Society of Wisconsin. Madison.

Johnson, A. A. Civil War Letters. Arkansas History Commission. Little Rock.

Johnson, Charles B. Papers. Arkansas History Commission. Little Rock.

Johnson, F. Roy. Papers. North Carolina State Archives. Raleigh.

Johnson Family Papers. Virginia State Library and Archives. Richmond.

Johnson, John A. Letters (transcript). Southern Historical Collection. University of North Carolina. Chapel Hill.

Johnston Family Papers (typescript). The Filson Club. Louisville, Kentucky.

Johnston, Joseph Sturge. Papers. Chicago Historical Society.

Jones, Charles Colcock, Jr. Collection. Duke University Library. Durham, North Carolina.

Jones, Edward. Papers. North Carolina State Archives. Raleigh.

Jones, Peleg Gardner. Letters (photocopies). Civil War Times Illustrated Collection. U.S. Army Military History Institute. Carlisle Barracks, Pennsylvania.

Jones, William W. Letters. Howard-Tilton Memorial Library, Tulane University. New Orleans.

Josey, J. E., et al. Letter. Arkansas History Commission. Little Rock.

Joyes, John, Jr. Diary. The Filson Club. Louisville, Kentucky.

Kearns, Watkins. Diary (photocopy). Virginia Historical Society (owner of the original documents). Richmond.

Keiser, Henry. Diary (typescript). Harrisburg Civil War Round Table Collection. U.S. Army Military History Institute. Carlisle Barracks, Pennsylvania.

Keitt, Laurence Massillon. Letters. Southern Historical Collection. University of North Carolina. Chapel Hill.

Kelley, Thomas. Papers. Duke University Library. Durham, North Carolina.

Kellogg, E. R. Recollections. U.S. Army Military History Institute. Carlisle Barracks, Pennsylvania.

Kelly, Williamson. Papers. Duke University Library. Durham, North Carolina.

Keywood, Franklin. Letters. Virginia State Library and Archives. Richmond.

Kimbell, Spencer S. Letters. Chicago Historical Society.

King, John Nevin. Family Papers. Illinois State Historical Society. Springfield.

Kingsbury, Marcus D. Letters (photocopies). Lewis Leigh Collection. U.S. Army Military History Institute. Carlisle Barracks, Pennsylvania.

Kinyoun, John Hendricks. Papers. Duke University Library. Durham, North Carolina.

Kirkpatrick Family Papers. Western Historical Manuscript Collection. Columbia, Missouri.

Kleinpell, Henry. Diaries. State Historical Society of Wisconsin. Madison.

Knight, Jonathan Thomas. Letters (typescript). Confederate Collection. Tennessee State Library and Archives. Nashville.

Kohout, Joseph. Letters. University of Iowa Library. Iowa City.

Kutz, Bently. Letters (photocopies). Harrisburg Civil War Round Table Collection. U.S. Army Military History Institute. Carlisle Barracks, Pennsylvania.

Kyger, Tilmon D. Letters. Illinois State Historical Library. Springfield.

Lang, Wendell W., Jr. Collection. U.S. Army Military History Institute. Carlisle Barracks, Pennsylvania.

Lawrence, Henry M. Letters. 6th Tennessee Cavalry Letters. Federal Collection. Tennessee State Library and Archives. Nashville.

Lee, John Walter. Letters. State Historical Society of Iowa. Iowa City.

Leman Family Letters. Howard-Tilton Memorial Library, Tulane University. New Orleans.

Leonard, James H. Letters. State Historical Society of Wisconsin. Madison.

Letcher, Governor John. Executive Papers. Virginia State Library and Archives. Richmond.

Lewis, John. Letter (typescript). Lewis Leigh Collection. U.S. Army Military History Institute. Carlisle Barracks, Pennsylvania.

Lindsay, Robert Goodloe. Papers. Southern Historical Collection. University of North Carolina. Chapel Hill.

Linscott, Andrew R. Correspondence. Civil War Correspondence. Diaries and Journals on Microfilm. Massachusetts Historical Society. Boston.

Linster, Robert. Collection. State Troops Papers. Duke University Library. Durham, North Carolina.

Lippitt, Charles Edward. Diary. Southern Historical Collection. University of North Carolina. Chapel Hill.

Locke, Joseph L. Letters. Illinois State Historical Library. Springfield.

Logan, Kate Virginia. Papers. Virginia Historical Society (owner of the original documents). Richmond.

Loudon, Dewitt Clinton. Papers. Ohio Historical Society. Columbus.

Lyman, Carlos Parsons. Diaries and Letters. Western Reserve Historical Society. Cleveland, Ohio.

Lyman Family Papers. Massachusetts Historical Society. Boston.

Lyndall, Mary S. Papers. Duke University Library. Durham, North Carolina.

Lyons, Mark. Letters (typescript). Alabama Department of Archives and History. Montgomery.

Mabry, Robert C. Papers. North Carolina State Archives. Raleigh.

Macon, Julius Montgomery. Letters. Louisiana Historical Association Collection. Howard-Tilton Memorial Library, Tulane University. New Orleans.

Madden, Cornelius. Papers. Ohio Historical Society. Columbus.

Makely Family Papers. Virginia State Library and Archives. Richmond.

Mangnum Family Papers. Southern Historical Collection. University of North Carolina. Chapel Hill.

Manson, Charles A. Letters. Lewis Leigh Collection. U.S. Army Military History Institute. Carlisle Barracks, Pennsylvania.

Marks, Samuel J. Letters (typescript). Civil War Miscellaneous Collection. U.S. Army Military History Institute. Carlisle Barracks, Pennsylvania.

Marsden, John. Journals and Letter. State Historical Society of Wisconsin. Madison.

Marshall, Eugene. Diary (typescript). Duke University Library. Durham, North Carolina.

Marshall Family Papers. The Filson Club. Louisville, Kentucky.

Marshall, John Wesley. Journal (typescript). Ohio Historical Society. Columbus.

Martin, John Marshall. Letters. Virginia Historical Society (owner of the original documents). Richmond.

Martin, William H. Letters. Harrisburg Civil War Round Table Collection. U.S. Military History Institute. Carlisle Barracks, Pennsylvania.

Mason, Daniel P. Papers. Howard-Tilton Memorial Library. Tulane University. New Orleans.

Mathews, John L. Letters (typescript). State Historical Society of Iowa. Iowa City.

McArthur, Henry C. Diary. State Historical Society of Iowa. Des Moines.

McCadden, Richard T. Papers. Tennessee State Library and Archives. Nashville.

McCaskill, Thomas L. Letters. North Carolina State Archives. Raleigh.

McClain, Byron M. Correspondence. University of Iowa Library. Iowa City.

McCole, George M. Collection. Indiana State Historical Library. Indianapolis.

McCoy, William. Papers. Western Reserve Historical Society. Cleveland, Ohio.

McCutchan, Charles Atcheson. Letters and Papers. Indiana Historical Society. Indianapolis.

McIntosh, David Gregg. Diary. Virginia Historical Society (owner of the original documents). Richmond.

McMichael, Paul Agalus. Papers. Southern Historical Collection. University of North Carolina. Chapel Hill.

McNair, Enoch Alexander. Letters. Virginia State Library and Archives. Richmond.

McNairy, W. H. Letter. Confederate Collection. Tennessee State Library and Archives. Nashville.

Mebane and Graves Papers. Southern Historical Collection. University of North Carolina. Chapel Hill.

Medary, Samuel. Papers. Ohio Historical Society. Columbus.

Medley, B. P. Papers. North Carolina State Archives. Raleigh.

Merriweather, George. Letters. Chicago Historical Society.

Metzger, Henry C. Correspondence (photocopies). Harrisburg Civil War Round Table Collection. U.S. Army Military History Institute. Carlisle Barracks, Pennsylvania.

Miller Family Papers. Virginia Historical Society (owner of the original documents). Richmond.

Miller, Wilson S. Letters. Federal Collection. Tennessee State Library and Archives. Nashville.

Mills, Caleb. Papers. Indiana Historical Society. Indianapolis.

Miltmore, Clarion I. Papers. Chicago Historical Society.

Miscellaneous Letters. Civil War Letters Collection. Alabama Department of Archives and History. Montgomery.

Mitchell, A[rchibald]. Letters. Louisiana Historical Association Collection. Howard-Tilton Memorial Library, Tulane University. New Orleans.

Mitchell, David L. Letters. Civil War Letters Collection. Alabama Department of Archives and History. Montgomery.

Mitchell, James C. B. Letters (typescript). Civil War Letters Collection. Alabama Department of Archives and History. Montgomery.

Mitchell, Robert, Jr. Letters and Diaries. Briggs-Mitchell Family Papers. Chicago Historical Society.

Mitchell, Samuel Clay. Letter. Confederate Collection. Tennessee State Library and Archives. Nashville.

Monks Family Papers. Western Reserve Historical Society. Cleveland, Ohio.

Montgomery, James H. Diary (photocopy). Civil War Miscellaneous Collection. U.S. Army Military History Institute. Carlisle Barracks, Pennsylvania.

Moore, Josiah Staunton. Papers. Virginia Historical Society (owner of the original documents). Richmond.

Moore, Samuel. Papers. Indiana State Historical Library. Indianapolis.

Moore, Samuel B. Letters. Civil War Letters. Mississippi Department of Archives and History. Jackson.

Moore, Thomas O. Collection. State Historical Society of Wisconsin. Madison.

Morehouse, Charles Ludlow. Diary. Ohio Historical Society. Columbus.

Morgan, Asa Stokeley. Collection. Arkansas History Commission. Little Rock.

Morey, Charles C. Letters (typescript). Western Historical Manuscript Collection. Columbia, Missouri.

Morrill, Justin Smith. Papers. Library of Congress. Washington, D.C.

Morton, Governor Oliver P. Papers. Commission on Public Records. Indiana State Archives. Indianapolis.

Moyle, Robert J. Correspondence. University of Iowa Library. Iowa City.

Mull, Oscar O. Diary (typescript). Virginia Historical Society (owner of the original documents). Richmond.

Munn, John. Diaries. Chicago Historical Society.

Murray Family Papers. Virginia State Library and Archives. Richmond.

Murray, John C. Diary. Howard-Tilton Memorial Library, Tulane University. New Orleans.

Murray, John William. Letters (photocopies). Virginia State Library and Archives. Richmond.

Musick, Michael P. Collection. U.S. Army Military History Institute. Carlisle Barracks, Pennsylvania.

Myers, A. C. Papers. North Carolina State Archives. Raleigh.

Myers, Frank M. Letters (typescript). Civil War Times Illustrated Collection. U.S. Army Military History Institute. Carlisle Barracks, Pennsylvania.

Nettleton-Baldwin Family Letters. Civil War Manuscripts Collection. Manuscripts and Archives. Sterling Memorial Library, Yale University. New Haven, Connecticut.

Newcomb, George Wallace. Letters. Civil War Miscellaneous Collection. U.S. Army Military History Institute. Carlisle Barracks, Pennsylvania.

Newhall, Horatio. Letters. Civil War Miscellaneous Collection. U.S. Army Military History Institute. Carlisle Barracks, Pennsylvania.

Nichol, David. Letters. Harrisburg Civil War Round Table Collection. U.S. Army Military History Institute. Carlisle Barracks, Pennsylvania.

Niles, James Barron. Collection. Lilly Library, Indiana University. Bloomington.

Northrop, John W. Diary of Prison Life (transcript). Western Reserve Historical Society. Cleveland, Ohio.

Norton, De Have. Papers. State Historical Society of Wisconsin. Madison.

O'Brien, John. Letters (photocopies). Civil War Miscellaneous Collection. U.S. Army Military History Institute. Carlisle Barracks, Pennsylvania.

O'Bryan, Joseph Branch. Papers. Tennessee State Library and Archives. Nashville.

O'Geran, Graeme. Collection. State Historical Society of Iowa. Des Moines.

Oldham, Kie. Papers. Arkansas History Commission, Little Rock.

Olds, William. Letters. Indiana State Historical Library. Indianapolis.

Olin, William Milo. Letters (typescript). Massachusetts Historical Society. Boston.

Olmstead, Charles Hart. Papers. Southern Historical Collection. University of North Carolina. Chapel Hill.

Opdycke, Emerson. Papers. Ohio Historical Society. Columbus.

Orear, Elisha. Letters. Louisiana Historical Association Collection. Howard-Tilton Memorial Library, Tulane University. New Orleans.

Orme, William Ward. Papers. Illinois State Historical Library. Springfield.

Osborn, Joseph Bloomfield. Correspondence. Library of Congress. Washington, D.C.

Owen, Henry Thweatt. Papers. Virginia Historical Society (owner of the original documents). Richmond.

Paddock, Elbridge E. Diaries. Civil War Manuscripts Collection. Manuscripts and Archives. Sterling Memorial Library, Yale University. New Haven, Connecticut.

Paine, Charles Jackson. Letters. Massachusetts Historical Society. Boston.

Palmer, William P. Collection. Western Reserve Historical Society. Cleveland, Ohio.

Palmetier, Charles. Letter. State Historical Society of Wisconsin. Madison.

Paris, John. Diary. Southern Historical Collection. University of North Carolina. Chapel Hill.

Parker, Frank M. Papers. North Carolina State Archives. Raleigh.

Parker, Leonard F. Diary and Letters. State Historical Society of Iowa. Iowa City.

Parmelee, Henry Spencer. Papers. Civil War Manuscripts Collection. Manuscripts and Archives. Sterling Memorial Library, Yale University. New Haven, Connecticut.

Parmelee, Samuel Spencer, and Uriah N. Parmelee. Papers. Duke University Library. Durham, North Carolina.

Parmeter, Nathaniel L. Diary (typescript). Ohio Historical Society. Columbus.

Parrott, James C. Letters. State Historical Society of Iowa. Iowa City.

Patton Family Papers. Southern Historical Collection. University of North Carolina. Chapel Hill.

Patton-Scott Family Papers. Western Historical Manuscript Collection. Columbia, Missouri.

Payne Family Papers. Virginia Historical Society (owner of the original documents). Richmond.

Peacock, William H. Letters (typescript). Civil War Miscellaneous Collection. U.S. Army Military History Institute. Carlisle Barracks, Pennsylvania.

Pedrick, Benjamin. Papers. Duke University Library. Durham, North Carolina.

Peebles, Thomas W. Letters (typescript). Civil War Letters Collection. Alabama Department of Archives and History. Montgomery.

Peel, William. Diary. Mississippi Department of Archives and History. Jackson.

Pegram-Johnson-McIntosh Family Papers. Virginia Historical Society (owner of the original documents). Richmond.

Perkins, Albert H. Letters (photocopies). Civil War Miscellaneous Collection. U.S. Army Military History Institute. Carlisle Barracks, Pennsylvania.

Perkins, Charles Ebenezer. Letters (typescript). Civil War Times Illustrated Collection. U.S. Army Military History Institute. Carlisle Barracks, Pennsylvania.

Perry, Leonard. Collection. Indiana State Historical Library. Indianapolis.

Perry, Matthew R. Letters. State Historical Society of Wisconsin. Madison.

Person, Persley. Papers. Duke University Library. Durham, North Carolina.

Petition from Officers of the 154th Tennessee Regiment. Mississippi Department of Archives and History. Jackson.

Philips, William H. Collection. Ohio Historical Society. Columbus.

Phillips, James Eldred. Diary (typescript). Virginia Historical Society (owner of the original documents). Richmond.

Pierce, Samuel B. Letters. Civil War Miscellaneous Collection. U.S. Army Military History Institute. Carlisle Barracks, Pennsylvania.

Pierson Family Papers. Rosemonde E. and Emile Kuntz Collection. Howard-Tilton Memorial Library, Tulane University. New Orleans.

Pirtle, Alfred. Civil War Letters. The Filson Club. Louisville, Kentucky.

Pittenger, William H. Diary. Ohio Historical Society. Columbus.

Pittman, Thomas Merritt. Papers. North Carolina State Archives. Raleigh.

Player, Fred K. Letters. Harrisburg Civil War Round Table Collection. U.S. Army Military History Institute. Carlisle Barracks, Pennsylvania.

Plumb, Isaac. Letters. Civil War Miscellaneous Collection. U.S. Army Military History Institute. Carlisle Barracks, Pennsylvania.

Poland, Samuel M. Diary. Ohio Historical Society. Columbus.

Polk, Trusten. Papers. Southern Historical Collection. University of North Carolina. Chapel Hill.

Pope, Albert Augustus. Journal (typescript). Civil War Times Illustrated Collection. U.S. Army Military History Institute. Carlisle Barracks, Pennsylvania.

Porter, John R. Correspondence (photocopies). Indiana State Historical Library. Indianapolis.

Porter, Styles W. Papers. Ohio Historical Society. Columbus.

Potts, Samuel J. Papers. Ohio Historical Society. Columbus.

Powers, Philip H. Letters. Lewis Leigh Collection. U.S. Army Military History Institute. Carlisle Barracks, Pennsylvania.

Price, Richard Channing. Papers. Virginia Historical Society (owner of the original documents). Richmond.

Prison Times (Fort Delaware) (handwritten). Williams Research Center. Historic New Orleans Collection. New Orleans.

Puffer, Richard R. Papers. Chicago Historical Society.

Pugh, James M. Papers. Southern Historical Collection. University of North Carolina. Chapel Hill.

Purdum, Nelson. Diary. Ohio Historical Society. Columbus.

"Q.M." Letter, May 29, 1862. Civil War Correspondence. Mississippi Department of Archives and History. Jackson.

Quiner, E. B. Papers: Correspondence of the Wisconsin Volunteers (microfilm). State Historical Society of Wisconsin. Madison.

Ragland Family Papers. Tennessee State Library and Archives. Nashville.

Ralph, James. Papers. Civil War Miscellaneous Collection. U.S. Army Military History Institute. Carlisle Barracks, Pennsylvania.

Randolph, Buckner Magill. Diary (typescript). Virginia Historical Society (owner of the original document). Richmond.

Rapson, William R. Collection. Western Reserve Historical Society. Cleveland, Ohio.

Resley, John. Collection. State Historical Society of Iowa. Iowa City.

Rich, Alonzo G. Letter. Civil War Miscellaneous Collection. U.S. Army Military History Institute. Carlisle Barracks, Pennsylvania.

Richards, Samuel F. Letter. Civil War Times Illustrated Collection. U.S. Army Military History Institute. Carlisle Barracks, Pennsylvania.

Richardson, George S., and William A. Richardson. Letters (typescript). State Historical Society of Iowa. Iowa City.

Riddle, Albert Gallatin. Papers. Western Reserve Historical Society. Cleveland, Ohio.

Riddle Family Papers. Virginia Historical Society (owner of the original documents). Richmond.

Rigby, A. A. Journal. State Historical Society of Iowa. Des Moines.

Ring, George P. Papers. Louisiana Historical Association Collection. Howard-Tilton Memorial Library, Tulane University. New Orleans.

Roach, Henry H. Letters. Virginia State Library and Archives. Richmond.

Robb, Robert. Diary. Federal Collection. Tennessee State Library and Archives. Nashville.

Roberts, Jesse M. Letters. State Historical Society of Wisconsin. Madison.

Roberts, William. Letters. Civil War Miscellaneous Collection. U.S. Army Military History Institute. Carlisle Barracks, Pennsylvania.

Robertson, William, and Ben Robertson. Papers. Mississippi Department of Archives and History. Jackson.

Robinson, Will. Letters. Indiana State Historical Library. Indianapolis.

Rockwell, Albert. Letter (typescript). State Historical Society of Wisconsin. Madison.

Rogers, Joseph C. Letters. Illinois State Historical Library. Springfield.

Romig, Milton A. Letter. Ohio Historical Society. Columbus.

Root, George W. Letters. State Historical Society of Wisconsin. Madison.

Root, Samuel H. Letters. Civil War Miscellaneous Collection. U.S. Army Military History Institute. Carlisle Barracks, Pennsylvania.

Roots, Logan Holt. Papers. Arkansas History Commission. Little Rock.

Rorer, W. A. Letters (typescript). Mississippi Department of Archives and History. Jackson.

Ross Family Correspondence. Virginia State Library and Archives. Richmond.

Ross, Levi A. Diary (typescript) and Letters. Illinois State Historical Library. Springfield.

Ross, William H. Papers. Chicago Historical Society.

Rowe, Louis. Papers. Civil War Miscellaneous Collection. U.S. Army Military History Institute. Carlisle Barracks, Pennsylvania.

Rude, William H. Letter. Indiana Historical Society. Indianapolis.

Ruffin, Thomas. Correspondence. Virginia State Library and Archives. Richmond.

"S.F.S." Letter. Williams Research Center. Historic New Orleans Collection. New Orleans.

Sale, John F. Correspondence. Virginia State Library and Archives. Richmond.

Sampson, Henry. Diary. Williams Research Center. Historic New Orleans Collection. New Orleans.

Sanborn, John W. Letters (photocopies). Civil War Miscellaneous Collection. U.S. Army Military History Institute. Carlisle Barracks, Pennsylvania.

Sanders, J. B. Papers. Mississippi Department of Archives and History. Jackson.

Sargent, A. J. Letters. Civil War Miscellaneous Collection. U.S. Army Military History Institute. Carlisle Barracks, Pennsylvania.

Saunders, J. C. C. Letters. Civil War Letters Collection. Alabama Department of Archives and History. Montgomery.

Saunders, Joseph Hubbard. Papers. Southern Historical Collection. University of North Carolina. Chapel Hill.

Saunders, William Laurence. Papers. Southern Historical Collection. University of North Carolina. Chapel Hill.

Sawtelle, Levander. Letters. Civil War Miscellaneous Collection. U.S. Army Military History Institute. Carlisle Barracks, Pennsylvania.

Sawtelle, Orlando P. Letters. Civil War Miscellaneous Collection. U.S. Army Military History Institute. Carlisle Barracks, Pennsylvania.

Scott, Henry Bruce. Papers (typescript). Massachusetts Historical Society. Boston.

Scott, Robert Kingston. Papers. Ohio Historical Society. Columbus.

Scripps, John Locke. Collection. Illinois State Historical Library. Springfield.

Scully, Dan. Diary. Louisiana Historical Association Collection. Howard-Tilton Memorial Library, Tulane University. New Orleans.

Sears, George E. Papers. Howard-Tilton Memorial Library, Tulane University. New Orleans.

Seibert Family Papers. Harrisburg Civil War Round Table Collection. U.S. Army Military History Institute. Carlisle Barracks, Pennsylvania.

Semple, Henry C. Papers. Southern Historical Collection. University of North Carolina. Chapel Hill.

Semple, Henry C. Papers. Alabama Department of Archives and History. Montgomery.

Settle, Thomas, Jr. Letters. North Carolina State Archives. Raleigh.

Sexton, Samuel. Papers. Ohio Historical Society. Columbus.

Shaffner, John Francis. Papers. North Carolina State Archives. Raleigh.

Sharp, Joseph C. Letters. Arkansas History Commission. Little Rock.

Shearer, George Marion. Diary. State Historical Society of Iowa. Iowa City.

Sheperd Family Papers. Virginia Historical Society (owner of the original documents). Richmond.

Sherman, Charles F. Letters. Williams Research Center. Historic New Orleans Collection. New Orleans.

Sherman, John. Papers. Library of Congress. Washington, D.C.

Shipman, Edward John. Letters (photocopies). Lewis Leigh Collection. U.S. Army Military History Institute. Carlisle Barracks, Pennsylvania.

Short, Luther. Letters. Indiana State Historical Library. Indianapolis.

Shotwell Family Papers. Ohio Historical Society. Columbus.

Shuman, George. Letters (photocopies). Harrisburg Civil War Round Table Collection. U.S. Army Military History Institute. Carlisle Barracks, Pennsylvania.

Simmons, Henry E. Papers. Southern Historical Collection. University of North Carolina. Chapel Hill.

Sinclair, James C. Diaries. Chicago Historical Society.

Skelly, Charles. Letters (photocopies). Harrisburg Civil War Round Table Collection. U.S. Army Military History Institute. Carlisle Barracks, Pennsylvania.

Slack, James R. Papers. Indiana State Historical Library. Indianapolis.

Smith, Arthur D. Letters. State Historical Society of Iowa. Iowa City.

Smith, Charles H. Letters. Civil War Miscellaneous Collection. U.S. Army Military History Institute. Carlisle Barracks, Pennsylvania.

Smith Family Letters. Louisiana Historical Association Collection. Howard-Tilton Memorial Library, Tulane University. New Orleans.

Smith, R. H. Letters. Alabama Department of Archives and History. Montgomery.

Smith, Robert A. Papers. Mississippi Department of Archives and History. Jackson.

Southwood, Virginia. Collection. Western Historical Manuscript Collection. Columbia, Missouri.

Sparkman, Jesse Roderich. Diaries. Confederate Collection. Tennessee State Library and Archives. Nashville.

Speed, Thomas. Letterbook. The Filson Club. Louisville, Kentucky.

Spencer, Charles H. Papers. State Historical Society of Wisconsin. Madison.

Sprake, J. D. Diary (typescript). The Filson Club. Louisville, Kentucky.

Stafford, Warren D. Papers. State Historical Society of Iowa. Iowa City.

Stanton, Edwin H. Papers. Library of Congress. Washington, D.C.

Stebbins, J. Webster. Papers. Lewis Leigh Collection. U.S. Army Military History Institute. Carlisle Barracks, Pennsylvania.

Steele, Robert. Letters. State Historical Society of Wisconsin. Madison.

Stegel, Overton. Letters (photocopies). Lewis Leigh Collection. U.S. Army Military History Institute. Carlisle Barracks, Pennsylvania.

Stephens, Hubert A. Letters. Mississippi Department of Archives and History. Jackson.

Stephens, Thomas White. Diaries. Western Historical Manuscript Collection. Columbia, Missouri.

Stern Family Papers. University of Iowa Library. Iowa City.

Steward, John M. Letters. Civil War Miscellaneous Collection. U.S. Army Military History Institute. Carlisle Barracks, Pennsylvania.

Stibbs Family Papers. Howard-Tilton Memorial Library, Tulane University. New Orleans.

Stone, Henry H. Diary (typescript). Harrisburg Civil War Round Table Collection. U.S. Army Military History Institute. Carlisle Barracks, Pennsylvania.

Storrow, Samuel. Correspondence. Papers, Diaries, and Journals on Microfilm. Massachusetts Historical Society. Boston.

Stowe, Johnathan Perley. Letters (typescript). Civil War Times Illustrated Collection. U.S. Army Military History Institute. Carlisle Barracks, Pennsylvania.

Stuart, John Lane. Letters. Duke University Library. Durham, North Carolina.

Stuart, Oscar E., and Family Papers. Mississippi Department of Archives and History. Jackson.

Sturtevant, Edward. Lewis Letters. Williams Research Center. Historic New Orleans Collection. New Orleans.

Sullivan, Thomas L. Diary. Confederate Collection. Tennessee State Library and Archives. Nashville.

Sumner, Allen. Papers. State Historical Society of Iowa. Iowa City.

Suter, John. Letters (typescript). Harrisburg Civil War Round Table Collection. U.S. Army Military History Institute. Carlisle Barracks, Pennsylvania.

Swain, Samuel. Papers. State Historical Society of Wisconsin. Madison.

Swank, Luther L. Letters (typescript). Virginia Historical Society (owner of the original documents). Richmond.

Swanson-Yates Family Papers. Mississippi Department of Archives and History. Jackson.

Tarbell, Eli M. Diary (printed excerpts). Harrisburg Civil War Round Table Collection. U.S. Army Military History Institute. Carlisle Barracks, Pennsylvania.

Tarleton Family Papers. Sterling Memorial Library, Yale University. New Haven, Connecticut.

Tarleton, S. B. Letters. Civil War Miscellaneous Collection. U.S. Army Military History Institute. Carlisle Barracks, Pennsylvania.

Taylor Family Papers. Virginia Historical Society (owner of the original documents). Richmond.

Taylor, Thomas S. Letters. Civil War Letters Collection. Alabama Department of Archives and History. Montgomery.

Taylor, Thomas Thomson. Collection. Ohio Historical Society. Columbus.

Terry Family Papers. Southern Historical Collection. University of North Carolina. Chapel Hill.

Thomas, James S. Letters. Indiana Historical Society. Indianapolis.

Thompson, Marcus A. Letter (photocopy). Lewis Leigh Collection. U.S. Army Military History Institute. Carlisle Barracks, Pennsylvania.

Thompson, William N. Letters. Lewis Leigh Collection. U.S. Army Military History Institute. Carlisle Barracks, Pennsylvania.

Thomson, James. Diary. Ohio Historical Society. Columbus.

Todd, Eli. Papers. Ohio Historical Society. Columbus.

Toney, Marcus Bearden. Diary. Confederate Collection. Tennessee State Library and Archives. Nashville.

Trimmier, Theodore Gillard. Papers. Tennessee State Library and Archives. Nashville.

Trumbull, Lyman. Papers. Library of Congress. Washington, D.C.

Trussell, John B. B. Commanders of Pennsylvania Civil War Regiments. Harrisburg Civil War Round Table Collection. U.S. Army Military History Institute. Carlisle Barracks, Pennsylvania.

Tuttle, Elizabeth A. Papers. Lilly Library, Indiana University. Bloomington.

Twombly, Voltaire P. Correspondence. State Historical Society of Iowa. Des Moines.

Tyrrell, Albert H. Letters. Civil War Miscellaneous Collection. U.S. Army Military History Institute. Carlisle Barracks, Pennsylvania.

Ullman, Rufus. Papers. Western Reserve Historical Society. Cleveland, Ohio.

Ulmer, Isaac Barton. Papers. Southern Historical Collection. University of North Carolina. Chapel Hill.

Underwood, Myron. Letters. University of Iowa Library. Iowa City.

Vail, John D. Diary. Ohio Historical Society. Columbus.

Vaill, George W. Letters. Civil War Miscellaneous Collection. U.S. Army Military History Institute. Carlisle Barracks, Pennsylvania.

Vairin, A. L. P. Diary. Mississippi Department of Archives and History. Jackson.

Vallandigham, Clement Laird. Letter, May 21, 1863. Ohio Historical Society. Columbus.

Vance, Zebulon Baird. Collection (microform). North Carolina State Archives. Raleigh.

Vance, Zebulon Baird, and Harriet Espy. Letters. North Carolina State Archives. Raleigh.

Vann, Samuel King. Letters. Alabama Department of Archives and History. Montgomery.

Van Vlack, Alonzo. Papers. Civil War Letters Collection. Alabama Department of Archives and History. Montgomery.

Vaught, William C. D. Letters. Williams Research Center. Historic New Orleans Collection. New Orleans.

Veatch, Simeon. Diaries. State Historical Society of Iowa City. Iowa City.

Veteran Banner (soldier newspaper). Ohio Historical Society. Columbus.

Vincent, John Bell. Diary. Virginia Historical Society (owner of the original documents). Richmond.

Wade, Benjamin F. Papers. Library of Congress.

Wade, Benjamin Franklin. Letters (typescript). Federal Collection. Tennessee State Library and Archives. Nashville.

Wade, Daniel P. Letters (transcript). Howard-Tilton Memorial Library, Tulane University. New Orleans.

Wade, R. W. Papers. Lewis Leigh Collection. U.S. Army Military History Institute. Carlisle Barracks, Pennsylvania.

Waite, Henry O. Letters (typescript). Civil War Miscellaneous Collection. U.S. Army Military History Institute. Carlisle Barracks, Pennsylvania.

Walkup, Samuel Hoey. Papers. Southern Historical Collection. University of North Carolina. Chapel Hill.

Wallace, James T. Diary. Southern Historical Collection. University of North Carolina. Chapel Hill.

Walters, Edgar A. Memoir (photocopy). Harrisburg Civil War Round Table Collection. U.S. Army Military History Institute. Carlisle Barracks, Pennsylvania.

Walton-Glenny Family Papers, 1855–1967. Williams Research Center. Historic New Orleans Collection. New Orleans.

Ward, F. B. Letter (photocopy). Lewis Leigh Collection. U.S. Army History Institute. Carlisle Barracks, Pennsylvania.

Ward, Joseph F. Letters (typescript). Chicago Historical Society.

Warner, J. Chapin. Correspondence. Civil War Correspondence. Diaries and Journals on Microfilm. Massachusetts Historical Society. Boston.

Warren, William H. Letters (typescript). State Historical Society of Iowa. Iowa City.

Warwick, Wiley. Letters. Civil War Letters Collection. Alabama Department of Archives and History. Montgomery.

Washburne, Elihu B. Papers. Library of Congress. Washington, D.C.

Waterman, Elijah. Collection. Indiana State Historical Library. Indianapolis.

Watson, Clement S. Diaries. Howard-Tilton Memorial Library. Tulane University. New Orleans.

Weaver, Amos C. Letters. Indiana Historical Society. Indianapolis.

Webb Collection. North Carolina State Archives. Raleigh.

Webb Family Papers. Southern Historical Collection. University of North Carolina. Chapel Hill.

Wheeler, Samuel Worthington. Collection. North Carolina State Archives. Raleigh.

Whitaker, Cary. Papers. Southern Historical Collection. University of North Carolina. Chapel Hill.

Whitaker, Stephen. Papers. North Carolina State Archives. Raleigh.

White, Joseph A. Letter (transcript). Civil War Times Illustrated Collection. U.S. Army Military History Institute. Carlisle Barracks, Pennsylvania.

Whitehorn, David A. Letters. Indiana Historical Society. Indianapolis.

Whitehorne Family Papers. Virginia State Library and Archives. Richmond.

Whitford, John D. Papers. North Carolina State Archives. Raleigh.

Wicker, Henry C. Papers. Chicago Historical Society.

Wildman Family Papers. Ohio Historical Society. Columbus.

Wilkens, John Adam. Diary (typescript). Indiana Historical Society. Indianapolis.

Willey, John J. Letters (typescript). Harrisburg Civil War Round Table Collection. U.S. Army Military History Institute. Carlisle Barracks, Pennsylvania.

William, Hugh P. Collection. Western Historical Manuscript Collection. Columbia, Missouri.

Williams, Enoch Pearson. Diary (typescript). State Historical Society of Iowa. Iowa City.

Williams Family Letters. Virginia Historical Society (owner of the original documents). Richmond.

Williams, James Peter. Letter (typescript). Virginia State Library and Archives. Richmond.

Williamson, John C. Papers. Ohio Historical Society. Columbus.

Wills, George Whitaker. Papers. Southern Historical Collection. University of North Carolina. Chapel Hill.

Wilson, Henry. Papers. Library of Congress. Washington, D.C.

Wilson, J. J. Papers. Mississippi Department of Archives and History. Jackson.

Wilson, John A. Letters. Mississippi Department of Archives and History. Jackson.

Winn, Mary Ann. Letter. Illinois State Historical Society. Springfield.

Winston-Clark Family Papers. Virginia Historical Society (owner of the original documents). Richmond.

Wise Family Papers. Virginia State Library and Archives. Richmond.

Withrow, Adoniram Judson. Letters (typescript). State Historical Society of Iowa. Iowa City.

Wood, H. B. Letter (typescript). Alabama Department of Archives and History. Montgomery.

Wood, Julius V. Correspondence. Western Reserve Historical Society. Cleveland, Ohio.

Woods, William Samuel. Letters. Eleanor S. Brockenbrough Library, Museum of the Confederacy. Richmond, Virginia.

Woodson, J. S. Letters. Eleanor S. Brockenbrough Library, Museum of the Confederacy. Richmond, Virginia.

Woodward, Samuel H. Letters (photocopies). Harrisburg Civil War Round Table Collection. U.S. Army Military History Institute. Carlisle Barracks, Pennsylvania.

Woolwine, Rufus James. Diary. Virginia Historical Society (owner of the original document). Richmond.

Worth, Alonzo K. Diary. Civil War Miscellaneous Collection. U.S. Army Military History Institute. Carlisle Barracks, Pennsylvania.

Wright Family Correspondence. Virginia State Library and Archives. Richmond.

Wright, John M. Family Papers. North Carolina State Archives. Raleigh.

Wynn, B. L. Diary (transcript). Mississippi Department of Archives and History. Jackson.

Wynne Family Papers. Virginia Historical Society (owner of the original documents). Richmond.

Yandell Family Papers. The Filson Club, Louisville, Kentucky.

Yates Family Papers. Illinois State Historical Library. Springfield.

Yellowley, Edward Clements. Papers. Southern Historical Collection. University of North Carolina. Chapel Hill.

Young, Emor. Letter. Harrisburg Civil War Round Table Collection. U.S. Army Military History Institute. Carlisle Barracks, Pennsylvania.

Zearing, James Roberts. Papers. Chicago Historical Society.

Zimmerman, James C. Papers. Duke University Library. Durham, North Carolina.

Index

election in, 181; troops deployed in, 181. *See also* Elections

Banditry. *See* Guerrilla warfare

Bankers (European), and prospects of Anglo-French intervention, 111

Banks, Nathaniel Prentiss, 51; and Red River campaign, 44, 161; chastised for conciliatory policy toward planter, 51

Barnard, John G., 134

Bates County, Missouri, 144

Baton Rouge, Louisiana, 72

Battalions. *See also* Regiments, consolidation of

"Battle Hymn of the Republic." *See* Citizen-soldiers: idealism of

Beaufort, South Carolina, 155

Bell-Everett ticket (1860), 132

Benton Barracks, Missouri, 52, 138

Beringer, Richard E., 83

Bertie County, North Carolina, 175

"Big picture." *See* Military situation

Blacks: Union recruitment of, and soldiers' views on, 2, 32, 51, 54–55, 72, 124; percentage supporting recruitment of, 54, 67; fighting prowess of, 55; Baltimore convention calls for arming of, 67, 89. *See also* Confederate States of America: proposals to enlist blacks; Emancipation; War aims

Blair, Frank, Jr., 160

Blockade, 99, 113; as war against civilians, 56, 148; likelihood of Anglo-British intervention to lift, 112, 114. *See also* Hard war

Bonapartism, 13, 108, 123–24; and left-wing tendencies among Confederate officers, 13, 125; political differences between officers and men and rise of, 13, 123–24; rumors of, among regular officers, 13, 123–24; officers' grievances leading to, 14, 124–25; resulting from alienation of army from parent society, 14; reverses in the field and rise of, 123;

Confederate and Union officers compared, 125. *See also* Confederate States of America: proposals to enlist blacks; Officers; People's armies; Regulars

Border states, radicalism of Confederate troops from, 2

Boston, Massachusetts, 140

Boston Advertiser, 65

Bounties, 6–8, 53; inflation of, viii, 111; and competition among communities for recruits, 7, 11, 53; jealousies between eastern and western soldiers over soldiers criticism of, 53; inequalities inherent in, 53–54. *See also* Conscription; Substitutes

Bounty men, viii, 8, 53; comparison with locally conscripted enlistees, 7, 18; citizen-soldier's attitude toward, 18, 53; reliability of, 18, 53. *See also* Conscription; Combat motivation

Bounty system. *See* Bounties

Bragg, Braxton, 13, 84, 86, 162; soldiers' opinions on, 48–49

Brayman, Mason, 104

Brazil. *See* Emigration, as an alternative to defeat

British regulars, 4. *See also* Combat motivation; Regulars; Long-service troops

Brown, Egbert B., 135

Buck River, Georgia, 135

Buell, Don Carlos, 134, 159, 161, 163

Buffaloes, 175–76

Bugeaud, Thomas, 165

Bummers, 154

Buncombe County, North Carolina, 131

Bureaucracy, 7; increasing size and efficiency of in recruiting troops, 7; compared to France's, 7. *See also* Conscription

Burnside, Ambrose Everett, 171–72, 180–81; Confederate assessment

of, 41, 110; rated by own troops, 43,
46–47, 91
Butler, Benjamin F., 123, 129–30

Caesarism. *See* Bonapartism
California, French designs on, 113
Camp Lawton, Georgia, 93
Canada, 111; as haven for deserters,
dissidents, and draft evaders, 174
Canton, Ohio, 180
Cass County, Missouri, 144
Catholic Church, suspicions in North
toward, 112
Cause, the: discussion of, as indicator
of scope of political awareness, 16, 36.
See also Combat motivation: political
convictions and patriotism; War aims
Cause of the war, 58; Northern soldiers'
opinions on, 59–60, 62; Southern
troops' ideas about, 60, 62–63;
Southern intransigence over slavery,
62, 73–74. *See also* Abolitionists;
Locofocoism; Slavery
Censorship: of newspapers reaching
troops, 139; of soldiers' mail, 139.
See also Newspapers
Centralia, Missouri, massacre at, 146
Chaffin's Bluff, Virginia, 88
Chambersburg, Pennsylvania, 160
Chancellorsville, Virginia, battle of, 47,
51, 113, 170
Chaplains, 15; political indoctrination by,
30, 140
Charleston, South Carolina, 3, 42, 85, 164.
See also Military situation: political and
electoral consequences arising from
Chase, Salmon P., 89; as potential
challenger to Lincoln for nomination
in 1864, 47, 49; rumored to receive
loan from Britian, 114
Chattanooga, Tennessee, battle of, 25,
44, 151; black troops salute Declaration
of Independence in, 105

Chester (Illinois) Picket Guard, 180
Chicago Convention of 1860. *See*
Republicans
Chicago Convention of 1864. *See*
Democrats
Chicago Times, 132, 139, 172, 180
Chicago Tribune, 30, 140. *See also*
Soldiers: as stringers for newspapers
Chickamauga Creek, Georgia, battle of,
44, 47, 49, 81, 151
Child, Lydia Maria, in *Mother's Book*
advocates naturalist method, 27. *See
also* Child-rearing practices: doctrinal
conflicts over; Rousseau, Jean-Jacques:
views on child-rearing in his *Emile;*
Mann, Horace
Child-rearing practices, doctrinal
conflicts over, 26–27. *See also*
Child, Lydia Maria; Mann, Horace;
Rousseau, Jean-Jacques: ideas on
child-rearing in his *Emile*
Choctaws, 159
Chouans. *See* French revolution
Christian Commission, disseminates
books and newspapers in camps,
30. *See also* Political socialization:
newspaper as source of
Christianity. *See* Citizen-soldiers: values
and virtues of
Church. *See* Political socialization: church
as source of
Cincinnati, Ohio, 172
Cincinnatus, defines citizen-soldier
ideal, 19
Citizen armies. *See* People's armies
Citizenry: military and political
obligations of, as components of
citizenship, 19–20, 22–25; political
participation by, 23. *See also* Politics
Citizen-soldiers, 2–4, 16, 46, 51, 55–56,
61, 66, 83–86; expectations regarding
parent society, vii, 51, 56, 166, 169–71;
political motivation of, vii–viii, 1–2, 4,

17, 19, 39, 57–58, 65, 73, 84, 91–92, 105, 121, 148, 156; resoluteness of, viii, 1–2; idealism of, 3, 18, 21, 24, 37, 58, 63, 65, 71, 81, 161; inchoate patriotism of, 9, 32–33, 36, 38, 57–58, 63; increasing effectiveness of, 14, 120, 153; values and virtues of, 11–12, 18–19, 21, 23–26, 61, 105; retain civilian outlook, 15, 43, 121–22; articulateness of, 16, 117–18, 161; courage of, 17, 20–21, 23, 37–38; bias against regulars, 18, 91; disdain bounty men and conscripts, 18–21, 34, 53–54; spurn pecuniary inducement, 18–19; ideal model of, 19–20, 23, 25–26, 91–92; reflective nature of, 20; and notion of death in battle, 21–22; literacy rates among, 28, 39; sense of political effectiveness among, 33, 37–39; significance of right to vote for, 91, 93–95, 117. *See also* Combat motivation; Political awareness; Political socialization; Soldiers

Civic competence. *See* Sense of political effectiveness (as indicator of political awareness)

Civic culture, 73, 81. *See also* Political socialization; Militia; Reconstruction; War aims: as radical revolutionary goals

Civil War: as a crusade, 15, 60–61, 67; as political revitalization, 20, 60, 65, 70–71, 79, 156; effect of size and scope on, 50, 63–64; plots and panics during, 50, 99, 104; as a punitive expedition, 50, 61, 62–63, 70, 78, 101, 108, 149, 152, 155–56, 163; as revolution, 50, 61, 63–64, 66–67, 70, 120; as a struggle for ideals and progress, 51, 60–61, 64, 112, 161; as a tragedy, 58–59, 61; as an apocalyptic clash between moral absolutes, 60–61, 63–64, 145–46, 149, 154; as battle against tyranny, 61; radicalization arising from, 61, 63,

65–68, 97, 99, 152, 156–57; as a melodrama, 61; ferocity of fighting, reason for, 63, 153; as a religious redemptive struggle against evil, 63, 70–71, 155–56; racism in, 73, 146. *See also* Clausewitz, Karl Von; Hard war: directed against civilians; Historical exceptionalism; Justification of the war; War aims

Clark County, Arkansas, 98

Clausewitz, Karl Von, on the nature of war, 10, 143, 153; service with Napoleon's Grand Army as new type of force, 10, 143

Cleburne, Patrick R., 125–26, 131. *See* Confederate States of America: proposals to enlist blacks

Cleveland Herald, 124

Cobb, Richard, 122

Cold Harbor, Virginia, battle of, 85, 144, 168

Collot D'Herbois, Jean-Marie, 152

Colored troops, review boards for selecting officers for, 11

Columbia, South Carolina, 174–75

Columbus, Ohio, 4

Combat motivation, viii, 25; camaraderie and small group bonding as, 57; bounties and pay as pecuniary inducements to enlist, 7, 12, 18, 57; fear of punishment, 18; glory and adventure, 57; political convictions and patriotism, 24–25, 37, 39, 57, 154; sense of duty, 7, 18, 24–25, 37, 57, 61, 91; unit pride and loyalty, 165; compared between citizen-soldiers and professionals, 14, 18–20, 25, 57, 165. *See also* Citizen-soldiers: values and virtues of; Long-service troops; Regulars: organizational and material incentives in recruitment of; Short-service armies; Volunteers

Courts-martial, and officers' disloyalty, 135–39. *See also* Disloyalty; Joint Committee on the Conduct of the War

Crater, battle of the, 55, 159, 174

Columbus (Ohio) Crisis, 180

Cromwellian Army. *See* New Model army

Cuba Station, Tennessee, 80

Curtin, Andrew Gregg, 120, 138

Curtis, Samuel B., 130

Danton, Georges Jacques, 85

David, Louis, 8. *See also* Citizen-soldiers

Davis, Jefferson, 88, 101, 129, 133, 179; and enlisting blacks, 13, 55, 75, 126; and peace proposals, 77; leadership assessed, 81, 85–86, 110, 144; denounced for favoring Bragg, 86, 131; calls for military overthrow of, 124

Davis, Jefferson C., loyalty questioned, 135

Dayton (Ohio) Empire, 180

Death, citizen-solder's image of, 21–22

Defeat. *See* Confederate States of America: soldiers' reflections on defeat of

Demi-brigades. See Mixed brigades

Democracy: army as embodiment of, 4, 37, 43; and citizen-soldier armies, 4, 61; introduction of in Southern society, 62. *See also* Civil War: as battle against tyranny

Democrats, 35, 65, 68, 72, 88, 94–97, 104, 106, 108, 117, 120, 124, 126–28, 130, 133, 137, 173, 180; party dissensions arising from the war, 35, 63–64; take control of state legislatures in Indiana and Illinois, 35, 70, 100, 177, 179; impact of 1862 defeats on electoral prospects of, 41; discomfiture over emancipation, 54, 72; position on conscription, 54; differences between Pendleton and

McClellan, 65, 90; views on hard war, 66, 90; Chicago convention and platform of 1864, 88, 96, 99, 107, 127; policies predicated on Union defeat, 88–90; Pendleton nomination as concession to conservative Vallandigham wing, 90; accused of treasonous ties to Confederacy, 100; effect of Early's 1864 invasion on electoral prospects of, 108. *See also* McClellan, George Brinton: refuses to subscribe to 1864 Democrat peace plank

Demosthenes, 21

Deserters, 53, 174–75, 181; soldiers' views on, 23, 61, 102; as indicator of declining enemy morale, 109

Desertion, 60; increase of in 1863, viii, 25

Disloyalty, 147; among troops, 1, 13, 36, 101–2; disloyalty at home discussed by troops, 32, 36, 38, 79, 99–105, 118, 170–74, 179; repression of, in army, 72, 131–39; conscription as a means of quashing, 182–83. *See also* Illinois: 109th Regiment, mutiny and political attitudes of; Dissent in enemy society; Copperheads; Home front

Dissent in enemy society, 84; soldiers gauge level of, in enemy society, 10, 42, 105–6, 108–9, 113, 123; Federal and Confederate level of interest compared, 105. *See also* Confederate States of America; Disloyalty

Doubleday, Abner, 129

Douglass, Frederick, 64

Draft. *See* Conscription

Draft evaders, 179, 181–82; Confederate assumptions of rising number in North, 7; in North Carolina, 175–76, 182. *See also* Stay-at-homes

Draft riots: in New York City, 112, 133; Confederates' reactions to, 111

Flanagin, Harris, 54, 179
Florida, 43, 162; soldier vote in, 97
Foreign intervention. *See* Foreign relations
Foreign relations, 84, 112; prospects of foreign intervention, 10, 81, 102, 111–15, 126; soldiers' interest in, 36, 76, 111–14; effect of Emancipation on, 67, 69; Confederate and Union interest in percentages compared, 112. *See also specific countries*
Forey, E. F., 112
Forrest, Nathan Bedford, 40, 114, 135, 146, 158
Fort Fisher, North Carolina, 101
Fort Gilmer, Virginia, 159
Fortitude, 1. *See also* Political awareness
Fort Pillow, Tennessee, 40, 146, 158
Fort Smith, Arkansas, 98, 185
Founding fathers, 119; views on public school system, 26
Fourteenth Corps, 135
France: mass political parties in, 1; intervention by, 10, 111–15; objectives in Mexico, 112, 114–15; Confederates overestimate power of, 114
Franklin, Benjamin, citizen virtues emulated by soldiers, 23
Franklin, Tennessee, traitors hanged at, 137
Franklin, William, character appraised by men, 45. *See also* Military leadership: moral character of, judged by troops
Fredericksburg, Virginia, Union repulse at, 41, 49, 109
Freedom, Civil War as reaffirmation of, 71, 146. *See also* Values: shared by army and society; War aims
Freemen. *See* Blacks
Frémont, John C., 129; admired by German troops, 89; as possible challenger to Lincoln in 1864, 89, 135. *See also* Military leadership

French revolution, 3, 8, 16, 148, 152, 163, 166; armies of, ix, 12–13, 20, 121–23, 149, 151–52, 168; political impact on citizens, 23; popular panics in, 99–100; spreading democratic ideas, 120. *See also* Citizenry: political participation by

Gallagher, Gary W., 49
Gates County, North Carolina, 175
General Order Number 10. *See* Missouri: political repression in
General Order Number 38, 181. *See also* Missouri: political repression in
Georgia, 12, 42–43, 48, 93, 147, 152, 163; soldier vote in, 97
German-American citizens, 89
German-American soldiers, 72; admire Frémont and Sigel, 45
German army. *See* Nazi ideology, as combat motivator
Gettysburg, Pennsylvania, battle of, 38, 45, 178; political arguments between prisoners and captors after battle, 12; soldiers views of significance of, 41, 49–50, 138. *See also* Militia: mustered in response to Morgan's raid and Gettysburg campaign
Gibbon, Edward, and unreliability of professional soldiers, 19. *See also* Citizen-soldiers: bias against regulars
Glasgow, Missouri, 183
Governors, 2, 11. *See also* Patronage; Recruitment
Grant, Ulysses S., 40–42, 104, 106, 113, 129, 144, 147, 162; Confederate soldiers' appraisal of, 41, 110; Union soldiers' appraisal of, 43–44, 46–48, 119, 132, 149; press relations of, 44, 139; as alternative to Lincoln candidacy, 127
Great Britain, 112, 114; prospect of intervention by, 10, 111–15; Union

soldiers' animosity toward, 63, 112, 114–15; Confederate soldiers sentiments toward, 102; Confederates overestimate power of, 114

Green Bay, Wisconsin, 177

Greenville, Ohio, 180

Grimsley, Mark, 144–45

Guerrilla warfare, 157–58, 162, 176, 183; as response to Southern defeat, 83

Habeas corpus, 65, 86, 97, 139. *See also* Confederate States of America: economic conditions in

Halleck, Henry Wager, 134; rated by troops, 45. *See also* Military leadership

Hampton, Wade, 40

Hampton Roads, Virginia, peace contacts at, 77

Hancock, Ohio, 102

Hard war, 48, 56, 90, 108, 142–43, 155, 157–58; in Europe, 3; directed against civilians, 14, 50–51, 64, 147–48, 152–57, 160–64; Confederate and Union views on compared, 50; as punitive endeavor, 50, 61, 63, 65, 67, 70, 78, 101, 145, 149, 152, 155–56, 163; soldiers call for, 50–53, 63, 88, 144–47, 149; political changes like revolution and democracy's effect on, 64, 156; rescinding prisoner exchanges, 64; and seizing slaves, 67, 153, 163; differences between professional officers and citizen-soldiers about, 122–23, 141, 143–45, 151, 163; technology impact of, 143; percentage of soldiers who supported, 144, 164; definition of, 146–48; political objectives in, 148–49, 152, 154–55, 161–63. *See also* People's armies; War aims

Haswell, Jock, 153. *See* Emigration, as an alternative to defeat

Hazen, William Babcock, 124

Hegelian view of the war. *See* Civil War: as a struggle for ideals and progress

Heintzelman, Samuel Peter, 178; troops' appraisal of, 46

Hertford County, North Carolina, 175

Hess, Earl J. (historian), on republican ideology, 22. *See also* Citizen-soldiers: values and virtues of

Historical exceptionalism, ix, 73

Holden, William, 180, as leader of dissidents, 35, 97–98, 103–4, 172

Holly Springs, Mississippi, 72, 101

Holmes, Theophilus Hunter, 84, 130

Holt, Joseph, 181

Home front, 17, 20; dissent and disloyalty, reactions by, vii, 10, 100, 163, 168–85; soldiers' ties to, 13–16, 121, 165; radicalization of, by war, 14, 64, 66, 173, 178; importance of in supporting a people's army, 14, 32, 38, 51, 56, 65, 84, 161, 165, 167, 184; pressure on its soldiers, 15, 24–26, 30–31, 99, 165–67, 170–71; indoctrination role of, 15, 168; aid at the front, 19, 167; political solidarity with army, 166, 170–71; succor for soldiers' families, 166–67; cost of living at, 167. *See also* Citizen-soldiers: expectations regarding parent society; Confederate States of America: dissent and disloyalty in; People's armies: relations with parent society compared with other countries; Parent society; Stanley, Henry Morton

Honor, importance of, 99. *See also* Citizen-soldiers: ideal model of; Political socialization

Hood, John Bell, 108, 144, 162

Hooker, Joseph, 126; Confederate opinions about, 41, 110; demands free hand in conducting campaign, 125; protests large number of Democratic officers, 129. *See also* Officers; Voting in the army

Houchard, Jean-Nicolas, 152

Hovey, Alvin Peterson, denounced as profiteer, 46

Hundred-day men, ineffectiveness of, 52. *See also* Militia

Hunter, David, 50, 129

Hurlbut, Stephen Augustus, 139

Idealism, 65, 152, 161. *See also* Citizen-soldiers

Ideas and values, 1. *See also* Political awareness; Values

Illinois, 43; 109th Regiment, mutiny and political attitudes of, 1, 47, 72, 101–2, 139; dissent in, 35, 70, 100–101, 104, 124, 174, 177, 185; political articulateness of soldiers from, 35, 37; blocks soldier voting, 91, 95; Democrat successes in, 100, 177; rumors of coup d'état in, 104

Implications of defeat, topic as indicator of soldiers' scope of political awareness, 36

Impôt du sang, 23

Independence. *See* Democracy; War aims

Indiana: dissent in, 35, 70, 100, 104; political articulateness of soldiers from, 35, 37; conscription in, 52; Republican 1864 success in, 96; Democrat successes in, 100; Copperheads in, 101, 132, 174, 184; legislature paralyzed in, 132, 179. *See also* Political socialization

Indicators for measuring political awareness (explained): political acuity, viii, 33–34, 39; scope of interests, viii, 33, 36, 39; sense of political effectiveness, viii, 33–34, 37, 39; percentage of soldiers who scored highly on all three indicators, 34, 39. *See also* Political awareness; Political

sophistication (as indicator of political awareness)

Industrialization and democracy, and rise of people's armies, 5, 154

Iowa, 43, 70, 127; political articulateness of soldiers from, 35; voting in the army, 94; dissent in, 104–5. *See also* Political socialization; Voting in the army: procedures for

Irish-American troops, 72

Irredentists. *See* Disloyalty; Dissent in enemy society

Irregulars, vii, 149, 153; repression of dissidents by, 183, 185

Jackson County, Missouri, 144

Johnson, Andrew, 89, 180; obtains exclusion of review board for Tennessee military appointments, 11; plans to liberate east Tennessee, 41; soldiers' opinions of, 115. *See also* Patronage

Johnson Island, Ohio, 73

Johnston, Joseph E., 86, 125, 128; stubborn defense of Atlanta causes tensions in Republican ranks, 42; soldiers' opinion of, 49, 144

Joint Committee on the Conduct of the War, 89, 146; checks caesarism in officer corps, 127–28; conducts inquiries on officers' disloyalty, 134–35

Jonesboro (Illinois) Gazette, 48

Juarez, Benito, 112

Justification of the war, 10, 62, 99; Southerners' claims of defensive war, 2, 62–63, 65; oppose extension of slavery, 15, 62; criteria of, 61–62; as legitimate democratic decision, 61–62; preserve democracy, 61–62; defend Southern minority's rights, 62; South's undemocratic nature and, 62. *See also* Indicators for measuring political awareness; Civil War; War aims

distinctions among Union troops, 43; Union and Confederate troops on compared, 43; moral character of, judged by troops, 45–46; persona of appraised, 45–46, 48, 119; corruption of, 45, 51–52, 54; Confederate assessment of enemy's, 48. *See also* Indicators for measuring political awareness (explained); Military situation

Military situation, 36, 38, 40–41, 49–50, 55–56; the "big picture," 9–10, 37, 40–43; political and electoral consequences arising from, 14, 40–42; effect on home front morale, 40–41, 160; percentage of soldiers showing interest in, 40; and enemy capabilities assessed, 41, 106–8, 110–11

Military tribunals. *See* Confederate States of America

Militia, 2, 4, 17, 120, 122, 174, 177; compared to French revolutionary formations, 5–6; compared with Europe, 6, 15; mustered in response to Morgan's raid and Gettysburg campaign, 6; number mustered into federal service, 6; universal enrollment in, 6; tradition in American War of Independence and Civil War, 19–20, 166. *See also* American political culture; Citizen-soldiers; Civil War: as an apocalyptic clash between moral absolutes; Confederate States of America: dissent and disloyalty in; English Muster Law; People's armies; Political socialization: militia system as instrument of

Millenialism. *See* Civil War; War aims

Milliken's Bend, battle of, 159

Milwaukee, Wisconsin, 177

Minuteman, as model of virtuous citizen-solder, 8. *See* Citizen-soldiers:

ideal model of; Militia: tradition in American War of Independence and Civil War

Mississippi, 43, 67–68, 72, 84

Mississippi River, 33, 40, 47, 77, 161, 167, 185

Missouri, 6, 43, 135, 140, 172; disloyalty of officer corps in, investigated, 130, 134–35; political repression in, 144, 161–63, 177, 181, 185; enrolled militia in, 185. *See also* Militia: universal enrollment in

Mitchell, Reid: community pressure on soldiers, 15; on republican ideology, 22; and minuteman ideal, 23

Mixed brigades, 7; compared with American formations, 5, 7

Mobile, Alabama, 74, 82; military situation, 42

Mobile Register, 86

Mobilization: and mass political parties, 1, 29; of citizenry for war, 148. *See also* Conscription; Political awareness

Mahoning (Ohio) Sentinel, 180

Monroe Doctrine, 77, 112

Montgomery, Alabama, 98

Morale: effect of defeats on, 41; factors influencing, 111. *See also* Hard war

Morgan, John Hunt, raid into Ohio, 28, 103, 184. *See also* Military leadership; Militia

Morgan County, Illinois, 52

Morrill, Justin Smith, 139

Morton, Oliver P., 104, 179

Mosby, John S., 158

Mouton, Jean-Jacques, 54

Murfreesboro, Tennessee. *See* Stone's River, Tennessee, battle of

Mutiny. *See* Disloyalty: among troops; Illinois: 109th Regiment

Napoleon III: seeks support of Austria, Spain, and Great Britain for armed mediation, 77, 113; ambitions in Mexico, 112; rumors of mediation by, 112; soldiers' attitude toward, 112, 114–15

Nashville, Tennessee, battle of, 153, 162

National Union Associations. *See* Union Leagues

Nation in arms. *See* People's armies: as nation in arms

Nazi ideology, as combat motivator, 9, 12

Neely, Mark E., Jr., 138, 147–48, 182

Negro Soldier Bill. *See* Confederate States of America: proposals to enlist blacks

Nelson, William, 135

New England: political articulateness of soldiers in, 35; abolitionism in, 179

New Hampshire, 127; political articulateness of soldiers from, 35

New Jersey, 43; 1864 election in, 96

New Mexico, French designs on, 113

New Model Army, ix, 20, 121

New Orleans, Louisiana, 74, 125, 167; Cajun and Creole loyalty doubted, 112, 113. *See also* Catholic Church, suspicions in North toward

New York, 18, 111

New York, 43; 1864 elections in, 96, 137; Copperhead activities press in, 103, 178–80

New York Herald, 139

New York Times, 64

New York World, 172

Newspapers, 15, 51, 102, 106–8, 113, 123, 140, 163; availability in camps, 15, 30; number extant at outbreak of war, 30; soldier correspondents for, 30, 139; pro-peace press, 65, 112, 139, 172. *See also* Christian Commission, disseminates books and newspapers in camps; Confederate States of America; Political socialization: newspaper as source of

Nevins, Allan, 52, 180

North Carolina, 43, 55, 73; dissent in, 97–101, 103–4, 138, 158, 173–76; elections in, 97; fears that central government threatens civil liberties, 97; peace movement in, 97–98, 172; soldier vote in, 97; economic conditions in, 98; draft evasion in, 175–76, 182. *See also* Confederate States of America

Northern society, Confederate perceptions of, 73

Northern Virginia, Army of, 47, 171

Northwest, old, 42, 161; rumors of secession by, 12, 179; significance of loyalty question in, 100. *See also individual state names;* Conscription: ineffectiveness of; Peace

Occupation policy, 146–47, 161–62. *See also* Reconstruction

Officers, 16–17, 46; civilian ties of, 2, 120–21; return to civilian pursuits, 4, 46–47; election of, 11; different ideas about the war, 13, 120, 122–23, 126, 128; share same political values with troops, 15, 18, 119, 121–23, 140–41; literacy of, compared to enlistees, 17; overrepresentation of, in dataset, 17; democracy of, 18–19; conservatism of, 78, 94, 120, 123, 129–30, 140; influence voting in the field, 94, 140; maintain political orthodoxy in the ranks, 119–20, 139–41; rank and file expectations of, 119–20; styles of command by, 119; Union and Confederate political views compared, 124–25; political differences among, 126–27, 129; as candidates in elections, 127; monitor elections in the field, 137–38; monitor troops' loyalty, 137, 139; attitudes toward tactical people's army's fighting style, 142–43. *See also*

Landed gentry; Military leadership; Political sophistication (as indicator of political awareness)

17, 21, 174; unit flags and insignia discouraged to increase political loyalty of troops, 13; relations with parent society compared with other countries, 13–16, 166, 169; comparison between, 23; defining attributes of, 23; school for citizenship, 23; war aims of, 63, 65, 77, 149, 151, 153; common outlook by soldiers and officers in, 66; effectiveness of, 66, 153; dissidence in, 99, 146; tensions between officers and men in, 121–23; romantic nationalism of, 143, 152–54; innovations in, 149–51; strategic unwieldiness of, 150–51; brutalization of, 154–160. *See also* Combat motivation; Home front; Patronage; Popular mobilization; Short-service troops; Spartacism; War aims

Perqimans County, North Carolina, 175

Petersburg, Virginia, siege of, 41–42, 56, 76, 106, 159, 164, 174–75; effect on 1864 elections, 42, 110. *See also* Military situation: political and electoral consequences arising from

Petitions from soldiers, 77, 139, 145–46, 171

Phillips, Wendell, 64

Pietism, and Southern acceptance of defeat, 81

Pillow, Gideon J., 166

Pine Bluff, Arkansas, 23, 98

Plato: objections to mercenaries, 19; sees the state as nurturing source for individual and community, 22–23

Plots. *See* Civil War: plots and panics during; Copperheads; Dissent in enemy society; Disloyalty

Poison Spring, Arkansas, battle of, 159

Political acuity. *See* Political sophistication; Indicators for measuring political awareness

Political awareness, viii, 2, 15–16, 19, 23, 33; definition of, 32, 34; sharpened by war, 16, 32; percentage of Civil War soldiers who showed, 16–17, 38–39; effect of war on, 38, 47. *See also* Political Socialization; Indicators for measuring political awareness; Politics: definition of

Political consciousness. *See* Political awareness

Political convictions. *See* American political culture

Political culture. *See* Civic culture

Political effectiveness, sense of, 37–38; complexity of, in the North compared to the South, 40–41. *See also* Indicators for measuring political awareness (explained): sense of political effectiveness; Pietism

Political empowerment. *See* Sense of political effectiveness

Political issues, 38; soldiers' interest in, 36, 38. *See also* Citizen-soldiers; War aims; Indicators of political awareness

Political leadership, 2, 16, 84, 117, 128; topic as indicator of scope of political awareness, 36, 84; competence of assessed, 38, 81, 85–88, 125; importance of, 83–84; disenchantment with, 84–85; percentage of soldiers who voiced confidence in, 84; confidence of officers' and soldiers' compared, 124

Political objectives, 3. *See also* Fighting style; People's armies

Political outlook. *See* Home front; Political convictions; Political socialization: community's role in; Political sophistication: in terms of coherence of worldview

Political parties, 1, 35

Political socialization: patriotic festivals and pilgrimages, 10; church as source of, 26–28; community's role in, 26, 29–32; extra-curricular school activities, 26: family as source of, 26–27; public school as source of, 26, 28; literacy rates and, 28, 39; effect of social class on, 29; militia system as instrument of, 29; and political participation, 29–30, 91–92; newspaper as source of, 30. *See also* Constitution; Home front: pressure on its soldiers; Political awareness; Indicators for measuring political awareness

Political sophistication (as indicator of political awareness), 3, 33; compared between the North and South, 29, 32, 34–35; in terms of coherence of worldview, 32–33; effect of social class and education on, 35–36. *See also* Combat motivation; Indicators for measuring political awareness

Political values. *See* Political socialization

Politics: definition of, 10; and war, 10; militarization of, 172–73, 176–78, 181–83, 185–86

Polybius, and his distrust of mercenaries, 19. *See also* Citizen-soldiers

Pope, John, 41, 134; rated by troops, 45. *See also* Military leadership

Popular mobilization, 148. *See also* People's armies

Porter, Fitz-John, 134; rated by troops, 45. *See also* Military leadership

Port Hudson, Louisiana, battle of, 157

Port Washington, Wisconsin, 177

Potomac, Army of the, 61, 138, 140; troops' attitude toward leaders, 43–48, 90–91, 126, 134. *See also* Military situation

Potter Committee, 178

Price, Sterling, 42, 157, 183

Prisoners of war, mock elections by, 20, 93–94

Professional armies. *See* Regulars

Profiteering, 105; transforms war to a struggle for the interests of the rich, 59–60; complaints by soldiers against, 16, 67, 85, 99, 101. *See also* Citizen-soldiers: idealism of

Provost marshals, repressing disloyal elements, 173, 180

Public schools. *See* Political socialization: public school as source of

Puritans. *See* New Model army

Putney debates (British Civil War), 20

Quakers, 180

Quantrill, William Clarke, 183

Racism, of Union troops, 73

Radicals, 16, 42, 65–66, 116, 124, 129, 176; call for disenfranchising ruling oligarchy and empowering poor farmers, 66, 89, 97; demand unconditional surrender, 97. *See also* Reconstruction; Republicans

Raleigh, North Carolina, 176, 180; riots in, 97

Raleigh (North Carolina) Standard, 97, 180

Randolph, George Wythe, 3. *See also* Virginia: landed gentry of; Ruling elites

Rank and file, relations with officers, 4

Rapidan River, Virginia, 106

Rappahannock River, Virginia, 24

Reconstruction, 16, 89, 97, 148; soldiers' views on, 2, 79–80, 115–16; and changing class relations in South, 64, 66, 80, 147; end of, in 1877, 66, 83; North's failure to carry out, 66; percentage of soldiers who commented on, 78. *See also* War aims

Recruitment: importance of, at local level, vii, 2, 4, 15, 25, 165–67; role of patronage in, 2, 17; decentralized system of, 8, 17, 165; waning of, 106. *See also* Conscription; Enlistments

Recruits. *See* Soldiers; Citizen-soldiers: politics and recruitment of

Rector, Massie, 179

Red River campaign, 44

Reenlistments: high level of, among citizen-soldiers, vii; soldiers demand right to elect officers as condition of, 11. *See also* Combat motivation: sense of duty

Regiments, consolidation of, viii

Regulars, 4, 83, 101; parent society's distrust of, vii; combat motivation of, 2, 14, 18, 57, 123; political differences between professionals and volunteers, 4, 18, 121–22, 146, 152; as cadres for people's armies, 5; citizen-soldiers' attitude toward, 18; compared to citizen-soldiers, 18, 93, 99, 121–22; types of wars fought by, 66; rarity of dissidence among, 99; organizational and material incentives in recruitment of, 121; fighting style limiting collateral destruction, 143; officers' detachment from parent society, 165. *See also* Armies, differences between professional and volunteer over purpose of; Bonapartism; Combat motivation of; Long-service troops; Manpower systems

Religion. *See* Political socialization: church as source of

Religiosity. *See* Pietism

Republic, the, 37; as beacon for the rest of the world, 58, 112

Republicanism: principle values and virtues of, 19, 22, 80, 132; as developmental nurturing democracy, 22–23, 26; dovetailing of child-rearing theories with, 28–29; Civil War as stage in progress of, 61–62; the South as Roman archetype of, 63, 74; and standing armies, vii, 119–20. *See also* Child-rearing practices; Citizen-soldiers: idealism of; Plato; Rousseau, Jean-Jacques

Republicans, 13, 35, 65–66, 72, 88, 96–97, 108, 112, 120, 126–27, 131, 177–78; disagreement over war aims, 35, 63–64, 66; Chicago convention of, 52, 95, 107; significance of emancipation for, 64; Baltimore convention calls for abolition, 89; reasons for favorable prospects in 1864 elections, 89–90, 95, 108; impact of military situation on electoral prospects, 106, 144, 162; in army, 126, 129–30. *See also* Abolitionists; Elkhart County, Indiana: Republicans' response to draft call in

République de la vertu. See Robespierre

Revolutionary ruptures, 66; and mass military organizations as agents of change, 1, 4; and change in defeated societies, 66. *See also* Reconstruction; War aims

Rhode Island, 6

Richmond, Virginia, 3, 42, 75, 77, 84–86, 90, 110, 114, 125–26, 134, 144, 159, 162, 171, 175, 179

Richmond Whig, 179

Roanoke-Chowan River region, North Carolina, 175–76

Robespierre, Maximilien, 61, 85

Rochester, New York. *See* Conservative Convention of 1863

Roman republic. *See* Rome (ancient)

Rome (ancient), 8; reliance on professional armies as cause of decline, 19. *See also* Citizen soldier: ideal model of; Gibbon, Edward

Rosecrans, William Starke, 136;

leadership assessed, 44, 47; as alternative to Lincoln as presidential candidate, 127

Rousseau, Jean-Jacques, 8; underrepresentation of poor in volunteer militia system, 8; ideas on democracy and military obligation, 22; on the state as transcendental value, 22–23; comments on citizen army as school for citizenship, 23; views on child-rearing in his *Emile,* 27. *See also* Citizen-soldiers: idea model of; Citizenry: military and political obligations of, as components of citizenship; Republicanism

Royster, Charles, 145

Ruling elites. *See* Landed gentry; Randolph, George Wythe; Lee, Robert E.

Runaways. *See* Contrabands

Russia, 16, 142–43, 163

Saint-Just, Antoine, 85

Salem Church, Virginia, battle of, 47

Sanford, Charles, 133

Schofield, John M., 185

Schurz, Carl, 130

Scope of political awareness, topics discussed by soldiers (as indicator of political awareness), 32–33, 36, 43; compared between regions of the North, 36; Confederates compared to Unionists, 32, 36; difference between, by social class, 36; officers and enlistees compared, 36. *See also* Indicators for measuring political awareness (explained)

Sebastian County, Arkansas, 98

Second Confiscation Act, 124

Second Corps, 77

Seddon, James Alexander, 181

Sedgwick, John, 47

Self-control as civic virtue. *See also*

Citizen-soldiers: values and virtues of; Mann, Horace

Sense of duty. *See* Combat motivation: sense of duty

Sense of political effectiveness (as indicator of political awareness), 37, 131; soldiers exhibit strong feeling of, 37; Unionists and Confederates compared, 37–38; effect of religiosity among Confederates on, 38. *See also* Indicators for measuring political awareness (explained)

Servile insurrection, 99, 146, 150, 179

Seven Days' battles, 43–44

Seward, William Henry, 77

Seymour, Horatio, 89, 93, 133, 172

Seymour, Truman, 124

Shenandoah Valley, Virginia, 40–41, 50, 160, 163

Sheridan, Philip H., destruction by, 147, 160

Sheriffs, 179, vetting political reliability of volunteers. *See also* Military commissions, monitering political reliability

Sherman, John, 65

Sherman, William Tecumseh, 42, 106; press relations with, 44, 139; hard war fought by, 48, 144, 147, 152, 156, 158; soldiers' opinion of, 48–49; criticized for armistice appeasing South, 51, 78, 128, 149; and Special Field Order Number 15, 163

Shiloh, Tennessee, battle of, 4, 26, 31, 38, 70, 81, 117, 127, 151, 153, 167

Shirking, 52; by substitutes and conscripts, vii. *See also* Stay-at-homes, soldiers' anger toward

Short-service armies, 1. *See also* Combat Motivation; People's armies; Volunteers

Sigel, Franz, 130; admired by German troops, 45. *See also* Military situation

Skocpol, Theda, 16

Slaveowners, soldiers' attitude about, 126. *See also* Contrabands; Slavery

Slavery, 68, 71, 81, 131, 146, 175, 179; as cause of the war, 2, 15, 41, 62, 64–65, 73–74, 155; soldiers' attitude on, 12, 64–65, 68, 74, 105; as key source of planter class' power, 41, 50, 64–67, 73–74, 83, 175; viewed as impediment to democracy and progress, 41, 64, 68; coming in contact with, increases soldiers' political awareness, 67–69. *See also* War aims

Social class. *See* Political socialization: effect of social class on

Social expectations. *See* Home front: pressure on its soldiers

Social Sciences, viii

Soldiers, as stringers for newspapers, 19, 30; conservative outlook of, 123. *See also* Citizen-soldiers: idealism of; Newspapers

Sons of Liberty, 174. *See also* Copperheads; Knights of the Golden Circle

South Carolina, 43, 71, 76, 85, 163

Southern society; a social structure of, 29, 60–61, 64, 67, 70, 73–75, 80, 83, 92–93, 175–76, 179; inequalities in and effect on soldiers' attitudes, 54, 58, 87; Northern perceptions of, 62, 108–9; 1776 revolutionary rhetoric of, 63, 73–74; need for reconstruction of, 64, 148; racism in, 68; marginality of small farmers in, 92. *See also* Confederate States of America; Landed gentry: domination of Southern politics by; *McGuffey Reader;* Reconstruction: and changing class relations in South; Slavery: viewed as impediment to democracy and progress; War aims

Spain. *See* Napoleon III

Spartacism, 14

Spears, James G., 136

Speculators. *See* Profiteering

Spottsylvania, Virginia, battle of, 153

Springfield, Illinois, 99

St. Louis, Missouri, 52, 130, 180

Stahel, Julius, 130

Standing armies. *See* Republicanism

Stanley, Henry Morton, pressured to join up, 31. *See also* Home front: pressure on its soldiers

Stanton, Edwin, 133–34

Statistical tests, ix

Staunton, Virginia, 160

Stay-at-homes, soldiers' anger toward, 15, 52. *See also* Draft evaders; Profiteering

Stone, Charles P., 134–35

Stone's River, Tennessee, battle of, 44, 47, 71, 81, 136

Stoneport, Illinois, 131

Storey, Wilbur D., 180

Strategy. *See* Fighting style; Military situation

Strong bands. *See* Union Leagues

Submissionists. *See* Confederate States of America: dissent and disloyalty in

Substitutes, 7; brokers role in finding, 7, 53, 170; denunciation of, 53; soldiers resentment of, 53. *See also* Bounty men; Bounties; Conscription

Summerville, Illinois, 176

Sumner, Charles, 64

Sunday schools. *See* Political socialization: church as source of

Tactics. *See* Fighting style

Tennessee, 40, 43, 49, 84–85, 89, 97, 101, 105, 116, dissent and draft evasion in, 98

Tennessee, Army of, 86, 108; divisions over arming blacks, 13, 74–75, 125–26

Tennessee, Army of the, 44

Tennessee River, 98

Territorial recruitment. *See* People's armies: politics and recruitment of

Texas, 161; French designs on, 113

Thirteenth Amendment, indication of radical definition of war aims, 65. *See also* War aims

Thomas, George Henry, 129, 132, 153

Tocqueville, Alexis de, 37

Tolstoy, Leo, *War and Peace*, 142, 186

Total war. *See* Hard war

Townsend, E. D., 178

Trans-Mississippi theater, 161, 169

Turchin, Ivan, 98, 159

Turchin, John Basil, 98

Tuskegee, Alabama, 31

Toombs, Robert Augustus, 85

Treason, 70, 90, 101–2, 104, 115–16, 118, 123, 131, 134, 137, 139, 149, 156–57, 171, 173–74, 177–78, 180–81, 184–85. *See also* Confederate States of America: dissent and disloyalty in; Copperheads; Disloyalty

Tuskegee (Alabama) South Western Baptist, 31

Tuttle, James M., 127

Tyranny. *See* Civil War

Union leagues, 13, 184–85; and vetting political reliability of volunteers, 130, 132, 134. See also *Comités de salut public;* Joint Committee on the Conduct of the War; Military commissions, monitoring political reliability

United States of America: Confederate perceptions of economic conditions in, 36; mass political parties in, 66; economic conditions in, 110–11; state of morale in, 111. *See also* Copperheads; Democrats; Dissent in enemy society; Disloyalty

United States Constitution, 62

Unrestricted war. *See* Hard war

Upton, Emory, 153

Vallandigham, Clement Laird (Copperhead leader), 35, 88, 90, 96, 102–3, 107, 111, 113, 136–37, 171–72, 180

Values: categories of, 12; shared by army and society, 15, 19, 168. *See also* Parent society; People's armies: relations with parent society compared with other countries

Vance, Zebulon Baird, 97–98, 137; receives reports of political disloyalty of some officers, 173–74

Verba, Sidney, 81. *See also* Indicators for measuring political awareness (explained): sense of political effectiveness

Vermont, 43, 51, 139. *See also* Political socialization

Vernon County, Missouri, 144

Vicksburg, Mississippi, 41, 109, 113, 161; 1863 Siege of, 33, 41, 49, 110–11, 123, 138, 156, 160; 1862 assault on, 44, 47. *See also* Military situation: political and electoral consequences arising from

Virginia, 3–4, 43, 69, 91, 96–97, 159; soldier vote in, 97; dissent and draft evasion in, 161–62, 179. *See also* Landed gentry

Virginia Declaration of Rights, 166

Volunteers: desertion rates, vii; as backbone of Civil war armies, vii, 1, 8; motivation of, 18–19, 39. *See also* Combat motivation; People's armies

Voting. *See under specific elections*

Voting in the army: soldiers petition for, 93; accusations of election fraud during, 94–95; procedures for, 94, 97, 140; Republican support for, 94; Union commanders influence, 94–95

Wade, Benjamin, 89, 129, 132, 150

Wade-Davis Bill, 89

Wadsworth, James Samuel, 130

Walker, William H. T., 13, 131

Wallace, Lew, 181

War. *See* Civil War

War aims, 10, 12, 14, 32, 63, 65–66, 76,
90, 99, 107, 120, 161; abolition as,
10, 12, 64–65, 69–70, 146–47, 178;
preservation of the Union, 10, 15;
as radical maximalist revolutionary
goals, 10, 16, 32, 50–52, 63–67, 72–73,
78–80, 85, 140, 147–49, 154–55, 163;
reactionary Southern ideas, 10, 50,
73–74, 148–49; mutual exclusivity of
in North and South, 16, 20, 65, 146,
157; as moral revitalization of the
republic, 20, 63, 79–80; effect of heavy
losses on, 65–66; impact of hard war
on, 72; people's armies and, 77;
dissension among soldiers over,
128–29; conditional surrender, 149,
154–55. *See also* Civil War; Combat
motivation: effect of radical war aims
on; Emancipation: redefines the
nature of the struggle; Hard war;
Republicans: disagreement over war
aims

Warren, Gouverneur K., 138

Washington, 72, 96, 134, 138, 171, 178;
political objective of Early's 1864
campaign, 42, 108, 125

Washington County, Wisconsin, 177

Washburne, Elihu B., 123

Weed, Thurlow, 66

Weldon, North Carolina, 175

West Bend, Wisconsin, 177

Wheeler, Joseph, 158

Whigs, 77, 131

Whitehall, Illinois, 151, 177

Wilder, John T., 151

Wilkinson, Rupert T., 26

William and Mary College,
Williamsburg, Virginia, 160

Wilmington, North Carolina, 99, 173

Winchester, Virginia, 160

Winder, John Henry, 179–80

Wisconsin, 39, 43; conscription in, 52,
177; disloyalty among troops from, 72

Women's Loyal Leagues. *See* Union
Leagues

Worldview, 32–33

World War II, brutality of, 156

Wright, Joseph A., 180

Yates, Richard, 37, 91, 139, 177; calls for
banishing supporters of dissenters, 80;
threatened with insurrection, 104

Yazoo River, Mississippi, 1862 expedition
on, 47, 160

"Year of Jubilo." *See* Citizen-soldiers:
idealism of

Yell County, Arkansas, 98